PA
for a
PURPOSE

a memoir

Barb Geiger

It's about the people, not the paddle!
Barb Geiger
John 13:34

ELECTIO PUBLISHING
first century principles.
a twenty-first century approach.

Paddle for a Purpose

By Barb Geiger

Copyright 2018 by Barb Geiger. All rights reserved.

Cover Design by eLectio Publishing. Based on photo by Gene Geiger (used by permission).

ISBN-13: 978-1-63213-488-2

Published by eLectio Publishing, LLC

Little Elm, Texas

http://www.eLectioPublishing.com

5 4 3 2 1 eLP 22 21 20 19 18

Printed in the United States of America.

The eLectio Publishing creative team is comprised of: Kaitlyn Hallmark, Emily Certain, Lori Draft, Court Dudek, Jim Eccles, Sheldon James, and Christine LePorte.

"Run, Mississippi, Run" song lyrics used by permission.

Publisher's Note

The publisher does not have any control over and does not assume any responsibility for author or third-party websites or their content.

This book is dedicated to my parents, Hal and Fran Hoops. I will be forever grateful to Dad for passing on his love of the water and to Mom for modeling faithful compassion and service.

CONTENTS

Photo galleries of our journey and an interactive map with links to the service organizations in the book are available at www.paddleforapurpose.net.

Chapter 1
Inspiration

THE WET VARNISH GLISTENED as we brushed it sparingly onto the curved slats, coaxing out the rich, golden grain of the wood. Every coat of varnish added even more luster to our kayak's finish. I cringed each time we scuffed the surface with sandpaper, reducing her shiny hull to a drab dusty shell. But the next coat always signaled a rebirth, magnifying the beauty of the craft we had meticulously stitched and glued together with our own hands. After this final layer of varnish, the long process of building our first boat would be complete.

I glanced at my husband, Gene, bent over the front cockpit, wiping away the bubbles and drips before the varnish began to cure. Although the boat was propped up on sawhorses, she came only to mid-chest on his six-foot-three-inch frame. It was hard to believe I started building this boat before I even knew him, and now, approaching our sixth anniversary, we were finishing her together. He squinted through his glasses, moving his head from side to side, examining the surface in the reflection of the sunlight streaming through the open garage door. Finally, he stepped back, straightened to his full height, and sighed. "She sure is gorgeous." He took the varnish brush from my hand, balanced it next to his on the edge of the nearly empty can, and wrapped an arm around my shoulder. "How's it feel to finally be done?"

"We still have to see if she floats," I joked, "but it's pretty awesome." I had no reason to believe that the boat wouldn't float. I read the directions so often I could quote them verbatim. Every step along the way was checked and rechecked. And when it wasn't clear, I called the company, just to be sure. I wondered if some of the operators at the help desk even recognized us by name. All the same, it would be a relief to get her in the water and see how she handled.

How many years has it been? I wondered. I tried to remember the year that Dad, Eric, and I began with nothing but a kit, directions, and a worktable we built out of sawhorses and plywood—just the right height for Dad's wheelchair—at my parents' home in Green Bay. I measured time by my son's age. *I think Eric was eight.*

My mind drifted to the cherry table in my parents' dining room, where I lingered after dinner with Dad, while Eric rushed outside to play and Mom busied herself in the kitchen.

"What's that?" I asked. Dad angled his magazine toward me. Displayed across the two-page spread were photos of wooden kayaks of various lengths and designs.

"I've always wanted to build one of these." Dad sighed. "Pygmy Boats have beautiful lines." He flipped the magazine closed. "But there's not much point anymore." I knew Dad was more realistic than dejected. He never was the type to feel sorry for himself, and wasn't about to start after a stroke at age sixty-six. Four years later, he managed just fine with his chair, drove a Grand Caravan with hand controls, and even designed a swiveling arm to lift himself into the cockpit of his sailboat, where he and his boat were one with nature's forces of wind and water.

"Just because you can't use a kayak, doesn't mean you can't enjoy building one," I said. His clear blue eyes looked questioningly at me as I continued. "We can build one together—up here."

Reeling from a divorce, I was learning to navigate my new life as the single working mother of a son I loved full time, but now only saw Mondays, Tuesdays, and every other weekend. Like Dad,

I was learning to be independent again. I was learning single-woman skills, like how to start a snow blower, how to change my furnace filter, and how to feel comfortable attending events without a man by my side. The two-hour drive from Waukesha to the refuge of my parents' home on the bay offered me comfort and solace, and the unconditional love that I craved. I brought Eric up to see his Grammy and Pappy when I could. "It could be a three-generation project—you, me, and Eric. You can teach us, and someday, it could be part of your legacy."

I reached for the magazine and we looked at the styles again, this time with excited anticipation. "What do you think about this one?" he asked, pointing to the Osprey Double.

Long and sleek, with a low profile, the boat in the picture had cockpits for two paddlers. A tandem boat seemed appropriate for our team project. I read the paragraph below the picture. "It's beautiful, Dad. And this says it's one of the most stable models they have." Stability felt important. "It'll be perfect," I said, excited about our new venture.

Gene was a late addition to the kayak project. He was also a late addition to my life and the answer to my question, "Will I ever be able to love again?" We met at church, developed a friendship there, and progressed to the next level—chatting online and talking on the phone for hours. Exhausted batteries often made the decision that we could not, saving some topics for future conversations.

One of our first family dates was a trip to the Milwaukee Boat Show. As Eric, then eleven, traipsed around one high-powered speedboat after the next, I told Gene about our never-ending kayak project up in Green Bay.

Gene's eyes widened. "You're building a *boat*?" he asked.

"We don't get much done at a time," I admitted. "The epoxy has to dry for at least twelve hours, so we only finish one step—or one little part of a step—each time we go up. The purpose of the project is to do it together," I explained. "I'm not really worried about how long it takes."

Gene shook his head. "I can't believe I'm dating a boat-building woman. How lucky can a man get?" I slipped my hand into his, and he wrapped his fingers around mine. Someone thought he was lucky to know me. It felt better than I remembered.

Now, as Gene helped me finish the boat, I recognized that he became as much a part of the boat-building team as the three of us who began it together. He also became as much a part of my life.

After the varnish dried, we attached the hardware and laced bungee cords across the deck in crisscross patterns. We mounted the rudder to the stern and bolted the seat backs to wooden support braces in the boat. On one side of each cockpit, Gene added an extra bungee cord and hook. "This wasn't in the plans," he said, "but I think it'll help solve the problem of where to put our paddles when we're not using them." He laid a paddle against the side of the boat, stretched the cord up over the shaft, and secured the bungee on the hook, like a big rubber band, holding the paddle tight against the hull. I did the same on the opposite side of the boat.

Walking around the kayak, I put an arm around Gene's waist. "Those finishing touches sure add a lot," I said.

"She's a beaut. I wish your dad could see her now."

"Me, too." I still missed Dad. He got sick a few years after our wedding. Before he moved to hospice, the doctor invited our family into the hospital room to show us his lung X-rays. White clouds of fibrous scar tissue filled the areas that should have looked clear. Pulmonary fibrosis. That's what they called the disease that ravaged his lungs with a vengeance, leaving no room for breath— for life. "Looks like I'm taking this better than you are," Dad said, upon noticing our tear-stained faces. "Don't worry about me. I've had a good life. I've gotten to do everything I wanted to do." *But I didn't get to do everything I wanted to do with you.*

I fingered the brass plaque we mounted on the wooden hip brace inside the front cockpit: "Inspired by and in memory of Hal Hoops." I yearned to talk with him, see his eyes sparkle, hear him say "It's be-you-ti-ful" the way he used to, articulating every letter.

I wanted to show him the plaque that dedicated the boat to him, but without the "in memory of" part.

"Dad would be proud," I said.

Later that week, Gene and I drove to Eagle Springs Lake to take the boat for her maiden voyage. I wished Eric could be with us, but he was busy finishing up his junior year at UW-Madison.

We lowered the boat carefully into the water from the end of the dock. "It floats!" I said. *Check one off the worry list.* I stepped into the front cockpit; the boat wobbled with every shift of my weight. "No pictures of me getting in or out until I can do it gracefully," I warned Gene. I wondered if that time would ever come. I lowered myself onto the inflatable seat cushion. My feet rested comfortably on the foot pegs, heels touching the bottom of the boat, knees bent. I adjusted the air in my seat, wiggling to get comfortable. My back pressed against the adjustable foam-lined backrest. *Good*, I thought, *the lumbar support feels fine.* I felt the boat jiggle as Gene took his place in the stern. I couldn't see him, but the boat responded under me to every movement he made. I gripped the edge of the dock to help us stabilize. My heart pounded. If we wobbled this much now, what would happen once I let go?

I pictured the four- and eight-foot strips of mahogany lying on our worktable, and remembered measuring the distance of each die-cut strip of wood from a chalk line down the middle of the table. "Measure carefully, and always measure twice," Dad advised, before we glued the wooden butt plates over the seams, which would later form the ribs of the boat. "If any measurement is off, even a little bit, it can affect the alignment." He smiled and winked. "We want her to go straight when she's done."

I pushed my paddle blade against the dock, easing us out toward the lake. The sunlight sparkled off the water, like tiny rhinestones bobbing on the rippled surface. Paddling tentatively at first, then gaining speed, I watched the bow cut effortlessly through the water. Our path was silent and straight. I'd have to remember to tell Eric our careful measuring paid off; the line of the hull was true.

It didn't take long before Gene became accustomed to steering with the stern foot pedals. "Want to give it a try?" he asked. We returned to the dock to trade places. Gene reached up inside the hull, moving the foot pegs to match the length of our legs. Then we slipped back in, more easily this time, adjusted our backrests and cushions anew, and shoved off for my turn at the helm.

My new foot pegs weren't stationary like the ones in the bow; they moved forward and back, attached to rudder cables that steered the boat. As I gently pressed my left foot forward, the right pedal moved back, like a child's seesaw, and the kayak began an arc to the left. I did a figure eight, to experiment with the turning radius. The turns weren't sharp, but the boat proved responsive and graceful. "Whoo-hoo," I shouted. "I love this!" We paddled around and between the small, treed islands in the center of the lake. I practiced matching the timing of Gene's strokes, dipping and raising my paddle in unison with his. He got to set the pace, but I got to aim the boat anywhere I wanted to go. We skirted along the edges of lily pad fields, white and yellow hues of future blossoms peeking out from tight peony spheres. We paddled past piers with boats much fancier and faster than ours, but today I felt no envy. Lake homes with picture window walls and smaller, quaint cottages peeked down from the hillside, their aprons of green spreading to the shore. I wondered if anyone inside watched as we passed.

The orange hue of evening tinged the water as we pulled up to the dock. I was satisfied, both with the boat's seaworthiness, and with our job of crafting it. Gene made no secret of the fact he felt the same. "That was awesome!" he said, as he raised himself out of the seat and climbed onto the dock. "I can't get over how straight she tracks and how easy it is to paddle. I can't wait to do that again!" I smiled in agreement, as I envisioned paddles in area lakes, lazy picnics by the shore, and maybe even a little fishing.

We began the ride home in tired, satisfied silence. Dad would have been happy to watch us today. He always loved the water. As far back as my memory reached, he taught us to love it, too.

Growing up, my two brothers and I learned to paddle, pedal, and sail a variety of boats, ranging from sailboards and canoes to paddleboats and sailing crafts of gradually increasing size. Mom preferred the ground under her feet and a good book in her hands, but no matter what the weather, Dad was always ready for a sail. White mustache and beard neatly trimmed, balding head covered with his white bucket hat, he proclaimed, "Any day's a good day to be on the water."

Gene broke into my reverie. "I think we should take her down the Mississippi."

"You think we should *what*?" *Where did that come from?* I shook my head, wondering if I heard him right.

He went on, as if his idea was perfectly reasonable, like going for a walk on a lovely day. "Now that we've finished her, we should take her on an epic adventure. I've always thought it would be fun to paddle the Mississippi River from the source to the sea." He cast a sideways glance and smiled. "It's all downstream. How hard could it be?"

His boyish grin would have been charming, if his idea wasn't so ludicrous. "Wait a minute. Do you even know how long the Mississippi River is?" I was trying to remember what I'd learned in school—how many miles it would be to travel all the way across the country by river.

"I know it's a little over two thousand miles. Maybe twenty-five hundred. I bet we could do it in a few months during the summer."

Twenty-five hundred miles. We just paddled what? Maybe a half mile on a lake. And somehow it makes sense to plan a two-thousand-mile trip, after one day of practice? Twenty-five hundred miles. Divided by ninety days. Twenty . . . something. Twenty-seven point something. Every day.

"Even downstream, that's a lot for people our age," I said. *Our age. Fifty-somethings.* "Let's practice a little before we decide." Not wanting to sound as inflexible as I felt, I added, "I'll give it some thought." But as hard as I tried, *it ain't gonna happen* was the only thought I came up with.

We practiced paddling in beautiful locales around our state, including glacially formed Devil's Lake and the cliff-lined Wisconsin Dells. I loved the beauty and solitude, but five-mile afternoon jaunts didn't compare to kayaking nearly thirty miles every day, for months on end.

As I often did when facing life's big decisions, I prayed. I remembered a scripture from somewhere in Proverbs. "Trust in the Lord with all your heart, and lean not on your own understanding. In all your ways acknowledge him, and he shall direct your path." *God, show me what to do.*

Gene was convinced that we could make the trip and began telling our friends, "Yep, we're planning to take her down the whole length of the Mississippi."

"Wow, that's amazing," or "I'm impressed," they replied.

"But we really haven't decided for sure," I hastily added to any conversations I overheard. *How many people was he telling when I wasn't around?*

I searched for encouragement from books written by adventurers who made it back alive. I read about weeks of rain, washed-away tents, wrong turns, monster mosquitoes, rough water, dangerous currents, and close calls with river barges. I was stuck between the desire to encourage Gene's dream, and the desire for comfort, safety, and sanity. Would surviving, even with bragging rights, be enough of a reason to make such a long, dangerous, and uncomfortable trip? Did we even have what it takes in the first place? I wondered how Gene could be so sure . . . so confident, when I had absolutely no idea what to do.

I didn't hear anything back from God. Would I recognize it if I did? I knew God worked in my life; it was easy to see that in retrospect. God gave us fifteen extra years with Dad after his stroke, accompanied me through an avalanche of emotions as my marriage crumbled, and afterwards, gradually healed the wounds, gently pulling off the scabs, revealing who I'd forgotten I was. But would God weigh in on this?

Weeks passed, and June became a memory. *It's probably too late to start now, anyway,* I thought. *Maybe this whole thing will blow over.*

***

One Sunday morning in early July, I sat next to Gene in the second pew, listening attentively to one of the first sermons by our new pastor. Tall and thin, Pastor Andy paced the floor in front of the altar hewn from a large, lightning-scarred crotch of a tree. The overhead lights shone off his shaved head, which, surprisingly, didn't make him seem any older than his thirty-six years. "Love isn't something you give or get," he said. "Love is a verb. It's something you do." He smoothed his trimmed beard with long fingers, laid his iPad on the small wooden podium, and continued. "Without action, love is just a feeling. Jesus calls us to take God's love outside our walls, to the hurting world." This man was going to shake things up, I was sure of it.

Then I heard it. "Make it a service trip." The idea was gentle, like a whisper in my mind. "You can do service in towns along the river." The thought came from inside me, but I knew it wasn't mine. I looked over at Gene; he was focused on the sermon. My mind raced too fast to concentrate. Could the message be from the Holy Spirit? I had felt that before, along with the nudging on my heart and the tugging at my mind—send a card, make a meal, encourage a friend. But sending me somewhere I had no intention of going? This was a first.

Doubt nagged at me. What if this was some crazy compensation my brain was trying, working overtime to find an answer to my predicament? Whatever it was, I knew I already felt different. Before this, thoughts of paddling the river filled me with anxiety. Now, I felt a growing sense of calm. I decided not to say anything about it right away—God might have to convince me of this one.

I didn't bring up the subject at home; Gene did. He opened the door to the guest room, where I sat on the floor, sorting pictures to add to a scrapbook. "How long do you want to take for this trip?" he asked.

I felt my pulse quicken. "Why?"

"Because," he offered, "maybe we could take six months instead of three, and stop to do service along the way."

The photos in my hands dropped to the floor. I felt shivers along my arms as goose bumps suddenly appeared, although summer's heat permeated the room. I stood up, reached for his hands, and asked, "When did you get this idea?"

"In church this morning. All of a sudden, it just came to me. Why?"

"Come sit down," I said, pulling him over to the edge of the daybed and pushing some photographs out of the way. "I got exactly the same message." We both let the news sink in. "I think we're supposed to do this," I said. Gene nodded.

Although some might say this was a coincidence, I didn't think so. In just one day, my attitude was transformed. I had no idea how we were going to pull this off, but I wanted to try.

"Maybe we could start a blog," I suggested. "We could write about the service organizations where we stop to work and give them some publicity."

"Do you even know how to make a blog?" asked Gene.

"Not yet," I answered, smiling.

"You know, this changes things," said Gene. "This trip isn't about us anymore."

"If it was about us, you'd probably be going alone," I reminded him.

He continued as if I didn't interrupt, making me regret that I did. "We've got to plan an itinerary. How do you want to choose the services?" On a roll, we brainstormed possibilities; the work ahead of us loomed large.

"Wow!" Gene exclaimed. "We've got a lot to do. How am I going to get six months off of work?" I didn't consider that. I was newly retired, but Gene still had a full-time job. And he wanted to keep it for a while longer.

"I think we should move forward slowly and do what we can to make this happen," I suggested. "If it's really meant to be, the pieces will fall in place."

The journey took on a new significance. It was no longer an adventure for its own sake, but became about serving others and listening for the Holy Spirit in our lives. We didn't know what the future held, but we trusted that we were in good hands. We were "all in."

We met with Pastor Andy, and the ideas that had swirled around in our heads since his Sunday message spilled out. I was excited and nervous at the same time. We hardly knew the guy. What would he think? After listening to our story, Pastor uncrossed his legs and leaned forward. "I think this has the fingerprints of God all over it," he said. "One of the things that helps to discern a call from God is that God gives us confirmation to let us know that we're on the right track. You've already gotten confirmation from each other, and now from me. If Gene's leave is approved, that'll be another one. You've told me you know the important thing . . . this trip isn't about you. Your job is to listen, follow, and point to God. God's the one who changes hearts." He paused, then added, "God might even change yours."

It was happening already. I wasn't sure what changed, but I no longer felt the same. I couldn't wait to dive headfirst into an experience that just last week terrified me—to force myself to put my trust in God.

Chapter 2
Preparations

CHOOSING A LAUNCH DATE was our first hurdle. I held out little hope for a six-month weather window with dry, comfortable days. A quick look at average monthly temperatures and rainfall for the states from Minnesota to Louisiana confirmed my suspicion. No matter how we framed the time period, we were bound to have some ugly weather. After checking with the Minnesota DNR about river depth levels, we decided to leave from Lake Itasca on June 1, 2013. The weather would be cool at first, but the spring rain and snowmelt would make the water high enough to make it safely through the bogs and the rapids at the headwaters. By the time fall temperatures arrived, we hoped to be well into the southern states.

Gene immediately wrote a letter requesting a leave from his convenience store management position until the end of November. A few weeks later, he returned from the mailbox, waving the envelope we'd both been waiting for. He sat down at the table and tore it open, reading silently.

"Well?" I asked, impatiently peeking over his shoulder.

"We better start planning," he said, with a grin. "Six months off! I just have to fill out these official forms." He scanned the leave request form. "This looks pretty easy. But it says here that leaves will only be granted for up to two months."

"And they gave you six?" I thought about what Pastor said about looking for confirmation—for things to fall into place. Gene's leave was three times longer than the two-month maximum. "I think that's a sign."

"Yeah," he said. "It's pretty impressive. Of course, it'll be unpaid."

"It'll be fine. We expected that," I reminded him. Weeks earlier, we crunched the numbers. We could buy the equipment we needed while we had his income. During the lean months, my pension would pay most of the household bills, and we had savings to help out. "We're probably not going to be spending much money on the river, anyway." I hoped that was true.

Fully committed to the trip, we had three seasons to prepare, and began to learn just how much we didn't know. If the recognition of our cluelessness struck me all at once, I might have been overwhelmed. Rather, the things we needed to learn arose casually and manageably. Our plan developed over time as well— one dinner conversation, one suggestion from a friend, one idea from a book, and one Google search at a time.

We began our initial itinerary planning at our kitchen table, with a world atlas and a tablet of sticky notes, dividing the roughly 2,500 Mississippi miles into monthly goals. "The current will get stronger as we get further down," Gene pointed out. "We won't cover as many miles in a day up in the headwaters. I don't think we want to set our goals too high the first month."

"I'm all for that," I said. I wasn't worried about the current limiting our mileage; I was worried about me. How many miles could I paddle in a day, one day after another? It wouldn't hurt to spend the first month easing into some longer stretches. In the meantime, we needed to get some serious practice on the water.

During the remaining summer months, we set off for the river towns of Prairie du Chien, La Crosse, Trempealeau, and Winona to get acquainted with the Mississippi. We spent whole days on the water, navigating with river charts and paddling between the channel buoys and the shore, avoiding the huge barges and power yachts. Weaving through the side channels, or sloughs (pronounced *slews)*, we paused to watch bald eagles soar overhead, and herons wade near the water's edge. We even practiced passing through two of the river's twenty-seven locks. The towering walls and huge metal doors became less intimidating as I learned the routine and felt the surprisingly gentle transition to the water level of the river pool below. In La Crosse, as the south gate of Lock #7 opened, we paddled out into the gorgeous panorama of Pool 8. Cotton clouds drifting through the cerulean summer sky reflected up from the river's surface ahead. Every so often, a lone vehicle caught my eye as it passed the verdant treed bluffs on ribbons winding along the shore. I found myself actually looking forward to more days like these.

During one river trip, we tried out our new camp stove, the Whisper Lite. Weighing less than a pound, the tiny stove had only one burner that used a small canister of IsoPro fuel to heat a single pot. It heated water quickly to cook our dehydrated Mountain House lasagna. "This isn't bad," Gene said, scraping the last of the noodles from the metallic bag, "but it wasn't cheap. I bet we could make our own meals."

After that, weekly grocery trips and visits to the farmer's market became more than opportunities to buy food for the week. We began to stock up for the future—fresh foods to dehydrate, protein bars, snack mixes, hot cereals, and cocoa packets. Soon our pantry morphed into Dried Food Central, shelves loaded with colorful mason jars of dehydrated carrots, corn, assorted peppers, green beans, peas, fruit, and a variety of meats. We experimented with online recipes, combining protein with rice or pasta and vegetables for a variety of one-dish skillet meals.

"We prob'ly should try one of these," Gene suggested, "before we finish making too many of them." The idea had merit, even if it did mean foregoing the fresh contents of our fridge in favor of rehydrated taco casserole.

"The rice is done, and the spices taste great," I said after my first spoonful. I rolled a piece of grit around with my tongue, wondering if it was meat or a lost filling. "I think the beef might need a little more simmer, though."

"Let's check YouTube," suggested Gene. "I bet we could make a cozy that would help us keep the water hot longer. It would solve our simmering problem, and save on fuel, too."

After several more dry runs with our new foam-and-duct-tape pot cozy, we zeroed in on our recipes and cooking procedures. Slowly, our collection of vacuum-sealed meals grew to meet our goal of 140 dinners. We packed them in prepaid Priority Mail boxes with serving sizes of hot cereals, protein bars, nuts, and dried fruit—enough for seven days out of ten. "I'm sure we'll want to stop at some small-town diners and an occasional Subway," said Gene. "Heck—we're paddling across the country. I'm gonna have to try all the regional dishes. I don't think I have a choice!"

The search for service opportunities and the development of our itinerary also evolved slowly, one connection at a time. The requirements were dictated by our only methods of transportation. "It's either kayak or Nike," Gene became fond of saying. I searched Internet listings of non-profit organizations within walking distance of the river, checked online maps for campgrounds or nearby hotels, and perused organization websites for those whose missions touched our hearts. Emails and phone calls ensued, and word of our upcoming trip spread. Requests came from people we didn't know, along with confirmations from most of those we asked. Things rarely worked out the way we first envisioned, but I took comfort that they fell into place the way they were meant to be.

With help from the Minnesota State Water Trail Guides, we made daily travel and lodging plans for the first ten weeks of our trip. Gene crafted a spreadsheet coordinating our daily mileage and lodging with service dates and contact information. We decided to leave an extra day, or flex day, in each stretch between service towns, in case of illness or inclement weather.

South of the Minnesota/Iowa border, the maps weren't nearly as detailed. "Let's leave our itinerary more flexible after the first two months," I suggested. "If we book ourselves too solid and something unexpected happens, we'll have a lot of plans to change. By the time we get to Iowa, we'll have enough experience to find the places we need." We sketched a rough plan to St. Louis that included mileage goals for long stretches between cities, and listed the camping options we found. South of St. Louis, we'd figure it out as we went.

Once we had some idea of what we were doing, we shared our plans with our four adult children, who had varying reactions to the news. Eric—my college junior—immediately offered to take care of the house and our pet chinchilla, Raji. "During summer break, anyway," he said. "It'll be good practice for when I'm a homeowner."

Gene's youngest son, Andy, volunteered to help Eric with the yardwork and send our food boxes as often as we needed them. "I can help with Raji once Eric goes back to school, too," he offered. "And if you need a ride home at Thanksgiving, I'll see about driving down."

"Just be safe," cautioned Cassie, Gene's daughter in Tennessee. "Let me know when you get down south," she said, "and I'll try to drive over from Nashville to meet you."

But Gene's oldest son, Nicholas, a personal trainer in California, had some reservations. "*I* wouldn't even think of doing a trip like that—and I'm in a *lot* better shape than *you* are," he chided. Okay. It probably wouldn't hurt to work out a little.

Although healthy, Gene and I both carried some extra pounds. His, around his middle, didn't show much on his lanky frame. Just shy of five feet eight inches, my Rubenesque features would have been considered ravishing in the seventeenth century. Growing up, I often wished for a body like the Barbies I owned, but didn't play with. We looked through my decades' worth of failed Get-Your-Perfect-Body-Quick DVD programs, choosing one to help strengthen our upper bodies.

Thus began our rigorous program of pull-ups, push-ups, and weight-lifting exercises alternating with yoga, plyometrics, and martial arts. Gene and I encouraged each other and commiserated together through daily workouts, determined to have visible biceps, triceps, and abs by June. Not far into the program, however, shooting pains in both my elbows made it impossible to continue. Tendonitis was the diagnosis and the treatment was rest.

"I don't know how I'll even paddle if this doesn't get better," I confided to Gene. I strapped elastic elbow braces around both arms, and switched to walking and cardio workouts to keep in shape.

Gene gave up his rigorous workouts, too, probably in an effort to be supportive. "We'll get a workout every day on the river," he said, plopping down beside me on the reclining loveseat. "Besides, it's all downstream."

"How hard could it be?" we both chimed in unison.

***

As the crisp chill of fall turned to the deep freeze of Wisconsin winter, we started our blog site, Paddle for a Purpose, on Wordpress.com. It was easy to manage and I soon felt comfortable creating and saving posts. Our site went live in January, with an introduction, posts about our preparations, and a countdown to our launch date. Now, it got real.

"Have you thought any more about a name for the kayak?" Gene asked, as he worked on adding pictures to our blog.

"I still kinda like The Love Boat," I joked. The moniker had popped up right away after our service trip plan was hatched in response to the sermon about love. "We'd have a melody for a theme song we could use and everything." I started to sing, "Looove Boat, exciting and new . . ."

"I like it," agreed Gene, "but it might not be the interpretation we're going for."

"What about a word for love in another language?" I asked.

"It should be a verb, like Pastor Andy said," Gene added. "It's kind of a theme of the trip."

We considered several options in many languages before Gene, Eric, and I agreed on a perfect fit: *Kupendana* (Koo-pen-dah'-nah) a Kiswahili verb for "love." We chose Kiswahili not only because of its beautiful sound, but because the people of Kenya had a special place in our hearts as a result of our travels there. The connotation was a perfect fit, too—love for one another, like the kind of love Jesus talked about when he said to his disciples, "A new command I give you: Love one another. As I have loved you, so you must love one another" (John 13:34, NIV). *Kupendana*'s formal name soon gave way to the nickname "Donna" when we talked or wrote about her.

We spent winter evenings making lists of equipment we thought we needed, and weekends shopping sporting goods sales. Weight and size of each item was balanced with cost. As the pile of supplies filled the corner of the room, Gene asked, "Do you have any idea of our maximum weight capacity?"

"Not really, but I can check the website." I read from the description of the Osprey Double. "It says here the maximum capacity is determined by its volume."

"So, basically, we can fill 'er up?" asked Gene.

"Sounds that way," I said, incredulous. "But I still think we should save weight wherever we can." Any extra weight would make it harder to paddle and to portage.

Soon, we effectively filled the boat. The bow, in front of the paddler's feet, held dry bags stuffed with our clothing. Mid-ship, we would store two plastic canister bear vaults for food, plus our mess kit, stove, and computer. The stern, behind the rear paddler, was reserved for our tent, mattresses, and bedrolls. Small items were stuck in every crevice and in deck bags clipped on top of the boat. Also housed on the deck would be a solar charger, a pop-up sail, and a set of portage wheels. I hoped the website was right.

***

As the weather warmed and the crocuses bloomed amidst the remnant snow of winter, we became eager for a taste of summer sport. "There's a big paddle expo in Madison this weekend. Let's go check it out," Gene suggested. Wandering through the exhibits at Canoecopia, we chatted with outfitters, experts, and other adventurers.

One paddler confessed to three unsuccessful attempts to paddle the Mississippi River with one of his best buddies. "Irreconcilable differences," he explained. "Each time, we got so mad at each other, it took a year before we could even talk."

His story reminded me of a friend's reaction to our upcoming trip. "How are you both going to survive in a boat together for six months?" she asked. "You're talkin' twenty-four/seven. If I tried that with my husband, I'd kill 'im." I laughed at the time, but her question lingered. Maybe we could avoid potential pitfalls by talking about them first.

After dinner one evening, I broached the subject. "Are you worried about getting on each other's nerves, spending so much time cooped up together?"

"Not at all," came his immediate reply.

"Would you tell me if you were?" I sat down next to him on the couch, laying a hand on his arm.

"Probably not," he said. "It'll all work out." His honesty was touching, but didn't make the conversation easier.

"I know we won't fight," I said. "Neither one of us does that. But you're stronger, and you might think I'm not doing my share of the work."

"There'll be times when I'm sore or tired, too. Like on our bike trips," Gene said. I remembered the bicycle vacations we took with Eric while he still lived at home. He continued, "It worked real well for the person who felt weakest to set the pace."

I had one more request. "And let's promise, no matter what happens, to try not to complain and not to blame each other."

"I'm sure we'll both do plenty of stupid things," Gene said, "but we're a team, and we're in this together." He pulled his hand out from under mine, as if ending the conversation. "I don't know if I can do six months without complaining, though," he added.

I grabbed the book I'd been reading and handed it to him—*A Complaint-Free World*, by Will Bowen. "I don't know if I can, either.

But there's an idea in here that might help. He suggests wearing a bracelet and switching the bracelet to the other wrist if you catch yourself complaining. I'm going to try it and I'll let you know what I think." I gave him a kiss and added, "Let me know if you notice a difference."

"I think I complain more than you do," he said. "Maybe I'll try it, too. But I really don't think we have anything to worry about. This is God's trip. We'll be just fine as long as we remember to let him control the rudder."

I knew what he meant. We both felt called to take this journey. It was comforting to trust that God would provide us with a common direction to face together.

Chapter 3
A Tough Start

May 31: Itasca State Park, MN

A HEAVY BLANKET OF CLOUDS made the late afternoon seem more like dusk as Gene turned his Mazda Tribute into the entrance of Itasca State Park. Eric, on summer break from college, reclined in the back seat. After seeing us off, he'd drive the Mazda home and *Kupendana*, Gene, and I would be on our own. We checked in at the Headwaters Hostel, where we would spend our last foreseeable night sleeping on beds with real mattresses, and then used the remaining daylight to scope out the site for our launch the next morning. We wound through the narrow forested roads to the Welcome Center, only to find it already closed. As I scanned the empty lot, searching for signs to give us a sense of direction, a green Chevy Tahoe pulled into the parking lot and crept slowly into a space not far away from where our kayak perched atop Gene's truck.

We must have looked as clueless as we felt, for the driver stepped out of his truck and offered an outstretched hand. "Can I help you?" he asked. "My name's Joel. I'm the campground manager here at the park." Joel's forest green hoodie was tucked underneath a pair of navy blue waders cinched up with wide elastic suspenders. We shook hands all around and introduced ourselves. Joel propped his sunglasses on his forehead, exposing calm, contented eyes, a good match for his welcoming smile. "Nice boat. Did you build it yourselves?" He pointed to *Kupendana*.

"Sure did." Gene grinned. He explained we were checking out the river for our launch the following day, then asked, "How do we get to the headwaters?"

Joel pointed to a path that began near the Welcome Center. "It's down that path, about eight hundred yards. You can't miss it." Then he smiled mischievously and continued. "If you have trouble finding it . . . I wouldn't even consider going any farther."

"You've got a point there," laughed Eric. I chuckled at the prospect of getting lost while trying to find the Mississippi River before beginning the trip.

"You picked a good time to start," Joel explained. "The water's high from the late ice melt. That'll help you with the current and the rapids. But it's not so high that you'll have trouble getting under the bridges."

"I'm just glad the water's open," I said. "Less than a month ago, we heard that Cass Lake still had three feet of ice."

"I was worried we'd need to put runners on the kayak," joked Gene.

"The water's still pretty cold, but the river's open and navigable," said Joel. "You should be fine. Just be careful. Every year, I meet a dozen or more people who try what you're tryin'. And lots of 'em don't make it, for one reason or another." He paused, giving me time to think about possible reasons I didn't really want to consider. Then he continued, "I hardly ever find out whether they do or not."

I stifled a twinge of doubt. For a moment, I thought about the wills we planned to update, but didn't. Maybe we should have. Then I pushed back any thought of quitting before we started. "We're going to be posting blogs during the trip," I offered. "You can check up on us once in a while and find out when we finish." I gave him a business card with our names, a picture of the boat, and our blog address.

"Thanks, I will," said Joel. He pulled a card from his pocket, pressing it into my palm. "You call me if you get in any trouble," he advised. I felt pretty sure we wouldn't need it, but was glad to have a safety net. I tucked the card into my waterproof wallet.

June 1–4: Lake Itasca to Bemidji, MN

Our launch day was nothing like I anticipated. We awoke early to a cold and windy morning. The mercury in the thermometer was trying, without success, to push itself up over forty. The weather app on my phone informed us that the high would be fifty-two degrees, but not until the afternoon. A misty drizzle from a blanket of gray clouds emphasized the misery of the date that we so excitedly chose long ago.

"You can shower first," I said to Gene. I pulled the blankets up over my head, stealing a final few minutes in the comfort of my toasty bed.

"You don't have to wait for me. There's a women's shower, remember?" *My, he was chipper at six-thirty in the morning.*

"Ohhhh," I whined. "You didn't have to remind me." Then, upset with myself, I changed my elastic bracelet to my other wrist, yawned, and dragged myself out of bed. I needed a cup of coffee. And an attitude change. Today was only the first of many during the months ahead. I fully expected to have days that were warm and sunny, as well as inevitable miserable days like today. We'd paddle through all of it. I showered, then donned double layers of wicking fabric on top and shorts on the bottom. We each had one dry bag of shorts, shirts, socks, and undies for paddling, but only one pair of lightweight sweatpants. I intended to keep those dry for sleeping. My legs would warm up soon enough, sealed inside the hull under my spray skirt.

After coffee and a quick breakfast, we donned our rain gear, drove to the lot, and unloaded Donna from the truck, strapping her onto the set of portage wheels. Even with help from Eric, it took half an hour to transfer all the gear into place and pull the entire rig to the river's source. We slipped into our bright yellow spray skirts. Suspenders held the tube-shaped bodice around my chest, but the hem, which would later seal around the cockpit, now hung down like an ill-fitting rubber dress. I zipped my blue rain jacket up over the top and pulled up the hood. With all the layers, I was actually quite toasty, but felt akin to a pudgy blue and yellow Teletubby.

We took a walk over to a carved post marking the spot where the mighty Mississippi began. A small stream of water trickled out of the northern finger of Lake Itasca, gurgling over moss-covered stones into a shallow pebbled riverbed only twenty feet wide. The river actually flowed north at first, but I knew from the maps we studied that it would meander east, then eventually turn south, like a big question mark, toward its final destination, the Gulf of Mexico. Posing in front of the sign, we pointed the way the river flowed. "Say cheese," Eric called, framing the picture.

"Nope," said Gene, pointing downstream. "Café au lait and beignets in New Orleans, baby! That way!" I laughed at his optimism. Here I was, thinking about getting to Coffee Pot Landing before nightfall, and Gene had already made reservations at Café du Monde for six months from now. I thought of the last time I had beignets—the melt-in-your mouth fried pillow-shaped doughnuts smothered in mountains of powdered sugar. Mmm. By the time we got to New Orleans, I'd have paid for those calories many times over and planned to enjoy every bite.

Several park visitors congregated to watch as we walked Donna down the boardwalk at the river's edge, removed the wheels, and lowered her into the reeds. Joel was right about the current. It wasn't easy to keep the boat from taking off as we strapped the wheels onto the deck, climbed aboard, and slipped into the cockpits. I stretched the elastic edge of my spray skirt over the raised wooden rim around the cockpit where I sat. The coaming would hold the waterproof fabric in place, sealing the cockpit, as long as we stayed upright. Gene did the same. In case of a wet exit—a paddler's fancy name for tipping over and falling out—we could pull the nylon loops on the front of the skirts to release them, allowing us to tumble out to safety. At home, we watched videos of wet exits and reentry methods, planning to practice once the water warmed up later in the summer. Eric walked on ahead to the pedestrian bridge to document our departure. We pushed off to begin our journey, filled with great expectations.

A mere 100 yards downstream, we met our first obstacle—the pedestrian bridge. I hoped Joel was right about having enough clearance to pass under it. The wooden beams supporting the walkway looked awfully low. I waved to Eric for a photo op as we approached. Then, holding my paddle down across the deck with one hand, I leaned as far back as flexibility allowed. I guided myself under the solid wooden beams with my other hand, my face inches from disaster. Just as I emerged from under the bridge, but before I could sigh with relief, I was rolling sideways. "What the heck?" I yelled, then my body hit the water. I had no choice but to reach forward and pull the release loop on my spray skirt. *Kupendana* handled the roll gracefully. Her contents stayed inside, but we both spilled into the frigid stream. While Gene turned the half-filled kayak upright and held her steady, I raced through the waist-deep water to snatch my paddle and hat, swept downstream by the rushing current.

"Are you all right?" Eric shouted from the bridge.

"Yep," I replied. "Just surprised." Glancing at the people lined up along the shore, watching our grand departure, I added, "And a little embarrassed." I looked downstream for a place to bail the boat. "We'll meet you by the steps next to the bridge, over there," I pointed.

As Gene and I pulled the boat over to the bank by the steps, I asked, "What happened? One moment, I was just coming out from the bridge, and the next thing I knew, we were rolling."

"I'm sorry," Gene apologized. "You laid back and went under the bridge just fine. But with my height, I knew I couldn't make it. I leaned sideways so I wouldn't crack my head against the bridge, and we went over."

"It's okay, hon. I'm glad you weren't hurt. I just didn't expect it." As an afterthought, I added, "We can check that wet exit off our to-do list."

Gene brightened slightly. "I think this might be one of the moments we'll laugh about later," he said. "But I'm glad Joel wasn't here to see it. He'd really worry about us if he knew we couldn't even make it out of the park without tipping over."

We spent the next hour removing all our bags from the boat, bailing the water with our cook pots, sponging it dry as best we could, and replacing all of the contents while standing thigh deep in the Mississippi. Eric helped from the shore and chronicled the whole event on his phone's camera.

"You didn't get a picture of us going over, did you?" I asked.

"I'm pretty sure I did." He chuckled. "Gene was under the bridge, but I got a great one of you." I threw a potful of water at him. He jumped back as it sprayed out a rainbow of water droplets. "Want me to send it to you?"

"Sure, it'll be funny to post it on our blog once we get to Bemidji." I wondered what I looked like in the picture. Scared? Maybe. Surprised? Probably. Graceful? Doubtful. To my knowledge, no one had ever used that word to describe me.

Finally, I climbed ashore to give Eric a wet hug. "Thanks for everything," I said. "Drive carefully going home."

"I will, Mom."

"I love you," I said. "I'll see you in a few weeks." Eric planned to drive up again to meet us at my brother's house when we passed through the Twin Cities. But Dave's home, less than four hours from Itasca by car, would take us five weeks to reach by kayak.

I climbed into the cockpit once more, this time a little colder, a lot wetter, and considerably more humble. "Look at it this way," said Gene, once we were under way. "The day has got to get better."

The first day's paddle proved to be a test of our patience and humor. Still wet from head to toe, we faced wind, cold, and rain. Once it was too late to turn back, my hindsight kicked in. "We probably should have changed into dry clothes," I said with a shiver. "I'm sure the Welcome Center was open by the time we left."

"I didn't think of it, either," admitted Gene. "I really just wanted to get out of there." He was silent for a few minutes, then continued, "I keep going over in my head if there was something I could have done differently, but I can't come up with anything. Maybe if we would have leaned different directions . . ."

"But there was no time to tell me." I tried to encourage him. "You did the right thing. And it gave us a great story to tell, too."

"Remember when I was worried that my pride would get in the way?" he asked. I did remember. We reminded each other often to keep service to others our focus, not our accomplishments. Gene continued, "I don't think that's an issue."

After a few hours, we approached our first portage around an old abandoned dam and rapids. We prepared for what was described on our map as a sixty-yard trail that would take us to the other side of the river obstruction. I hoped our wheels would make it an easy walk around the rapids. Once I saw the steep, boulder-strewn and rutted hill, I knew the wheels would be useless. First, we took multiple trips up the rough, rocky path and down the other side of the hill with our gear. Then, we carried our empty sixty-pound boat to the launch site, repacked her once more, and finally resumed our paddle over an hour later.

The next set of rapids—a four-mile stretch of sandbars and rocks—could not be portaged. If the water level was low, we might have worried about the sandbars. But with the river running high and fast, the underwater rocks were our biggest concern. We began to steer Donna through the rolling water, swerving to avoid what could be our second catastrophe of the day. We knew that any one of the rocks could turn the boat sideways to the current, overturning it with a powerful surge. Our twenty-foot craft struggled to make the quick turns necessary to slalom around the rocks. "It's shallow enough here for us to walk the boat through this part," Gene suggested. "It might be better than scratching the heck out of it."

Once again, we found ourselves in the chilly river. The strong current clawed at us, sweeping us to and fro in water that dropped from knee to chest high without warning. The best we could do was to scramble over the boulders in the uneven riverbed, using our legs as bumpers, guiding and protecting our wooden boat. I felt like a Mario Brothers video game character, my legs churning while I leaped over some obstacles and crashed into others, the controller in the hands of the Mississippi current.

Finally, we climbed back in to finish our first day's paddle. I wished that I could enjoy the scenery, but what might have looked spectacular on another day only looked dismal through the gray mist that dripped from the brim of my hat, speckled my glasses, and collected on my coat. Even though I wore my arm braces, my elbows began to ache and I found myself needing to take more frequent breaks. Late in the afternoon, after nineteen long miles, we finally spotted Coffee Pot Landing. The only available campsite was across the river, so we locked *Kupendana* to a tree and took several trips over the bridge with our gear. After the day on the water, it felt good to walk. Each time we passed over the bridge, we paused, leaning on the railing to watch the river flow by.

"I wonder how much water flows past here every minute," Gene said. "It's gotta be a lot, at this rate." I tried counting to sixty as I watched the water flow under the bridge. Gene continued, "It's hard to believe that this volume of water can just keep flowing at this rate, every day, twenty-four/seven, without draining the lake."

"The Mississippi watershed is huge," I said, remembering what I read. "Thirty-one states and even part of Canada feed into this one river. It's pretty amazing."

"Well, she really beat up on us today, didn't she?" said Gene. We both looked down at our cut and bruised legs. "Let's go get a fire started and warm up. Then I'll make you hot cocoa and some dinner."

We awoke the next morning feeling every one of our fifty-plus years. My elbows ached, and my legs were mottled with red, black, and blue from their abuse in the rapids. We took inventory of our injuries, and then started the day with Aleve.

Gene dressed and went out to start breakfast while I rolled up the mattresses and bedrolls. "Barb, look at this!" he called. I peeked out of the screen door to see Gene rapping his paddle glove on the picnic table. Clunk! Clunk! Our wet gloves, left on the table to dry, were frozen stiff. The night was chilly, but I didn't expect a hard frost. After all, it was June! While we waited for the frost to burn off and the tent to dry, we enjoyed a warm, hearty oatmeal breakfast and steaming cups of hot cocoa.

Soon, patches of bright light among the foliage announced good news—the cloud cover had dissipated. We quickly tied our clothesline between two trees and hung up our wet belongings while we broke camp. The warmth and light brightened more than the foliage; it bolstered our spirits as we looked forward to our first dry and sunny day on the river.

The river transformed from the forested terrain of the previous day into an endless maze of wetlands and bogs. Reeds and cattails obscured our view to the sides, enticing us forward. Frequent loops and switchbacks gave us a false sense of progress. The channel was so narrow that I pushed my paddle against the reeds to complete the tight turns without grounding.

Often we came to forks in the river with two or three different options. At each fork, only one of the directions followed the main channel. Paddling down one of the other channels could lead to a backwater maze with an ultimate dead end. We needed to choose carefully; getting lost and backtracking would waste precious time.

We slowed as we approached a triple fork in the river. One direction was easy to eliminate. The water was still. But I noticed V-shaped ripples from the current around the stems of cattails edging both remaining choices. "The main current's one of these two." I pointed with my paddle. Droplets of water slid off the blade, their ringlets quickly absorbed by the river sliding by. I remembered reading that when in doubt, the best way to determine the true channel was to check the underwater vegetation. "Can you see the bottom?" I asked.

"No. It's too deep here," Gene replied, "but I'll steer us over to the side." He swerved to the nearest bank.

I strained to see past the surface glare. The seaweed leaned downstream, swaying gently, as if pushed by a summer breeze.

"There's a little current, but let's check the other bank," I suggested. Gene steered over to check our second option. Long green ribbons of seaweed, rooted into the riverbed, lay nearly flat against the silt river bottom. "*This* is it," I said. "No doubt about it."

With clouds, but no rain, we witnessed more wildlife than the previous day. Trumpeter swans, startled into flight, sounded their warning calls. Canada geese and great blue herons watched us pass with wary eyes. Beavers swam along the edge of the reeds, and loons disappeared under the water only to pop up again hundreds of yards away.

"Look—ahead on the left—what is that?" whispered Gene. We stopped paddling and drifted. I was used to the rhythmic cadence of our paddles dipping into the water; without it, the soft swish of the river against our hull was the loudest sound I could hear.

I scanned the river ahead, but saw nothing unusual. Then, in the dappled shadows of the reeds on the left, I made out the tufted head silhouette of a merganser—then a second. Zigzagging behind them were several miniature versions. I didn't answer Gene, but pointed to the family. I started to count the ducklings to myself, but before I could finish, I realized we were spotted. As the male took flight, the female dove beneath the surface. The babies mimicked the diving escape, rejoining their mother near the bank and scrambling into the safety of the reeds.

"I think those were mergansers," I said, as we resumed our work. "That was awesome. Did you see the way the male distracted us while the rest of the family took cover?"

"And Dad'll circle back around and join them after we're gone," Gene said. I looked around, but couldn't see the male. I wondered how far he went. Unlike us, I was sure he'd have no trouble finding his way around. This was his backyard.

Minutes stretched into hours of paddling, and I felt a familiar ache in my elbows. As I continued to pull, the ache developed into a searing pain. Each paddle stroke stabbed spikes into my tendons. My eyes watered. I backed off, paddling with my elbows in a fixed position. Minor relief came at the expense of efficiency. My torso stiffly twisted back and forth, sacrificing valuable range of motion. I was sure Gene noticed my contorted technique. "Sorry I'm not much help," I said, craning my neck and speaking into the air over my shoulder. "I'm trying everything I can, but my elbows are screaming at me."

"It's okay," encouraged Gene. "Take a break whenever you need one." I was thankful that he still felt strong. I rested my paddle on the coaming until my arms stopped throbbing, but when I felt ready to begin again, merely stretching them out produced wrenching pain.

I silently mouthed a prayer. "Lord, you know my heart. You know I'm all in and don't want to quit. But I know I can't last six months with this much pain. Please help me complete the work you called us to do. Amen." I prayed with confidence, but the immediacy of my relief still caught me by surprise. My pain was gone. I glanced up and smiled. I began to paddle slowly, with a full range of motion. No pain. I closed my eyes, concentrating on each elbow movement. Nothing.

"Feeling better?" Gene asked from behind me.

"No pain right now," I said. "But I'm taking it easy." I'd tell him the whole story later. I wanted to make sure it was true. I believed my release from pain was an answer to my prayer. But what if it came back?

A few miles later, I felt a dull ache in my elbow. I braced myself for the searing pain, but it never came. I can live with this, I thought, and whispered, "Thank you."

After eighteen miles of wiggles and waggles, we pulled over to the grassy shore at Pine Point. The sprawling campground was deserted. "This looks like a good place," said Gene, pointing to a grassy site near a wooden lean-to sheltering a picnic table.

We set up our tent and stretched the rain fly over the top. Rain wasn't in the forecast, but the extra covering of fabric would keep us warmer and keep the morning dew off the tent. I crawled inside and unfolded one of the lightweight, crinkly space blankets we brought along, laying the silver side up to reflect our body heat from below. I removed the Velcro straps from around our air mattresses and watched them slowly unroll as they self-inflated. I was glad we decided to spend the money and allocate the extra weight for the three-and-a-half-inch-thick pads. If I wanted to last more than a week out here, I'd need my sleep. Closing the valves of the mattresses, I spread out our two fleece blankets and melted into the soft cushiony bed. *Ahh. This was heaven.*

"Doin' okay in there?" Gene asked, peeking through the door.

"Yep. Just relaxing. I'll blow up the pillows and be right out." I placed the pillows at the head of the bed and spread the second space blanket on top, this time silver side down. Sandwiching ourselves between two heat-reflective layers kept us warm the night before, even though temperatures dipped below freezing outside. It would be cold tonight, too, but this time, we were dry.

"Just in time," Gene said as I emerged to find the picnic table set with our plastic bowls and insulated mugs. "I took the liberty of preparing dinner." My stomach growled. Gene took the foam off the insulated pot cozy. He lifted the cover of the pot as a chef might lift the silver dome off a platter of Coq au Vin. "Quinoa with peppers, in a tomato sauce." Quinoa never tasted better.

As we ate, I told Gene about the relief from my tendonitis. "I know my prayers have been answered before," I said. "But usually there's some wait time. Today was different."

"So, you have no pain at all?" asked Gene.

"Not right now," I assured him. "And nothing like the stabbing pain I had. But I didn't pray for no pain at all. I asked God to help me finish the trip."

Gene took my hand in his. "When you were hurting so much, I was afraid we might have to stop the trip. It would be okay with me if we have to, you know."

"I know. If we need to stop, we will," I assured him. "But now, my aches are small ones I can handle. I've decided, when I get them, to let them remind me to back off and be grateful I can continue."

After dinner, we walked up to the bluff and watched the setting sun turn the wetland water trails from orange to pink to deep purple, before turning in for the night.

When I awoke on Monday, the tent was already uncomfortably warm. Darn! This would be another late start. Our plan, from the beginning, was to be on the river by eight each morning. So far, we hadn't made it yet. I rolled over and pushed back the space blanket. Drops of condensation clung to the underside. It kept us warm, but didn't breathe worth a darn. I couldn't wait for warmer nights.

Gene stirred. I sat up and reached for my dry bag to change out of my pajamas. My fingers wouldn't bend to snap open the latch. I stretched them out, and was surprised to see swollen knobs where my knuckles used to be. *Great.* "Honey," I said to Gene, "look at my hands. I can't bend my fingers." I tried to make a fist, but managed only a claw.

Gene sat up and held out his hands. "Me, too. I bet it's from all the paddling." I expected sore muscles—maybe even blisters—but no one had prepared me for zombie hands. Gene unzipped the tent. "I'll get some Advil from the first aid kit."

"I'll take two," I said. I downed my double dose of anti-inflammatories, massaging my fingers in a vain attempt to speed the effect. Groans and moans accompanied nearly every movement. I veiled my complaints in a sad attempt at humor. "I'll change my bracelet . . . once I can pull it off." Zipping was a formidable challenge and rolling up the mattresses was nearly impossible, but within half an hour the meds kicked in and my hands were useful once more. Fueled by a breakfast of oatmeal with nuts and raisins, we broke camp and packed the boat for day three on the water.

Since Gene took the stern-steering responsibilities the first two days, he adjusted the foot pegs for me to get some rudder time. As I slid into the cockpit, my heart pounded. I wanted to take my turn at the helm, but after all Gene went through the first two days, was I ready? The only way to get the practice I needed was to muster the courage to shove off.

As it turned out, I got plenty of practice steering. New wiggle-waggles provided a challenge for Donna's turning radius and our paddling skills. We kept our eyes on the underwater grasses for directional guidance. We took one wrong turn and, after a few twists, found ourselves in a dead end shallows.

"I can see the channel right there, through those reeds," said Gene. "Think we could get through?" He pushed his paddle down to check the depth. The water barely covered the blade. "It's a couple of feet," he assessed. "But it looks like it gets shallower in the middle of the cattails."

I considered the silt on his paddle blade. "I don't think I really want to get out and push if we get stuck in that," I said.

"Me, neither," Gene admitted. "All I can picture is Humphrey Bogart, covered in leeches, pulling the *African Queen* through the muck." We backed out and retraced our steps to find the main channel, and were on our way.

Our river map indicated a change from the "wild" section to the "scenic" section of the headwaters. What I noticed was the change from a wetland to a woodland habitat. Unfortunately, much of the area was devastated. "Looks like a pretty bad storm blew through here," said Gene.

We paddled past long lines of trees whose trunks were broken, leaning over as if a giant dog ran through a flowerbed, bending, then breaking every stem at the same height.

In the afternoon, we passed through a six-mile stretch listed on our map with "numerous stump fields." It proved to be a maze of fallen trees extending into the water from both banks, combined with a minefield of stumps jutting out from random locations in the middle of the river.

The continuous twists and turns of the river made it difficult to plan ahead. "We need to paddle faster than the current for the rudder to steer," Gene reminded me. From the bow, he determined the best route past each new set of dangers and shouted the directions back to me. At some of the turns, pools of calm water behind the bend gave us a gift of time. We paused in the backwater, decided on a plan, and then gained speed to slalom the section safely.

Being a sea kayak, Donna was designed for open water and large rivers, not slaloming through obstacle courses. Gene and I successfully avoided collision until a stump caught the port side of our boat, turning it sideways to the current. Donna started to roll. Rushing water poured into my cockpit. Oh, no—not again!

Gene twisted to look back at me. "Are you all right?" Before I could answer, he slipped from the bow cockpit into the rushing water.

We had our half skirts on—the ones used for nice weather. They covered only the front half of the cockpit, allowed for ventilation, and should have made it possible to climb in and out without removing the skirts from the coamings. I tried to pull myself out, but the cook kit tumbled in the crash, and my feet were wedged between it and the side of the boat. "I can't get out," I yelled. The rushing water pressed the half skirt down on top of my thighs. I reached forward and pulled the nylon loop to release the skirt from the coaming, then pulled myself out of the rapidly filling boat into the raging current. Clinging to the side of the boat, I watched my half-skirt bob downstream.

Water pounded against my back. Gene clung with one arm to a fallen tree, grasping the bowline with the other. Donna was wedged between a log jamb next to the shore and a stump fifteen feet away. She was held captive by the current pushing against the deck and pouring into both cockpits. I stretched my feet down, but they found no bottom. I knew I couldn't let go.

"I think I can make my way to the stern," I shouted over the rushing of the water. "If I push the stern off the stump, maybe you can pull it to shore." I glanced down to find the cord that would inflate my life vest with CO_2 if I needed it. Hand over hand, I moved toward the stern. The raging current pasted my legs to the hull. Only my fingertip grip on the cockpit coaming prevented me from being swept under the boat. "Bad idea," I admitted and headed back to safety by the shore.

We hoisted ourselves out of the water onto what seemed like a beaver dam in the making, patched together with a jumble of floating logs and debris. Some of the whittled logs were partially supported on shore, and others were wedged among the debris. The bank itself was a soggy, sandy wetland; there was no dry land to pull the boat up and figure this out. Balancing on the logs, Gene wrestled to rotate Donna right side up. He removed the gear he could reach and I piled it on the soggy shore. "I think we lost one sponge to the river," he said. I found the other, but it didn't offer much promise for bailing a literal boatload of water. Once again, we used pans from our cook kit to bail the boat. Now, Donna was lighter, but facing the wrong direction.

"Let's not launch upstream," I suggested. "I've already flipped us once."

"We've still got the clothesline, right?" Gene unzipped the sport deck bag and pulled out the bundled sixteen-foot camouflaged cord. He tied it to the rudder bracket, handed me the line, and gave the bow a shove. The current took it from there. In a matter of seconds, Donna was pointed downstream. Hugging her close to the beaver logs, we finally reloaded our gear. "Ready to go?" asked Gene.

I hesitated and briefly considered asking Gene to steer. My confidence was shaken. This whole debacle was my fault. But I knew if I asked him to steer he would. I wanted another chance. I pushed down my fears and climbed in the stern. I wasn't about to be defeated by a river—not on my first day at the helm. Gene must have read my thoughts. "You got this," he said. He stepped in the bow and pushed us out into midstream.

My confidence returned as I easily maneuvered Donna through the stump field and around the next few river turns. Five minutes later, we pulled into Silver Maple Campground.

"Really?" Gene said. "We roll the boat a tenth of a mile away from our campsite?" I was glad it wasn't farther.

Everything was soggy—again. We set to work. There was firewood to gather, camp to set up, dinner to cook, and the contents of all our bags to check through. Before long, damp and dripping belongings hung from the clothesline and sat propped up against every tree. The small Bible that we brought along was soaked, its pages stuck shut. I briefly considered it a loss, but left it out to see how it would fare.

After dinner, I called Jenilynn, our contact in Bemidji, to confirm our arrival the following day. Her organization, called Fishing Has No Boundaries, held an annual fishing weekend for individuals with special needs. I was excited to begin the service part of our trip—the purpose for our paddle. I also looked forward to leaving the rapids and stump fields behind, paddling on wider and calmer waters.

"Remember looking at all those pictures of the serene streams of the headwaters?" I asked, as we prepared for bed. "I expected us to take our time, drifting along, working on our suntans. This has been *nothing* like that."

"I know," said Gene. "I wouldn't have predicted all this trouble either. But I did learn something today, about us, that makes me think we're gonna make it." I flopped over on my side to face him and propped my head on my hand as he continued. "Even though it was scary, both of us figured out one problem after another. For over two hours, we worked together to get through it safely."

"We did, didn't we?" I was surprised that I wasn't petrified. "I knew it was serious, but I wasn't scared. Somehow I knew we'd be okay." Gratefully, I thanked God for watching over us and settled into Gene's arms to get some much-needed rest.

The next morning, I reached out of my fleece cocoon, unzipped the inner fly of the tent, and peeked out the screen door. Cloud cover, but no rain. Good. I could tell it was still early by the dim light and the crisp, cool air. My arm was already chilly, but before pulling it back under the blanket, I reached for my dry bag, unclipped the top, and pulled out the bottle of Advil, clean underwear, a pair of shorts, and two shirts. Today was a day for layering. I retreated back under the covers and waited for my cool clothes to warm up before wriggling into them under the blanket. "You *are* a freezy-cat," laughed Gene, awakened by my undulations. He tossed off his side of the covers, exposing his merely boxer-clad body. "Ahhh."

Cold air hitting my bare skin was only an *Ahhh* moment during the dog days of August. "And *you're* crazy. But I love you anyway." I leaned over and gave him a kiss. I handed him his morning anti-inflammatory and checked the time on my phone. "It's almost seven. I'm going out to see if our stuff is dry."

Our clothing and deck bags were damp, but no longer drippy. I pulled our clothing off the line and rolled each piece into a tight little cylinder. Consolidating my few remaining clean paddle clothes with my still-dry service clothes, I began to pack the now empty bag with the damp laundry items.

I looked forward to spending the day in town. We were only a couple hours' paddle from Bemidji. My wish list was ready: a

Laundromat, a hotel with a bed, shower, and flush toilet, and good coffee. After three days without coffee, I began to question our decision to go cold turkey during river days rather than drink instant. We couldn't afford the weight or the space for a brewing system, and decided to get coffee as a special treat when we were in towns. Even with teabags and hot cocoa packets, I missed my morning coffee more than I expected, and wondered aloud if Bemidji had a Starbucks.

As Gene started CoCo Wheats for breakfast, I checked on the Bible that we left out to dry. The damp pages remained plastered together; they opened only at one place. I sat on top of the picnic table, my feet propped on the bench, to read the only passage available—First Corinthians, Chapter 2. I was struck by verses 4–5 (NKJ): "And my speech and my preaching were not with persuasive words of human wisdom, but in demonstration of the Spirit and of power, that your faith should not be in the wisdom of men but in the power of God."

I was nothing like Paul. I often hesitated to talk about my faith to people I didn't know. I was terrible at memorizing Bible verses, and had no confidence in my ability to explain the mysteries of faith. Our friends knew that we were taking this trip in response to the nudging of the Holy Spirit. But how would I have the courage to try to explain this to people who might think it's crazy? Just maybe, if Paul didn't rely on his own expertise, I wouldn't have to, either.

"Hey, Gene. Look at this." I showed him the soggy pages. He handed me breakfast and hopped up on the table to join me. After grace, I read the passage aloud.

"That's a timely scripture," he said. "But Paul was such a great example of humility and faith; I don't think I can compare myself to him."

"Me neither. And I'm certainly not wise or persuasive. But it's comforting to think that even Paul didn't rely on himself."

"There's no doubt that God's been with us the last few days," Gene added. "In spite of our screw-ups." We held hands and prayed for God to guide our path, put people in front of us that God wanted us to meet, and give us words to say." Then I tucked the Bible into my deck bag. Even if it never opened to another passage, I had a feeling I'd be coming back to this one.

After we paddled a short stump field section with no complications, the river opened up into the small, but beautiful Lake Irving. Due to strong winds and waves, we avoided the deep water, working our way north along the east shore. We paddled past one lake home after another, but the clouds were spitting now and no one was outdoors. I noticed a two-story contemporary home, with windows extending to the peak of a vaulted ceiling. The warm glow of the lights made me wish we could stop for a visit. "I'll take that one—with the tall windows and the dock," I said.

Gene gazed along the line of lake houses and pointed to a ranch home, situated farther back on its lot. It looked older, but had a wrap-around covered porch. I wasn't surprised when he called over his shoulder, "That one's mine." We changed our minds as fast as the next home came into sight. Before we knew it, we put dibs on a half dozen lake homes, and found ourselves paddling under the bridge onto Bemidji Lake.

Jenilynn was meeting us at a volunteer recruitment fair after she finished her workday. This gave us a few hours to look for lodging, dry our clothes, and get caught up on our emails and blogs. We turned east along the south end of the lake and stopped at the closest beach, the property of Hampton Inn.

Leaving Donna on the vacant swimming beach, we entered the lobby. I checked my appearance in the gilt-framed mirror behind the marble front desk and felt immediately out of place. My long, blonde hair was pulled back in a damp ponytail, a few unruly strands framing my wind-reddened face. The transition lenses of my prescription glasses were speckled with water droplets. I looked like I'd been through a spin cycle of the washing machine that my clothes now needed so badly. Gene was a taller version of bedraggled, the brim of his Outback hat flopped down in front of his face. Maybe we should have shaken ourselves off outside. The thought of us doing a wet-dog shake made me smile.

"May I help you?" asked a tall young man, meticulously dressed in a crisp white shirt, black suit, and tie.

"Do you have a room for one night?" I asked, trying to look nonchalant.

He sized us up, then checked his computer screen. "I'm sorry. We're full tonight." I looked down at the pools of water forming around our feet from our wet paddle shoes. Footprint puddles on the polished floor marked our entrance. Even if there was an available room in the place, I wasn't surprised to hear the opposite. I imagined the cleanup crew that would appear in the lobby the minute we left.

Gene glanced at the attendant's name badge. "Hi, Randy," he said. "We've come by kayak from Itasca, and will be in town for one night. I noticed you have a canoe rack by the beach. If we find a room somewhere else, could we leave our boat here for the night?"

"Wait here. I'll ask my manager for you." Another awkward wait. I removed my wet rain jacket and noticed that I stopped dripping. But now, I had air-conditioning goose bumps along my arms and legs. I rubbed my hands together, then along my arms to warm them.

Soon, another well-dressed gentleman approached, shook hands with Gene, and offered, "I hear you're in town for a night with a kayak? You can leave it on the property, over by the canoes. But you need to put it on the grass above the beach. And we can't be responsible for your boat or for its contents if you decide to leave it here."

"Thank you. We have a lock and covers for the cockpits," said Gene. "We'll take our valuables along with us. I'm sure the rest will be okay. Is there a Laundromat near here?"

"The road in front of the hotel leads to town. You'll find all sorts of things along that stretch, including a coin laundry. Do you need change?"

The new quarters jingled in Gene's pocket as we walked outside to secure the boat. I looped the shorter of the two lasso-shaped cables over the bow. Gene slid his loop over the stern, wrapping the extra cable length once around the trunk of a tree, then padlocked the ends of the two cables together. I gave the looped ends each a tug. They fit snugly around the bow and stern. No one was going anywhere with our Donna.

Just down the street, we hit the trifecta . . . a Laundromat, Ace Hardware, and Dunn Brothers Coffee Shop, all within a couple blocks. While the laundry tumbled, we bought some extra cotter pins for our emergency repair kit, and full-fingered gloves to warm up our frozen hands. Then we enjoyed fresh bakery and hot coffee, plugging our devices into as many outlets as we could find. While Gene changed the clothes to the dryer, I ordered a second sugar-free mocha and started typing our headwaters blog post. Four days had passed since our launch at Lake Itasca, and we knew our friends and family awaited news of our safe arrival at "the first city on the Mississippi."

By now, it was raining again. There was a campground six miles across the lake, but I was dry now, and wanted to stay that way. "Let's spring for a hotel," I suggested.

It took Gene only a few minutes on the Internet to find out that there was a convention in town, and nearly all the hotels were full. "I guess there really was no room at the inn," Gene joked. We called a cab and headed to the only available hotel—Ruttgers Lodge at the north end of the lake—with our dry bags full of freshly laundered clothing, excited to shower and meet our hosts.

June 4: Fishing Has No Boundaries

Rejuvenated by a hot shower and shampoo, I flopped on the floral comforter of our queen-sized bed. "Oh, yeah," I sighed. "Sweetie, can you throw me my service clothes? I don't want to move." On the way to the shower, Gene tossed me the dry bag that held my two dressy outfits for use in civilization. And by dressy, I mean compared to shorts and wicking tees. I propped up the pillows, sat cross-legged on the bed, and read some of the messages written on the outside of the bright orange bag—good wishes written in permanent marker by guests at our going-away party just weeks before. I smiled as I read a message from my neighbors that said, "Stay warm. Stay cool. Stay AWESOME!" So far, we'd been both warm and cool. I wasn't so sure about awesome. Another message, printed in primary script by one of my former students, said, "Missis Giger do not be gone long i miss you."

"I'm glad we had people write these messages," I said, as I snapped open the clip and unrolled the top of the bag. "They bring a little bit of home with us." I forced myself off the bed and pulled on a pair of black capris and a short-sleeved print top. A pair of bedazzled flip-flops completed my summer casual look. I longed for toenail polish, a selection of jewelry, and makeup, but those were casualties of our space and weight limitations. Foundation with sunscreen, a necklace with Eric's birthstone baby ring, and small gold hoop earrings that went with everything became my signature summer and fall look. My elastic beaded bracelet provided variety, but only because my one bracelet still changed wrists regularly.

"You ready?" Gene asked. "Jenilynn's boyfriend, Jason, is waiting down by the desk." Gene cleaned up nicely. Like me, he had two service outfits. He chose khaki tan pants with a short-sleeved moss-green shirt. I was surprised to see he had even shaved. I slid my hand seductively down the side of his face.

"Mmm. You feel nice." Then I glanced at the bed, with my flop marks still on the comforter. "You sure we have to go?" I teased.

Gene pulled me toward the door. "Come on, before you change my mind. This is the reason for all the fun we've had paddling." He opened the door and waited while I went first. "I'll try to get you home early."

Downstairs, Jason shook our hands and led the way to a black, four-door, quarter-ton pickup under the portico. I climbed in the back so Gene could have some guy talk. Sure enough, as soon as we got on the road, he commented, "Nice truck!"

"Thanks. It's Jeni's," said Jason. "She's driving my ol' beater so I can pick you up in this."

Outside Elite Performance and Fitness, families strolled the grounds and waited in line at an inflated bouncy house. "The open house started earlier this afternoon," Jason explained. "But Jeni came right from work. There she is. Come on, I'll introduce you."

Jeni strode over and gave Jason a hug. "Thanks for picking them up," she told him. Then she offered us her hand. Jeni was casually attired in jeans and a colorful, spiral tie-dye T-shirt, her curly blonde hair pulled back in a ponytail. "I'm Jeni. You must be Barb and Gene." Her smile was wide and easy, like the cover of a brochure in the dentist's office. It added sparkle to her face.

Jeni introduced us to a few members of the board of directors who came to meet us. "Jeni told us a little about your service trip," said Bob, the board president. "What made you decide to work with Fishing Has No Boundaries?"

"I'm familiar with it," I answered. "One year, our Bible School raised money and donated fishing equipment for the Milwaukee chapter."

"We really like what you do for people with special needs," Gene added. "And who doesn't like to fish?"

"Well, we thank you for coming. I wish you could be here for our fishing weekend, but it isn't until the end of June. Fund-raising and volunteer recruitment is a year-long job, though. Jeni works like crazy, especially now, when we only have a couple of weeks left to sign up over a hundred volunteers. How many do you have so far, Jeni?"

"About eighty," she said. "But we're going to sign some more up tonight!"

We said good-bye to the board members and followed Jeni and Jason inside to a table set up in the foyer of the club. She gave us each a FHNB hat to wear and showed us magnets, pamphlets, and registration forms we could hand out to guests. "Remember to tell people they don't have to be able to bait hooks or clean fish," she said. "We also need people to help with the food, the boats, and the equipment." It took a lot of people together to orchestrate a whole weekend of fishing, complete with lodging and meals.

"How many participants sign up?" I asked.

"This year, we have eighty anglers," she said. "The youngest is eight, and the oldest is ninety-three. Each one of them brings an attendant, so we need pontoon boats, supplies, and food for over a hundred sixty."

Jason, Gene, and I mingled with the guests, handed out materials, and sent potential volunteers over to Jeni to sign up. During the slow moments, Jeni shared stories of past fishing weekends. Her eyes lit up as she told tales of anglers catching fish for the first time.

"Out of all the different charities, what made you decide to become involved with this one?" I asked.

Jeni flashed a spontaneous smile. "It suits me," she said. "I love being outside and I love the water. In fact, that's what I do for my job. I'm an aquatic biologist for the DNR." She thought for a moment. "But I think the reason I really stick with it is because of the people. Many of the anglers come back year after year. I've gotten to know them and enjoy helping them do something they love. Fishing seems so easy for you and me, but this is the only time during the year when some of these folks get a chance to get out on the water."

Turning to Jason, I asked, "How 'bout you?"

With a twitterpated grin and a head tilt toward Jeni, he said, "I do it for her. She asked me if I wanted to help. How could I say no?"

At the end of the evening, Jeni and Jason took us out to dinner at an area restaurant that specialized in thick, juicy burgers and craft beers.

"How are the headwaters this year?" asked Jeni. We shared stories of the pedestrian bridge, the rapids, and the bogs. "A couple of years ago, I canoed from Itasca to Bemidji with some girlfriends." She chuckled. "We got lost for hours in those bogs."

Gene told her how we looked at the water plants under the surface to find the strongest current. "Oh, the plants you're talking about are probably vallisneria," she informed us. "They're sometimes called eel grass, or tape grass." She laughed and turned to Jason. "Next time I'm in the bogs, I'll have to be sure and check the underwater plants, huh?"

As we prepared to part ways, Jeni thanked us for our help. "I wish we could be here to help with your fishing weekend," I told her. "But we'll be well on our way to the Twin Cities by then. Hopefully, we can get you some publicity with a story about Fishing Has No Boundaries on our blog. We'll tell about what you do and about how people can volunteer to help. We've got a link to your website, too, so people can volunteer or donate that way. We'll work on it tonight and have it up tomorrow before we leave town." I gave her one of our business cards with the blog address.

"I'm not working tomorrow until noon," said Jason. "I can give you a ride to your kayak. I'd love to see it!" We made arrangements to meet early the next morning.

June 5: Back on the Water

Our next day began with—no surprise—more rain. Jason drove us to our boat and helped us pack it up with our bags of clean, dry clothes. Then, since we planned only a short fourteen-mile day, he dropped us off at our favorite coffee shop to grab a final cup of joe while proofreading the blog post and waiting for the rain to subside. Finally, the deluge gave way to drizzle. We dragged *Kupendana* through the wet sand and pushed off onto Bemidji Lake. We paddled along the south edge of the lake, turning north to follow the shoreline. The river channel was midway on the eastern shore of Bemidji Lake, but was obscured by the rainy haze and the jagged shoreline scattered with inlets, each of which looked like a possible channel opening. The last thing we wanted to do was bypass the entrance to the channel. Finally, just beyond a spit of green, the Mississippi reappeared and ushered us farther east, toward Cass Lake.

Our water-resistant garden gloves from Ace Hardware made fairly cozy paddle gloves, and two miles after a long, but uneventful portage around the Otter Tail Power Dam, we arrived at Island Point Landing campsite. We were actually lucky to see it . . . it was on a cliff thirty feet *up*. A fallen tree barricaded the landing, so we pulled the boat up to the shore, then scaled the lumber retaining wall steps—several times—with all our gear. In the late afternoon, the weather cleared up, giving us a gorgeous panoramic view of the river and a chance to dry off once again.

June 6: Catastrophe!

We awoke to a morning that promised a glorious day. The sun was out and the chill in the air quickly disappeared. We broke camp faster than usual, eager to get on the river. Soon after launching, we noticed adult and juvenile bald eagles soaring overhead. We were now nearing the Chippewa National Forest, with one of the greatest densities of bald eagle populations in the forty-eight contiguous states. I pulled out my Nikon and snapped a few quick shots. I looked forward to spotting more eagles during our peaceful float downstream. I placed the camera back in the dry bag, then rolled up and snapped the waterproof opening. We had just one little half-mile stretch of rapids, and then we would be free to enjoy the rest of our day.

Compared to the rapids and the stump fields of the first three days, this short section initially seemed as simple as a backyard Slip 'N Slide. The river was fast and high, but its increased width offered space to maneuver. We successfully bypassed boulders that rose above the surface, and avoided submerged danger by watching for riffles, or disturbances, caused by water pushing up off rocks lurking inches underneath the surface. Even so, I was relieved to see the overpass ahead that indicated the end of the rapids and the beginning of the easy part of our day.

Before we got to the overpass, our world fell apart.

We were paddling slightly across the current, on a line to slalom around a riffle. With a good vantage point from the bow, I could see the ominous shadow of a large boulder. Gene steered upstream of the riffle, but the strong current increased our drift. It was pushing us directly toward the rock! I stopped paddling, pointed left, and yelled, "We're not going to make it! Turn downstream!"

"We can make it!" Gene encouraged. He didn't turn, but started paddling even harder. I picked up my paddle and churned with quick strokes as powerfully as I could. As we neared the rock, I noticed the riffle was caused by a sharp edge, like the ridge of a mountain range. I prepared myself for a lurch and the inevitable roll. I felt the hard, granite boulder push against the hull under my legs, bending the fiberglass-covered wood upward. I held my breath as I listened to the scraping sound of hull against rock.

And then, with a gentle push, the rock released its grip, sweeping us back into the current. I breathed a sigh of relief. Remaining upright, we slipped right over the crest of the rock. I imagined the scratches we would need to sand out once we got home.

Then I felt it—water sloshing around my legs and seat cushion. "Can you pass me the sponge?" I asked Gene. "I think we took on some water." I looked down at the tops of my shorts, fully expecting to see them darkened by a splash that found its way past my half skirt. My legs were bone-dry on top. How did water get inside the boat? This couldn't be good.

"I don't think the sponge will help," answered Gene. "I'm sitting in water, too!" We looked around for the closest place to pull ashore. Thankfully, to our right was a grassy bank, sloping up to the highway overpass bridge. As Donna rapidly took on water, we made a mad dash for shore.

We pulled Donna onto the grass, spread out our damp gear, and propped the boat on its side. On the port underside of the hull, a little left of center, a gaping hole shattered all hope of continuing. It was the size of my fist and jagged around the edges, where pieces of laminated wood had succumbed to the cutting and tearing of the rock ridge. Extending about eight inches back from the hole toward the stern, I surveyed a trail of lightning cracks. Like reversed stained glass, the light shone around the pieces of wood, held together by the translucent layers of fiberglass. I sat down on our dampened mattress bag and allowed myself to fall into a moment of grief. My eyes pooled with tears; I tried to blink them away. From somewhere deep inside, despair welled up, drowning the optimism I managed to keep through our earlier trials. I lost the battle for self-control. Tears slid down my face, washing away my resolve. How would we continue now?

By the look on his face, I could tell Gene was working out his own feelings, but he sat down next to me and offered a silent embrace. The sounds of water rushed by, as the river continued without us. We sat in stunned silence.

How did this even happen? If he had listened to me, we'd be beyond the overpass and in the clear. That would have to be a conversation for later. If I opened my mouth, I risked an eruption of frustration and perhaps even blame. Even if I measured my words, it was a discussion I wasn't willing to risk.

Gene leaned back to rest on the sloping hillside and closed his eyes. "You okay?" I managed.

"Yeah," he said. "I will be." I wondered for a moment if he blamed me. After all, I second-guessed his line and stopped paddling to tell him what to do. Would we have been fine if only I had kept paddling?

Gene sat up and sighed. "So what do we do now?" His question pulled my mind into the present, and back into problem-solving mode. I felt more comfortable there. We'd have time to process later, but it was still early in the day, and we had to decide what to do.

I thought about the area. "This is northern Minnesota. There have *got* to be marinas around. They might be able to do a fiberglass repair in a couple of days. We could find a hotel nearby until it can be fixed."

"I was thinking even a car repair place would be able to do a fiberglass job," added Gene. "What we need is someone who could recommend a place around here to get it done."

Finally managing a weak smile, I reached for my phone. "We just met someone." Jeni's boyfriend, Jason, was the only one I knew who might have contacts that could get us going on repairs. Like my other Mississippi River contacts, he was entered in my phone under the first letter of the town where he lived. I quickly found "Bemidji Jason." Please answer, I thought as I made the call.

Jason's phone rang only once before I heard his voice. He answered my question about repair shops with one of his own. "Why would you want to have someone else fix it? You built it; you can fix it. I'll come pick you up. Where are you?"

When I gave him the number of the overpass highway, he seemed surprised. "I'm at my grandma's, only five minutes away. Be right there."

I clicked off the phone and gave Gene an update. "He's got a place for us to fix the boat ourselves. I think he's got more faith in us than I do."

Jason arrived shortly, and suggested we bring the kayak to his grandparents' home, where he lived in a trailer on their property. He would take us to buy supplies and we could repair the boat ourselves in the garage. "Are you sure your grandparents won't mind?" Gene asked.

"No, they're cool," assured Jason. "I'm always doing projects for them. I'm sure they'd like to help friends of mine." Jason's confidence was just what I needed. Mine was almost gone. For the first time since the accident, I dared to believe that everything would be okay.

June 6–9 Back in Bemidji

Jason's grandparents were fine with us using their garage and even offered us a spare bedroom in the house during our stay. "But, if you stay, you're part of the family," said his grandma. "You help yourself to whatever you want. I've got too much to do around here to entertain guests." Kind, honest, and outspoken. I liked her style.

"Thank you," I said. "And let us know if there's anything we can do for you while we're here. We're used to being busy, too."

We set to work immediately. While Jason and Gene set the kayak onto a couple of sawhorses and plugged in heat lamps, I called the assistance number for Pygmy Boats. Kelly, the help line technician, calmly explained the steps needed to patch Donna well enough to finish the trip. I wrote down her step-by-step directions and made a shopping list. "Not all hardware stores carry wood flour," Kelly warned. "If you can't find it, unbleached wheat flour will work instead."

While the heat lamps coaxed the moisture from the kayak's river-soaked hull, we set off to visit the familiar folks at the Bemidji Ace Hardware. We picked up a large sheet of fiberglass fabric, epoxy resin, hardener, and brushes. As Kelly predicted, they didn't stock wood flour, a powdered sawdust material mixed with liquid resin to make wood filler. Grateful for Kelly's foresight, we stopped at a health food store and picked up a bag of wheat flour as a suitable substitute.

Gene got to work cutting away the delaminated fiberglass, inch by inch, until it no longer pulled away from the wood. To cover the entire area, our fiberglass patch would have to be two feet wide and three feet long! Our next step—and the trickiest—was to insert the remaining shards of wood into the empty space in the hull. Temporarily supporting the patch with plastic wrap on the outside of the hull, we fitted the remaining pieces together the best we could. It resembled a puzzle with several missing pieces—probably still floating downstream, I thought. Then we slathered the hole with wood filler made from the wheat flour and epoxy resin.

Once the wood filler dried, we removed the plastic wrap and sanded the makeshift wooden plug, relieved that it nicely filled the hole. Jason pitched right in to help us cover the exposed wood on the inside and outside of the hull with new layers of fiberglass, filling the weave with epoxy resin. "How long will this take to dry?" asked Jason.

Gene studied the resin can. "Each coat takes twenty-four hours to cure completely," he explained. "But we could flip the boat and alternate coats on the inside and outside every twelve hours."

"Good idea, hon," I acknowledged. "Kelly said three coats would be optimal, but two are enough to get us through the trip. We don't want to skimp on the curing time, though—that could be disastrous." I mentally calculated that we could finish the final coat in two more days. Twenty-four hours after that, we'd be good to launch.

Jason stepped back and looked at the glistening hull. "I've thought about building a boat of my own someday. This isn't so hard."

"You should," said Gene. "I hope you know how much we appreciate what you're doing."

"I'm just glad I could help you guys. But maybe I'll have to autograph the patch when we're done."

"You should," I said. I pulled an orange dry bag off our pile in the corner. "But for now, how 'bout you and Jenilynn sign one of our bags?" I asked.

"Really?" he asked. Jason found a Sharpie, sat down with the bag, and wrote, "You're awesome people and it's a privilege to have met." Jenilynn added, "Safe Paddling!" After they signed their names, Jason swished the bag in the air to dry the ink, then handed it back to me. "There! Now you won't forget us."

"Like that would ever happen, after you saved our whole trip," said Gene.

We became optimistic about our chances of getting back on the water and decided it was finally time to write a blog post about the accident. I plugged in the Chromebook, opened it up, and pressed the power button. Nothing. The charger light glowed, but the indicator on the keyboard remained dark. Oh, man. Our string of bad luck wasn't long enough? I put it in a bag of rice to try to pull out any moisture, but suspected that the repeated dousing proved to be too much for the electronics. "That's what we get for trying to save a buck," sighed Gene.

I regretted the moment when we decided to forego an iPad with a watertight, LifeProof case in favor of the lightweight, inexpensive Chromebook. "What were we thinking?" I asked.

"It seemed safe enough to keep it inside the boat," said Gene. "But then, I never expected to roll the boat twice and nearly sink it, all in the first week." Neither did I. My stomach dropped as I recalled the damage we caused Donna. I still had unresolved feelings about that day, but wasn't ready to talk about it yet. Maybe when the repairs were complete, grace and forgiveness would be easier to find—for both of us.

Jason's grandma let us use her home computer, and I wrote a vague description of the accident, stressing our progress on repairs. No need for our family to worry any more than they already did.

On Saturday, we arose early to apply our morning coat of epoxy. Fishing Has No Boundaries was scheduled to help sell food at the Walleye Classic fishing tournament in Bemidji, and Jeni asked us the night before if we'd like to help with their fund-raiser. You bet! We were in town anyway. And we were glad to have an opportunity to do more to help their cause.

We accompanied Jeni and Jason to the downtown lakefront, just north of the huge statues of Paul Bunyan and Babe the Blue Ox that had welcomed visitors to Bemidji since 1937. Long white tables were already set up, end to end, to serve picnic fixin's to hungry fishermen, up since dawn, and to spectators enjoying the revelry of the day. The scents of grilled burgers, hotdogs, and brats mixed with the spicy aroma of simmering pulled pork.

"Welcome back," greeted one of the board members. I recognized him from a few days before, at the fitness fair, but didn't remember his name. "I'm sorry to hear about the trouble you had with your boat."

"Thanks." I smiled back. Jeni must have explained why we were still in town. Good. I didn't feel like going there. "How can we help?"

Gene put his height to good use attaching the price list menus high on the arched wooden supports of the super-sized pagoda that sheltered our serving station and several green wooden picnic tables. I helped set out the plates and plastic utensils and walked down by the shore to find some rocks to hold the stacks of napkins in place. I noticed half a dozen fishing boats already beginning to line up at the pier with their morning catch.

When I returned, everything looked ready. "Gene, do you want to help serve the pulled pork?" asked Jeni. "And Barb, could you help with the pop?"

"Sure." I hoped she interpreted my grin as willingness to help, not the amusement I got from her regional label for cans of soda.

Soon, a steady stream of customers had us working at a frantic pace. "I'm sure glad you could help today," Jeni said. "Most of the board's here, but it's great to have extra hands." I was glad to hear our help was needed. At the fitness fair, the value of our presence felt negligible, but today, we were really going to pull our weight.

Occasional lulls in the action gave me a chance to strike up conversations with customers as they waited for their meals. I noticed a woman wearing a pin with a picture of a small child. "Who's that cute little boy?" I asked her. "A relative?"

"No," she replied. "This little guy is struggling with cancer. Our whole community of Grand Rapids came out to help him with a fund-raiser, so I bought a button to help."

"That's an awesome story," I said. I told her about our trip. "We plan to stop in Grand Rapids to get a new box of food at the post office. We'd love to stay for a day, but haven't made a service connection yet. Do you know of anyone that might want our help?"

"Oh, you *have* to stop there," she said. "I can't think of a particular place right now, but it's a caring town. I'm sure there are charities that would love to have you."

I wrote my phone number on the back of one of our blog cards. "Please give us a call if you think of anything."

Saturday night, we put the final coat of resin on the inside of the hull. The patch looked good and felt solid. Another coat would make it stronger, but we were itchin' to get back on the water. "What are your plans now?" Jason asked. "Jeni and I both have tomorrow off and can drive you wherever you'd like to launch."

"If we put in where you picked us up, we'll be three days behind schedule," said Gene. "We can use our flex day, but we might miss some of the services until we get caught up."

"And Cass Lake and Winnibigoshish are in that stretch," I added. "If the weather's bad, or if the wind is strong, that could add another day or two." I worried about Lake Winnie. We'd read story after story about its wild weather and dangerous conditions.

"You can't put the boat in the water until Monday morning anyway, right?" Jason asked. "Where were you planning on camping tomorrow night?"

I pulled our itinerary out of our zip-lock map bag and checked the dates. "Sunday, hmmm. Schoolcraft State Park," I informed him. "If we left Monday morning from there, we'd be back on schedule."

"Then how about we drop you off there tomorrow?" asked Jason. "Don't worry about missing the lakes. Cass Lake is nice, but Winnie can be awful. One time, I was fishing out in the middle and all of a sudden, a storm blew up. We made it back, but barely. I thought we were goners."

I wasn't disappointed to skip the paddle through the two lakes. Based on the weather so far, our chances of having fair winds weren't good. But I hated to miss river miles already. We wanted to do the whole river, and before a week passed, we were already planning on skipping part of it. "What about the river? Will we regret it later if we skip some of the mileage?"

"I look at it this way," said Gene. "On this trip, the paddle is just the hook. It's the reason people want to hear about what we're doing, and why they read our blog. But the trip isn't about the paddle. It's about the people—the people we meet, and the people who help others every day working at the services where we stay. I don't mind sacrificing some river miles to keep the services first."

Sunday turned out to be yet another rainy day. We packed our belongings in the truck, tied Donna on the roof, and rode with Jeni and Jason to Schoolcraft State Park. We chose a campsite near the launch area for the next day, hastily set up the tent, and waved until the truck disappeared behind the trees.

It was still early, but a blanket of mottled gray clouds dimmed the sky, making it feel much later. All was ready for our launch the following day, so we hunkered inside the tent and played a little cribbage. We had no board, so we played a few hands, but didn't keep track of wins or losses. As I put the cards away, I noticed they had thickened so much from the humidity that the deck refused to be squeezed back into its box. I wound a hair scrunchy around the pile, and made a mental note to pick up a new deck at the next available store.

This was as good a time as any to have the conversation that I suspected we both knew was coming, but neither of us wanted to initiate. I turned toward Gene and took his hand in mine. "Honey," I began, "before tomorrow, I think we need to talk."

"I know." Had the accident been on Gene's mind, too? What did he think? Did I really want to know?

I took a breath, and then started. "I've thought a lot about what happened in the rapids."

"Me, too." Gene squeezed my hands and then folded his in his lap, waiting for me to continue.

"When we were paddling cross-current to get around that last riffle, we were sliding sideways so fast it scared me. Then I saw the rock under the water and panicked . . . because I didn't think we could make it on the upstream side. That's why I shouted for you to turn downstream."

"That's not exactly how I remember it," Gene replied. "I thought you were making a suggestion."

I chuckled. "If it was, it was a really *strong* suggestion," I said. "But, if I wouldn't have stopped paddling, maybe we could have cleared it, too. Once you said, 'I think we can make it,' I paddled like mad, but it was too late. I'm sorry."

"I'm sorry, too," Gene admitted, wrapping an arm around my shoulder. "It wasn't one person's fault, but together, we could have avoided it. What we need is a better system for quick calls so it doesn't happen again."

Considering different scenarios from our first week, we decided the person operating the rudder would be primarily responsible for choosing the line. If there was no rush to make a decision, we could collaborate. But in an emergency, the person in the bow, with the best vantage point, would be the one to give orders.

"Thanks, sweetie." I gave Gene a tender kiss. "I feel better now that we talked."

"Me, too," he said, as he leaned over me, gently pushing me down onto my back. "But it's still early. Now what will we do?"

"I bet we could think of something," I whispered in his ear as raindrops landed softly on the tent.

Chapter 4
River Angels

June 10-11: Schoolcraft Park to Grand Rapids

IN THE MORNING, MY WORRY was not the overcast weather, but whether the patch would hold fast. The epoxy seemed fully cured. The patch overlapped the old fiberglass by over an inch, and the edges were sealed. My confidence was tempered by the fact that I was in the bow today—I would know first if anything went wrong. We pushed the loaded boat into the water, my eyes on the floor. It looked dry. I stepped in, centered my weight, and lowered onto my seat cushion. As we began to paddle, I glanced down between my knees—no moisture. I began to relax. Donna appeared to be river ready. We would know after the eighteen miles of our day's paddle if we had repaired her as well as we built her.

Bald eagles were plentiful. Sometimes, we heard a high-pitched warning screech before we saw its source. Other times, we noticed a spot of white amongst the greens and browns lining the shores, or a majestic silhouette soaring on air currents, effortlessly gliding in silent command of the sky. Rounding a bend, I spotted an eagle regally perched on a high branch, its bleached head the only giveaway to its presence. Upon our approach, it swooped off its perch and led us down the river in a graceful arch. "There he goes," said Gene. "It's like we have an eagle escort."

Mid-afternoon brought us to the portage around the Pokegama Dam, which wound through a recreation center of the same name. Compared to the rustic campgrounds we had used, this one was the Taj Mahal. It had tent and electric sites, blacktop trails, and a shower house with flush toilets. By now, I was equally willing to use an outhouse or the privacy of a bush, hill, or tree when the need arose. But few things pamper a camper quite like the smooth seats, porcelain tanks, and satisfying flush of a nice, clean loo.

We chose a campsite at the top of a hill, with a perfect launch point below the spillway for the next morning. Gene scouted for a good tent location as I began removing bags from inside the hull.

"Looks like you're on quite an adventure."

I turned toward the voice, which belonged to an elderly visitor. He seemed every bit the camper in his work boots, black pants, and flannel lumberjack coat, which hung open over his worn T-shirt. It was the black beret tilted over his graying temples that set him apart, lending him an artistic flair.

"We sure are," I answered, offering an outstretched hand. "I'm Barb and that's my husband, Gene." I nodded in Gene's direction.

"I'm Mike Turner," he said. "Where ya headed?" I gave him the short version of our paddle plans as Gene walked over. "Well, it sure is a pleasure to meet you both," he continued. "My camper is the one right over there." He pointed to the fifth wheel situated in the next campsite. "Is there anything you need? Anything at all?"

"We're actually fine. We couldn't fit one more thing in the boat," I replied. "But we could use your prayers."

"Well, I've got lots of those," he said. "I'm a gospel folk singer. I'd be happy to pray for you. In fact, I just finished giving two concerts in the last two days. I'll be havin' a little campfire tonight. I'd love you to stop over. I need to rest my vocal cords, so I apologize right now that I won't be able to sing for you, but it'd be nice to talk with you more."

We agreed to stop by later, and returned to our picnic table to choose dinner from our bear vault. Even before we started heating the water, Mike returned, carrying a paper plate filled with crackers, cheese, and sausage. "Just thought you might like a little appetizer," he explained. "This is my own deer sausage. I hope you like it."

"Thanks, I'm sure we will," I said. At this point, anything fresh was a real treat.

He left, calling over his shoulder, "Don't forget. Tonight . . . later . . . come over when you see the fire."

The appetizers were gone in no time. As Gene started our dinner, a woman approached with a toddler in tow. "You're the kayakers from Bemidji!" she exclaimed. "And this must be your boat. It looks just like the picture on the card you gave me."

"I remember you, too, from the walleye tournament," I said. She touched the pin on the lapel of her coat. "Gene, this is the woman from Grand Rapids I told you about," I said. Gene secured the top on the pot cozy and wiped his hands on his shorts before joining us.

"My grandson and I love to go for walks in this park," she said. "What a nice surprise to meet you here!" We followed the toddler over to the boat and Gene lifted him onto the bow while the woman continued, "I thought of a service in Grand Rapids you might want to call when you get in town. It's a homeless shelter called Grace House. They're doing some wonderful things."

"Thanks. I'll call today and give them a little advance notice," I said. The woman took her grandson's hand and waved good-bye.

I placed a quick call and then reported back to Gene. "They'd love to have us. We can stop in to meet the director tomorrow when we get into town and work with them Wednesday."

After dinner, we heard the soft sound of a banjo from the next campsite. We walked over and took places in folding camp chairs by the fire. Unlike Gene's blazing tepee fires that lit up the night, Mike sat by a small bed of wooden embers next to a single log. He placed two cut planks across the embers to fuel the small controlled burn, then sat down again. "I know I wasn't gonna sing tonight," he said. "Usually, I'm exhausted after a couple nights of concerts, but your trip reminds me of a song I wrote. It's about the river. I'd like to share it with you, if it's all right." We sat back and let his pickin' and singin' drift over us, like the river's current . . .

"Run, run, Mississippi, run,
Run on down to the land of the sun.
Run, run, Mississippi, run,
Run, run, run.

From Itasca where you start,
'Til your banks grow wide apart,
Mile to mile and state to state,
You're nature's work of art.

You're more than just a river.
You're more than water grand.
You're more than man can reason.
You're God's wonder in our land."

– "Run, Mississippi, Run" by Mike Turner

Between verses, Gene and I joined in with the catchy refrain. Then our voices drifted off and the soft crackle of burning wood lent rhythmic accents to the distant splashing of the spillway. "Thank you," Gene said softly.

"Have you met any river angels yet?" Mike asked. He must have noticed our questioning look, for he continued. "Around these parts, that's the name for people who help out river trav'lers like you. It's like God just knew you needed something, and placed 'em right there in front of you—like angels." River angels. I liked that idea.

"As a matter of fact, we have," I said. We recounted the story of our tragic encounter with the now infamous rock and the much-needed assistance we got from Bemidji Jason and his family. "I don't know what we would have done without their help," I added.

Between songs by the light of the fire, Mike told us about the call he felt to share his gift of music and praise around the country. It seemed that every topic of conversation brought a song to his mind, which he then felt compelled to share with us. He accompanied our personal concert with his banjo, acoustic guitar, Hawaiian steel guitar, and Autoharp. "I'm starting to feel old," he admitted. "I miss my family when I'm on the road . . . but I'm gonna keep singin' as long as God wants me to."

As the embers settled into white dusty hills at his feet, he told us, "God drew me to you this afternoon. I knew I had to go talk to you, even though I didn't know why. You've eased my loneliness and been a blessing to me through your fellowship. Thank you."

"I'm pretty sure it's you who's the river angel," said Gene. "We've had a pretty rough first week on the river, but you helped me remember why we're doing this." Mike insisted that we take some of his CDs and closed the evening with a prayer for our safe travels.

On Tuesday, a short paddle brought us to Grand Rapids. The portage around the Blandin Paper Mill Dam zigzagged through town on a course of hilly streets. Grace House was close to the portage route, so we kept a lookout for a hotel that would allow us to park our boat nearby. There we were, walking up the steep sidewalk on Pokegama Avenue, pulling our twenty-foot kayak behind us, when a middle-aged, jeans-clad gentleman bolted toward us, feet flying across the uncut field between his yard and the street. His arms waved wildly as he shouted, "If you're looking for the river, you're going the wrong way!" I laughed at the sight, then reassured him that we knew where the river was, but didn't intend to finish the whole portage today. Once we explained the purpose for our stop, Dan kindly offered to store Donna in his yard while we were in town and gave us directions to both Grace House and an inexpensive nearby hotel.

June 11–12: Grace House

We settled into our small no-frills hotel, then walked over to meet Sherry, the executive director of Grace House. She gave us a short tour of the cozy individual guest rooms, separated from the central living area only by floor-length privacy curtains drawn back for the day. At each end of the building were two larger spaces for families. "Guests only stay here for thirty days," Sherry explained, "so they need to be out looking for employment every day. We provide temporary shelter, but more importantly, we provide assistance with job and housing searches and we connect guests to appropriate resources and social service agencies."

As we were talking, a nicely dressed young woman in a business skirt and white blouse stuck her head in the office. "My interview went great!" she said. "I think maybe I got the job." Sherry introduced us, but was careful not to mention the guest's name. Turning to us, the woman said, "This place is great. They care and they really want to help. You know . . ." She hesitated. "When I had a home and a job, I used to stop by an' donate stuff here. Now I find myself in a situation where I can't make a go of it. And they're helping me get back on my feet."

"We can't do it alone," Sherry said, once the woman left. "The whole community is behind us. We depend on over a hundred and twenty volunteers who are an essential part of the support and assistance we give. And we work closely with community groups, too. In fact, I've got a meeting with some area pastors in a few minutes, but we could really use your help tomorrow. Can you stop by at nine?"

It was still early, so we walked downtown to get our box of food from the post office. I hoped it was waiting for us. We still had a few days' worth of food in our bear vaults, and there were plenty of stores in Grand Rapids, but after months of meal preparation, it would be a shame if our system didn't work.

It felt good to walk briskly without lugging a boat behind us. Crossing the bridge over the Mississippi, we stopped to watch the water. No matter how much time we spent on the river, it held a magnetism that was difficult to explain. Every view was different, but each was as fascinating as the next.

On the east side, past the Central Square Mall, towered the old post office building. We approached the counter, and Gene announced, "I'm here to pick up a general delivery package for Barb and Gene Geiger." The man disappeared into a back room. I held my breath, hoping Eric sent it on time. Hoping it got here.

Hoping we had food for the next leg of the trip. And then I recognized the box that we had packed with assorted dried meals, bars, oatmeal packets, and refill bottles of soap, shampoo, and sunscreen. The box that I had addressed long before I ever knew what our days on the river would really be like. "That would be the one!" said Gene, to the congenial postal employee. "Thanks!" He lifted the box to his shoulder with a grin. "That worked well!"

The next morning, we arrived at Grace House just before nine. Sherry and her staff were preparing for a special event, which exemplified her message from the day before about connecting with the community. "Tomorrow, we're teaming up with the Judy Garland Museum to co-host an event called 'There's No Place Like Home,'" she explained. "It'll kick off at the museum with tours, wine, and appetizers. Then everyone will be bused out here for a soup line fund-raiser."

"Sounds like a great event," I said. "I wish we could see it."

"I do too," Sherry agreed. "The problem is, we've got a lot of work to do before we're ready to entertain people here. That's where you come in. The parking lot is a mess. It needs to be swept. And the grass is overgrown, but our lawnmower and trimmers aren't working. Do you think you could look at them?"

"I'll see what I can do," offered Gene. As Sherry led us to the shed, I scanned the property. The lawn was indeed overgrown, and the gardens and shrubs were brimming with weeds. Sherry had a point.

Gene did some maintenance on the lawnmower and bought fresh gas for the two lawn trimmers while I picked up trash and swept leaves and cigarette butts from the parking lot. Next, we worked together for hours—mowing, trimming, and weeding the nearly three-acre property, transforming the overgrown hayfield back into a manicured lawn. Then we retired downstairs to the cool kitchen and made four gallons of chicken noodle soup for the next evening's event. As the soup simmered, I borrowed the Grace House computer to work on our blog.

Sherry joined us outside on the patio after our work was finished. "This place hasn't looked this good in a long time," she said. "Could I talk you into staying a little longer? Like a month, maybe?"

Everyone laughed, but the compliment in her request was touching. Our efforts had made a visible difference at just the right time. I could tell Sherry was grateful for our help.

"We've got to get back on the river," I said, "but I'm glad we could help. Good luck with your event tomorrow. We'll be thinking of you."

June 13–19: Grand Rapids to Deerwood, MN

"Wow! Look how high the water is," Gene said, as we readied Donna for our launch. "Musta been all that rain we paddled through." Sure enough, the river now strained against both banks and carried us with newfound urgency.

Our itinerary for this stretch included a variety of potential campsites, depending on the weather and water conditions. Many of them were DNR river sites, accessible only by water and identified with a small wooden sign displaying a yellow painted tepee and canoe. The river sites we used upstream were lovely, with boat landings, plenty of firewood, and sometimes even shelters. Now, with the slope of the shore erased by high water, one of our challenges became campsite accessibility. The other challenge was bugs.

One of our sites was aptly named Ms. Keto. With the warm, damp June weather, the swarming bloodsuckers were such a problem that, despite the heat, we tucked our long pants into our socks, zipped up our jackets, and velcroed our cuffs around our wrists. We even broke out the silly-looking beekeeper head nets I made fun of before we left. "I never thought we'd really have to use these," I told Gene. "But it's better than being eaten alive."

After a quick dinner, we dove into the tent to escape being dinner ourselves. "I thought the mosquitoes in Wisconsin were bad," Gene complained. "I think they breed them with vampire bats here." I didn't even remind him to change his bracelet. Some things just merit complaining. One thing I knew for sure—our environmentally friendly lemon/eucalyptus insect repellent wasn't going to cut it. Deet was now on my shopping list.

I plugged my phone into the solar charger and checked my email. One was from Becky, the contact for our next service in Deerfield, giving us directions to her home located just off the river. The other was from a man named Jason, who lived further south near Brainerd. "I read about your trip in the newspaper," he wrote. "I'd love you to stop at our home on your way through the Brainerd area. We can offer you a steak dinner, a comfortable bed, and the use of our laundry. All I ask is that you talk with our two children about what you're doing. They're eight and ten—a good age to learn about the value of service to others."

"Listen to this." I read the email to Gene. "If we can, I'd love to find a way to stop there." Jason's children were the same age as the students in my school. From one little glimpse into his parenting values, I wanted to meet this dad as much as his kids. We pulled out our maps and made some tentative adjustments to our plans. We'd have a few long paddle days, but it just might work.

Settling in for the night, I thought about Grace House. "I wonder how the No Place Like Home event went," I said. "I kinda wish we could have stayed for that."

"I don't think we were meant to," said Gene. "If we stayed another day, we wouldn't be able to stop at Jason's." He turned onto his side and rested his head on his hand. "Did you ever stop to think how many things fell into place to bring us to Grace House? The hole in the boat, the walleye tournament, you meeting the lady there, and then seeing her again at Pokegama? I think Pastor was right. God's fingerprints are all over this. It's cool to be a part of it."

Mosquitoes weren't the only bugs that we found plentiful in Minnesota. June was prime tick season, and they were everywhere. During our daily tick check, Gene picked a wood tick off his leg and threw it outside the tent door. "How come you hardly get any, and I have two or three every time?" he asked.

"It's gotta be all that leg hair," I guessed. Even after the tick check, I itched all over. I couldn't wait for a campsite with a shower.

It wasn't to be. The next campsite offered no bathhouse, but plenty more bugs. We pulled up to a normal-looking water site, marked with the familiar wooden sign. I wrapped the bowline around a stump and began unloading our gear. By the time I arrived for another load, the line was crawling with caterpillars. They were only about an inch and a half long, with large heads and prominent stripes. Individually, they were actually kind of pretty, but clumped together in a writhing mass, their appearance morphed right into disgusting. I brushed them off of the line and grabbed a couple more bags. Back at the campsite, caterpillars literally fell from the trees. I looked up through the oak leaves to see hundreds of munching machines stripping the leaves. We kept our hats on for the rest of the day, covered our food, and swept caterpillars off the tent each time we went in or out. As we packed the boat the next morning, we flicked them off the deck. "Let's not paddle under any overhanging branches today," suggested Gene. I steered away from the bank, happy to oblige.

The river widened, but continued to snake back and forth like a Chutes and Ladders game board. Before the trip, I read that the Mississippi was constantly changing. Here, I saw the reason why. The river continually carved and built its banks at every corner. On the outside banks, exposed roots, toppling trees, and clumps of sod halfway down muddy cliffs provided a real-life science lesson on erosion. Partly submerged stumps of fallen trees required constant vigilance on our part. Conversely, on the inside corners of the bends, I noticed deposits of silt and mud, often accompanied by new growth of young reeds and willows.

The high water and muddy shore conditions made it hard to find places to pull over and stretch. During a typical day, we took breaks every two to three hours to walk around a little, get something to eat, take a country pee, and relieve our sit muscles.

One afternoon, I noticed Gene wiggling to shift his weight. "Feeling pressed?" I asked, a polite way of saying, "Gotta pee?" that we learned in Kenya.

"That, and I need a stretch," he replied. I began scanning the shore for a place to stop. After what seemed like an eternity, Gene pointed to the left bank. "It looks like a sandy beach over there." I steered over to the inside curve and let the bow drift onto the shore. As Gene swung his leg out to pull Donna farther up, his foot descended into thick mucky silt, which oozed up around his calf, nearly to his knee. "I guess I don't have to go that bad," he said, wrestling his muddy leg out of the silt and washing off his shoe.

I couldn't help but chuckle as I watched the mucky water drip from his shoe. "I'm sure glad you went first."

Occasionally, we passed homes with backyards overlooking the river. Chairs and swings offered peaceful scenic views. They were almost always empty. "If I lived here," I said, "I'd be sitting outside whenever I could." If I really lived here, I thought, I'd be out there all day, and nothing around the house would ever get done. I began a photo collection of these riverside seats; each was different, but the sense of tranquility never changed.

Transitioning from Itasca to Aitkin County, we found several nice county campgrounds. Accessible by road as well as water, these had modern camping conveniences—a choice of sites, bathrooms, and showers. We arrived at Berglund Campground after a long thirty-six-mile paddle. A young couple canoed in about a half hour behind us. Adam and Madelyn, also on their way to New Orleans, left Itasca a few days after we did. They were making better time—paddling about thirty miles every day and stopping neither for volunteer work nor boat repairs. At the campsite, we shared stories of our headwaters adventures.

"Did you do Lake Winnibigoshish?" Gene asked. He explained that we missed that part because of our repairs.

"Oh, we did it all right," said Adam. "The winds and waves were terrible!"

"That's gotta be even more dangerous in a canoe than a kayak," said Gene. "We can close ours up with our spray skirts. But I imagine you get the waves right in the boat."

"Yeah. We got pretty wet," Adam admitted. "We were glad to put that one behind us."

The next day, our younger counterparts were already launching when we arose. I wondered how much easier this trip would be if we were in our twenties, instead of our fifties. I handed Gene his daily Advil, and downed my own with a swig from my water bottle. Time to get moving.

Thirty-one miles lazily drifted past. The landscape was rural; past the tree-lined shore, farm fields stretched for miles. The river's bends brought the highway near enough to hear traffic, then took us away again into wilderness. There was plenty of wildlife—waterfowl, muskrats, turtles, and deer—but our rhythmic paddle splashes alerted them to our presence. I often glimpsed only their backsides as they slid, scampered, jumped, or flew to safer locations. Getting a good photo required advance notice, time to get the camera from the dry bag, and a fast enough shutter speed to compensate for the movement of the boat in three dimensions, as well as that of the subject. So, the pursuit of good wildlife photos often took a back seat to the opportunity to sit in hushed awe as we observed an unexpected sight. "Thank you," I whispered, as we glided past, memories the only souvenirs of the moment.

As we neared a bend in the river, I pressed my left foot against the rudder pedal to start our turn. I felt it give way under the pressure of my foot. "Uh-oh. I lost rudder control," I warned Gene. I gently pushed my right foot, and the boat began to swerve right. "It'll turn right, but not left."

"It has to be a problem with the port-side cable," said Gene. "Can you make it over to that shore?"

I pulled the cord to lift the rudder out of the water. If it didn't turn in both directions, it would only be in the way. I steered to the shore the old-fashioned way, using J-strokes and sweeps. Gene checked the cables. Sure enough, the line to the left pedal was frayed. "The cable snapped. I can jerry-rig it for now, but we'll need to buy some parts to do it right later." Gene twisted the cable around the bolt and screwed it tight. "I think that'll hold," he said. "But don't push the pedals too hard until we get it fixed." I was careful to gently steer the last few miles to Aitkin Campground. Pulling Donna up to the campsite, we saw that Madelyn and Adam's tent was already set up, their canoe resting nearby.

All settled in and showered up, we set out to get a real meal in town. We headed toward the rustic bar/restaurant recommended by the first resident we asked. Adam and Madelyn were a few minutes and a drink ahead of us. We bought them another, and chatted about our day on the water. "We just took a walk through town," Madelyn said. "There's a great place for breakfast called the Birchwood Café. The pancakes are huge!"

I told them about our rudder failure. "I think we'll use our flex day to stick around and fix it," I said. "We probably won't see you after that, though. You're movin' faster than we are." We traded contact information. "Keep in touch, okay?"

The next morning, we filled up with pancakes the size of the plates. "Madelyn sure called that one," said Gene, contentedly leaning back in his chair. It was a good thing we filled up our tanks, because the rest of the morning was spent trudging all over town on errands. We mailed our Chromebook home; it didn't make sense to lug it around. I used the library's computer to catch up on our blog while Gene did laundry across town. Then together, we shopped for some much needed cooking fuel, killer mosquito repellent, and parts for the boat.

Finally back at the campsite, Gene installed metal loops called ferrules on each rudder cable. He squeezed the cables tight with the only pair of pliers we had, tugging them for good measure. "They'd look a little better if I had a crimper," said Gene. "It isn't pretty, but this should do the trick."

We knew from our weather app that Wednesday would be our last sunny day before a system of thunderstorms came through. We had two days to make it to Becky's, so we decided to do the lion's share of the paddling on Wednesday and get to the Lone Pine Creek DNR river site. Our rudder cables held tight and we enjoyed a leisurely, twenty-one-mile paddle. During the night, we heard the predicted front coming through. The thunder rolled, far away at first, and then closer. In the morning, I awoke to a full-fledged storm. The sides of the tent shook, but it held firm. The sound of the pelting rain was oddly soothing. "We're less than five miles from Becky's," I said. "Wanna wait it out?" No answer. I rolled over and went back to sleep.

June 20–21: Salem West and The Mustard Seed

Eventually, the rain and thunder subsided. We rolled up our wet tent, broke camp, and kayaked to the Highway 6 landing. The boat ramp was covered with a thick layer of Mississippi mud deposited by the receding floodwaters. Gene steered Donna nose first into the gloppy goo, but she stopped well short of solid ground. Gene laughed from behind me. "Your turn to go first," he said. "Don't lose a shoe."

I tried to ignore the muck oozing around my ankles as I pulled Donna onto shore. "Just wait," I said as Gene climbed out. "I get the stern next time." We pulled Donna to a grass patch in the middle of the circle drive.

Just then, a dark blue minivan crept past us and came to a stop at the top of the boat ramp. We set Donna down and watched curiously. What brought people here on this cool, drizzly day with no boat? We waved in greeting as an elderly gentleman and woman who I assumed was his wife climbed out of the car and walked to the river, pointing and talking in hushed tones. They returned to the car. The man opened the sliding door and addressed two children, who I could now see were girls, both engrossed in video games. I guessed they were about ten and twelve. "Come look!" said the gentleman. "This is the Mississippi River. The one Mark Twain wrote about in *The Adventures of Huckleberry Finn*."

"Aw, Grandpa," whined one of the children. "It's raining."

"At least come take a look," the man urged. "We drove all this way just to show it to you." I glanced at the car to see where they came from, but couldn't see the license plate.

The girls put their phones on the seat and hopped out of the car, raising their jacket hoods. They skittered down to the ramp, peered around the shrubbery, and ran back to the shelter of the car and their waiting games. "That's nice, Grandpa. Thanks for showing us," said the younger girl.

As the older one climbed in the car, I heard her say, "It looks like a river to me."

I wished I could show her how different this river looked from the small stream of its origin. Explain that when it finally meets the sea, its flow will be a hundred thousand times as strong as its headwaters. That long ago, it was navigated by this land's native people, and then by European explorers who came to make this place their home. That the Ojibwe people believe that it is the lifeblood of Mother Earth. That wildlife depends upon its waters for their lives and humans for their livelihoods. But the river visitors rolled away. The Mississippi was not just like any other river—not to me, not anymore. I hoped someday to share this river with our own grandchildren.

We pulled Donna across the highway, right into the driveway of the hosts for our stay in Deerwood. Becky and Gary's property was landscaped with an abundance of gardens and bird feeders. In the side yard was a fishpond, surrounded by natural stones, ferns, and perennials. Under a wooden bridge, orange koi swam amongst water lilies and reeds.

Our hosts greeted us warmly. Becky, dressed casually in a bright pink shirt and off-white shorts, invited us into the house. The first thing that caught my eye was a wall of windows showcasing the backyard, with even more bird feeders scattered about. A flash of red and black flew down from the tree line and lighted on a hanging feeder. The bird was at least a foot tall, mostly black with bold white stripes down its neck, and a flaming red crest. "That's a pileated woodpecker," explained Becky. "He comes around just about every day."

"How do you ever get anything done?" asked Gene. "I'd just sit and watch out the windows all day."

"We do enjoy the wildlife around here," said Gary. "I'm a retired game warden. I worked outside all my life."

It was hard to imagine him in a uniform, rather than his white T-shirt and comfortable khaki shorts. "Retirement looks good on you," Gene said. "Barb's retired, and she's enjoying it so much, I can't wait."

After showering up and changing into clean clothes, we joined them in the living room to get acquainted. After we answered several questions about our trip, the conversation turned to our Deerwood service. "I was surprised to get an email from Greg inviting us to Deerwood, since it's a few miles off the river," I said. "He said the Little Falls Chamber of Commerce sent our contact information to surrounding non-profits, and he thought we might like to see what you're doing here."

"We're no different than other small communities that way." Gary smiled. "Word gets around."

"We found out about you through our church," said Becky. "Salem Lutheran runs Salem West and The Mustard Seed under the umbrella of our Social Ministries Board. In church, they asked for people to host you; since we live right here by the ramp, we volunteered."

"Thanks, it sure was easy for us," I said.

On Friday morning, Gene joined a group of men to pick up donations for Salem West, while Becky dropped me off at The Mustard Seed. The storefront was similar to other businesses in the small strip mall, but I stepped inside a cozy little boutique. Furniture was arranged in settings, with plates, stemware, and centerpieces on the dining table, pillows and throws arranged on the sofa, and accents on end tables and ottomans. Shelving units displayed artistic arrangements of ceramic vases, baskets, jewelry, and folk art. Picture arrangements adorned the walls, and lamps softened the lighting in the room. An adjoining room offered more utilitarian items, such as kitchen utensils, appliances, and books.

Deb, the manager of the store, welcomed me and introduced me to the morning's volunteers. "Your first priority will be to assist customers with anything they need," she told me. "Cleone will handle the cash register. And you can help Barbara and Kristy to fill any empty display areas with new items. Then, if you have extra time, you can help clean and price some of the new things that come in."

Kristy called me over to the furniture grouping by the storefront window. "The first thing we need to do," she said, "is to price the furniture in the window. We had a bedroom set there yesterday when the store opened, and it sold in only a couple of hours. We put a new living room set here yesterday, but still need to price it."

"The bedroom set must have been priced pretty well," I said, "to go that fast."

"We try to price things to go quickly," she explained. "But another reason they go so fast is the way we display the merchandise. The store's only open to the public on Thursdays through Saturdays. Each Tuesday and Wednesday, Deb comes in with a few volunteers, and they redesign the floor, shelves, and window areas. Every week, customers come by to see the window displays and check out the new look of the store. If something doesn't sell, sometimes it's just a matter of displaying it in a different setting."

Barbara agreed. "If people can visualize an item looking nice in their home, they'll be more likely to buy it. Sometimes they even buy the coordinating items, too."

Kristy, Barbara, and I priced the sofa, chair, and ottoman, and then went to the back storage room to find accent pieces. I found an afghan with the same color palette and a tray for the ottoman. Kristy added some decorative candles to the tray and Barbara found a framed print to hang on the wall. As customers made purchases, we filled the empty spots with items from the storeroom, combining them in appealing new ways. The creative challenge kept us busy and entertained as customers came and went, getting good deals while assisting the needy in their community.

In the afternoon, Gene returned from his work at Salem West. "What'd you get to do?" I asked.

"I met with the director and some of the volunteers," he said. "They explained that people donate all kinds of things to Salem West. Some of the stuff is cleaned up and given right away to those who need it. The extra donations are sent over to The Mustard Seed, and the money raised here helps people with their utility bills or pays for needed things that didn't get donated. After our meeting, we made a trailer run to pick up some donations from an estate all the way in the next county."

"What kinds of things did you get?"

"Mostly furniture. But it filled the whole trailer. They get plenty of donations, but they're really hurting for more volunteers. Everything's gotta be cleaned and categorized before anything can be given out or sent over here to be sold."

I was impressed with the way these two organizations cooperated so closely to help the community. In order to make everything run smoothly, I could see they depended on reliable volunteers. But, at The Mustard Seed that day, it was clear to me that the benefits of service were mutual. The ladies I worked with were delighted to use their creative talents to help their neighbors in need. As was I.

June 22-24: Deerwood to Brainerd, MN

On Saturday, we launched in the rain, fully expecting to be wet all day. Much to our surprise, the drizzle dried up early and the rest of the day was warm and overcast. We bypassed our planned river site campground, paddling onward to meet the second Jason of our trip and his family. I mentally reviewed ideas about service that parents might want their children to learn about—ideas that might be worth a promised steak dinner and laundry facilities.

Jason's dock was just off the Mississippi on a backwater channel. We picked our way through the wild rice paddies to the bay, keeping our eyes out for the bright orange life jacket he told us would be on the end of his dock. The stems and leaves of the rice plants were just beginning to emerge through the water's surface, which made it easy to maneuver through the maze. As we approached, two children ran down from the house to greet us at the dock. Jason soon came down the path with his tractor and boat trailer, greeted us, and pulled Donna into his oversized garage.

True to his word, Jason and his wife, Tammy, prepared a delicious grilled steak dinner. We ate around a long wooden table in the great room of the contemporary summer timber home. Tall picture windows offered a view of wooded hills and the bay off the slough.

After Jason said grace and we started eating, he asked, "Would it be okay to ask you some questions about your trip? We've asked Matt and Macie to think of some things they'd like to ask you."

"Of course," Gene said, turning to the kids. "What would you like to know?"

Matt put down his fork and looked up at us. "How do you fit all your stuff in the boat?" he asked.

"That's a great question," replied Gene. "There's actually a lot of room inside the hull. We push our air mattresses, tent, and bedrolls in the back. Way up in the front, we have our clothing bags, and in the middle, between us, we keep our food, our mess kit, and our burner stove. On top, we have a deck bag for each of us, for things we use during the day, and a solar charger."

"What do you use the solar charger for?" he asked.

"Our phones, mostly. The trickle charge is too slow for our camera, so we charge that when we get into towns."

Macie summoned up her courage next. "What do you eat?"

"We dehydrated all kinds of healthy foods before we left," I explained. "We combined them into meals, and packed them in boxes. We keep about a week's worth of food in the boat at a time. My son sends us a new box of food whenever we ask him to."

"Any other questions?" Jason encouraged.

"When you get to the end of the river," said Matt, "how will you get back home?"

"We're not sure yet," I admitted. "We won't paddle back—that's for sure. If my son can take time off from college—"

"Or if my son can get off of work—" interjected Gene.

I continued, "One of them might drive down to pick us up. Otherwise, we might rent a car. We'll have to wait and see how it works out. But you can follow us on our blog and we'll let you know."

"If that doesn't work out, just call me and I'll come with my truck," offered Jason. I appreciated the offer. It was too early to worry about it, but it felt nice to have options.

"What kinds of services have you done so far?" Tammy threw in a question of her own. She must have noticed, too, that most of the questions so far were of a practical nature—mostly about the boat. I followed her lead and turned the discussion toward our service experiences in Bemidji, Grand Rapids, and Deerwood.

As the questions died down, it seemed like a good time to keep our promise to Jason. "Matt and Macie," I started, "do you like to help other people?"

"Sometimes," Macie answered.

"Yeah," said Matt. "Sometimes our parents ask us to do stuff that isn't fun, though." He looked at Tammy, then Jason. "But we do it anyway." Tammy smiled, which seemed to give him silent encouragement. Matt grinned back at her, then lowered his eyes.

"Why do you help your parents, even when it's not fun?" I pressed.

"So we don't get in trouble!" Matt's eyes got big. Then he added, "And we want to make them happy." Another glance, this time at Jason.

"Because we love them," Macie chimed in.

"I can tell you do," said Gene, joining in the conversation.

"How do you know when people need help, like your parents here at home, or a friend at school?" I asked.

"That's easy," said Macie. "They ask us to help with something, like the dishes."

"Or a math problem," added Matt.

"Can you ever tell that someone might need help before they ask?"

There was a pause. Then Macie said, "Sometimes my friend looks sad." The corners of her mouth turned down and her eyes were empathetic. "And I ask her what's wrong and try to make her feel better."

"Well, then, you already know a lot about service . . . and you're doing it right now. You're helping others because you care about them. You're helping when you're asked to, and offering help when you think someone might need it."

Jason looked at his children. "We're proud of you," he said.

"Your mom and dad did the same thing, too," Gene said. "They found out we were on the river, and offered to help us by giving us a place to stay. With thunderstorms coming tonight, I'm really glad to be here instead of in a tent."

Jason helped bring the point home. "God wants us to love him and to love each other . . . not just our friends, but anyone who needs help." He turned to us. "Thanks for a great lesson." It felt good to have a part in the conversation, but I realized the lessons that Jason and Tammy were teaching their children came through their day-to-day example of caring for others—even for two strangers paddling through their neighborhood.

After dinner, we discovered God's timing could not have been more perfect to have shelter. The weather turned nasty. We relaxed in the warm steam of our basement suite sauna, showered up, and snuggled on the sectional to watch Game 5 of the Stanley Cup play-offs. Then we collapsed into a warm bed to sleep out another storm.

We had a flex day before our Monday date in Brainerd, so Sunday morning brought us a chance to attend a church service in Merrifield with our host family. Joyful hymns preceded a sermon about following God's law, not because it is written on stone, but rather allowing him to write it on our hearts. The minister ended saying, "If you give God control, you will find that he'll change you from the inside out." This sermon wasn't just words. I knew from experience that it was true.

After church, Jason drove us to Best Buy, where we picked up an iPad and a Bluetooth keyboard to replace our Chromebook. This time, we purchased a LifeProof case. Then, at Caribou Coffee, settled between my sugar-free mocha and Gene's chai tea, we set up our new system and caught our readers up on our travels.

Monday morning, Jason backed his trailer down the ramp and *Kupendana* slipped into the water. "Before we go, do you want to take her for a little spin?" I asked.

"Are you serious?" Jason asked. "I'd love to!"

"Take my seat in the stern," I said, handing him my life vest. "That way, you can get a feel for the steering. Just push the right foot pedal forward to turn right, and use your left foot to go left. It's pretty intuitive."

He stepped down off the dock, his tall thin body sliding easily into place. I wondered if I would ever look that graceful. My agility and balance had definitely improved with practice, but I still hoped no one was watching each time I perched on the coaming, swished the mud off my shoes one at a time, shook off the water, and jiggled into the cockpit. "See you soon," Gene called. He shoved the bow away from the dock and Jason initiated a graceful turn toward the backwaters.

I watched them disappear around a corner and listened to the rhythmic splash of the paddles until I could hear it no longer. I checked the weather forecast on my phone—highs in the low eighties, partly sunny, with winds out of the south at five to eight miles per hour. Looked good. After no more than a Facebook minute, men's voices softly floated over the water, alerting me to their return. As they glided alongside the dock, a huge grin spread across Jason's face. "It handles as great as it looks!"

"I thought you'd like it," I said. "You're our first honorary member of the *Kupendana* crew." Jason handed me my life vest, and we switched places. Thanking him once more for his hospitality, we picked our way back through the sprouting rice paddies to the main channel for the short, six-mile paddle to Brainerd. I wondered what it would be like to live this far north and harvest wild rice each fall from the waters right outside my door. As we rejoined the main channel, I counted the bays as we passed, comparing them to the outline of the shore on our map. I savored the views of the tranquil water and the emerald tree-lined shore snaking in and out. I closed my eyes to imprint the memory of this pristine place, then opened them to check my memory against reality. Reality was better. "I wonder how many people give up their journey down the river and make a home around here," I mused.

"It's tempting, isn't it?" said Gene. "I do know I want to live by water someday."

"Me, too," I agreed. "But further south, where the water doesn't freeze." Ocean, bay, lake, or river? I didn't know yet. I suspected it didn't matter. Each had its own personality. But all shared the same elements of beauty, tranquility, and life.

My thoughts shifted to the destination ahead . . . the city we almost dismissed. Brainerd offered several interesting service organizations, but had presented a quandary when we planned our itinerary months ago. There was no place to pitch a tent. There was a park near the river with RV sites that looked beautiful. But they didn't allow tents.

We had sent emails to a couple of organizations that looked promising, but heard nothing. Rather than force-fit a match, we'd planned to camp on an island in the area, then push on downstream.

Several weeks later, we received a surprising email from Let's Go Fishing. This organization, like Fishing Has No Boundaries, provided angling experiences, but its mission was different. Rather than one large weekend event for disabled anglers, Let's Go Fishing offered pontoon boat excursions to seniors of any ability. These half-day fishing trips were scheduled all summer long—free of charge.

"We saved your request to discuss at our board meeting," the email explained. "We'd love to have you join us for a fishing trip." They designated a volunteer to be our contact and chauffeur, and arranged for us to help at a nearby camp for the developmentally disabled. It even got better—they offered us our own cabin at the camp to use while we were in the area.

Approaching Lum Park, I called Les, our contact, to give him our ETA. "I've arranged to pick up a trailer to bring your boat to the camp," Les confirmed. "A friend of mine is a photographer for the *Brainerd Dispatch* and wants to come and take a picture of your arrival. I hope it's okay. We should be there within an hour."

Already within sight of the park, we decided to wait for them onshore. A stretch would feel good; we could always paddle back out to stage a reentry for the local newspaper photographer once he arrived. We tied the kayak to a dock, bought a couple sodas and a dozen worms at a nearby gas station, then returned to wet a line and pass some time. We shared our worms and some stories with two local boys, their bicycles parked nearby. When Les and the photographer arrived, we paddled out to reclaim the bobber I snagged in the weeds, then posed for a few publicity shots as we glided back to shore.

June 24–26: Confidence Learning Center

Soon, we arrived at Confidence Learning Center, affectionately called by its original moniker, Camp Confidence. Les parked the sixteen-foot trailer next to our cabin and helped us carry in our bags. The cabin was aged, but was many times larger than our tent. There was no closet, so the oversized pine coffee table and the sagging green and burgundy plaid couch served as our dressing area. I spread my service clothes on the couch, hoping the wrinkles would flatten out by tomorrow. It was still June, and I was already getting tired of wearing the same things over and over. Two bottoms and two tops didn't offer much to mix and match. With eight hours of exercise daily, I secretly hoped that my clothes would start drooping on my new, fit body. Oh, it would be fun to go shopping for new outfits. I tugged at the waistband of my shorts. It felt looser, but far from danger of falling off my hips. No shopping yet.

Off the living and kitchen area, we had a bathroom with a shower and our choice of two small bedrooms. The choice was moot. Both rooms were identical—two sets of wooden single-mattress bunk beds against the wood-paneled walls, and a curtained window opposite the door. I sat down on one of the bottom bunks. The springs sagged; I knew I'd need more support for my back. I pulled the mattress off the bottom bunk. "I'm sleeping on the floor. Want to join me?" I asked.

"How can I pass up an offer like that?" Gene answered. Once he set another mattress next to mine, it left no floor space to walk around, but created a king-sized bed smack in the middle of the room.

The best part was the view from the small stone patio outside the cabin. I found myself looking down on the rest of the world, through the top-most branches of an oak forest, to sparkling Sylvan Lake below. Two chairs beckoned for us to sit, rest, and enjoy a quiet afternoon. I took a rain check; we had to go.

Les drove us to the main camp office, where we met Bob, the program director. He thanked Les for his help and then turned to us. "How'd you like your cabin? It's kinda old and tired, but we're in the process of renovating. Yours'll be one of the last. At least you have a place to stay, and some privacy while you're in town."

"Thanks," replied Gene. "It's far more than we need, but after cooking one-pot meals on a camp stove, I can't wait to use four burners again."

"And a real shower," I added.

In the main lodge, Bob explained a little about the organization and its mission. "We offer year-round outdoor activities for developmentally disabled campers of all ages. A family member or caretaker comes along with each camper. Our programs aren't canned weekly camps where everyone does the same thing. Each camper or group is assigned a program specialist, who customizes the activities to each camper's needs."

Bob walked us through a nature center with real artifacts and live animals, an astronomy room complete with black lights and glowing constellations, and a craft room decorated with colorful painted handprints signed by past campers. "We offer lots of sensory activities, both inside and out," Bob told us. "Outside, we have a wildlife sanctuary, a swimming beach, boat rides, harnessed tree climbing, archery, hayrides, and a super slide." *What? A super slide?* I looked around, but saw only wooded trails. Bob continued, "In the winter, the campers can go snowshoeing, tubing, and cross-country skiing."

As a teacher, I was impressed with the thought that went into planning visual, auditory, and kinesthetic experiences for the campers. "Do you have formal training in special needs?" I asked.

"No," he said. "My training is in environmental education. But I've been overseeing camp programming here for twenty-four years, and have picked up a thing or two about the campers we serve, just from working with them. Lots of times, people focus on what the disabled can't do. That limits our expectations, and theirs. We start with what they can do, and then get them to try something new. Sometimes their caretakers, who have worked with them for years, are shocked at what they find out they do when they try something new."

"What can we do to help while we're here?" asked Gene.

"Just relax for tonight," said Bob. "You've gotta be tired. Tomorrow I'll introduce you to Mary, our volunteer coordinator. She'll have some jobs for you."

In the morning, Bob handed us off to Mary. "Volunteers are an integral part of what we do here," she said. "I try to match volunteers with positions that are fulfilling for them, while meeting the camp needs. I think it's important for volunteers to grow personally, as well as giving their time and talents to help us."

"I think I usually get more than I give," Gene shared. I thought of The Mustard Seed, and had to agree.

"That's great," said Mary. "Then you're doing the right things. Are you ready to get to work?" I nodded.

"Whatever you need," said Gene. This became our go-to offer—help without conditions. It summed up the reason we were here, but it also opened us up for some pretty long and tiring days.

"Well, then . . . we'll start with the most difficult job," she said, lowering her head and casting us a sideways glance, almost apologetic.

I gave Gene a "Now we're in for it" look, just as a young woman in jean shorts and a tank top joined us, exchanging a smile of greeting with Mary.

"We have a group of campers coming tomorrow," Mary explained. "Their favorite activity is the giant slide, but with the wind and rain we had recently, it's not ready to use. I'll need you to help us clean and wax it, so it's ready for tomorrow." She put her hand on the young girl's shoulder. "This is Anna, one of our student interns. She's done this before, and will help me show you the ropes."

"Aw, I hate this job," Anna complained with a pronounced pout, followed by a sly smile. She flipped her long brown hair over her shoulder, turning to lead us down the narrow camp road to the giant slide. When she traipsed off the main road, following a mulched walking path into the woods, we got a glimpse of the "hardest work of the day." Built right into the slope of the hill was a giant, six-lane metal slide. Wooden steps along the side led to a landing at the top. The surface of the slide was littered with leaves, mostly congregating on the flatter sections near the middle and bottom of the gigantic structure.

For the next hour, Gene and I chatted with Mary and Anna while helping them ready the huge play area for company. First, we swished burlap bags back and forth at the bottom of the slide to send the leaves swirling back to the forest floor. Patches of silver glittered in the dappled light, but the metal felt cool to the touch. After the slide was free of debris, we climbed the steps to the top. Mary pointed to three-leaved plants with shiny foliage along the edges of the stairway. "Watch out for the poison ivy," she warned.

"We're pretty careful, but I don't think I need to worry," said Gene. "I never get poison ivy. In fact, when I was a Boy Scout, I mowed down a patch of it with a push mower, and didn't have any reaction at all."

"You're lucky," said Mary. "It's miserable. We'll bring the goats out here later, before the campers arrive. They love to eat poison ivy, and for some reason, they're immune to its oils. It's a win-win for us." I knew goats weren't known for their discriminating palates. But poison ivy?

Once we reached the top, Mary gave us each a strip of waxed paper. "Put this under the burlap bag," she said. "It'll wax the slide a little more each time we go down."

My first trip was a disaster—starting and stopping like an old jalopy and stalling halfway down on the flat section. Gene's ride looked no easier, but he was ahead of me, his heels pulling him onward to the next descent. I refused to give up; after all, I was here to help. We rode our burlap waxing sleds down each lane of the slide, time after time, until we nearly launched off that plateau, coming to a stop only feet from the end of the slide. Anna challenged us to several races. She was good, but Gene and I held our own. Finally, the gleaming slide awaiting tomorrow's campers, we strode out of the woods.

Feigning exhaustion, Gene wiped his brow and glanced at Mary. "Whew. Anna was right," he said. "That was rough. I hope all the jobs you have planned for us aren't that demanding."

"No, the next one's easy," interjected Anna. "Have you ever sexed rabbits before?" At that, Mary took her leave, and Gene and I followed Anna to the wildlife sanctuary, where she taught us how to determine the sex of baby bunnies. The litters born in spring were ready to be separated into different hutches. One by one, we cuddled them, held them gently on their backs to check their genitals, and then placed them in the corresponding hutch. Several campers who came to enjoy the animals joined us at the sanctuary. We held the bunnies for them to pet and sometimes taught them how to hold them alone.

That afternoon, Bob took us to a storage shed to explain our next project. "We'd like to paint the floor inside," he explained, "but it needs a little prep work. Sort what you can, and just leave the stuff you don't know what to do with out here." He pointed to a fence by the corner of a walkway. "We'll find a place for it." The shed was so full we could hardly see the floor. We emptied, sorted, and organized the contents—then realized what a mess it was going to be to clean. Moisture from a leaking freezer unit saturated the floor. Flaking paint, mixed with dirt and mud, was everywhere. Spider webs hung from the exposed rafters.

With a broom, Gene knocked down the webs, sending creepy crawlies running for cover. Then we used metal brushes and paint scrapers to slowly chip away the rust and old paint. Finally, we swept and washed the floor. At the end of the afternoon, it was prepared for painting, but would need days to dry out completely. Once again, we wouldn't be around to see the results of our work, but I was satisfied that our presence helped—not only with the fun things like waxing the slide, but with the grungy work as well.

Showered, tired, and satisfied, we joined the campers for a campfire sing-along.

Tuesday morning, we assisted some adult campers who came with chaperones from their group homes. We spent time in conversation and accompanied them to the animal sanctuary. One tall, thin woman with short-cropped dark hair reminded me of pictures of my mother when she was younger. Smiling, she watched the ducklings and chickens strut on the path, eating the pellets that campers scattered about. I cupped a tiny brown and tan rabbit in my hands and held it out to her. "Would you like to pet a baby bunny?" She reached out, gently touched it with one finger, and smiled again. "Would you like to hold it?" I asked.

Her chaperone took her elbow. "Sit down over here, Betty," she said, helping the woman to a wooden bench by the chicken coop. Betty took a seat and cupped her hands near her chest. I gently nested the bunny in her hand and she placed her fingers on top of its back.

"You've held animals before, haven't you?" I asked. "You know just what to do."

"Betty used to live on a farm," explained her chaperone. "This is her favorite place at the camp." Turning to Betty, she asked, "How many years have you come here now, Betty?"

Without looking up from the baby bunny in her hands, Betty replied, "Four. Four years now. Camp is my favorite part of the summer." Her eyes searched the pond and the forest inside the nature area. "Where's Mama?"

"Let's go see," her chaperone gently answered. She turned to me. "Mama is the resident doe. She's very gentle and Betty loves to watch her." She pointed toward a wooden bridge over a small pond. "There she is." I took back the bunny and snuggled it to my chest, watching the pair walk down the path toward the bridge. A tan, white-tailed deer slowly approached along the path. Betty stood still and watched as Mama crossed the bridge, ambled along the path into the trees, and lay down on the grass.

Later, we visited with a group of adults at the beach. A variety of activities were going on at once—swimming, playing in the water, tie-dyeing shirts, and sitting in beach chairs and wheelchairs by the waterfront. Mary was taking small groups out on the lake in a glass-bottomed boat. "Can you help invite people for our last boat ride?" she asked. Gene pushed wheelchairs to the end of the pier, and I helped campers step down onto the boat while he returned their chairs to the shore. The campers sat on benches around a glass window in the middle of the floor, gazing at the silky green strands of seaweed drifting in the currents under our feet. Mary piloted the boat, asking questions about aquatic life and habitats, and adding commentary and stories to make the trip more interesting. We viewed plant life, fish, and even an old sunken rowboat.

As we pulled back to the dock, a bare-chested man swam underneath the boat, turned face-up, and waved to us. His brown hair flowed like the seaweed, changing direction with each movement of his head. Instead of legs, he sported a glittery green tail, swishing back and forth as he swam. "Look, everyone!" Mary shouted. "It's Tony the Merman! He's come to say hello." Some of the adults on the boat waved to Tony, some shouted out his name, and others just grinned from ear to ear. In no time at all, the merman was gone.

Twenty feet away, a two-legged camp counselor climbed up a ladder onto the dock, a dripping bag slung over his shoulder. As the excited campers rose, Gene and I helped them step up onto the dock, where counselors waited with wheelchairs for those who needed them. I watched Tony's friends surround him with handshakes and back slaps. These young people gave me hope. It was obvious to me that their joy came from the joy they gave. I could see why campers like Betty returned here year after year.

June 25: Let's Go Fishing!

After lunch on Tuesday, Les drove us to the Cragun's Resort Marina on Gull Lake. I couldn't wait to get firsthand experience with a Let's Go Fishing outing for seniors. "How old do you have to be to sign up for a fishing trip?" I asked Les.

"We'll take any seniors, fifty-five on up," he said.

"That's not so old," I laughed. I was fifty-six, and Gene, less than a year older. It was hard to believe that we already qualified for free fishing charters. I followed up on my question. "You use pontoon boats, like Fishing Has No Boundaries. Do many of the seniors have disabilities?"

"Some do," he said. "The pontoon boat is just easier all around. But this service is based more on gratitude than on need. We try to express thanks to seniors for all the time they've given to others and respect for their value in our community. Lots of the people who sign up are fit as a fiddle like you two. They just don't have access to boats or fishing gear and it gives them a chance to spend an afternoon out on the lake."

"Do people just call to sign up?" I asked.

"Individuals can register themselves as often as every other week. But a lot of our people sign up through churches and senior citizen groups; even nursing homes and assisted living centers bring groups out. We really offer any senior the chance to get out on the lake, even if they don't participate in the fishing."

"And it's all free of charge?" Gene asked.

"It is," Les confirmed. He turned into the driveway of the marina. "There's one hired staff member who takes care of all the registration. But other than that, it's entirely run by volunteers. Our pontoon boat was donated and advertising on the boat pays for our gas and supplies. Gary and Kathy can tell you more about it. Come on. I'll introduce you."

We hopped out of the truck and walked down the gravel drive to the pontoon boat tied up at the dock. I could see the advertising placards Les mentioned along the outside of the railing. Two people wearing yellow T-shirts were puttering on deck. The woman finished loading water bottles in the cooler and closed the lid. Wiping her hands on her gray shorts, she extended one to me. "Welcome," she said. Her short brown hair was tucked behind her ears, and her spectacles were shaded under the brim of her white cap. "You must be Barb and Gene. I'm Kathy." She turned and pointed to the tall tanned man, with a cap matching hers, standing by the captain's wheel. "And that's my husband, Gary." Turning back to us, she noticed Les. "Thanks for bringin' 'em over, Les. We'll be back in about three hours."

"Okay, then," said Les. He shook Gene's hand. "I'll be here when you get back. Say—if you don't have plans later, I'd love for my wife, Lucy, to meet you. Can we take you to dinner tonight?"

"That'd be nice," said Gene. We waved good-bye and stepped aboard. The boat was outfitted with six generous-sized well-padded swivel chairs. Like fishing from lounge chairs, I thought approvingly. Two elderly ladies occupied the seats in the back. On the stern railing between them was a sign, which read, "Giving Back to Those Who Have Given So Much." I loved the fact that the mission statement was posted right here on the boat. I was only here as a volunteer, and yet the sign still made me feel welcomed and appreciated.

Overhead, the canvas Bimini top shaded the deck. Hanging from plastic clips attached to its frame were about a dozen fishing rods. It was hard to imagine enough people on this boat to use them all. The mental image of crossed lines, bobbers, and hooks made me cringe. Gene went to talk to Gary and I walked back to chat with the ladies in the stern.

"Hi, I'm Barb." I told them about the reason we were there. "Have you taken these fishing trips before?"

"Oh, I come all the time," said one of the women. Tall and thin, she was seated comfortably, but her face, framed by closely cropped curly white hair, exuded energy. Judging by her wide smile, I was sure that there was plenty of sparkle in the eyes that hid behind the oversized dark glasses wrapped around her face. "I even bring my own life vest." She straightened, proudly displaying her fitted sleeveless black vest. "The ones they have here aren't nearly as comfortable as mine. I'm Helen," she said. "And this is my friend Elaine." Elaine smiled politely. Her hands were folded in her lap, over her pink tank top and light blue shorts. Her gray, layered cut and thick glasses gave her a librarian look. I wondered, if not for Helen, if she wouldn't be just as happy sitting at home with a good book.

Soon, another couple, Tom and Marlee, joined the crew. They were new volunteers in training, and were coming along to learn from our experienced captain and first mate. Tom reminded me of a tanned Jimmy Durante, with a weathered face that couldn't help but make me smile. Marlee, a few inches taller than Tom, was just as infectious. "How can I help?" she asked. Kathy took her up front and began to show her around.

Just as we readied to shove off, the last senior boarded. Jimmy looked like he might be the oldest one of the bunch. Tentative in his step, but walking without assistance, he looked to be in his seventies. "I haven't been fishing in years," he confided, as he took a seat. "I sure hope I catch something."

Kathy and Marlee passed out life jackets to those who needed them. Gene and I wore our lightweight vests from the kayak. "What can we do to help?" I asked Kathy. With six golden-ager volunteers to help three independent senior anglers, it didn't look like we'd be very busy.

"As volunteers," she explained, "our job is to make it a good experience for the seniors. You can help them if they need help, but mainly, just enjoy the day. The reason most of us volunteer is because we love to be on the water fishing and we want to share the experience with others. So feel free to throw in a line yourselves."

Gary knew the lake well, having fished it himself many times. He drove the pontoon boat to several hot spots around the lake, where everyone—even Elaine—threw in a line. As we passed one beautiful lake home after another, I thought of my parents' home on the bay, a family gathering spot and vacation rolled into one. A place for frolicking, fishing, Packer games, birthdays, holidays, and family reunions. The place where Dad handed us his binoculars to watch the loons dive and the pelicans glide. Where we stitched together the kayak we now paddled. But Dad was gone. And Mom could no longer remember the laughter echoing over the water, the glassy surface painted with pink and orange at the end of the day, the smell of warm apple pies she baked each time we came to visit. After Dad died and Mom moved to Memory Care, we sold that empty waterfront house, but I saved the memories like souvenirs. I pressed my crossed hands to my chest to stop the ache, and refocused on the present.

The hum of the engine died as Gene helped Gary lower the anchor. I busied myself passing out worms and leeches to those who needed bait, and then threaded a redworm on my hook.

Bobbers began to jerk, and we reeled in some sunnies, smallmouth bass, northern pike too small to keep, and even a bullhead. Gary filled a five-gallon bucket with water, and we put all the keepers in it together. "I'll take anyone's fish that they don't want to take home," offered Helen. "I brought my own bucket, in the car, to take 'em. I love to eat fish, and I don't even mind cleanin' 'em."

"Fish on!" I heard Jimmy yell. Excited for him to have his first bite of the day, I looked over the side and watched his line cut through the water in a zigzag pattern.

"Keep the tip up," Gene reminded him. "Don't let the line slack." The other lines were reeled in, so as not to tangle with Jimmy's.

I alternately watched the fight and the gleeful grin on Jimmy's face as he played the fish. Finally, he brought the fish to the boat and Gary netted it. "A large-mouth bass!" he told Jimmy. He took hold of its mouth and gills, gently pulling it out of the net and handing it to Jimmy. "Wow! It's at least eighteen inches, and look at its girth. It must run at least two pounds."

"Hold it up for a picture," I said, as I quickly framed and clicked.

"Jimmy, you got the biggest catch of the day!" congratulated Gene.

On the way home, Gary asked Tom, "Do you want to drive? You'll be doing it by yourself before long, so you may as well get some experience." I knew Gene had experience driving his dad's pontoon boat, and suspected he would have liked a turn. But he seemed comfortable just being a part of the crew.

Back at the dock, we said good-bye to the seniors, helped clean and organize the boat, and talked about the day. "This was fun!" Gene said. "I could see us doing something like this someday." I had to agree; it felt like a natural fit.

June 25–26: Sertoma Club

After we made a quick trip to our cabin to clean up, Les took us home to meet Lucy. She was a good fit for Les, similarly gentle and kind and equally strong in spirit. If I thought of a stereotypical grandma, she'd fit the role—shorter than the rest of us, dressed in comfortable clothes and shoes, hair in the process of turning from brown to silver. Their home was modest, but nestled into nature with the woods for a backyard. As she finished getting ready, I busied myself looking at the framed family pictures arranged cozily on the walls and the kitchen counter bar. It didn't seem to matter whether design rules for groupings were followed; what seemed more important was that everybody was included. "Shall we go?" Lucy asked and Les gently put his hand on her back as we walked down the steps to the car.

At the restaurant, Les announced, "You can have whatever you want, but we always get the buffet. There's plenty of food, and all of it's good."

"That sounds good enough for me," Gene said, rubbing his stomach. Gene loved buffets. When I met him, he took pride in going back to fill his plate for seconds . . . at least twice. I joked that restaurants made money on me at buffets, because I tried to watch my portion sizes. "They lose money on me," he said. "I'm surprised they let me in the door."

Over dinner of ribs, chicken, fish, pizza, and all the fixin's, we shared stories about our families, hobbies, and adventures.

Too full for dessert, I pushed back my plate. "Thank you. It was as delicious as you told us," I said.

"Mmm-hmm," agreed Gene, enjoying his sampling of small bars and cakes.

Les laughed. "It's our pleasure. What do you have planned for tomorrow?"

"Laundry," I answered.

At the exact same time, Gene said, "Blogging." He gestured with his hand for me to speak first.

"Actually, both. Bob said we could use the laundry machines in the lodge. And that's the only place that has Wi-Fi. So, we'll hang out there for most of the day."

"We've got several posts to do." Gene counted on his fingers. "One about the trip here from Jason's, one about Camp Confidence, and then Let's Go Fishing!"

"Will you have time for me to take you to lunch?" asked Les. We looked at him quizzically. He'd already spent too much on us. "I'm a member of the Brainerd Chapter of Sertoma. That's short for service to mankind." He wrote it down on a napkin—SERvice TO MAnkind. "We raise money for lots of charities in the area, and we do some other projects, too. Our monthly lunch meeting is tomorrow. I'd love to introduce you to the other club members, and show you what Sertoma Club does."

"How can we refuse?" Gene laughed. "We'd love to. But you'll have to get us back early; that'll be another post we'll have to write."

"Oh, before you go, I have something for you," said Lucy. She reached into her purse and unfolded a newspaper clipping. It was the picture of the two of us paddling into Brainerd. "I thought you might like this."

"Thank you," I said, holding the picture up to look at it closely. The caption underneath told briefly about the reason we were in town and gave our blog site address. "We've been in a couple different newspapers, but so far, we haven't been in town long enough to see them. Even back home in Waukesha, an article came out in the *Freeman* right after we left for Minnesota."

From the beginning, Gene and I had agreed that we would try our best not to allow our pride be an issue in this trip. So far, that wasn't a problem. It was hard to feel like proficient paddlers when we spent so much time in the water—or doing repairs. We focused on the organizations and the good they did, so it was pretty easy to ignore the publicity we received.

But I did like this picture. It was beautifully composed. Both of our paddles were perfectly in sync, and we looked focused, but content. I was rarely pleased with the way I looked in photographs, but in this one, we both looked strong and fit. "Your photographer friend does nice work," I told Les. I folded it and slid it into my pocket. Maybe we could keep this one souvenir.

When Les and Lucy dropped us off, it was still early, so we brought the iPad and keyboard down to the lodge. We had time to start one of the posts before tomorrow. Gene settled in—it was his turn to compose. "I like it better when you do it," he told me. "It takes *forever* to think of just the right words to say exactly what I mean."

"That's why we're doing it together," I reminded him. "We get to help each other and our readers get both perspectives."

Gene set to work. I went to get a cup of coffee from the vending machine. Mmm. This was just what I needed after dinner. I took the picture out of my pocket and looked at it again. Maybe I could put it in with the maps. It wouldn't take up much room and would stay flat and dry. I set it down on the floor and balanced my Styrofoam cup on the wooden arm of the chair. Then I turned my attention to Gene's writing. As I shifted in my seat, the cup tumbled to the floor. Coffee cascaded onto the carpet, soaking the newspaper clipping. "Ohhhh," I groaned. "It's ruined." I rushed to the bathroom to get some paper towels to blot the carpet, and held up the soaked newspaper by one corner.

"Don't worry about it," said Gene. "It's just a picture."

I dropped the photo into the wastebasket. It fell on top of the rubbish, doubled over and stuck to itself. "We don't need it," I said. "But it didn't hurt to see how much better we're startin' to look." I gently squeezed his bicep.

Shortly before noon the next day, Les gave us a reprieve from our laundry and writing to drive us to the same restaurant where we'd eaten the night before. In a back room, eight long tables were set, and people mingled in a pre-meeting social hour. "There are lots of place settings, Les. How many Sertoma members are there?" I asked.

"There are over a hundred of us, but they don't all come to every meeting," Les replied. "Many of them are local business owners, but some are just people that want to help support local charities."

Gene entered the conversation. "Like what charities?" he asked.

"Oh, you'd recognize most of them: United Way, American Cancer Society, Red Cross, Salvation Army, and Junior Achievement." Les went on to explain, "We have a few major fund-raisers that have gotten to be traditions. One of our biggest is a drive-through Winter Wonderland of holiday lights and displays set up at the arboretum." I thought of a similar tradition in our hometown. Cars lined up every night throughout the holiday season to drive through lanes with lighted displays.

Les continued, "We also have some year-round fund-raisers, like contracting with businesses to display American flags for patriotic holidays, and renting pipe and drape kiosks for conventions. But my favorite things are our week-long camp for the deaf and hard of hearing right here at Camp Confidence, and our holiday toy drive for children."

Les introduced us to some of the people who sat around us at the table, and after lunch, there was a short business meeting. There were the usual business items, like elections of officers and thank-yous for help with projects. Then a list was read of the organizations that received recent checks from Sertoma. The striking thing to me was the number of them that were donated anonymously. It was nice to meet people dedicated simply to service, often for people they will never meet, not for recognition, but to make their communities welcoming and strong.

Chapter 5
Fast Water

June 27–28: Brainerd to Little Falls, MN

DURING THE THREE DAYS that we stayed in Brainerd, the rains of early June continued their water cycle journey into the streams and lakes of northern Minnesota and from there into the Mississippi. Runoff from the seven counties through which we paddled now added to the river's volume and speed, like powerful jets at every turn of a gigantic water slide.

"Look at that current!" exclaimed Gene, as we climbed out of Les's truck at a boat ramp south of the Brainerd Dam. I watched the water slide by, bending the grasses along the bank. I wasn't sure whether I was excited that the miles would fly by, or nervous that this meant less time to react to our surroundings. Probably both.

"You be careful," cautioned Lucy, who rode along with Les to say good-bye. They were going to the Cities today to see their daughter. It still made me smile that with the plethora of communities in the world, everyone in Minnesota knew that the Cities meant Minneapolis and St. Paul. The rest of the country knew them as the Twin Cities, as they were so close in proximity they grew into each other over time and their borders became mostly irrelevant. To Minnesotans, the names seemed to be equally superfluous.

"We will," I promised. We joined hands at the bank before boarding—our own little prayer circle. I felt the warmth of Lucy's hand in one of mine and the soft padding of Gene's leather paddle glove in the other.

Les took the lead. "Lord, we thank you for your servants, Barb and Gene, and for the chance to meet these new friends and be part of the work you are doing through them. We place our trust in you, knowing that every day they are in your presence, and asking that you keep them safe. We pray these things in Jesus' name. Amen."

"Thank you," Gene said. "For everything, but especially for this." I felt him squeeze my hand, and knew he was squeezing Les's hand on his other side. "There isn't a better way to start a day," he said. We exchanged hugs all around and then I hunkered down into the cockpit for a wild ride.

It seemed in no time, we approached the bridge and landing at the Kiwanis Park. Drawing near, I noticed a photographer aiming his camera at us from the walkway atop the bridge. "That's Les," I said. "On the bridge!" We rested our paddles momentarily and waved for another picture I figured we'd never see. Then, as Les continued to click away, we focused our attention on the bridge ahead. Gene steered toward the center opening between the two bridge supports. If we paddled too close, the swirling currents could suck us into a concrete confrontation that we wouldn't win. "I'm squaring it up . . . get ready!" Gene announced. *Kupendana* was positioned perpendicular to the bridge, her bow pointed toward the center, where we could ride the current straight through. We passed under the bridge, our paddles churning, and the river spat us out into calmer waters.

I glanced back toward the park. Lucy stood at the railing of the overlook, her hand raised in a wave. I couldn't turn far enough to see if Les was still on the bridge, so I waved over my shoulder to both of them. "I'll miss them," I said.

"Me, too," replied Gene. Even though Les and Lucy had somewhere else to be, they took the time to drive down the road and wait for us, just to watch us pass and wave good-bye again.

"When we do get home," I told Gene, over my shoulder, "I want to be more like the people we've met."

"How so?" he asked.

I rested my paddle. "I don't want to be too busy to go out of my way for other people," I said. "Les chaperoned us all over, took us to his home, and even out to dinner. That was over-the-top hospitality."

"I know what you mean," said Gene. "Like Jason and his grandparents, letting us stay with them, helping us fix the boat, and then driving us all the way over to Schoolcraft. I don't know what we would have done without their help."

I thought of our other river angels, Bemidji Jason and Jeni, Pokegama Mike, Deerwood Becky and Gary, and just recently, Brainerd Jason and Tammy, providing us shelter from the storm. In less than a month, so many generous people were blessings to us. I hoped, when we did get home, we could find ways to do the same for others.

The city disappeared behind us, and the river spread out to more closely resemble a swamp. "Look at all this water," I said over my shoulder. It looked like the riverbanks had surrendered, unable to contain the onslaught. Entire banks were submerged, grasses growing out from the surface of water turned chocolate with churned up mud. In the middle of the river, trunks of trees sprouted up from the river's surface. "I think that's an island," I called to Gene.

"Not much land left on that is*land*," he said, emphasizing the last syllable. True, there was no ground to be seen. The trees shaded the surface of the water, making it look deeper brown than the milk chocolate color of the sun-soaked river beyond. Branches and debris, snagged by the grove of water trees, hugged the bottoms of the trunks.

About twelve miles downstream, we arrived at Crow Wing State Park in the early afternoon. The banks were higher here, and didn't yet succumb to the rising water. We pulled the boat up the ramp, locked it to a nearby canoe rack, and set out on foot to locate the campsite area. We followed the paved camp road, which curved past a picnic area, a swampy, flooded pond, and historic mission sites. Where were the campsites? I felt the afternoon heat emanating off the blacktop; I was definitely not interested in pulling the kayak over these hills and double-broiler roads. If we left the boat by the river, how many trips would it take to unload all our gear? How would we get an early start in the morning? We finally got to the camp office, and inquired about the nearest campsite to the boat ramp. She unfolded a map, circled the camping area with her yellow highlighter, and ran her finger along a dotted line. "This trail will take you along the waterfront right to the boat ramp. It's only about a hundred yards long."

"We walk through the whole park, and the campsites are only a hundred yards from the boat ramp the whole time?" asked Gene, incredulous. If I weren't so hot and tired, it would have probably seemed a lot funnier. But I still had to chuckle at the irony. "I guess we got our exercise," he added.

Putting a positive spin on tough situations was nothing more than a change of perspective. It became easier with practice—and we got a lot of practice. An added benefit was the chance to air our problems without technically complaining and changing our bracelets. Strong headwinds were easier to handle when we thought about the workout they gave us, strengthening us for times ahead. Long paddle days became tolerable when we realized how much we could eat for dinner. We learned to think of rain as refreshing, and cold, invigorating. Admittedly, these mental gymnastics would have bordered on annoying at home, but staying positive was a survival technique on the river. It gave us the strength to keep going and helped us remain grateful for the chance to do it together.

We picked out a campsite that had mixed shade and sun, with a flat space for the tent. The newly discovered path was short, but hilly, so we brought just what we needed to the site. We were set up in a jiffy. Since we had already explored the campground, we bought two bundles of firewood and spent the afternoon and evening relaxing around one of Gene's blazing campfires.

Well rested, we rose with the sun to get an early start. Our next campsite was over twenty miles away. The current raged, which made for easy paddling, but not so easy steering. Gene acclimated himself to the response of the rudder in the swirling water. I heard the swishing sounds of the water against the sides of the boat as we rounded a bend in the river. Then I felt the back of the boat begin to slide to the right and for a moment, I was turning toward the shore. Another swish of water against the rudder and the stern fishtailed back to the left, as I faced out again into midstream.

"That was awesome! There should be a water park ride like that," I said, raising my paddle in the air. I was glad Gene was steering first in new river conditions. "How'd you do that?" I asked.

"I'm just figuring it out, but when we go around a turn, the faster water's on the outside bank. The stern has a tendency to swing wide. In the middle of the turn, I counter-steer to control the swing and keep the faster water from turning the boat sideways."

"You're nice to have around," I said. "I would have just turned left."

Signs of high water were everywhere. Birch clumps I presumed were standing on the bank last month were now growing ten feet off shore. We passed branches and huge logs floating downstream, ripped from their rightful place on land. They posed little danger for us, since we traveled faster, but Gene steered as far from them as possible. I was already watching for snags and riffles. Now, I had to add floating debris to my worry list. I heard the sounds of splashing water. "What's that?" I asked.

"Just a log jam," said Gene. "Over by the bank." Dozens of branches, entangled along the shoreline, swayed in the rush of water, straining to get free. Bubbles of froth, whipped up like egg whites, were trapped between the crisscrossed limbs. Water splashed up over a precariously balanced log at the edge of the jam. "We better keep an eye on it, though. Looks like that one log is about to break free." I watched the log teeter-totter as we glided past, hoping it wouldn't be chasing us down the river anytime soon.

Looking through the trees on the other side of the river, I saw no land. "That looks like the top of a sign," I said. "Try to get closer." We paddled over to where the shore should be. The top of a metal sign protruded above the surface. A red oval on a black background held bold white lettering that said DANGER. I couldn't see the part that probably told what the danger was. "Uh-oh," I said. "What do you think that's about?"

"I don't know," Gene said. "It might just be an underwater cable or something. But if this sign is on a regular post, the water's gotta be over three feet higher than usual."

We heard explosions. "Sounds like mortar drills," Gene said. "There's a military training facility near here. The map says Fort Ripley." I felt like we were paddling through a war zone. It was unnerving to hear the blasts overhead, not knowing where they were being aimed. I hoped not at the river.

In the distance, a churning froth appeared. "There's something ahead," I said, pointing. "I can't tell if it's rapids or not. I don't see any rocks, but there's a lot of turbulence. I'll watch for anything, but let's take it easy through here."

I checked the wind direction by looking at the tree branches. We were traveling the same direction as both the current and the wind, but the waves on the top of the water were coming toward us, whitecaps breaking. We entered a chop, forces coming at us from all directions, while listening to mortar blasts from the nearby military camp. I paddled tentatively, half expecting to bump into something, and was relieved when we didn't. Every so often, I jabbed my paddle into the water to see if I could gauge its depth. The paddle plunged down to my handgrips, but didn't hit bottom. That was good. We were floating right over whatever was down there. Gene kept us near the center of the river where it seemed to be less wild, but I still breathed a sigh of relief when we left the chaos behind us.

"What was THAT?" Gene asked.

"I don't know, but there was *something* under there." I checked the map. "It says that in low water, there are some dangerous rapids along here," I said. "I bet we floated right over the top." I imagined a mountain range of boulders underneath the water, stretching up toward our boat, unable to reach us. Each one I pictured had a razor ridge on top, like the one we grazed just past Bemidji. The one that kept us off the river for three days. "Thank God."

"And thank you, Les," added Gene, "for the prayer for safe passage."

After twenty miles, my tailbone was looking forward to a break at Fletcher's Campsite, our intended stay for the night. "Fletcher's should be coming up any time now," Gene said.

I checked the map. "About a half mile, I think."

"This one's a private one, right?" he asked.

"Yep. That's what it says. And you know what that means?" I envisioned some of the private campgrounds I'd camped at in the past. "At the very least, showers!"

"And probably a camp store with mosquito repellent!" Gene said.

"If there's a camp store, they'll have firewood, and the fixin's for s'mores. Maybe even a pool!"

Gene added to the fantasy that was now in full swing. "And those strings of colored lantern lights. And hammocks!" I laughed at the thought of a fancy Camp Hilton. I hoped at least the shower part would come true.

But when we got to the location, there were no campsites . . . only some private homes and a cracked cement boat landing. "I'm sure this is the right spot," said Gene.

We pulled Donna up on the grass next to the landing and walked over to a man, busy cleaning up debris from a tree that had fallen against his home. He stepped down from his ladder, wiped his hands on his jeans, and shook Gene's hand. "Can you direct us to Fletcher's Campsite?" Gene asked.

"Oh . . . there is no Fletcher's anymore," he offered. "It burned down. But that was *years* ago." He continued, "If ya need a place to camp, though, there are plenty of islands around here. I see canoes and kayaks over there all the time." He pointed to an island just downstream.

We thanked him and walked over to the steps by the old landing. The grass around the stairs was overgrown. Weeds grew through the cracks in the aged cement. Watching for poison ivy, we cleared off a place to have a late lunch, come to grips with the loss of our fantasy, and decide what to do next. I got the water bottles; Gene brought over a foil packet of salmon, a sleeve of crackers, and a variety of protein bars. He cut a slit in the salmon packet and folded back the top. The smell of food reminded me how hungry I was. I took a squirt of anti-bacterial spray, rubbed it between my hands, and passed it to Gene. I wondered if it did any good. Here we were, out in nature, skipping showers for days, dipping our hands in the Mississippi, and peeing behind bushes. I supposed every bit of hygiene helped.

Occasionally interrupted by the sighs of satiety, we examined our only options. "It's still eight miles to Little Falls," said Gene. "We could camp on one of these nearby islands and get there tomorrow in the morning."

I looked at the island directly across from the landing. It would be free, but certainly not accommodating. "The ones I see from here don't have any high ground," I said, "and there's no place to pull Donna up out of the water." I imagined our kayak banging around in the current all night, or even worse, breaking loose and tumbling downstream.

"Or," Gene continued, "we could just paddle into Little Falls tonight. Since we haven't used our flex day, we'd get into town two days early. We're not due at the state park until Sunday night, so we might have to get a hotel for two nights and find something to do in town."

"Let's see . . ." I put my hands out like a scale, and raised and lowered them to weigh the options. "Sleep on an island and worry about the boat all night." I changed the position of my hand scale.

"Or paddle a little longer, pay a little extra, and have a bed, a shower, and maybe that pool. Little Falls, it is."

We made awesome time—traveling between six and seven miles per hour according to Speed Tracker, my GPS speedometer. Our map showed the Little Falls portage to be on the east bank, just above the dam and immediately after the Highway 27 bridge, so we stayed to the left. After the day's disappearing campground, however, my faith in the DNR river map was shaken. As we rapidly approached the orange floating balls serving as dam markers, across the face of the highway bridge were several large signs. "Danger, Dam Ahead. Do Not Enter." With the roar of the huge waterfall directly ahead and our little boat rushing forward in strong current, I couldn't see where we were supposed to go!

My senses were on high alert. My seat in the bow meant I was the lookout. It also meant I'd be the first one over the dam if we weren't careful. *Kupendana* wouldn't survive a drop over a spillway and there was a good chance we wouldn't either. "Hug the shore," I told Gene, but realized he was already doing that. "There! On the sign! Portage left," I yelled, as I pointed to the left side of the bridge. Gene steered through a small water corridor to a landing on the left bank. We wedged Donna between a couple of the boulders scattered in front of the concrete steps and I let my adrenaline subside.

Gene climbed out first and held the boat for me. "I don't *ever* want to cut it that close again." His body gave a shiver.

"Me neither!" I wondered if God ever got tired of keeping us out of trouble. It was beginning to seem like a full-time job.

We locked *Kupendana* securely to a tree in a park by the river, and watched the wild water pouring over the dam, just yards downstream of our landing. All the gates were wide open, and the spillway was mesmerizing as water poured through the open gates, then cascaded down, splashing into the foaming, rolling cacophony of waves. The roar was deafening. I took a video to post on our blog.

"I wonder where the launch point is below the dam," I said. "I hope it's well downstream."

At the police headquarters, we asked about leaving our boat in the park for the weekend. "There's no law against it," the officer said. "We'll check on it when we do our rounds, but we can't be responsible if anything happens to it." That was better than I hoped, and easier than pulling Donna three miles to the hotels at the outskirts of town.

"We'll check on it, too," Gene assured him. "I'm sure we'll be walking into town at least once a day. And we'll take all the valuable stuff with us." He turned to me. "If someone wants my stinky paddle shoes, they can have 'em." We thanked the officer, then decided to check out the downtown. It was, after all, a Friday evening in June. Tonight, in our hometown of Waukesha, residents would flock to our historic downtown streets for Friday Night Live, a weekly summer block party. Gene and I often rode our bicycles downtown, dined at one of the many small eateries, and listened to live bands at different locations around town.

As we began to work our way up and down the main streets of Little Falls, however, I realized we were now in Smalltown, America. The town was preparing to call it a day at 4:45 on a Friday afternoon. We managed to find a bakery and bought a delicious mint brownie to share just as the doors were locked behind us. Then, except for the bars, all was quiet.

We ambled through the streets to get our bearings. I peeked inside the windows and doors as we passed. There was activity inside American Legion Post 46. "Let's stop in here," I suggested. "I'll buy you a drink. And maybe we can find someone who can recommend a hotel."

Gene studied the American Legion symbol on the door. "They might know a place we can do service this weekend, too," he said. "We aren't scheduled to work with Kinship until Monday and we're in town anyway. We might as well help out if we can."

Kinship of Morrison County was the reason we stopped in Little Falls. Similar to Big Brothers and Big Sisters, it was a mentorship organization for children of single parent families. A touching video on their website prompted me to call from home and ask if they'd like us to visit. "I'd love that," said Aaron, the director. "I'll plan our monthly meeting for when you get into the area, and maybe even think of something fun that ties in with your trip." Aaron outdid himself. He planned a triathlon for the kids and their mentors, with canoeing, bicycle riding, and hiking. I couldn't wait. But now we had two extra days before Monday's triathlon. Gene was right. If someone else in town could use our service, we had plenty of free time to help.

Returning to the table with two gin and tonics, Gene said, "The bartender thinks the Commander might have some ideas. She'll send him over when he has a minute." I squeezed the lime slice, then dropped it into the glass, which was already beginning to perspire on the outside from the humidity. I was so thirsty—I should have ordered water first. Resisting the temptation to guzzle the entire thing, I made some phone calls, looking for the closest, least expensive hotel in town. My only requisites were laundry facilities, a pool, and a hot tub. We found all three at the Country Inn, only a little more than a mile's walk from the boat.

As I finished the reservation, the waitress set two more drinks on the table. "Bill wanted you to have these," she said. "He'll be over as soon as he can." So much for nursing my one drink. At least I wasn't driving—not for several more months, anyway.

Before long, the Commander approached. "Hi, I'm Bill," he said, offering his outstretched hand. His appearance and unpretentious manner did nothing to betray his rank. Close to my height of five feet eight, he wore a short-sleeved dress shirt with several buttons undone at the top, I surmised due to the heat. Dockers and brown loafers completed the Friday-night-at-the-Legion look. "I hear you're floatin' the river," he began. "And you're staying for a couple days in Little Falls?" We updated him on our trip, our plans to work with Kinship on Monday, and the extra time we found on our hands. "Well," he started, "there's a Veterans Home a few blocks from here. They don't get a lot of visitors, and would probably enjoy talking with you. The place is called the Pine Edge Home. It used to be a fancy hotel, back in the day. Charles Lindbergh even had a dinner there in his honor. About 'twenty-seven, I believe." He smiled and added, "But that was before my time."

"Ours, too," I chuckled. I figured that Bill was probably close to our age, but didn't ask.

I emptied my second drink as we chatted about the Legion, our adventures, and some of the places we had served so far. "Can I get you another drink?" Bill asked.

"Thanks, but I'd better not." I was starting to feel lazy already and still had far too much to do. I couldn't afford a Friday night bar buzz. "We still have to get some of our things out of the boat and head over to the hotel," I added.

"I'm about to leave in a few minutes myself. Can I give you a lift?" *That* we could accept. Gene and I walked back to the boat, pulled out our clothing bags and ditties, and recovered the cockpits. Soon, Bill arrived with his pickup and delivered us to our weekend abode.

Clean and relaxed after a steaming shower, I hopped up on the cozy queen-sized comforter and crossed my legs to check out our website and start our travel blog entry. I checked the stats page first. "Hey, look," I called to Gene. "We've got views from twenty-eight countries." I showed him the world map, with orange, yellow, and red countries representing nations that viewed our site. I wondered if anyone in all these foreign countries was really following our trip, or if they just happened upon it during Google research about kayaks, food dehydrating, or the Mississippi River. Probably the latter, but it was fun to imagine our trip being discussed at dinner tables across Europe, Africa, Asia, and Australia.

I received a notification of a message for us to approve before it could be posted. It was from a Brainerd resident who knew many of the people we met there. "I don't know if you heard," he wrote, "but the locks in the Twin Cities have been closed due to treacherous waters from the flooding. Be careful." I read the message to Gene.

"When are we scheduled to get there?" he asked.

"Not for a week or so," I said. "We leave here on Tuesday and have six travel days to Dave's." Our next stop was my brother's house in a suburb of Minneapolis, where we were scheduled to help with Habitat for Humanity.

"Maybe the water will have gone down by then," he said. "No use worrying about it now." Judging by the water cascading over the spillway downtown, it didn't seem like the river level would go down anytime soon.

June 29-30: Thank You, Veterans!

The Pine Edge was about an hour's walk from our hotel, but it felt good to move. As we entered the lobby, the first thing I noticed was the rich dark wood lining the walls and an intricately carved wooden railing which led my eyes to an upstairs hallway lined with aging wallpaper. We introduced ourselves to Abby, the front desk attendant and cook on duty at the time. "I'm making lunch now," she said, "so I don't have any projects for you. But the men outside might enjoy some company and conversation."

Extending the length of the building, the long screened-in porch served as a gathering spot for the veterans. It was cheerily decorated with hanging pots of colorful flowers, which contrasted with the solemn mood of the residents, sitting silently, lost in their own thoughts. Quite a few were smoking, flicking the ashes into coffee cans half-filled with sand, placed between the chairs along the length of the porch.

Our presence seemed to be met with initial skepticism. I remembered what Bill said about not getting many visitors. I walked up to an elderly man seated by a small table. Extending my hand, I made the first move. "Hello! My name's Barb and this is my husband, Gene. Okay if we sit down?"

Giving my outstretched hand a half shake, he answered, "Name's Frank. Suit yourself." His eyes seemed wary, as if he really wanted to know, "Why are you here?"

I sat down in a chair on the other side of the table. Gene chose one near me. In answer to his unvoiced question, I continued to make small talk. "What a beautiful day! We have some extra time in Little Falls and thought you might like some company."

Frank got up. "Gotta go to lunch," he said. "Want to come?"

Abby didn't invite us to eat and I wasn't sure she made extra food. "No, thanks," I replied. "We'll get something to eat later."

Frank shuffled inside, followed by four other residents who had listened quietly to my rather pathetic attempts at conversation. I looked at Gene and shrugged.

"Do you want to leave?" he asked.

It would have been easy to leave, but we decided to stay. We came for these men. We needed to give them enough time to warm up to us, not leave without showing them that we cared. So I relaxed and sat back to enjoy the day.

Soon the screen door opened, and several veterans came back from lunch. Frank looked at us. "You still here?" he asked.

"Yep," I answered. "How was lunch?"

"It was good," Frank said with a smile. "That Abby sure can cook! Where'd you say you were from?" I brightened. It seemed we made it past the barrier of mistrust. I was glad we stayed.

"We're from Wisconsin," Gene answered. "We're kayaking the Mississippi and are in the area for a couple of days. Yesterday, we met Bill, the American Legion Commander, and he suggested we might want to see your place. What branch of the service were you in?"

Frank pulled himself up a little straighter in his chair. "Air Force," he replied. "I served in Korea."

"My dad served in Korea, too," offered Gene. "He was in the Navy." Gene stood up and shook Frank's hand. "Thank you for your service to our country."

The conversation continued. Before long, others moved closer and joined in. Our presence and interest now seemed to be a welcome change to their daily routine. We listened to stories of their memories, service, and hopes for the future. We thanked each one for his service and shared some stories of our own.

As we departed, I thought about the moments we would have missed if we left at lunchtime. God led us to another truth about service. There isn't always a project and nobody deserves to feel like one. Our service was only a well-intended fail until those men knew that we really cared about them. But then, just our presence was enough.

Bill called on Saturday night to check up on us. I listened to Gene tell him about our day as I rolled up my freshly laundered paddle clothes and fitted them into my dry bag. "It was great. I think they were glad we visited . . . That'd be awesome! See you then." After hanging up, Gene began packing his things. "Bill offered to pick us up tomorrow morning," he said, "and take us with him to church. He'll even give us a ride to the state park in the afternoon."

After worship the next morning and lunch at a local diner, Bill borrowed a friend's trailer, picked up *Kupendana*, and gave us all a lift to the Charles A. Lindbergh State Park. We chose a cart-in campsite on the south end of the camp. It was near the shelter for the following day's activity, but more importantly, near the canoe landing for an easy launch into Pike Creek on Tuesday.

July 1: Kinship of Morrison County

On Monday, we walked into town again, this time from the park, and introduced ourselves to Aaron at the Kinship of Morrison County office. I didn't expect him to be so young—I guessed in his early thirties. His facial hair was the first thing I noticed, a mustache and a beard so full, it seemed like he was going for the

North Woods lumberjack look. "Kinship," he explained, "matches children from single-parent families with volunteer mentors. Even though it starts out as a one-year commitment, most kids and mentors make strong bonds and their matches continue until the child is eighteen and no longer eligible. Each month, we have at least one group activity, but the 'Kinkids' and their mentors choose to do other things together as well."

"What kinds of activities have you done?" I asked.

"We try to do some fun things, but we also do educational and service activities," said Aaron. "Last year, we did curling on a frozen lake, a firearm safety course, fishing, and model rocket launching. We've also had board game and movie nights, and even a chili cook-off."

"That's a nice variety. I think your idea of a triathlon for this month is perfect," I said, "especially since there's no running." I told Aaron about the triathlon that Gene and I trained for a few years before. I loved to swim, so I helped Gene build his endurance. He helped me with the skill I dreaded—running. We were both in good shape for the biking. On the day of the race, the swim was cancelled due to the water conditions, an extra run put in its place. I was devastated, but we made it across the finish line . . . but only a few minutes ahead of the winner of the Eighty-Plus division.

"So what's the plan for today?" asked Gene.

"Can you be at the west-side boat ramp by five?" Aaron asked, handing Gene a map with the landing circled. "The first leg will be a four-mile canoe paddle on the river. Everyone's coming to the start right after work and school, but I'll need you and Barb to help with the transition area to the bikes, if that's okay. You'll meet the paddlers at the dock, help them get out, and load the canoes on the trailer."

"The water's really fast. Is the transition area near the dam?" I asked.

"That's why we're using the west-side landing," Aaron said. "We've warned all the adults to stay near the right bank on the approach, so they'll see the dock right away. I'll have an extra canoe for you on the end of the dock, in case you need to go chase anyone, but they should be fine." I pictured Gene and me trying to catch a runaway canoe and turn it around in this current. I hoped we wouldn't have to.

Aaron continued, "Then, there's a two-mile bicycle ride to the state park followed by a choice of a half-mile or a two-mile hiking trail at the park. Some of the kids might be tired by then, so each group can decide which walk they want to do. It doesn't matter what they decide; it's not really a competition. We'll end up at the park shelter, where my wife will have dinner. Then I thought you might like to tell the kids and mentors about your kayak trip and show them your boat."

Leaving Aaron to his paperwork, we found a coffee shop to have lunch and work on our blog. Later that afternoon, Gene and I walked over the bridge and up the road to the transition area. I was no longer worried about the current; we were quite a ways north of the dam. We tied a banner with brightly colored flags to the dock, and then scanned the river for the flash of aluminum that would signal the arriving canoes. We flagged down the paddlers, helped them exit their canoes, and put the boats on trailers while they got ready for the bike ride to the state park.

Many of the kids, as well as some adults, wore bright yellow T-shirts with the Kinship Motto on the back—Making a difference . . . one friendship at a time.

Once everyone arrived, all the bicyclists headed to the park together. Bikeless, we hitched a ride on one of the trailer trucks to meet the Kinship pairs for a hike in the park. Ty, the park manager and himself a Kinship mentor, led our group on a two-mile hike along well-kept trails through the forested terrain. I learned that many of the mentors felt they got as much out of the relationship as the Kinkids did. I met one mentor whose three former matches stayed with him until they became adults. He was there with his fourth match. "I do it for the relationships with the kids," he said, "but all the activities help keep me young, too. I wouldn't have done half the things I've done if it weren't for Kinship."

After a picnic of grilled chicken, salad, and dessert, we shared about our kayak trip—some of the people we met, the challenges we faced, and the satisfaction of helping others through service. We pulled Donna onto the grass outside the shelter and invited the kids to take turns sitting inside the cockpits. Shutters clicked as the youngsters pretended to paddle down the Mississippi, and their mentors recorded memories.

One of the young girls pulled our small spade from its storage space behind the wooden seat brace. "What's this?" she asked.

"Oh, that?" replied Gene. "That's how we go to the bathroom."

She pointed to the bowl of the spade. "You pee into THIS?"

"No," explained Gene. He stifled a grin and answered as seriously as she asked, "If we have to pee, we go in the grass behind a tree or bush. But if we have to poop, we dig a hole in the ground, go in the hole, and scoop dirt on top of it with the shovel."

A look of disgust crossing her face, she held the shovel up with her thumb and forefinger, then dropped it back into the boat. "Ewwww!"

As our friends wished us well and left for home, I thought of how important caring, significant adults are in the life of every child. I admired and respected these folks who gave so much of their time to create lasting, supportive friendships. Gene said, "I'd like to check into the Big Brothers organization when we get home. I've always thought that sounded rewarding and fun, but haven't ever taken the time to sign up. After today, I'm pretty sure it's something I'd like to do."

"You should," I encouraged. Gene was heavily involved in scouting as a youth, earning the rank of Eagle Scout. "With scouting, you've had lots of experience and know how to do so many different things, it would be fun for you to share that with someone." I thought about Gene's love of adventure, his willingness to try new things, and the positive values he showed every day. "You'd be a great mentor, and could really make a difference for a child."

"I think I'll look into it," he resolved.

We pulled *Kupendana* down the hilly trail to our campsite in the descending darkness, avoiding the ruts carved by all the recent rains. I felt well rested after three full days in Little Falls, but hit the hay early nonetheless. Tomorrow, we would follow Pike Creek back to the Mississippi to begin the next leg of our paddle—our journey to the Twin Cities.

July 2-8 Little Falls to the Twin Cities

Despite our early start, by mid-morning it was already in the high eighties. With no clouds in sight, it was going to be a scorcher. Our map showed three dams that we'd need to portage, as well as a mile of rapids . . . all within the next three days. We knew the length of the portages in yards, but nothing about the terrain. Depending on the ease of the approach, the slope of the hills, and the composition of the trails, each portage could be a matter of minutes or hours. I wasn't worried; after a month on the river, we settled into the pace of taking things as they came. But I was looking forward to the Twin Cities, where the locks and dam system began. Once we made it to the first lock in St. Paul, Minnesota, if it was open, we'd be able to stay in the water and be lowered inside the locks down to the next pool. The end of tiring portages was in sight—only a little more than a hundred miles away.

I heard the familiar ring of Gene's cell phone behind me, and a snap as he unclipped it from his deck bag. "Gene here." Without both of us paddling, Donna slowed down and I settled into the new pace. "Hi, Adam! How are you?" The only Adam I recollected was the one we met in Aitken County. He and Madelyn were somewhere ahead of us. "Oh, we're fine . . . struggling a little in this heat." Wait a minute! Who was struggling? With my better, stronger half on the phone instead of his paddle, the river turned from water to mud. I stopped stroking, content to drift in the current, and listened to half of the conversation. "Where are you? ... La Crosse? Wow! You made good time!" They were already over 250 miles ahead of us? When we saw them, they were averaging an ambitious 30 miles a day. I remembered a few days when we did that kind of distance, and came limping into campgrounds like bow-legged cowboys from an old western movie. But those two young'uns seemed none the worse for wear. I wondered if the canoe made it easier to stretch and change positions during the day, or if it made more difference that we were over twice their age.

I heard Gene say, "Thanks for calling and warning us. Good luck with the rest of your trip."

"Warning us about what?" I asked over my shoulder as he clipped the phone back to his bag.

"They're almost to La Crosse already," he replied. "Adam called to warn us about the portage at Blanchard Dam. He called it the portage from hell."

"Oh ... great, that's the one today. Did he give you any details?"

"Just that the take-out is hard to find, and the portage involves several hills, lots of steps, and crossing a bridge over a stream." I felt the boat lurch forward as Gene dug his paddle into the river, deep and strong. I was glad for his physical strength on this trip. I wondered how far behind I would get each day if we were in two separate boats. He'd be constantly waiting for me, that was for sure.

"I guess we don't have much choice." I resumed paddling to help out. "We'll just have to take lots of trips." I didn't like that idea. It meant leaving our bags and boat unattended at one location while we walked back and forth to get more loads. But we couldn't assess the situation until we arrived.

"That's not all," added Gene. "Adam said the locks in the Twin Cities are still closed. The water's so high and fast, it's dangerous to put boats through. They're still open for commercial traffic, as far as he knows, but the locks are closed to recreational boats. They had to portage there, too."

"Bummer." I empathized with them, but wasn't worried about us. My brother planned to meet us at a park south of the locks in a week; we could change our pick-up location with one quick phone call.

We saw the steep hill with railroad tie steps before we actually spied the portage take-out sign. "Adam wasn't kidding," said Gene as he steered the bow ashore. "Look at that hill!" I hopped out of the boat; my feet squished into the spongy uneven ground. "We've gotta get to the top to scout it. How do you want to do it?" Gene asked.

"The wheels'll just dig in down here where it's swampy, but I think we should use them once we get to the bottom of the hill. That seems better than emptying her and carrying everything up the steps." We pulled and slid Donna to firm ground at the base of the hill. Then Gene lifted the stern so I could center and strap on the wheels. Straddling the edge of the steps and coordinating our lifts, we pulled and pushed our unwieldy load, foot by foot. We finally reached the summit—a gravel road at the crest of the hill. I wiped my forehead with the back of a sweaty arm, not sure that it helped. "Which way?"

"I have no idea," said Gene. "But I'll go check it out." We parked Donna in the shade of a tree and I remained behind with her while Gene disappeared down the road. At half an hour past bored, I started to worry. I couldn't call him; Gene's phone was still clipped onto his deck bag. This was a three-hundred-yard portage . . . roughly a quarter mile. Even walking slowly through rugged terrain, a half-mile round trip shouldn't be too much longer. Keeping an eye on the boat, I walked to the edge of the path where Gene disappeared. I knew why Adam called to warn us. Narrow, wooden steps zigzagged down to a rippling stream. There was no room next to these steps for Donna's wheels. Everything would have to be carried in several trips. A narrow bridge over the stream led to a high grassy hill far in the distance, but the path was hidden by foliage. And Gene was nowhere to be seen. I returned to the boat to give him fifteen more minutes. Gene was unencumbered by gear. How long would it take us to make several trips loaded down with our bags, tent, mattresses, and food? And then, with our boat?

Gene finally returned and gave me the low-down. "Across the stream, more steps lead up the other side," he explained. "Then a long path winds downhill through some woods. I don't know how we'll even carry a twenty-foot boat through there, with some of those tight turns. After the woods, there's still an uphill through a field, and a second gravel road that leads down to the river access."

We sat in the shade to weigh our options. Gene looked down the road in the opposite direction from the portage route. Our gravel road connected to a paved roadway heading east. "Where does that road go?" he asked. "On the other side of all the hills is a road that goes down to the spillway. Maybe they connect."

I pulled out my phone. I-map showed they did, in fact, connect via a county highway. This gave us a chance to bypass the hilly portage by road. It would be more than a mile. But we'd only have to do it once. We opted for the road. Gene fashioned a second handle from the rope of our bowline so we could both help pull from the front. The heat of the midday sun radiated from the blacktop surface like a convection oven. Our load was heavy—the rope handle cut into my fingers, and my elbows ached from hyperextension. "Rest stop," I announced each time I saw a fluffy-looking spot of shade on the side of the road. The air was noticeably cooler in the shade of the few trees along our route. We filled our empty water bottles from our supply, chugged half of the freshly filled bottles, and traded handles to switch arms.

A little over an hour later, we arrived at the launch area, a mere fifty yards below the dam. Fallen trees stuck out from the rocky shore into the crashing waves of the spillway. I sighed. "All that walking, just to end up right below the dam."

Gene sat on one of the fallen trunks, his legs dangling. He slit open a foil pack of tuna salad and slathered it onto the last of our fresh bread, handing me a slice. I waded as I ate; the cold water felt refreshing. I shuffled my feet through the pebbles, scanning for rare staurolite crystals, one of Blanchard Dam's claims to fame. A dark reddish-brown mineral, staurolite often crystallized in a twinned manner, producing cross shapes. A woman at the Confidence Center called them "fairy stones," and showed me some that she had found below the dam. I discovered some small single crystals and a couple incomplete crosses. I wanted to keep searching for a complete crossed crystal, but Gene was fidgety. After the long portage, I could tell he was eager to get going. I dropped the few I found into my waterproof wallet. We didn't have room for many souvenirs, especially rocks. But these crystals were small, and they felt special. I would mail them home as soon as I had a chance.

After lunch, we considered our options for launching. All of them were scary. Just getting into the boat with the waves pushing us toward the rocks was enough to make me want to launch further away from the dam, but there was no riverside road. Even if we boarded safely in the swirling surf, we would still have to navigate the chaotic foamy current on the spillway itself. We had no choice but to give it a go. Before climbing in the boat, we held hands and prayed for a safe launch. Suddenly, I knew what we had to do. "We have to walk the boat under that tree," I told Gene, pointing to a fallen trunk at the south end of the launch area, which extended into the fray. I knew nothing about what was beyond the tree, but trusted the message I received.

"Okay," he said without hesitation. "Let's do it." We waded into the waves, past some shallow water brush and around intimidating boulders jutting out of the foam. Water swirled around me as I lowered myself into the cold Jacuzzi and ducked under the trunk, guiding the boat beside me. Gene followed suit at the stern. We found ourselves in a shady waist-deep pool. Shielded from the waves, the water was nearly still. "Wow!" Gene said. "I had no idea this was here."

"Me neither." We pushed Donna's stern against the soft mossy shore, boarded, tightened our spray skirts around the coamings, and made a safe entry into the frothy current. "God is good," I said.

"All the time," I heard Gene answer from behind me.

A few miles later, we pulled into the Two Rivers Campground, located at the Platte River confluence. The basic tent campsites were on the point of land right where the two rivers met and would have been our choice, were they not cordoned off due to flooding. We chose one farther downstream on higher ground. The camping fee seemed extravagant, but the riverside site, showers, and lodge with Wi-Fi made me feel better. And the fact that they sold ice cream treats sealed the deal.

The next day, we had cooler weather, an easy paddle, and a second portage, this time around the Sartell Dam. Compared to Blanchard, it was a cakewalk. In fact, most of the route was along a sidewalk that passed right by a city pool and a few businesses. The Riverboat Depot seemed like a nice spot for lunch. We parked Donna on the grass near the parking lot and ordered lunch. As we worked on our super-sized plate of nachos, the waitress asked us about our trip. "We get a lot of people stopping by here during portages," she said. "But you better keep an eye on your boat. Last summer, a really nice guy stopped in for lunch, and while he was eating, someone took his canoe, with everything in it."

I jumped up and half-walked, half-ran out the door to check on *Kupendana*. "The boat's fine," I announced when I returned, slightly embarrassed by my fearful reaction. "What did the guy do?"

"He was going to give up and go home," she said. "But the people of Sartell took up a collection to replace the boat and gear so he could continue."

"That's an amazing story," I said. But I wasn't as surprised as I would have been a month earlier. I was learning, from experience, the culture of community along the Mississippi River—different from others I'd known. The river had a kind of magnetism that attracted people to it. It had happened for generations. People living along the river couldn't imagine living anywhere else. And they loved to share the experience with others who were drawn to it. Every year, adventurers floating the river encountered these river angels, who helped them out by sharing their homes, giving advice, and offering meals, supplies, kindness, stories, and encouragement. On the river for only a month so far, I couldn't count the number of angels we met. It didn't surprise me at all that a river community like this would come out to support a traveler in trouble.

After lunch, we arrived at the city park boat ramp, complete with the ultimate luxury—a boat dock. We pulled Donna into the water without getting ourselves wet, transferred the wheels to the top, and stepped right into our cockpits from above, keeping our socks and paddle shoes dry and comfy—at least for the time being.

That afternoon brought us to Sauk Rapids. Just the name of the town struck fear in my heart. This stretch of river was reputed to be even more treacherous when the water level was high. And high it was. We stopped at the park to scout the rapids from land. The telltale froth and riffles looked navigable, but our previous experiences with underwater rocks gave me pause. "I'd rather avoid rapids whenever we can," I said. "Besides—what's one portage more or less?" As we walked, we began to look for a campsite for the night. It was still early enough not to panic, but it would be nice to find a spot along our route. I checked the park hours. It closed at 10 o'clock, which meant no camping here. I returned to find Gene perched on a stone fence, pocketing his phone. "I called the police station," he said, "to see if we could set up a tent anywhere for the night. They told me that if we set up on public land we'd not only be ticketed, but jailed as well."

"You're kidding," I said. Gene's expression was one of shocked disbelief. "You're *not* kidding." After our previous experiences in river towns, it felt strange to be warned instead of welcomed. I wondered if other travelers had left bad feelings in their wake. "It's still early. Let's keep going. Maybe we'll find someone who can help us."

"And as a last resort, we can go to jail," said Gene. "At least we'd have food and a place to stay."

"It'd make a great story," I added. We walked along a road between the river and a set of old railroad tracks. It looked like there might be some businesses up ahead. Where there were businesses, sometimes there were hotels.

As we passed an apartment building, I noticed a young man with a plastic garbage bag headed for the dumpster. "Excuse me," I shouted. During introductions, I learned his name was Adam—our second Adam in a month. Gene told him about our trip, and recounted our search for accommodations. "It looks like camping might be out. Do you know of any hotels in the area?" I asked.

Adam threw his bag in the dumpster and let the lid shut with a clank. He pointed the way we were walking. "There used to be a hotel just up ahead, but it burned down a couple of years ago. I know there's one in Sartell."

"We just ate lunch in Sartell," Gene explained. "We won't make it all the way back there. But thanks, anyway."

"Sorry I couldn't help you more," Adam said. "Good luck."

"I wonder what's up with everything burning down?" I asked as we continued.

"It's weird," agreed Gene. "Makes you wonder if there's insurance money involved." That, or an awful lot of bad luck.

As we continued up the road, Gene spotted a VFW post. His dad was a member of the VFW. Maybe they'd be able to help. At this point, we were ready to set up our tent in the parking lot if they'd let us. I stood in the street with the boat while Gene walked over to make friends at the VFW. Before he returned, however, Adam came jogging up the road.

"I'm sorry I didn't think of this earlier," he apologized. He moved his sunglasses to the top of his head. Without them, he reminded me of John Ritter with a mustache and goatee. "My fiancée and I are leaving for the Fourth of July weekend. You could stay at our place!" My face must have registered the shock I felt, because he went on to explain, "I went back in to tell Brittany about meeting you and it hit me. You could stay here tonight and just hide the key when you leave. I checked with Brittany and it's okay with her."

Gene returned, disappointed that no one at the VFW could be of help. When Adam repeated his offer to Gene, he looked flabbergasted. "Really?" he asked. "That's an incredibly generous offer!"

"I just became a Christian a year ago," explained Adam. "I think it's what God wants me to do."

We backtracked with Adam to his apartment, where he introduced us to Brittany, a petite brunette, every bit as gracious as he. "Oh, it's fine with me," she said. "I'm proud of him for thinking of it." We learned that they were getting married in August; I made a mental note to send a card from wherever we happened to be.

Gene and Adam agreed on a place to leave the key in the morning. We thanked them for their kindness and watched them drive away, leaving us their home. What an awesome demonstration of love and trust! We walked over to the VFW for some supper, set up our bedrolls on the living room floor, and enjoyed nice, hot showers, grateful once again to people we barely knew.

In the morning, Gene said, "I've been thinking all night about our portaging procedures." I had too. "I think we should make some adjustments." To reduce the weight on the bow, we packed the boat with all the heavy items behind the axle in the stern. Then, Gene moved the stern handle to the bow, so both front handles would have comfortable grips.

I took hold of the bow handle and the front of the boat rose with little effort. "I can't believe we didn't think of this earlier," I said. "I learned about fulcrums and levers in grade school. In fact, I *taught* it in grade school. It's not like this is rocket science." I looked forward to a much easier portage.

As we got started, we peeked again at the river through the trees. The rushing water splashing up from boulders, stumps, and fallen logs cemented our resolve to stay out of this watery pinball game. We studied the map. A couple of miles past the end of the rapids would be the St. Cloud Dam. Rather than putting the boat in after the rapids, taking it out to portage the dam, and putting it back in again, we decided just to walk through town. It was only a few miles. We had the boat weighted for walking now. Once we put it back in the river, we'd be good until the Cities.

Residents of towns along the Mississippi often saw boaters, both in and out of the water. Even so, we received plenty of waves and stares pulling Donna through the streets of town. One helpful soul even leaned out of his second-floor apartment window, pointed toward the river, and hollered, "If you walk a block down that way, you can float it!" I smiled, giving him a thumbs-up. He could have been trying to be helpful, but it sounded more like a joke. Either way, it *was* funny.

Our route through town was beautiful. As with many Mississippi towns, the streets were designed to take advantage of the gorgeous view. Passing one park overlooking the river, I noticed blankets already dotting the lawn, staking out territory for the evening's Fourth of July fireworks.

A dark-colored sedan slowed down as it approached. "That's the second time that car passed us," said Gene. I looked at the driver. A graying man, perhaps in his late forties, was staring at us. As he neared, he pulled closer to the curb and rolled down his window.

"Where're you headed?" he asked.

"Just south of the St. Cloud Dam," replied Gene, approaching the vehicle.

"My name's Tod, and this is my wife, Linda." For the first time, I noticed he had a companion. Leaning forward, a woman with gray shoulder-length hair and a pleasant smile waved to me. I smiled back.

"The dam is a long way yet. We live just down by the river," he said, pointing back the way we came. "You're welcome to put your boat in at our house."

Gene explained our reason for the long portage. "Do you know anything about the launch site south of the dam?" he asked.

I wouldn't suggest it. The west side of the river is much calmer. It would be a longer walk, but you could cross the bridge by the university and there's a nice spot to launch safely south of campus. A paved trail from the bridge'll take you right there." Tod continued, "You're welcome to stay at our home tonight, if you have the time. We have some guests coming over for a little get-together to watch the fireworks and would love for them to meet you. You could get an early start in the morning."

"We did build in an extra day," Gene admitted, "but I'm not thrilled with backtracking just to walk all this again tomorrow."

"A friend of ours lives off an alley just up ahead," Tod offered. "Let me see if he'll store your boat until tomorrow. We'll be right back."

"We're not going anywhere fast," Gene laughed. "You'll find us." Once we were alone, he asked, "What do you think?"

"We have plenty of time to walk over to the university and keep going today. But it is the Fourth of July; it'd be fun to see the fireworks."

Gene glanced around, as if checking for the car. "It feels a little strange that he's so persistent," he said.

"I know what you mean," I replied. Learning to let God direct out path took more trust than I was used to. Lots of people had helped us out so far, but no one had put this much effort into convincing us to stay with them. What if God wasn't whispering to us, but to Tod? Would that explain his persistence? "I think Tod may be feeling pulled to help us," I told Gene. "Like Mike was, in Pokegama, and Adam, yesterday. We can't just listen when the Spirit leads us and ignore it when it's leading others. I think there's a reason we should stay with them tonight."

Gene agreed. "If he does have a friend nearby who'll keep our boat, I'm sure it's fine."

Tod and Linda returned, giving us directions to a home a few blocks away. "Jim's a retired postal worker and a good friend of mine," said Tod. "We'll drive over and meet you there."

At first glance, I could imagine Jim dressed in his letter carrier blues, greeting people by name as he handed them a stack of envelopes at their door or waved from the mailbox by the side of the road. Today, though, he was dressed for retirement in pleated khaki shorts and a yellow Golden State Warriors T-shirt. A shock of gray sprang forward from his widow's peak. He chatted with us as we gathered our dry bags and ditties and locked *Kupendana* to a tree in his backyard. "Don't you worry 'bout your boat—I'll be here 'til morning." Any residual worry about our decision to stay overnight faded; I knew we were in good hands.

On the way home, Tod drove us along the route we would walk the following day—across the St. Cloud Bridge, down a spiral ramp, and through the campus to the university launch. It would be a long walk, but a beautiful one.

We got settled in the guest bedroom, then sat on bar stools at the wide kitchen island as Tod and Linda finished the preparations for their evening guests. The conversation didn't rest in the casual, but moved right to deeper topics that I'd expect from friends with a long history together—family, faith, and purpose. I was deep into the conversation, but Gene began to fidget. I wasn't surprised; of the two of us, I was more the talker. He asked, "What can I do to help?"

"Nothing," said Linda. "Just relax."

"Whenever we aren't paddling, we're used to working. It doesn't feel right to just sit around. Are you sure there's nothing I can do?" Gene stood up and paced, as if to illustrate his point.

"Sometimes there's value to rest, too," replied Tod. "Thanks for your offer, but we would love it if you could just relax while you are here."

"Okay, I'll try," said Gene, taking his seat on the stool next to mine.

Linda stopped cutting fruit. "Quiet times are often a gift from God." She smiled mischievously. "The rest may prepare you for something you'll need to face later." Gene and I shared a look that could only be mutual apprehension. But I knew Linda had a point. We had been falling into bed exhausted each night, sometimes after paddling all day, and other times after doing service, laundry, and blogging. But we hadn't planned any time to just rest. So that evening, we allowed ourselves to unwind, met many wonderful people, and enjoyed a spectacular fireworks display from the porch swing.

At breakfast, Tod shared his morning devotion with us. Afterward, he said, "You know, you two have been an answer to my prayers. Lately I've been feeling unconnected—I've been praying for renewed passion in my faith. And then I saw you and knew I had to meet you. Now I know why. What you're doing has given me the spark that I've been missing. Thank you."

"All we're doing is planting seeds," Gene replied. I recognized the allusion to his favorite parable about the sower who planted seeds in different environments. Some never sprouted, because they were cast upon rocks. Others grew, but had weak roots, or became strangled with weeds. Still others were fruitful. "We just breeze in, help a few people, and connect them to others. We don't get to see the fruition of the things we do. But we still believe that God is using us in ways we may never know."

"Planting seeds," Tod replied. "I like that parable, too."

"You've inspired us, as well," I added. "We do okay with the helping part, but aren't very disciplined with study and devotion. I love the way that you two schedule time to read and pray together. I hope, once we're home, we can do more of that."

After breakfast, Tod and Linda took us to Jim's. We packed the boat, Tod said a prayer for safe travel, and we set off for the university launch. Only a few days and we would be paddling into

Minneapolis, where we would reunite with family for the first time since leaving Itasca. After this, we would rarely, if ever, need to portage so often or so far. But Tod and Linda taught us lessons we would take down the river and back home again. Trust others. Learn and grow together in faith. And don't forget to rest.

It didn't take long for us to discover why we needed to be well rested. The next two days presented us with another challenge—wild winds.

It was common for the prevailing winds to travel up the Mississippi corridor from the south. As the river widened and straightened, strong headwinds could cancel any advantage of the current and even stir up hazardous waves. "I guess we know what the rest we got at Tod and Linda's prepared us for," said Gene as we donned our yellow Teletubby rain skirts—not because it was raining, but because they completely sealed the cockpits.

Mile after mile, we pushed on, steering at a right angle into any waves that blew up. We had occasional breaks from the wind when the river turned east or west; then we paddled closer to the lee shore and the trees on the bank shielded us from the gale. But when the fickle river turned again, our respite ended, testing our training for a complaint-free world. We veiled annoyance in optimism, trying valiantly to put this trial in a positive light. "This sure is a good workout. I feel stronger already," Gene said semi-brightly.

"We're going to be ready for anything after this!" I replied, between grunts befitting a weightlifter.

After one bend in the river, Gene stopped paddling. "Eagle!" he said, just loudly enough for me to hear over the wind and the lapping of the waves. I looked up at the branches of the trees. They were waving, bent over in the wind, but I didn't see the trademark white head that I became accustomed to spotting among the browns and greens of the foliage. "On the ground!" Gene added. Sure enough—on the riverbank stood an eagle, feathers ruffled, talons gripping its shiny silver prey, taking cover from the gale. Even the majestic bald eagles were grounded in this wind.

Each day, I watched the miles on the map, doing the math, counting down to our arrival in the Twin Cities. Finally, the winds shifted. After one river bend, I glanced at the trees on shore, bent over in the direction we were headed. "Hey, I think the wind's finally behind us for a stretch. Wanna try the sail?" The sail we bought at Canoecopia in early April sat on the bow, still neatly folded, waiting for the perfect tail wind that eluded us—until today. "We could sail right up to that sand beach ahead." I imagined the beachgoers stopping to watch the unusual sight as we came into view, gliding smoothly up on the sand.

"Are you sure you want to?" asked Gene. "It seems a little gusty. And I'm not interested in a bath."

"It'll be fine," I reassured him. "Wait'll you see how fast we go with this wind." We clipped our paddles to the deck with bungee cords. I released the strap restraining the billowing sailcloth. Up popped the circular sail, immediately filling with the strong breeze. I held tightly onto the sheets—thin cords on the port and starboard, controlling the angle of the sail. The boat lunged forward as our hull speed dramatically increased. "Whoo-hoo!" I shouted. "We'll be there in no time!" Before I could enjoy the fulfillment of my beach-landing daydream, a sudden gust of wind grabbed at the sail, dipping the lower edge into the water. The frame twisted as the sailcloth pocket filled with water, effectively putting on the brakes, and Donna began to list to starboard. I let go of the sheets, reaching over to grab the flexible sail frame, as Gene turned the boat upwind. Struggling to lift the heavy water-filled fabric, I drained the sail and flattened it on the foredeck. "Okay, not my best idea," I admitted. "I hope we're too far away for anyone to have seen that." If anyone did see, they were probably shaking their heads—or boarding their boats to rescue us. I folded up the sail to try again another day.

Chapter 6
Twin Cities

July 7–11: Family Reunion

We broke camp on day thirty-seven with excited anticipation. As we paddled toward a family reunion in the Twin Cities, I realized my son, Eric, was simultaneously driving the 300 miles from Waukesha to see us. Traveling with him were Gene's parents, Herbie and Delores. We were all meeting at my brother Dave's home in Edina, MN, where we planned to stay with his family, do service with Twin Cities Habitat for Humanity, and visit my mother in her memory care home.

The St. Anthony Lock was still closed to recreational traffic, so we altered our rendezvous point. Dave now planned to meet us at a park in Champlin. A gentle breeze was the only remnant of the previous days' winds; the miles slid by in idyllic fashion. We arrived at the park around noon, called Dave, and then spread out a blanket in the shade of a tree to wait for our ride. I gazed at the emerald canopy of leaves fluttering gently above me. Sounds of water lapping at the shore lulled me to the edge of sleep. The breeze, blowing off the river, caressed my skin. Maybe I'll just close my eyes for a minute, I thought.

"Dave's here," I heard Gene say, only seconds later. He jumped up and started over to the sidewalk where we parked the boat, flagging the Honda Pilot toward what seemed to be a rather obvious destination. I watched Dave pull up into a parking space near the boat, walk over to Gene, and shake hands. Unlike me, Dave had inherited the tall, thin frame of my mother's side of the family. I waved, folded up the blanket, and carried it over.

"Good to see you," Dave said, bending slightly to wrap an arm around me. "I thought you said paddling the river was hard work. Doesn't look hard to me."

I kissed him on the cheek. "It's a piece of cake when people don't interrupt my nap." I smiled, enjoying fully the sibling banter we never outgrew. "Thanks for coming." We tossed our gear in the back and strapped Donna to the roof.

Twenty minutes later, we turned into the driveway and Dave's family helped us carry in our things. My sister-in-law, Karen, and my two teenage nephews, Robert and Christian, looked over poor *Kupendana*, covered in scratches. "So where is the patch?" asked Christian. Gene pointed out the five-square-foot patch on her hull. Christian's eyes widened. "That's awesome!" The boys helped to carry her gently into the garage; later, we would give her some TLC.

Soon after we arrived, Eric drove up. Herbie and Delores piled out of the car, beaming as they wrapped us in hugs and covered us in kisses. "We were worried about you," Herbie said. "We saw on the news that there's lots of flooding down in Missouri. You should see the pictures. There's water everywhere."

"It's a little high here, but we're fine," Gene answered. "We won't be in Missouri for another two months. By the time we get down there, it'll all be gone." I hoped he was right.

Eric gave me a hug, then stood back, holding me at arm's length. "You're so tan!" He turned to Herbie. "You don't have to worry about Mom and Gene. I've been on bike trips with them. They can handle just about anything." I don't know if it was Eric's vote of confidence or the fact that we were still breathing that comforted Gene's parents more.

After dinner, we out-of-towners went to visit Mom. Her eyes lit up and she clapped as she watched us fill her room. I doubted she recognized all of our faces, but her exuberance showed that regardless of her memories, she enjoyed the company. She accepted hugs from all, with smiles and nods of greeting. "Gene and I are paddling our kayak down the Mississippi River, Mom," I explained again, knowing that my last visit was long forgotten.

"That sounds fun!" she said. Her eyes, the same brown hue as mine, scanned the room, moving from face to face.

I waited to respond until she got back to me, then looked into her eyes as I talked. "It's fun for us, but I don't think you'd like it very much." I remembered Mom's fear of water, her attempts to brave it through our family sailing vacations with the help of Dramamine and the decision, once we were grown, to enjoy the water with her feet on the ground.

Mom's voice sounded indignant. "I would, too! I'd love it!"

I smiled. Maybe forgetting fears of younger years was a blessing. "Okay. Maybe someday, after our trip, you can come for a ride with me." I gave her a hug. Without her memories, Mom wasn't the same, predictable parent I knew, but I loved to be with her. I understood that five minutes after I left her room, she might not remember my visit. But, somehow, this made every minute of time together a gift of presence for the moment. Even in my retirement years, I was still learning lessons about love from my mother.

July 8–10: Twin Cities Habitat for Humanity

The construction site for our next two days of service was in Crystal, MN, only about a twenty-minute drive from Dave's home. Eric and Gene's parents planned to return to Waukesha later that day, so we said good-bye before heading to the Habitat for Humanity building site. Upon our arrival, we met our site supervisor, Eric. "It'll be easy to remember your name," I said. "It's the same as my son's."

"He must be handsome, too, right?" He laughed—an easy, infectious chuckle. Somewhere in his fifties, our leader was dressed for the day's task in a gray T-shirt and work pants. A bright red sweatband across his brow added a splash of color. But the thing that set him apart was the wide, unpretentious smile that energized all his other features and made it impossible not to smile back.

If we got to pick our boss, we couldn't have done better. With his friendly, laid-back style, Eric introduced us to his college-age son, another father-son team—Elliot and Jacob—and four other single volunteers. Then he explained that Habitat's vision was to create a world where everyone had a decent place to live. "You're doing something important today," he told us. "Thank you for being here."

We followed him inside, where he demonstrated the technique for installing insulation—our job of the day. "Remember to fluff it, not stuff it," he said, placing a section of fiberglass between the studs. "The air pockets are what'll keep the house warm." We cut the rolls of insulation to size and trimmed it to fit around windows, doorframes, and electrical outlets. Gene's height came in handy for the top of the walls and areas that were tough to reach in the stairwell. Eric stopped by frequently to answer questions, help out, and sprinkle in encouragement, wit, and wisdom. When he noticed insulation sagging at the top, he explained, "Start at the bottom. That way, gravity helps hold it in place instead of working against you." Sometimes he just stopped by to ask, "Are you having fun? Your goal is to help. Mine is to make sure you have fun while you're doin' it."

Next, we wrapped the interior of the house in poly, a plastic layer that kept the warm inside air from escaping and condensing between the walls. Staple guns popped and duct tape ripped as we secured large plastic sheets to the studs, overlapping and taping the edges. Many hands made light work and we finished early for the day.

We stopped at a boat supply store on the way home to pick up some epoxy resin and fiberglass tape. Our patch was holding fast, but we still needed to add an extra two-inch strip of tape down the inside and the outside of the keel to protect it from rocks, sand, and the abuse of being repeatedly set on the ground during portages.

In Dave's garage, we carefully epoxied new tape onto the keel line at the bow and over the patched area. With the several days we planned here in Minneapolis, we had plenty of time to add more coats of epoxy, inside and out, to strengthen *Kupendana* for the remainder of our journey.

After dinner, Gene and I went to visit Mom. As we entered her room, she stood up from her seat at the edge of the bed, wide-eyed with surprise. "Barb!" My heart rejoiced at the sound of my name. I was afraid of the day that I knew would come, when there would be no flicker of recognition in her eyes; I pushed it to the back of my mind. Somewhere along the pathways of our lives, the wise caretaker and comforter of our youth became an innocent and trusting dependent. But she would always be Mom. As we exchanged hugs, she gave me an exaggerated kiss. "I love you!"

I touched her cheek and looked into her eyes. "I love you, too, Mom." I turned to include Gene. "Eric and Gene's parents had to go home; they said to say good-bye. But Gene's here."

Mom arched her willowy frame slightly to look up into Gene's face, then turned toward me. "Look at this big guy!" Gene's eyes met mine and we shared a smile. Mom was five feet ten herself, but always seemed surprised to come up short next to Gene.

"Let's go for a walk, Mom," Gene suggested. He offered his arm and Mom slipped her hand around it, every bit the princess on her way to a royal ball. Gene had a chivalrous way of making her feel special. As he escorted her past the staff and other residents, she tapped his arm and said, "Look what I found!"

We took seats in the stuffed armchairs. "Barb and I are paddling down the Mississippi River in our kayak," Gene reminded her. "We stopped to see you and to help build a house with Habitat for Humanity."

"That's nice," Mom replied, staring forward with a faraway look in her eyes.

I took Mom's hand in mine, rubbing it gently. Her skin was soft and cool, but thin—not like the strong, sturdy hands that rolled out pie crusts, sewed her only daughter polka-dot dresses with ties at the waist, and tied red velvet bows on crafts for the church bazaar. "It's good to be with you, Mom."

She smiled, then turned back to her private thoughts. What did she think about? What did she see? I wished she had the words to tell me. I hoped it was happy.

The next day, most of the volunteers returned to the construction site, with the addition of a couple of new faces. One was Elliot's father, John, who flew in from Manhattan to join his son and grandson for a three-generation volunteer day. "My son and I built Habitat homes together for a long time," John told me. He pulled a hand through his scraggly white beard in an apparent attempt to tame it. "We're trying to get Jacob interested in continuing the tradition. Right now, I can't say he loves it—he's a little shy—but I really hope it'll grow on him."

"You're already flying back tomorrow?" I asked. I found the thought of flying halfway across the country for a day amazing.

"Yes," he said. "It's worth the price of a plane ticket to be able to do this together and to show Jacob the satisfaction of helping." Maybe Jacob didn't appreciate it yet, but he had one heck of a role model.

The entire day was spent putting up drywall. After a short lesson in Sheetrock installation, Eric sent Gene and me downstairs to work on lining the closets. We measured each piece several times, cut the Sheetrock to the right size, and then screwed it into the studs and the joists. Often the studs weren't square, and each dimension needed to be measured and cut separately. One time, as we tried to force a piece into place, the corner cracked. Deflated, we lowered it down to save it for smaller scrap pieces and cut a new piece. I heard footsteps dancing down the stairs.

"Hi! How's it going?" Eric's brightly wrapped head popped around the corner, a broad smile gracing his countenance. "Do you need anything?"

"We're okay," Gene replied. "But it's going pretty slowly." He told Eric about the problems we had fitting the drywall sections together perfectly.

"Don't worry about that," comforted Eric. "In construction, things rarely fit perfectly. We'll hire a team to tape and spackle all the seams; the experience they bring to that job is worth it. They'll do the whole house on Friday—no one'll ever see that." He pointed to a gap at the top of the closet. "It'll look beautiful."

Despite his encouragement, I was concerned with our snail's pace. "At the rate we're going, the *closets* might not be done by the end of the week." I quietly changed my bracelet to my other wrist.

Gene noticed and gave me a side hug with a second little squeeze. "It looks like we'll get to be alone in the bedroom closet for a while." Turning to Eric, he asked, "When does the Sheetrock go up on the main walls?"

Eric's face lit up. "Oh, that'll go fast!" he exclaimed. "I like to do all the little, more difficult areas first, and end with the easy part. If we get all the closets done today, the rest'll go up tomorrow in a couple of hours!"

I raised my drill in salute. "Then, since we won't be here tomorrow, we'll get this done today, boss."

Eric smiled. "The important thing is that you have fun, and that you feel like what you are doing is valuable. A family of nine will be able to call this house their home because of what you are doing. Thank you for that." Boy, he's good at his job, I thought. I was one part of a crew for two days. I knew my role was minimal, but my crew leader made me feel like Wonder Woman—with a drill.

As Eric bounded up the steps to check with other volunteers, I stepped carefully over the closet threshold into the tiny space that was becoming more claustrophobic by the minute and readied my drill. Gene reached in, opening his hand to reveal a pile of shiny hardware. He asked with a wink, "Need a screw?"

"As a matter of fact, I do," I replied, putting the handful into my work apron pocket and puckering my lips to send him an air kiss.

At the end of the day, we thanked Eric for a great experience, added a coat of epoxy to Donna's keel line at Dave's, and went to see Mom after dinner. This time, she was resting in bed. Her eyes were closed, but she heard us enter and turned to us with a tired gaze.

"Hi, Mom! It's Barb. Gene's here, too. How are you?"

"Not so good." Her reply was barely audible.

"I'm sorry. I'm glad you're resting. I hope you feel better soon." Gene sat in the chair across the room, but I climbed onto the unused side of her bed, propping myself up at the headboard next to her. "I'm tired, too. Today, we worked hard at Habitat for Humanity. We got to put up drywall. It's starting to look like a house now, with real walls and everything!"

"That's nice."

"Mom . . ." I rolled on my side and propped my head on my hand so I could look into her eyes. "The reason I love to help others is because of you. You showed me how to care about people and do whatever I can to help them. I remember when you'd take me along to deliver Meals on Wheels." At the name Meals on Wheels, Mom brightened. I remembered how much she loved visiting homebound folks, chatting while she heated up and served them prepared meals. "You were always helping with something at church," I continued. "And remember how much you loved being a Hospice volunteer?"

Mom nodded. "I liked doing that," she said softly.

"I love you, Mom."

"I love you, too," she whispered, as she returned to sleep. I gently kissed her forehead and we quietly left, pulling the door closed behind us.

Our third day of work with Habitat was at the ReStore in New Brighton, MN. Upon our arrival, we met Grant, a sales assistant, who gave us a short tour and introduced us to the staff of five. "The ReStore helps support Habitat," he explained, "by selling donated new and used building materials and home supplies. We price the donations at approximately fifty percent of retail value and sell them to the public. Both contractors and do-it-yourselfers love it. They get to purchase things they need at a great price, while helping the community. It's a win-win."

After getting acclimated, we started by accepting donations at the drive-up dock. We carried in used windows, lamps, tools, and furniture, writing out donation receipts. Later, after the items were priced, we helped put them on display. The store was clearly labeled in sections, and items for sale changed constantly as things on the floor flew out the door and new donations were stocked. Had we not been traveling by kayak, there were several things I might have purchased.

My signature blue worker's vest clearly identified me as a volunteer, so customers constantly stopped me to ask questions. I settled on an effective go-to response: "I'm not sure about that, but I'll find out for you." I had no idea whether or not the table saw really worked or how to install a vinyl window. My design talents were valuable for creating displays at The Mustard Seed in Deerwood, but with his background in retail sales and total lack of fear when it came to home repair, it was Gene who was in his element here. He seemed happy as a lark, organizing sinks by composition and color, straightening displays, and helping customers with knowledge and confidence that I lacked.

Near the end of our shift, Grant asked if we could do one more project. "Sure—whatever you need," answered Gene. We followed him back to a corner of the store where I saw pyramids of paint cans—mostly used.

"As a service to our customers," Grant explained, "we let people drop off paint cans in a bin out in front. We're behind in sorting these. Some of them are usable, but most of them need to be taken out to the disposal area by the dumpster. They'll get picked up later this week."

"What's the best way to do that?" Gene asked.

"Leave any full or mostly full usable cans here," said Grant. "You can pile the other ones in this bin and take it down there with the pallet dolly." He showed us a metal bin on top of a wooden pallet.

Gene and I sorted through the cans. One unopened can in the good pile, five or six nearly empty cans with paint-spattered labels in the disposal pile. When we were finished, our bin was brimming with multicolored cans of latex waste. "Do you know how to drive a pallet dolly?" I asked Gene.

"Of course," he said. Feigning shock, he added, "You don't?"

"Can I try it?" slipped out of my mouth before I knew it. The controls to lift and lower the fork proved easy to use, but the steering had a steeper learning curve. With several fits and starts, I rather awkwardly maneuvered the bright yellow electric dolly, loaded with five hundred pounds of paint, through the parking lot to the dumpsters.

"Good job, babe." Gene high-fived me. "You didn't even bump any of the cars." Dolly driving wasn't likely to be a skill I needed again; I considered it a win.

That evening, after slathering on Donna's last coat of epoxy, we stopped to say good-bye to Mom and then spent a quiet evening with Dave's family. Our volunteer work, boat repairs, and visits with Mom, as well as Dave's job and family activities, made for a very busy week. We packed our dry bags with the clean laundry Karen washed for us and organized our supplies, then discussed what to do with the rest of the evening.

"How 'bout we watch a movie?" Dave suggested. "We could make some popcorn. I've got *Deliverance*," he teased. "I think it's about a couple of people taking a canoe trip on a river."

I laughed at his wry sense of humor and wished, once again, that we lived closer. "Thanks, but the last thing I need is a Dueling Banjos earworm. How 'bout a friendly game of Trouble?"

Chapter 7
Barges and Big Boys

July 12–21: Twin Cities to La Crosse, WI

SOUTH OF ST. PAUL, the character of the Mississippi River changed, due in large part to the system of locks and dams built by the Army Corps of Engineers to facilitate recreational and commercial navigation. Dams contained the water in numbered pools, lowering the river's elevation in a series of steps. Locks, located next to the dams, allowed boats to travel from one pool to another by raising or lowering the water level within the lock. With these changes, the ever-widening river became a thoroughfare for a variety of boats, from small muscle-driven canoes and kayaks like ours, to motorized fishing boats and pleasure yachts as well as tugboats pushing behemoth barges. No longer did we need to portage around every waterfall and dam. But no longer were we paddling alone in tranquil waters. We were now sharing the river with boats we affectionately called the "Big Boys."

The next leg of our journey involved over a week of paddling to get to La Crosse, where we planned to work with the Salvation Army and the Myrick-Hixon Eco Park. It was our longest river section so far, averaging about twenty miles a day.

Friday, Karen dropped us off at the Twin City Marina in downtown St. Paul. We optimistically stretched our sunny-day half skirts around our coamings. With a new replacement for the one I lost in our rapids, we could both, once again, have the ventilation of a half-open cockpit. Two miles into our idyllic paddle, the river doubled back on itself, providing no lee shore to protect us from easterly winds we didn't expect. "That was nice while it lasted," Gene called, as waves began crashing over the bow. The barges, tied up along one shore, sounded like a percussion ensemble of metal drums, as waves slapped the sides of their empty hulls. Ventilation was a liability in waves like this. Carefully, we paddled between two of the moored barges. Shielded from the wind, we took turns sculling to keep the boat in place while changing into our familiar yellow bibs. Then, out into the wind and waves we went.

After a very long five miles and ready for a change of pace, we took a narrow channel detour to explore the secluded Pig's Eye Heron Rookery. Named after Pierre "Pig's Eye" Parrant, the first settler in what is now St. Paul, it was known for being one of the largest heron nesting sites in the state. Its small bays and narrow channels provided a perfect respite. Around every corner, we made new discoveries . . . a stately great blue heron standing perfectly still among the reeds at the bank, its long white neck hidden in tight folds, and a line of herons perched on a low branch, searching the water below for their Friday fish fry.

"Look! Up in the tree." I pointed ahead, as we drifted toward a towering leafless tree. Perched on seemingly every branch, herons alternately extended their wings as if to take flight, regained their balance, and refolded their wings, in a graceful ballet to an inaudible beat.

Rested and inspired, we rejoined the main channel. Before long, I heard the low hum of an engine accompanied by a high-pitched whine. "Hear that?" asked Gene. "There's a barge coming. Can you see it?" I stopped paddling, alert for the source of the new sound. Three flat maroon-colored hulls emerged from the bend ahead, joined together side-by-side as one. They were one, really, hitched together like a team of horses. The barges crept slowly closer, a row of small white waves at the water line the only indication of movement. Another set of three barges appeared behind them, then another. A single towboat, centered behind the barges, expertly guided them around the bend, then straightened them back out again.

I pried my eyes away from the approaching giant long enough to resume paddling. "Let's get out of the channel and find a place to watch." Gene steered us over toward the shore, then turned the boat to face the channel. We drifted lazily as we watched.

The barge's apparent slow speed was deceiving. As it passed, I realized it made good time, but its size and the lack of water disturbance made it seem like it barely moved at all. I waved to the captain standing at the controls, high on the glassed-in bridge of the white towboat. His name was painted in red below the side window—Robert. He didn't wave back. Was he oblivious to our presence? If he couldn't see us, it could present problems. As the sound of swirling water began to compete with the fading engine noise, I was surprised that its wake was no monster at all. In fact, it dissipated to small rollers before it arrived. My first barge experience inspired awe and respect, but not fear. We could do this.

Along with the increase in commercial river traffic came a helpful navigational benefit—channel markers. Because the commercial and recreational boats required deep water, the river channel was dredged to a depth of nine feet. Red and green buoys marked both outer edges of this safe zone for the Big Boys. Because we were traveling downstream, the green buoys were all on our right, and the red buoys were on our left as we paddled south. *Kupendana* didn't need the deep water, but the fastest current could be found in the channel. By paddling just inside the channel markers on either side of the river, we took advantage of the current and could easily veer into shallower waters if Big Boys came along.

Determining our location on the river also became easier, thanks to mile markers, now found regularly along the edges of the channel. Bold black numbers on metal signs corresponded with our position on all of our maps, and helped us easily calculate the miles we traveled and the distance to upcoming destinations.

The next day, we approached our first lock and dam. The map showed its location on the right side of the river, so we paddled along the green channel markers. Soon, we saw huge numbers posted on the shore, counting down the distance to the lock entrance. Moments later, a concrete wall loomed on our side. The signal rope hung near the beginning of the wall. Gene steered over and I tugged the rope to signal the lockmaster that our vessel waited to lock through. I wondered how he would even see us . . . a thirty-inch-wide craft tucked in the shadow of the concrete wall. But he did. The lock doors slowly swung open, inviting us inside. When the doors finished moving, we paddled into the gaping enclosure.

I waved to the lockmaster standing on the walkway above us. He ushered us forward and dropped each of us a line. Holding the rope loosely with one hand, I used my paddle as a bumper to keep Donna from scraping against the concrete. A deep rumbling sound accompanied the pair of huge metal doors closing behind us. Then slowly, the water began to drain out of the lock, lowering us to the level of the next pool. I let the rope slide through my fingers and watched the receding water expose white paint markings every foot up the side of the lock wall. The darkened color of the damp walls rose as we were lowered gently down, down, down. Ten . . . eleven . . . twelve feet. As we lowered, the blue sky receded and our lone vessel seemed to shrink into the depths of the darkened cavern. Then the sound of a motor, and the doors in front of us swung open. Behind us, the towering gate held back twelve feet of water, but the doors ahead ushered us out into the sunshine. The water was choppy—the effect of drainage from the lock. We paddled straight out into Pool #3, being careful to stay far enough away from the lower entrance wall not to be pushed into it by the bobbing water. I heard a shout from behind me. "Whoo-hoo! A lot easier than a portage!"

On Saturday night, we pulled into Leo's Landing, a famous landmark in Prescott, WI. This small dock and marina had been a fixture at the confluence of the Mississippi and the St. Croix River for as long as many of the residents could remember. I became acquainted with the current owner, Dick, on the phone before leaving home. A more affable and helpful man would be hard to find. As we floated up to the gas dock at the front of the highly decorated blue façade, Dick emerged. He led us to a protected slip behind the store and entertained us with river stories. "Me? I've done the Mississippi twice, as a young man. Not in a small boat like that . . . I had a day cruiser. But if I did it again, I wouldn't stay on the Mississippi the whole way down to the Gulf. It's gotten more dangerous and most of the marinas have moved over to the Tenn-Tom Waterway. The only thing you'll find now on the Lower Mississippi is big industry."

"Do you think we should reconsider our plan to stay with the Mississippi?" I asked Gene later. I knew friends who took their powerboat down the Tennessee-Tombigbee Waterway, a route that ended up in Mobile, AL, instead of New Orleans. But I wasn't familiar with the route itself.

"I don't know," said Gene. "If it is safer, maybe we should consider it. We still have plenty of time to decide. I'm sure we'll meet other people along the river we can ask."

On Sunday, we passed though the next lock, near Red Wing, MN. Once again, we had it all to ourselves. We paddled through the steel gate and slipped up alongside the cement wall. The lockmaster dropped down our lines and asked, "Where ya headed?"

"South," replied Gene. I drew in a sharp breath. That seemed like a cheeky response, considering he was answering an employee of the US Army, who could obviously see the direction of our heading. But I also knew why Gene said it—I could no longer keep count of the people who asked our destination. To avoid routine, we began varying our answers: "New Orleans," "the Gulf of Mexico," "salt water," sometimes even just "That a-way."

The lockmaster apparently took no offense. "All the way?"

"Yes, sir—unless there's a job opening for a lockmaster on the way down. I sure do think I'd love *your* job, workin' on the river."

"It gets pretty busy sometimes, when the barges come through, but most days, it's still real nice," said the lockmaster.

"How many barges can you lock through at once?" Gene asked.

"This enclosure is average sized—six hundred feet long and a hundred ten feet wide," he explained. "We can fit a three-by-three, if the towboat locks through separately. We've gotta take anything bigger than that apart and lock it through in stages. If you ever have to wait for one of those, you might be waiting for a couple hours."

"This is the first week we've had to deal with barges," Gene admitted. "Got any advice? Would they prefer us to be on one side or the other when they come through?"

"It doesn't matter which side you're on," he answered. "Just don't get in front of 'em."

I chuckled at his grasp of the obvious, but it was actually pretty good advice. As I let the rope slip between my fingers and watched the water-stained lock wall rise beside me, I imagined the entire space filled with those nine barges, each thirty-five feet wide, and one hundred ninety-five feet long. I remembered the barge that passed us a few days ago, and I realized why Robert didn't wave back to me. His was a huge responsibility. With nearly six hundred feet of cargo in front of him, he would never have seen our little boat, and we certainly wouldn't have been able to outrun him.

The lock doors slowly swung open. "Hey, babe," I called to Gene, as I dropped my line and started to paddle toward the next pool. "Let's make sure we remember his advice . . . about the barges, okay?"

"That's a deal," he said.

Monday night's campground was located on an island across a channel from Red Wing, MN. As we paddled under the mainland access bridge, everything looked quite normal, except that the campground was located directly beneath the huge, four-lane Highway 63 bridge. How did we not notice that on our maps? The sites were nearly all occupied, most by campers and fifth wheels at seasonal sites. Vacationers buzzed around the property on golf carts, "roughing it" in the surreal shadows of a bridge that spanned two states. Ours was the token tent site—a patch of grass at the intersection of two gravel roads, complete with a picnic table and one tree. No chance of seeing wildlife here—the sounds of wheels clamoring over the metal roadway grids continued through the night. In the morning, I couldn't launch fast enough.

Approaching the western end of Lake Pepin, we watched the weather reports carefully. Lake Pepin was the widest natural section of the Mississippi River, and itself an actual lake. The speed and direction of the wind were critical for a safe and timely crossing. Starting at its western end, Lake Pepin bent gently around nearly eight miles of Frontenac State Park shoreline to continue in a southerly direction. The weather looked good. We decided to follow the Minnesota shore past the park and stop in Lake City for the night.

It was still early afternoon when we turned into a small bay and spied the pebbly beach of Hok-Si-La Campground. Swimmers dotted the shallow water and sunbathers lay on towels spread on the beach. A few small boats were pulled up to the shore. We debated continuing on, since it was still early and the weather was good. But the siren song of the beautiful beach was too strong. I steered *Kupendana* to the shore.

Several swimmers and sunbathers turned and gazed with casual interest at our wooden kayak, loaded with gear, and then at us, faces and arms bronzed by the sun, red life jackets already faded to a dark shade of pink, and pale legs pulling out of the cover of our cockpits. Gene gave up shaving weeks ago, and was sporting a full salt-and-pepper beard—mostly salt. Jason's words replayed in my mind, all the way from Bemidji: "Sooner or later, if you go all the way down, you'll start to look like real river people." At the time, I wasn't exactly sure what he meant, but now, I figured we were well on our way.

A middle-aged blonde woman with a broad smile and an outstretched hand bounced over to greet us. Shaking my hand, then Gene's, she announced, "Hi. I'm Jeri. It looks like you're travelin'. Where'd you start?"

"Up at the headwaters in Itasca," Gene responded, telling her briefly about our trip. "This is a beautiful beach. This is Hok-Si-La Campground, right?"

"Sure is," Jeri answered. "Prettiest beach around." She stopped to call her husband, cooling his feet in the water. "Jeff! Come on over and meet these people." Beach pebbles crunched under his water shoes as he headed our way.

"Pleased to meet you," he said. "That's a beautiful boat you have there."

"Thanks," I responded. "Are you camping here? Can you tell us the way to the camp office?"

"We don't actually camp here," explained Jeri. "We own a bakery and deli in town. But after work, this is our favorite place to come and relax. We just lie around, swim a little, and spend a couple of hours winding down before supper. The office is right up that path. If you want to go on up there and register, we'll watch your boat for you."

I was only half-listening since the word *bakery*. Just that one little word, and I voted to stay here tonight. *Bakery*. That meant fresh bread in the morning, and maybe even some for lunch the next day.

On the way to the office, we checked out the facilities . . . flush toilets *and* showers! That sealed the deal. We reserved a lakeside campsite.

We returned to the beach to paddle Donna over to our home for the evening and thanked Jeri and Jeff for watching her. "Any time," said Jeri. "We're meeting a couple of friends for dinner tonight. We'd love for them to meet you. Can we pick you up after you set up camp and treat you to a dinner in town—say about six thirty?"

Dinner in Lake City was an unexpected treat—a swanky restaurant meal instead of campfire cooking. We exchanged stories about the trip, our towns, our children, churches, and faith. "You should really stop and see the Lake City Marina," Jeri suggested. "It's the largest 'small craft marina' on the Mississippi. It's just a couple miles from the campground, across that bay." She indicated a point of land across the water.

"What's the name of your bakery?" I asked. "We'd love to walk over and buy breakfast from you tomorrow before we leave."

"It's called Marien's Deli," replied Jeff. "But it's too far to walk. Call us when you get to the marina. We'll deliver some breakfast sandwiches and hot coffee there for you. On the house. We won't take no for an answer."

As the morning sky over Lake Pepin changed from rosy pink to pale blue, we set off across the bay. An early start meant we could get a couple of hours in before the midday winds strengthened. There were still fifteen miles of Lake Pepin to cover before we were scheduled to meet a hometown friend at the Wabasha dock for lunch.

Lake City Marina certainly lived up to its reputation for size, with over 600 boat slips, most in the outer marina, formed by a long breakwater, and the rest in an older marina located on the interior of the land peninsula. We walked along the docks, admiring hundreds of sailboats and motor vessels—mansions compared to our tiny water home. We snooped around inside the modern administration building. Returning from the bathroom, I caught Gene perusing the ads on a bulletin board for used boats. Holding up a flyer for a thirty-eight-foot cruiser, he chuckled, "I bet we could get to New Orleans a lot quicker in this one!"

"You're not really thinking about cheating on Donna, are you?" I asked. "Getting there fast isn't the point, is it?"

"You can't blame a guy for looking," he said with a smile as he slid the flyer back in the rack.

Jeff arrived, bearing gifts of fresh steaming coffee, hot breakfast sandwiches, and astronomically caloric treats. "Jeri wanted me to include a caramel roll and some carrot cake. We're kinda famous for 'em," he said. "Have a safe trip." After thanking Jeff and waving good-bye, we gobbled down the filling breakfast. I thought about saving the desserts for later—but only for a second. We divided each of them in half. I savored the rich, gooey caramel and the spicy, melt-in-your-mouth cake with buttery cream cheese frosting. Good thing I planned a long workout.

For the rest of the morning, we kept to the west side of the lake. There was no reason to stay near the channel. Lake Pepin was nearly three miles wide at this point, and the channel crossed over to the Wisconsin side. Following the points of land along the western shore, we bypassed the bays and inlets that could have added miles to our day, sticking with the most direct route to the south end of the lake.

Finally, the shores pulled closer together. Paddling felt effortless as the wide waters of Lake Pepin, now joined by the Chippewa River, were funneled back between two riverbanks. I scanned the western shore. My good friend and colleague, Karen, had traveled to her aunt's home in Wabasha to see us and would be waiting for us by the dock. Coming around a bend, I heard a gleeful shout. "Barb! Gene!" Standing in the water in front of a small sand beach, Karen flailed her arms. We stopped paddling and drifted in. She waded out, gave me a hug, and then held the bow in place against the current. I dug my paddle into the sandy bottom on the downstream side of the boat to stabilize it.

"It's great to see you! Have you been waiting long?" I didn't even try to keep the supersized grin off my face. We had been on the river for six weeks and met hundreds of new faces. But here was a long-time friend who drove across the state to see us, to support us, and to be a part of our journey. Just for lunch. I was touched.

"Just a little while," she answered. "I stayed at my aunt's house last night and then decided to hang out at the beach while I watched for you. It was so exciting to see you come around the corner."

"Are you hungry?" asked Gene. "I'm starving!"

"Slippery's Bar and Grill is just a couple blocks down." Karen pointed downstream to a large white two-story building with full-length porches facing the river on both floors. Famous for its role as a gathering place in the *Grumpy Old Men* movies, it was a "can't miss" attraction. "They have a dock right out front. I'll meet you down there."

Slippery's was a fun and friendly luncheon locale, decorated with *Grumpy Old Men* memorabilia. Both the movie and its sequel played simultaneously on TV sets facing the dining area. We caught up with news of home and ate lunch in air-conditioned comfort. On the way to the bathroom, I meandered through the hallway displays. The pictures of scenes from the movies brought back amusing memories of Walter Matthau and Jack Lemmon fighting over the affections of ebullient and flirtatious Ann-Margret.

After lunch, we walked a few blocks south to the National Eagle Center. Situated right on the river, the Eagle Center was an attraction I didn't want to miss. The modern building held educational displays and housed five rescued eagles. The naturalists on staff held live eagle programs daily. We could make the 1 o'clock program if we hurried.

Scott, the education director, told us about the recovery of the eagle population and its removal from the Endangered Species List. He explained about eagles' development, average size, wingspan, and weight, as well as their behavior. We learned that the brown eagles we saw along the river were not golden eagles as we thought, but juvenile bald eagles. "Their dark brown color remains until they are four to five years old," explained Scott, "when their characteristic white feathers grow on their heads and tails." We heard shrieks from the next room; they were familiar eagle cries we heard upstream on the river. "Bald eagles are very territorial," said Scott. "When they see other eagles in their air space, you'll know it."

In came Harriet, the eldest of the residential bald eagles. Scott held a fish in his gloved hand. Harriet tore it apart with her razor-sharp beak, easily breaking the bones and gulping down large chunks. Scott explained Harriet's predatory adaptations and her rescue. "Harriet lived in the wild for her first seventeen years," he said, "but in 1998, she was hit by a car. She can't survive in the wild anymore." He lifted her crippled wing gently. It only spread partway out. "She's famous, though," he bragged. "She travels all over the country as an Eagle Ambassador. She's been to veterans centers and Washington DC, and she's made appearances on *The Tonight Show* with Jay Leno. Her picture was even used to make these plates." He held up a patriotic license plate with Harriet's image at the corner. I'd seen some like it before, but never even thought about where the picture came from. Now, I knew I'd never see one without thinking of her.

After the program, we wandered around the displays. On a platform in one corner of the room, fashioned out of sticks and easily six feet across, sat a life-sized replica of an eagle's nest. Karen and I climbed inside and posed as young eaglets. From hundreds of feet below, eagles' nests looked to be quite precarious, but the model showed they actually offered plenty of safety and room to move about. I would have loved stay longer and attend one of the center's eagle viewing trips, but we still had several hours of paddling ahead.

I locked Karen's arm in mine as we walked out to the dock. "Thanks, Karen. It means so much to me that you drove out to see us."

She squeezed my arm. "I'm glad I did. I'm proud of you for what you're doing. I follow you and read all your blogs. It's nice to share a little part of your experience." She stopped and turned toward me. "Before you get too far down the river and before school starts, I want to come meet you again. Maybe in Dubuque? You're stopping there, right?"

I nodded, picturing our itinerary. "We're scheduled to be there at the beginning of August. We'll be working at a free clothing ministry called The Clothes Closet."

"That would be perfect. But I don't just want to visit this time," she said. "I want to share your experience—to spend the whole day with you and help you with the service. We can work it out when you get closer, okay?"

"I'd love nothing better." I gave her a hug and slipped into the cockpit. I felt a twinge. Was it homesickness? Probably not. I didn't have time for that. But amidst the challenge and excitement of the unknown, her loving presence was a touchstone. And that sustained me.

The next five miles flew by. With renewed vigor, we crossed over to the Wisconsin side. After a quick descent through lock number four, we tied up at Alma Landing. The blacktop drive led to a marina office, already locked up for the evening. But from there, a gravel trail led to a bathhouse and city beach with two lifeguards on duty. A picnic area and sand volleyball court completed the small-town picture. Cheers floated over from beyond the bathhouse; a baseball game was in progress. I briefly entertained the idea of buying some popcorn and watching the game. But we had to get our camp settled before dark. I scanned the beachfront. "That's a perfect spot!" I whispered, pointing to a grassy area by the picnic table. "We could bring Donna right up on the bank."

"We can't set up 'til the beach closes," answered Gene, "unless we ask permission first."

I read the sign posted by the bathhouse. "The beach closes in half an hour. But I do think we should ask." Both lifeguards were young women, looking tanned and fit. "You go ask," I urged Gene. "You're cuter."

"Yeah, right!" he answered. But the smile he flashed back as he walked over to the guard's chair told me he appreciated the thought.

Gene returned, pulling his fist back in a characteristic gesture. "Score!" he announced. "We can set up over in the picnic area and use the bathhouse too. It stays open all night."

While we ate dinner, I watched from the picnic table as a team of young athletes celebrated their win, splashing in the cool water, their parents congregating on the sand. Soon the beach emptied, leaving the park lights reflecting off the calm water. Stars twinkled through a canopy of leaves.

As I tucked under my fleece for the night, I heard new voices. The two lifeguards had returned for a late night dip. I considered staying up for a swim, but only for a second, before I drifted off to the soft splashing sounds of their strokes and easy laughter.

Wednesday was predicted to be a scorcher, but we only planned a short seventeen-mile paddle. We worked our way through several backwater sloughs, crossing over to the Minnesota side. The sun beat down mercilessly. Freeing my neck shade from its pocket under the brim, I dipped my hat in the river, letting the cool water drip over my face and down my neck. Momentarily, I wondered how many gross little organisms might be in that hatful of river water, but decided not to dwell on that thought. On hot days like this, keeping hydrated was a bigger concern. Gene stopped paddling and fiddled with his phone. "I'm setting the alarm to ring every twenty minutes," he said. "Whenever it rings, we make sure we drink, okay?"

"Great idea." I was glad he thought of it. The last time I allowed myself to get dehydrated was years ago, during a bicycle trip. But the memory was still vivid—the oppressive heat emanating from the blacktop roadway, the smell of tar, my clammy skin, the nausea, dizziness, and fatigue. Nope—I never wanted to go through that again. I unhooked my water bottle and took a good swig.

Approaching Lock and Dam #5, I maneuvered the boat alongside the looming cement wall and Gene yanked on the chain to announce our presence. A few minutes later, the doors swung open, and once again, we were alone in a lock. The high, damp walls offered a short reprieve as we descended, but in about twenty minutes, we found ourselves back under the sweltering sun.

The day's destination was Merrick State Park, along the Wisconsin shoreline. We stayed there on a bicycle trip several years ago and were eager to revisit. The route to the park by water was trickier than by road; we needed to cross the channel to the east side of the river, then weave our way through a series of sloughs and small lakes to the park peninsula. "We should see Devil's Door soon," I announced. Devil's Door was a corner with a reputation for claiming boats that underestimated the power of the rapids rushing around and between the rocks on each side, but it was the best route to the park.

Gene read the map and guided me through the backwaters. We turned left into Kieselhorse Bay and scanned the right side for the telltale boulders that would signal our turn. "There it is," I shouted. Ahead and to the right, a stream of water swirled its way around several huge boulders, disappearing into the foliage in a rush of whitewater. The rippling sound of water cascading over rocks would have peaceful if I were sitting in a lounge chair in the shade, reading a good book. But sitting in the helmsman's seat, it was nerve-wracking. I took a deep breath to calm myself.

Gene coolly talked me through it. "Square it up first." I started a gentle turn to the right to set our boat up at a ninety-degree angle. "Go!" said Gene. We paddled quickly, entering the middle of the stream as it rushed through Devil's Door. The tumbling water pulled us with it, through the one safe opening between two intimidating piles of rock. Our stern swung to the left. I pressed the foot pedal on the same side to compensate and the bow swung left, centering the boat once again. The water calmed from rapids to a fast-moving stream. We were through.

"That was amazing!" my adrenaline shouted. "Let's do that again!"

"Good job," said Gene, raising his paddle over his shoulder so I could touch it with mine in a paddle high five.

Soon, walking paths, scenic overlooks, and a boat ramp appeared along the left shore. We pulled up to the dock, next to an aluminum fishing boat. The two occupants looked in their late thirties or early forties: a generously tattooed man in jeans and a dark blue T-shirt and his blonde companion, whose white Daisy

Duke shorts and low-cut stretchy top seemed in stark contrast to his comfortable outdoor ensemble.

"Hi! Have you been fishing, or are you just going out?" Gene asked.

"Oh, we ain't fishin'," answered the man. "We're just on our way out to check our turtle traps."

"Turtle traps?" I asked.

"Yass'm. Snappers. Me an' my wife got twenty-five yesterday. We're just goin' out to check the traps again today."

I was fascinated. I didn't even know that there was a snapping turtle season. I once snagged one when I was fishing for northern pike. I remembered netting it, then watching as it snapped through the webbing and scrambled to the end of the dock, escaping with a splash. I couldn't imagine twenty-five sets of snapping jaws in one boat. And, with exposed skin, to boot.

"People pay good money for turtle meat," explained the woman. "I hope the traps are full." She held up crossed fingers on both hands.

"Good luck," Gene called, as we shoved off.

We paddled along the shore, checking out the campsites. At the first one with a grassy landing area, we pulled Donna's bow up onto the bank. "Before we take her all the way out," I suggested, "let's walk down to see if there are any sites we like better."

We strolled down the trail, hand in hand, reminiscing about the last time we camped there. After bicycling seventy miles, we had arrived in the dark to find our campsite was next to a friendly group of Harley riders. "Remember?" asked Gene. "They invited us to stop by in the morning with our mugs for some hot coffee—but we didn't have any mugs."

"Yeah, and I suppose now that we have mugs, we won't get any offers." I laughed.

We were shaken out of our shared memories by the roar of an engine and blaring speakers. Peering out at the slough, we saw the source of the ruckus. A ski boat sped toward us, swishing back and forth, pulling a water skier in tow. Rock music blared from two huge speakers on deck, and an enormous wake crashed against the shore behind the one-boat demolition crew.

"Idiots," grumbled Gene. I would have probably made him change his bracelet, except for a more urgent, frightening thought. They were headed toward our boat! Gene must have had the same thought, because we both began to sprint, hurdling over a chain fence and crashing through the bushes. We arrived back at the campsite just as *Kupendana* rose with a huge swell and slammed against the bank. Rushing into the water, we each held one end of the boat away from the shore until the waves subsided, then pulled Donna entirely out of the water. I was livid. How could anyone be so self-centered? So oblivious? "They're not even looking for other boats," I muttered. "And they probably don't even care what they're doing to the shoreline."

"They're not thinking about any of that," said Gene. "They're just having fun—really fast an' loud fun. I'm sure they didn't even see our boat." He was probably right, but it made me sad and angry at the same time. Immersed in the river ecosystem, appreciation of God's creation was now a part of our everyday existence. Reckless fun might not be illegal, but it seemed out of place.

Gene helped me set up the tent, then asked, "What would you like for dinner, love?"

"Hmmm, how about juicy steak and a baked potato?" I joked.

"I'll see what I can do."

I left him to his culinary challenge and retreated inside to ready the bedrolls. As I reemerged, Gene announced, "Supper's ready." He presented me with my orange plastic plate from our mess kit, filled with a base of instant mashed potatoes and a topping of chili. "It's as close as I could get," he explained. "There's beef in the chili."

I leaned over to give him a kiss. "You spoil me." We ate dinner to the banging bass of "Sexy and I Know It," watching the rock 'n' roll waterski party make several more passes.

The next day, the scenery changed to spectacular views of towering dolomite and limestone cliffs. South of Winona on the Minnesota side of the river, I easily spotted Great River Bluffs State Park. Two of the most prominent bluffs, named King's and Queen's Bluff, rose five hundred feet above the Mississippi to showcase sheer stone peaks. On the opposite side, round-topped limestone bluffs appeared in the distance like a roller coaster horizon, painted in hazy shades of forest green, azure, and violet. Gene pointed to the left. "There's Trempealeau Mountain, in Perrot State Park." A cone-shaped bluff rose into the sky, surrounded by water at its base. I read that the name of the mountain came from the French explorers, who called it "the mountain whose foot is bathed in water." I loved that derivation, even more after seeing it from the river. I wondered if knowing what it meant in French would help me spell *Trempealeau* correctly. There sure were lots of vowels.

We pulled into the Trempealeau Marina, just above Lock and Dam #6. This time the tent stayed in the boat. Our home for the night would be a modest place on a hill north of town called the Little Bluff Inn, an overnight stay last year during one of our river paddle practices. After dinner and local live music at Mrs. Sippy's Diner, we walked up the hill hand in hand to showers, a real mattress, and an air-conditioned evening.

Our last travel day to La Crosse started early Friday morning with a three-minute paddle to the lock. Gene called the lockmaster from the marina and we scooted around the concrete corner, right into the open doors of the enclosure. "Easiest lock entrance *ever*," I sang.

"This whole day should be pretty easy," said Gene. "We paddled this stretch last summer. I've been looking forward to doing it again."

"Except this time, we'll watch out for the wing dams," I reminded him. Wing dams were underwater rocks piled in lines extending from the shore. They helped to direct river water toward the channel while preventing shore erosion. Their location was marked on our river maps—at least in most cases. The previous summer, while taking a shortcut in a side slough, we found a wing dam that wasn't on the map. Unfortunately, we found it by grounding, scratching up the bottom of the boat in the process. I paged ahead on the map. Yep, there were the notations I made after the unmarked shallow rocks brought us to a grinding halt. STAY IN MAIN CHANNEL.

Seventeen scratchless miles and one more lock and dam later, we tied up at the Pettibone Boat Club on the south end of Barron Island. Once owned by Buffalo Bill Cody, the island was now the property of the La Crosse Park System. Besides the boat club, the island included a campground, picnic park, Frisbee golf course, and expansive sand beach.

Gene found the manager over at the gas dock. "We're traveling the river," he explained. "We have camping reservations starting Sunday, but we're two days early. Is there any chance we could tie the boat up here until then?"

The manager glanced at *Kupendana*. "That shouldn't be a problem," he said. He pointed to a narrow space between the shore and a dock that ran parallel to it. "You think you can pull it into the space over there? No one uses that side, so there'd be no charge."

I leaned over the edge of the dock to see the space. It was only about four feet wide, but plenty long. Donna could easily tuck in there. "Looks perfect," I said. "We really appreciate it."

We floated the boat around the end of the dock and pulled it into our private slip. Gene wrapped the lock cable around Donna and through the metal frame under the deck boards. With the boat secured, Gene called our friends, Terry and Donna, who had invited us to their farm for the weekend. Soon, Gene was back on the gas dock, chatting with a couple that motored in. Their two children explored the piers with long loping steps and swinging arms that seemed to celebrate their freedom from the confines of their boat. I know how they feel, I thought.

I felt an arm slip around my waist. "Can I buy you a drink, good-lookin'?"

I felt anything but good-looking, but loved the fact that my husband thought I was. We celebrated our long week's voyage from the Cities with drinks and a deluxe large pizza at a table across the room from the motorboat family.

Later, as Gene took out his wallet, the waitress surprised us. "Oh, there's no charge. Your bill was paid by the man over at that table." The table was empty. I glanced down at the gas dock in time to see the couple and their children board their boat.

We ran out of the clubhouse, toward the gas dock. "Thank you!" I shouted, waving. As the boat turned out of the marina, the man waved back. The generosity of river residents obviously wasn't exclusive to the North Country.

We spent the weekend doing nothing but visiting with good friends from our hometown church at Terry and Donna's farm—or rather, their thoroughly modern home built on Terry's family's farmstead. The farm was on the highest point of land in the area. I could see why they loved it and wanted to retire there. Situated as close to the sky as the land allowed, the view was spectacular. Remembering Linda's words about the importance of rest, we did just that, sightseeing in the area, meeting friends and family, and spending an evening out at a favorite restaurant in town.

On Sunday, Terry and Donna drove us back to Pettibone. I rode to the campground with Donna while Terry and Gene paddled across the small bay. "That was fun," Terry said, as he climbed out of the bow. He turned to his wife. "That boat handles *really* well."

Before *Kupendana*, I tried paddling plastic rental kayaks, often struggling to keep a straight line. But now, I realized I was spoiled. "I think people are unduly impressed when they hear what we're doing," I confessed. "Sometimes the wind and waves can make it difficult, but most days, it's a lot less work than people think."

"After all, it *is* all downstream," added Gene, with a wink in my direction.

We set up our tent, and gave them a quick peek into our riverside home. Then I listened to the gravel crunch under the wheels of Terry's van as it disappeared around the bend. We wandered over to the camp office, pleased to learn that there were plenty of bar tables and free Wi-Fi. We had some blogging to do.

July 22: Salvation Army, La Crosse, WI

Early Monday morning, we walked a mile across the bridge from Barron Island to the city of La Crosse, and then hoofed two more miles to the Salvation Army, arriving just before 9 a.m. This was a service chosen for us by the owner of Gene's company. Before we left for the trip, Gene wrote a letter, thanking Don for the generous leave of absence, and asking if he had any specific service requests in La Crosse, the location of company headquarters. Don's response was clear. "The Salvation Army."

We met with Jeff, the volunteer coordinator, and filled him in on the details of our trip. "We'd like to get an idea of the ways that people get assistance from the Salvation Army programs, and help out today in any way we can," I explained. "We'll write about our time here, and the services you provide. If you have any specific needs for donations and volunteers, we can include those."

Jeff leaned back in his chair. His orange and white plaid button-down shirt animated his diminutive stature, emphasizing his youthful appearance. I wasn't fooled, though. His was a big job, coordinating all the volunteers for the Salvation Army's many offerings. "We have programs here for clients with all kinds of needs," he began, "including a shelter, meal program, food pantry, and worship programs. We also provide social, health, and financial assistance. But I thought you might be interested in starting out this morning helping with a program called Feed the Kids."

"Sounds good to me," said Gene. "What do we do?"

"You'll be helping to make bag lunches for children from low-income families," Jeff explained. "At school, these kids get something to eat each day through the free and reduced lunch program. But during the summer—when they're not in school—we want to make sure they get something healthy too. So every weekday, all summer, volunteers make bag lunches and we deliver them to their homes."

"That's awesome! I'd love to help," I said. As a teacher, I couldn't imagine a more perfect assignment.

Several volunteers began to arrive. They all seemed to know each other, but looked at us questioningly. "Hi," I said. "I'm Barb, and this is Gene. We're helping out today, too. Where are you from?"

"We're all from St. Paul's Lutheran Church," replied an elderly man, with a firm handshake. "We make lunches every Monday. We sometimes have different people join us, but it's usually the same group."

It soon became obvious just how well this bunch worked together. Everyone took up their places around a huge table organized into piles of grapes, sandwich fixings, bags of chips, pudding cups, and water bottles, each with their own specialized job. Gene was stationed behind an aluminum bowl of plump purple grapes and assigned to cut them into small bunches. My job was spreading jelly on the top of sandwich buns. To my right, my partner spread peanut butter on the bottoms, and then plopped hers together with mine, zipping them into plastic bags. I wondered if we'd make some with just jelly, due to all the peanut allergies nowadays. Across the table, more volunteers snapped open brown paper bags, filled them with one of each item, folded the tops, and packed them in plastic bins.

In an hour and a half, we finished our goal of assembling two hundred seventy-seven bags. "We'll send out two vans," explained Frank, behind a pushcart piled high with bins. "With different routes around the city, we can get the lunches distributed faster. You two'll get to ride along with Linda."

Outside, Frank showed us to a black van and we helped him slide the bins in back. Two women approached. "Hi, I'm Linda," said the younger looking of the two. Her hair was pulled back in a ponytail and side bangs framed her face. The black frames of her glasses matched her short-sleeved blouse and onyx necklace. She shook my hand and then swept hers toward her friend. "And this is my partner, Jane." Jane was as colorful as Linda was classic. Her transition lenses appeared violet in the bright sunlight and matched her blue and purple snakeskin print shirt. "We've driven this route together every Monday, now, for ... ?" Linda looked at Jane, questioning.

"Going on three years now, I think," said her friend. "But it doesn't seem that long."

Linda drove the van slowly on its well-known daily route through neighborhoods and trailer parks, lightly tapping the horn to signal families of our presence. Children, sometimes with parents in tow, ran out to the van, eagerly awaiting the lunch bags handed out the window. Linda often talked to the children by name, asking about their parents and siblings. It was rewarding to see the big smiles, hear the shouts of thanks, and watch the children unfolding the sacks to peek at the contents—a gift from caring community members and businesses, perhaps their only food for the day.

By 12:30, we were back at the Community Center and ready for our next project. Jeff walked us down to the kitchen where we met Angel, a volunteer cook. "I started out helping in the kitchen here while I was recovering from an injury," Angel told us. "Now, I cook dinner for a hundred twenty hungry men, women, and children four times a week. It's so rewarding, I can't imagine ever stopping." The night's menu sounded delicious—roasted chicken, corn on the cob, and mashed potatoes.

The deli department of Festival Foods had donated thirty rotisserie chickens the night before, so Gene and I were given the task of quartering the birds. Donning hairnets, gloves, and aprons, we used butcher knives to cut them apart and placed them in huge baking pans. Once we finished, Angel slid the three large stainless trays of chicken into the oven.

I took off my gloves and hairnet, figuring we were done in the kitchen, but Angel wasn't ready to give us up yet. "I'm expecting more trays of daily donations to arrive soon," he said, "but there's a little problem." He opened the cooler door. Inside were piles of food trays, each marked with stickers. "The cooler needs to be sorted and organized to make room for the new food. I haven't had the time to go through it all. I sure could use your help." We checked the expiration dates, scooping expired food out of containers into a huge stainless steel sink. Tacos, meatloaf and gravy, dips, and vegetables coagulated together in a heap, gurgling down the disposal. I vowed never to let any food in my refrigerator expire—ever again.

We sorted the unexpired foods by type and date, stacking them neatly back in the cooler, leaving plenty of room for new donations. By the time we finished, the afternoon was nearly gone and the dinner guests were filing in. "I'm exhausted," I confessed. "And we still have a three-mile walk back to the campground."

"I know," said Gene. "But it's a good kind of tired. When I think of the Salvation Army, I think of a red kettle and a bell. It's a lot more than that, isn't it?" I agreed. I knew I'd long remember the smiles on the faces of children clutching lunch bags filled with love.

During the walk back through town, my cell phone rang. It was our next-door neighbors from Waukesha, Sarah and Manuel. "Manuel has a few days of vacation," said Sarah, in her familiar English accent. "We're at a hotel in La Crosse tonight. Where are you staying? We'd love to come visit you, if you have time." Hearing Sarah's voice put a spring back in my tired step. I gave her directions to our campground and made plans to meet them at the camp office. Later, Manuel bought a pizza and treated us to cocktails. While rain poured down outside, we caught up on back home neighborhood news.

July 23: Myrick-Hixon Eco Park, La Crosse, WI

Play. Learn. Repeat. The philosophy of our next service, the Myrick-Hixon Eco Park, resonated with me. Located in a beautiful outdoor forest and marsh setting, it was a place where children and families were encouraged to splash, climb, dig, and explore adventure playscapes while learning about the area's ecosystems. Gene and I found this treasure by accident while exploring La Crosse the previous summer. The park was still in its infancy, but a poster showed the vision for its future. Plans included a center for inside learning activities, outdoor adventure playscape areas focusing on water, forest, prairie, and farm ecosystems, a marsh touching pool, and nature trails. "I want to try to help out here on our way through La Crosse," I told Gene at the time.

The Eco Park was a half mile farther from our campground than the Salvation Army. Once again, we hiked from our campsite, arriving early in the morning to meet Jean, the executive director. I was eager to find out how much of the plan had been completed since we last visited.

"We've got the Eco Park Center up and running," Jean explained, pointing out the various areas within the modern building. I noticed colorful seating areas with stuffed animal classification activities, drawers of objects from nature, an artifact room, and several aquariums with live animals. In fact, there were so many interesting things around, it was hard to maintain eye contact and listen attentively to our host. Temptation was everywhere. I just wanted to explore and play. Jean led us outside as she continued on, either oblivious to my attention disorder or accustomed to the effect of such engaging activities. "These trails wind through the Hixon Forest and go around the marsh," she explained. "You can see lots of wildlife almost any time you go."

"Have you finished any of the outside play areas since last year?" I asked. "I'm especially interested in the Wild Water area. It looked like so much fun."

"That's operating now," confirmed Jean. "And the Forest Scramble area will be opening soon. We still need to get the safety check for the canopy walkways, tree houses, and netting. The other two areas are still under construction. The Prairie Mystery area will be a maze of tall grass prairie plants, and the Farm Play area will be a kid-sized farm." She pointed to a troll-sized stone cottage with a footbridge leading to a miniature stone pagoda. "That'll be the duck house. We saved it from the city zoo, which used to be right here on this property. The zoo was a special place to many people and they love that we saved a little piece of it to be used here."

We turned the corner to see a gardener, waist-deep in prairie plants, tying colored ribbons around bunches of stems. "This is Andrea, one of our volunteers. Tomorrow, we're having some Scouts come help us to weed the butterfly garden. She's marking the native prairie plants that we don't want them to pull." Andrea looked up and waved. Nearly every inch of her skin was covered, from her long pant cuffs tucked into her socks, to her floppy wide-rimmed hat that cast her face in shade.

"Don't come in here," Andrea called. "The stinging nettles are pretty scratchy. I'll come out in a few minutes."

"So what can we do for you today?" I asked, secretly hoping that we'd get to help maintain the Wild Water area or finish the Forest Scramble.

"What we really need is help weeding this entryway to the Center." Jean pointed to the front walkway, lined with a mix of plantings and overgrown weeds. "It's planted with native prairie plants, but the weeds have gotten out of control. Andrea can help you if you're not sure which plants are weeds."

"I recognize a lot of the weeds from our perennial gardens back home," I said, "but we'll be sure to ask if we don't know." I'd hate to find out too late that I pulled out a whole patch of rare prairie plants.

After she left, Gene shrugged. "I don't have a clue," he sighed.

"Then let's stick together," I said. "You want to take that side of the walkway? I'll start over here." Inch by inch, we dug, plucked, and tilled, leaving an orderly border in our wake. We learned in addition to being a prairie enthusiast, Andrea worked as a naturalist for Perrot State Park. She answered our questions about which plants not to pull, sprinkling in obscure botanical facts and classification trivia that would have impressed Alex Trebek.

As we worked, we watched families and groups from daycares and YMCA programs come to enjoy the activities. A senior citizen fitness class arrived to exercise in the classrooms area. Families passed us on the walkway, reading from check-off sheets for a wetland scavenger hunt. Inside during a drink break, I watched children eagerly examine artifacts, watch a video about peregrine falcons, and sort stuffed animals into boxes. A group of students sat on balcony chairs, reading books in the library overlooking the center. This place certainly got plenty of use.

Two hours later, we finally reached the end of the walkway. "I think I'm done," said Gene, removing his gloves to wipe his brow.

"Me, too," I agreed. "This is harder than paddling. My hand even hurts." I pulled off my gloves. In the middle of my right palm was a large popped blister. A torn flap of skin unsuccessfully covered the raw red patch where the end of the spade rubbed the glove against my skin. "Now I know why it's sore," I said, extending my arm.

"Ouch," said Gene. "No more work for you. I'll go return the tools and get you a Band-Aid." I agreed to rest the hand. In one more day, I'd need it to paddle again.

Gene bandaged me up with the tenderness of an RN and we said our good-byes to the staff. "Before we go, let's hang out in the Wild Water area for a bit," I suggested. Now that it was operational, I couldn't wait to watch.

The stream began with a fountain at the top of the hill that flowed with the mere press of a button. Water tumbled down the streambed between stony riverbanks. Children ran up and down the hill, balancing on the rocks at the edge of the stream, opening and closing dams to control the water flow.

Gene squatted next to one of the junior lockmasters. "How high do you think the water will get before it flows into that channel?" he asked, pointing to a pathway swerving around the dam. The young boy touched the metal door to indicate his guess. "I think you're probably right," Gene agreed. The water rose, and sure enough, before spilling over the top of the dam, it began to trickle to the side, around the bend, and into the dry streambed below.

My attention turned to two children laughing and following a foam flip-flop down the stream. The sandal boat stopped, lodged between two rocks. "The water's not fast enough to sail it over the rocks," said the older boy. "Let's try again." He retrieved the sandal and scurried—half bare-footed—back up to the dam.

The smaller boy followed close behind. "Let me try," he said.

"Okay, but I'll tell you when." The older boy gently floated the foam flip-flop behind the metal gate, then stepped on the rocks in the side channel, preventing the rising water from finding another route. I could see his mind working through the problem, and knew from his actions he was trying to build up the greatest possible force of water before releasing the sandal into the stream. This is why I love teaching, I thought. Nothing beat this excitement of discovery. "Not yet . . . not yet . . . NOW!" Just as the water reached the top of the door, his companion pulled it up. Water tumbled down the streambed, the sandal boat gliding along on top of the wave. The boys ran down to the rocks where their boat stalled the time before. The sole scraped on the rocks, but lurched over the top and down the hill.

Joyful shouts erupted. I clapped too, celebrating their achievement, while recognizing that I was still only a stranger to the boys. Somewhere, parents were probably watching. I hoped they saw the promise that I did in their young engineers.

We climbed to the top of the hill. A three-year-old, totally drenched, blond hair plastered to his head, danced around under the fountain, tongue extended to catch the spray. "Want a hug, Mom?" he called. Dripping and giggling, he chased his mother, until they collapsed together in a wet embrace.

Gene and I started our trek back to the campground. We both looked forward to catching up on errands the following day. River travelers called it a "zero day." Zero miles. We would spend the day doing laundry and blogging at the campground. Then we planned to check out the city bus routes, head out to company headquarters for the food box Eric sent, and visit the Sprint store to pick up a replacement for Gene's cell phone, which became soundless—and thereby useless—a week before.

We meandered along the beautiful, brick-paved river walk downtown and stopped for dinner at a café along the way. As we climbed the grated metal steps to the bridge, the rosy glow of evening began to color the sky. We stopped on top of the world, leaned on the railing, and admired the beauty of the moment. The river was peaceful and calm, gliding effortlessly onward toward the sea. A variety of pleasure crafts moved along in different directions, enjoying entertainment the river offered . . . fishing, tubing, cruising.

Gene nudged my arm. "Look." He pointed. "Kayaks."

We watched as two kayakers paddled near the shore of Pettibone Island. Their tiny yellow and blue vessels scooted along the surface, turning easily as they paddled into coves and around points of land.

"They look so small . . . like toothpicks in a bathtub," I said.

"A really looong bathtub," added Gene.

"It's funny. When we're down on the water, the river doesn't seem this big," I mused. "I suppose we see one tree at a time, one house at a time, one boat at a time, as we pass. But in the big picture, we're really pretty small." The enormity of our undertaking pressed in on me, squeezing the breath out of my lungs for just a moment. I took a deep breath, letting it out slowly as we started walking again, hand in hand. I liked the view from the water better. It was easier to be brave.

July 25–27: La Crosse to Ferryville, WI

After a restful and productive zero day, we boarded Donna from the shore by our campsite and shoved away, once again, from the familiar toward the unknown. It was exciting to arrive in each new place, meet people, and learn our way around. But it was also exciting to leave, to get back on the river, not knowing what awaited us in a new town downstream. This I did know—we were headed toward Ferryville, Wisconsin, a small riverside town, and would be there in only three days. I didn't even know where Ferryville was until a former member of our church emailed me the offer of a place to stay and connected us with a service opportunity at the Sugar Creek Bible Camp. Soon after that, we settled on a date and added it to our plans. "That'll be a perfect time to come," said Marilyn, upon hearing the date we chose. "It's a festival weekend in town. If you can get here in the morning on Saturday, I'll bring you to the tractor pull."

"I'd love it," I answered back. "I'll see how it goes, and call you when we get close." I put her cell number into my phone— Ferryville Marilyn. I had heard about tractor pulls, but didn't know people still had them. My hometown of Green Bay was near several small farming communities, but I had never attended a tractor pull. Heck, the closest I came to even driving a tractor was having a roommate once who grew up on a farm. This was going to be fun.

The first day back on the river started out sunny and pleasant, but we remained wary of the sky and clouds. Storms were predicted for mid-afternoon. The distance we could travel and the campground we would use depended on how long the storms held off.

We made good time. Between the threat of bad weather and the fact it was midweek, there were few boats on the river. I selfishly hoped that any bad weather would confine itself to the nighttime hours. We didn't plan any flex days on this super-short leg of the trip.

Paddling a short distance from the right bank, we approached the Root River confluence. Like all the streams and rivers that emptied into the Mississippi, this one would help fuel its push southward. As we paddled past the last point of land that separated the two rivers, I looked behind me to the right. A new and different stripe of water, lighter, almost greenish-brown in color, squeezed in between the sandy shore and our faster, darker, familiar Mississippi. Once again, the distinct line between two bodies of water mesmerized me—two colors flowing side by side. Eventually, the Big Muddy relented, allowing the waters of its lesser sibling to comingle, stripping the Root River of its former identity, finally integrated into the Mighty Mississippi. One color, one river—stronger than either was before.

The clouds soon began to darken and the few fishermen still on the river headed for cover. It was only about one o'clock, but the Wildcat Campground, just ahead, was as far as we would get. We pulled into the dock. A retreating angler greeted us. "I hope you're not going too far. They just issued a severe storm warning."

"I guess this is it for today, then," replied Gene. We claimed a campsite next to a shelter with picnic tables and electricity. Within minutes of setting up camp and sealing Donna's cockpit covers, the show began. From our picnic table under the shelter, we had a front row seat to watch the storm. Jagged bolts of light lit up the darkened sky, and raindrops pelted down on the surface of the river, dimpling the waves already churned up by the wind. Water splashed and puddled all around us. Safe and dry in the center of the shelter, we charged our phones with the outlets in the rafters and played a few hands of gin rummy, thankful to be off the water for the night.

More thunderstorms were predicted the following day. We set off in the morning with our eyes once again on the sky. "Let's keep near the shore," suggested Gene, "in case bad weather blows up."

Even the wildlife seemed on edge. A line of seagulls kept watch from a driftwood log, stripped and polished by the river, and brought to rest by an island of sand blocking its downstream journey. Geese—too many to count as we passed—patrolled another sandbar, their squawking sounds overlapping like damp fingers rubbing on dozens of inflated balloons, the cacophony fading in pitch and volume as we paddled past.

"Eagle, up ahead, on that stump," Gene whispered loudly enough for me to hear in the bow. Sure enough, a bald eagle perched atop a protruding tangle of roots. "Let's see how close we can drift," he said.

Noiselessly, I secured my paddle to the deck and picked up my camera. Gene steered us on a line toward the root stump, where the eagle paced, head down, more concerned with what was below the water than above it. "He's fishing," I said, unsure if Gene could hear, but not willing to raise my voice. As it raised its wings for balance, I focused my lens on its long feathered legs and strong claws, gripping the arching roots with curved, razor-sharp talons. We drifted nearer and my model, aware now of our presence, alternated over-the-shoulder glances and cocked-headed stares in our direction with its predatory quest. I snapped pose after pose of my silent subject. Even the soft click of my shutter seemed intrusive.

Finally, through my lens, I watched the eagle spread its wings and lift off. "There it goes," said Gene. The huge bird tucked its feet under its tail feathers, its enormous wings fully extended, as it skirted above the water in the opposite direction from ours. I was sorry we interrupted its fishing session, but glad our paths crossed.

When we stopped for a lunch break, the weather still looked threatening, but the next lock was on the Wisconsin side of the river. "We'll have to cross sooner or later," I said, trying to convince myself as much as Gene. The map showed the section of the river above Lock and Dam #8 to be three miles across. If a storm blew up when we were out in the middle, there was nothing we could do. I just hoped there wouldn't be lightning. Soon after starting the crossing, I noticed a huge, ominous cloud following us like a kite on a string. We paddled faster, but the dark gray mountain centered itself right above us and opened up. The downpour was brief, but effective. We paddled into Blackhawk Army Corps Park, wet and tired, but safe, and chose a campsite on a spit of land near the river.

"This wind's really whipping," Gene said, as we set up the tent. "Let's stake 'er down well." We used every tent stake in our arsenal. It was a good thing we did. The wind howled through the night, tugging at the fabric of our tent and shaking the walls well into the morning.

The meditative sounds of water gently rippling over rocks on the shore eased me into consciousness. I concentrated on the sound. It occurred to me that I didn't even hear the waves over the wild winds the night before. Then I heard soft clinks of metal, and the whoosh of our little gas stove. I rolled over and patted the spot where Gene should have been. Uh-oh, I thought. How long did I oversleep? I stumbled out of the tent door. Everything was soaked from the storm. But the sky was clear and the air smelled clean.

"Good morning, sweetie." Gene handed me a cup of hot cocoa. "What do you want for breakfast? We have . . ." He held up zip-lock bags, one at a time. "Oatmeal with strawberries, oatmeal with walnuts and brown sugar, orrrr . . ." He paused for dramatic effect, then held up a bag of what looked like brown sand. "CoCo Wheats!"

"The next time we do this," I began, wondering if we would ever do something like this again, "we really have to get more creative with breakfasts." I picked the bag with CoCo Wheats—at least it was chocolate—and helped make breakfast. I used to love oatmeal and looked forward to adding a variety of ingredients to change it up. But we had packed seven bags of oatmeal or CoCo Wheats in every food box for twenty weeks. I wasn't sure how many years it would be before I made either one again.

We planned a short paddle day into Ferryville in order to arrive by noon, meet up with Marilyn, and attend the River Bluff Daze Antique Tractor Pull. We just had one little obstacle . . . weedy Winneshiek Slough. In order to get to the landing, we needed to navigate through a long and winding maze of islands and channels along the Wisconsin side of the river. We used a combination of our river map, our I-map app, the direction of the grasses and reeds, and advice of some local fishermen to slowly pick our way. Eventually, the slough opened up to Winneshiek Lake. I spotted Ferryville in the distance. The path to the tiny waterfront town was a maze of massive weed beds. The long strands grabbed at our paddles, slowing our progress and wrapping around the rudder, hindering my efforts at steering.

"It looks clear over there." Gene pointed to a water path, the surface unbroken by stems of water plants, at least for a short distance. Paddling with shallow strokes and gliding when we could over the weed patches, we slowly made our way toward the shore.

We arrived at the landing about forty-five minutes late and pulled Donna onto the boat ramp and up the street. At the top of the marina lot was a set of railroad tracks—a common sight. Trains constantly chugged up and down the Mississippi Valley, transporting goods across the country. We saw and heard them frequently from the river during the day, and even from our tent at night. But this time, the crossbar lowered in front of us and the bell began to clang. Gene grabbed his phone camera to record the irony of the moment. Late, in a hurry, and on the street with our boat in tow, we were stopped for a train.

One hundred forty-six rail cars later, we walked Donna down Main Street. A friend of Marilyn's lent us the key to his garage, where we stored the kayak for the duration of our stay. Finally, we walked down to the fire station to find the tractor pull in full swing. Marilyn met us, having already finished her turn pulling a weighted sled down the lane until her tractor bucked up, refusing to pull another inch. "Sorry we missed you," I said. "We got held up by all the weeds."

"And stopped by a train," Gene added, pulling out his phone as proof.

We met some of Marilyn's friends and even ran into Donna and Terry from La Crosse. Together, we watched a variety of other antique tractors flexing their muscles in an attempt to out-perform each other with feats of power.

Marilyn took us home for a tasty homemade meal with several of her friends, and then back to town once more to enjoy the riverfront fireworks. We joined other revelers at an establishment claiming to be "One of the Three Best Bars in Ferryville." "There are ONLY three bars here," whispered Marilyn. We didn't stop at all three to check which was best, but managed to celebrate past our usual river bedtime.

July 28: Sugar Creek Bible Camp

On Sunday, Marilyn packed bag lunches, and after church, drove us to the Sugar Creek Bible Camp. Along the entrance road, I saw telltale signs of flooding. Sticks, grasses, and even entire tree limbs encircled the trunks of pines lining the road. From the height of the debris, I guessed the floodwaters reached about three feet up the trunks. "When you two were dealing with the Mississippi flood stages in June, Sugar Creek was pretty high up over its banks, too," Marilyn explained. I knew that flood cleanup was a chore for the small towns along the Mississippi, but never really thought much about the tributaries flooding, too.

Don, the executive director of the camp, greeted us and took us on a short tour of the 660-acre grounds. He explained that the camp simultaneously ran programs for different ages. Even with hundreds of campers on a given week, programs retained their small-group focus because they took place in separate areas designed for varying age levels. He pointed out platform tents in the Pathfinder Village for fifth graders, a sixth grade Covered Wagon Village, and even a frontier town, where seventh graders stayed in wooden cabins with facades resembling sets of western movies. High school campers took week-long excursions on Mississippi riverboats, paddled the river in twenty-six-foot Voyageur canoes, and pedaled bicycles on the Elroy-Sparta Trail.

We walked with Don to the entrance road; I didn't remember seeing the empty wagon and pitchforks there when we arrived. "If you don't mind, we could sure use help cleaning up debris from the June flood." He pointed to the piles of branches strewn about on the lawn. "We haven't been able to get to this area, due to it bein' so low." As we walked, my shoes occasionally sunk into still-spongy sod and were soon caked in mud. Deep ruts crisscrossed the sparse grass, indicating the failure of premature efforts at cleanup. "Just collect as much as you can and throw it right here in the wagon," he said. "We'll have someone dispose of it later."

Next, Don walked us past the storage shed to a small creek. It was hard to believe this little stream caused so much havoc. But the eroded sand banks bore witness to the height of its flood stage. Piles of new fresh sand stood nearby. "If you have any extra time, it'd be great it if you could spread this sand around the area by the creek to re-contour the banks. There are rakes in the storage shed. Help yourself to whatever you need." Thanking us again, he left to get his staff ready to welcome a new crop of campers for the week.

We found some gloves in the storage shed and set to work. With no way to move the wagon around the field, we started with the trees that were farthest away, planning to work our way back. I loaded my pitchfork with twigs and branches trip after trip, unwrapping the trunks of trees one by one. The larger limbs had to be dragged and heaved up over the sides of the wagon. Some of the heavier ones even took both of us working together. I was so busy making trips that I didn't notice when Gene slipped away. But I couldn't miss the smile on his face and the jingle of keys as he returned. "Look what I found!" he announced, holding up the keys to a nearby John Deere front-end loader like a prize ribbon he won at a fair.

"Do you think we should?" I asked, furtively looking back over my shoulder.

"Why not?" Gene shrugged. "Don said to help ourselves to whatever we need. The keys were right out in the open. And it sure will make the job easier." He climbed up behind the controls and started the engine—and he was off! Driving down to the far end of the field, Gene looked like the proverbial kid in a candy store. We loaded up the front end with debris, and he drove it back, lifting the bucket and dumping the contents into the wagon. I had to admit, it was considerably more efficient. After a few loads, he asked, "You want to learn how to drive?"

I looked at the ruts that he made in the soft dirt just by efficiently maneuvering the monstrous machinery. Steering a pallet dolly was one thing; this was a tank. I imagined what the ruts would look like after I got done lurching through the gears. "I think the ground's a little soft for newbies. Maybe another time."

When the scattered piles of brush finally transformed into a heaping wagon of debris, we eagerly stopped for a lunch break, then traded our pitchforks and keys for shovels and rakes. We took turns shoveling sand from the piles into the ruts eroded by the floodwater runoff and raking the bank smooth. "It's almost like spending the afternoon on a golf course," Gene joked. He feigned surprise. "Oh, no! In the sand trap again!"

I handed him my rake. "Here ya go, then. Gotta rake your own divots." Picking up the shovel, I threw more sand in front of his rake. I enjoyed the easygoing way we worked together. It seemed no matter what our chores, we kept a sense of humor that made everything tolerable, even fun.

Soon, we saw dramatic results from our efforts. The previously pitted and worn slopes transformed into smoothly contoured banks beside the clear, babbling brook.

As we put the final touches on our sandscape, families drove by, dropping off their campers at the registration area nearby. Youthful, friendly faces appeared everywhere, helping direct traffic, assisting nervous campers with luggage and anxious parents with registration. Laughter floated up from the field below the lodge, where games broke the ice and counselors waited for their young charges.

We cleaned our tools and stowed them in the shed. With an hour to spare, we walked to the lodge to mingle with the campers and staff while waiting for our ride. Soon, Don joined us. "The cleanup looks wonderful," he said. "Thank you for all your work." He held out two folded T-shirts. "I hope you can use a couple of shirts. I'd love to be able to give you more."

"We couldn't fit more in the boat, believe me," I said. I unfolded a shirt. The name of the camp was on the front. I read the slogan on the back. Live the Story. "Thanks—this is perfect."

Don lit up. "The story of Jesus is a timeless one, isn't it? It's as true now as it was two thousand years ago. Here, kids learn that God's Word gives direction to our lives, and the Holy Spirit empowers us to live abundantly in faith."

I didn't have Don's eloquence, but I could relate to his awe of Christ's love and grace. "I would have liked to come here when I was growing up," I said.

"We don't just have programs for kids," Don answered. "Lots of church groups come here for retreats. We also have family camps and even camps for special groups, like crafters."

"I'll remember that," I said. "It would be nice to come back someday."

On the way home, from the back seat of Marilyn's truck, I glanced at the banks of Sugar Creek and the rows of pine trees lined up in the field by the entrance road. Everything looked tidy. Satisfied, I leaned back and closed my eyes, listening to Gene talking with Marilyn in the front seat. Tomorrow, we'd be paddling again, but tonight would bring a much-needed shower and a good night's sleep.

July 29–Aug. 1: Ferryville, WI to Dubuque, IA

The trip from Ferryville to Dubuque turned out to be an easy four-day paddle in idyllic weather conditions. For the most part, we were out of the sloughs and back in the big river again. The current was a welcomed old friend. We paddled just inside the channel, next to either the green or red buoys. When the line of channel buoys swerved close to shore, leaving us little space to maneuver, we paddled to the other side. It was the beginning of the week, so we had little boat traffic, other than an occasional fishing boat looking for another prospective hot spot.

Sand beaches and islands offered plentiful rest stops and camps. Near the end of the first afternoon, Gene pointed out an island shore. "How about that for a camp tonight? It looks like there's some sand high up over there."

Paddling past the north end, I scanned the island, dense with foliage. A few dead and leafless trees towered like sentinels near the tip of the island. The shore was a mix of sand and gnarly roots exposed by erosion, but the golden, sandy plateau in the center looked like a perfect spot to throw up a tent. "Looks great to me," I agreed, and swerved over to the bank.

We pulled Donna as far up as possible onto the narrow shore, and tied it to the clumps of exposed roots. Gene scrambled up the fifteen-foot sand dune to scout the campground at the top. Soon, his head peeked over the sand cliff. "It'll be perfect," he called. I climbed partway up the hill to hand him our tent bag and mattresses, and then hung our electronics bag around my neck, grabbing hold of shrubs and exposed roots to help pull myself up. It was a perfect site. There was a flat, sandy area for the tent, a fire ring, and a picnic table. But the best thing was the view. High above the river, we could see for miles in both directions.

I gazed through the canopy of leaves at the still blue early evening sky. Something gazed back. "Hey, look up there," I whispered to Gene. Above us perched a juvenile bald eagle. It had no white head or tail, just some mottled brown and white feathers. It appeared mostly brown, and, were it not for our eagle lecture in Wabasha, I would have mistaken it for a golden eagle quite easily. The junior eagle stayed to watch us while we set up the tent, started a fire, and even made dinner.

"I wonder if its parents have a nest around here. Maybe after dinner, we can try to find it," Gene suggested.

Scouting the island sounded like adventure to me. "I saw some dead trees at the north end of the island," I said. "Let's head up that way."

After dinner, we found a path that led from the shore into the center of the island. Off to the left, I noticed a small clearing with all the requirements for my bathroom—bushes for privacy, clear spaces to walk without worrying about poison ivy, and distance from our campsite. We continued past my commode and turned north. Here, we found no path at all. Gene forged his way through the thickets and held aside the branches so I could follow, but we made slow time. I wasn't worried about getting lost—it was an island, after all—but I did worry about what we might be walking through.

Gene must have been thinking the same thing. "I don't think we should go too far without any trail," he said. "We don't know what's in here." We retreated, putting safety before adventure this time around.

As we paddled along the Iowa shore the next morning, my mind wandered back to another hometown friend, Kathy, whom I met when her children were in my class years before. Upon hearing that I was planning a Mississippi River trip, Kathy called. "I love the Mississippi," she told me. "I was raised there, and I met Dave during a canoe trip on the river. We even spent our honeymoon on a steamboat." Kathy gave me contact information for her Iowa relatives. "Any of them would love to help you out with a place to stay if they can," she said. Her father planned to be in Florida when we passed through, but offered us the use of his cabin in Guttenberg for an overnight stay.

Burnell's cabin was easy to find, at mile marker 617, along Abel Island. We let ourselves in, pulled the boat in his garage for the night, and called to let him know that we arrived safely. "Glad you found it," he said. "I'm happy to help." It was a treat to stay inside his cozy cabin, watch the eagles soar over the water from the huge picture window, and see the barge traffic from a different perspective. After dinner, I heard the distinctive low rumble of an approaching barge. I rushed to the window to watch it pass, fascinated as its sweeping floodlights pierced the darkness, searching for familiar reflectors that served as landmarks for the twists and turns of the river at night.

Our last night was at Finley's Landing Park, in Sherrill, Iowa. We settled on a small, easily accessible campsite, and enjoyed some afternoon sun on a strip of sandy riverside beach.

We paddled into the American Yacht Harbor in Dubuque the following afternoon. Prepared to pay a slip fee for Donna's safe storage while we did service in town, we were surprised to hear there was no charge for kayaks. The attendant even gave us a weekend pass to the yacht harbor pool and laundry. No time to swim yet, though. First, we needed to call Pastor Jay, our contact from St. John's Lutheran Church.

"My wife and I would love you to stay in our home tonight," he offered. "She's in town today, and can come pick you up." We agreed on a time, covered and locked Donna, and waited amidst our heap of colorful bags on the front lawn.

Soon, a woman parked, exited her car, and approached us. "You must be Barb and Gene. I'm Barbra. How was your trip?" Barbra was petite, but her personality was extra large. Her blonde hair was tied back in a ponytail like mine, but with bangs. She wore tortoiseshell glasses, with large, nearly circular lenses. Her smile was wide and easy.

We traveled north, watching the hills of Iowa pass by our windows, and occasionally catching a glimpse of the river. We passed a sign that read "Finley's Landing Park." "Hey." I pointed. "That's the campground where we stayed last night."

"That's really funny," said Gene. In the front seat, he turned from the scenery to face Barbra as she drove. "We paddle all day to get from this park to Dubuque, and then take a half hour car ride to come right back here and stay at your house." It did seem weird. Being on the river for two months had changed my frame of reference for time and distance. Going everywhere by car, twenty-five miles seemed like no distance at all. In a kayak, it took most of the day.

We pulled up to a beautiful old farmhouse on the top of a hill. Like Terry and Donna's farm, I could see no higher ground anywhere around. The panorama was gorgeous in all directions. Jay walked out of the house to join us. "Welcome," he said, extending his hand first to Gene, then to me. His handshake was firm and warm. Pastor Jay towered over me, and even had a few inches on Gene. He must have gotten home from work recently— still dressed all in black, but his white cleric's collar removed and shirt unbuttoned at the top. His shaven head and trimmed beard made it hard to judge his age. His mustache and beard were partly gray, but I figured we had him by a few years.

Jay and Barbra showed us around the yard. "We bought this house because of the land," Jay confessed. "We love it here. Our field of view is so wide, we can enjoy both the sunrise and the sunset from the same spot in our yard." We walked up the front steps into the kitchen. It no longer looked like an old farmhouse. The interior was a mix of old and new—huge spaces, high ceilings, and expansive windows. My eyes immediately rose to the copper ceiling panels, which gave the room an exotic air. "We've spent years remodeling much of the house," Jay explained. "We've almost got it like we want it."

"You've still got a few things that aren't finished," Barbra reminded him.

"Just like all of us." I smiled at Gene. Back at home, we were still working on replacing some carpet in the basement and needed to refinish a bathroom. But what did we do instead? Head off down the river in a kayak. "Everything in its time, right?"

Barbra and Jay immediately made us feel at home, treating us to a delicious steak dinner, plenty of conversation, and a wonderful night's rest. I was eager to see the church in the morning, and learn more about the work St. John's was doing to provide shelter and clothing to those in need.

Aug. 2–3: The Open Closet, Dubuque, IA

Early Friday morning, Pastor Jay took us to his church in downtown Dubuque and introduced us to Amanda, the executive director of the Guest House and The Open Closet, two of the community outreach programs facilitated by and housed in the church. Amanda wore a simple black, V-neck tee tucked into her jeans, her dark brown hair pulled back in a ponytail. She was younger than I expected, perhaps in her late twenties, but demonstrated wisdom and empathy that couldn't be measured in years.

Downstairs at the Guest House, we found a cheerfully painted twelve-bed section used as an overflow shelter for men from October through May. The beds were all covered with beautiful quilts made by crafters from another area church. "The men take their quilts with them when they leave the shelter," Amanda explained. "That way, they have something warm that was handmade especially for them." She shared with us plans to expand the mission of the Guest House to include areas for men with children, as well as transitional housing for families. "We have an extra room upstairs that we're currently using for storage," she said. "We're looking for someone with some carpentry skills to build suites that would give family groups nicer, private bedroom areas . . . like they would have at home."

"That sounds like what we saw at Grace House in Grand Rapids, Minnesota," I shared. I took out my phone and showed Amanda a photo of one of the homey bedroom areas there. "You might want to call and talk to Sherry. I can give you her number. Since she's doing what you want to try, it might be a good way to get some ideas."

Next, Amanda took us downstairs to the basement. "This is our Open Closet," she said, "where you'll be helping out today and tomorrow." Gently used clothing was organized by type and size on shelves around the room. More hung from racks filling the space in the center. Another volunteer was already at work, stocking some of the newer donations. I introduced myself, and found out that her name was Barb, too.

"Tomorrow morning, over a hundred customers will come in for free clothing," Amanda continued. "Our goal is to make their visit as much like a shopping experience as we can. Just because they can't afford to pay retail prices for clothes doesn't mean that they can't have a fun day of shopping. So today, we'll make sure the store is organized and attractive and then tomorrow, we'll assist them with finding items and sizes and help them through the process. At checkout, we count the items for our records; we just don't take any money."

I looked around with new eyes and noticed attempts to make the church basement look welcoming. The walls were clean and looked recently painted. Clothes were placed in different areas around the space and in small side rooms, which lent a department store feeling. Some updated display racks would help, I thought. And some oversized, colorful posters to brighten up the space. But I was sure they had no Macy's budget. "Where would you like us to start?" I asked.

Amanda led the way to the racks of women's clothing and asked us to make sure that the pants and jackets were labeled and organized by size. "Customers come looking for specific sizes for themselves and members of their families, so we make them as easy to find as possible," she explained. Once again, she had the customers in mind.

From opposite sides of the racks, Gene and I checked sizes and moved errant hangers to their proper locations. Just as I finished the last of five rows, Amanda appeared. "That looks great," she said. "I think we're ready for the fun part!" Barb laughed at what I assumed was an inside joke. Gene and I exchanged puzzled glances. Amanda continued, "We put together sample outfits to hang on the ends of the racks. Find some cute things, hang them together, and accessorize them as much as you can. We don't have mannequins, but coordinated outfits dress up the place and give our customers some new fashion ideas, too."

Oh, no. Accessorizing might seem like fashionista fun to others, but was a foreign language to me. My friend Karen would love this. She was more than my friend; she was my personal fashion consultant, and did her best to steer me away from T-shirts, elastic pants, and fleece. But she wasn't due until tomorrow, a day late for this emergency. I put on a brave face and assembled a toddler's pink and purple outfit with a flouncy ruffled top over some size 3T yoga pants. Cute enough with no accessories, I decided. Gene did better—and seemed to enjoy it, too—putting together a classic women's outfit, with slacks, a blouse, jacket, and matching scarf.

By noon, the store looked inviting enough for what we hoped would be a large group the next morning. "Let's catch some lunch and check out downtown," suggested Gene.

We heard from several friends along the river that a "can't miss" place in the city was the Mississippi River History Museum, so we headed there first. Videos, artifacts, and interactive displays chronicled the history of steamboats on the famed river. I found myself especially fascinated by the historic photos and Mark Twain quotes.

I found a display with interactive satellite imagery of the Mississippi. I rolled my hand over the trackball control to retrace the path we took from Lake Itasca and then continued to view the remainder of the Mississippi. Below St. Louis, barge docks and industry were commonplace. "Come look at this," I called to Gene. Together, from a bird's-eye view, we explored the river ahead. We hovered over barges, barge docks, and foundries, but found few marinas, campgrounds, or small towns.

"This gizmo doesn't make the rest of the river seem very inviting," Gene said, his voice edged with disappointment. "I don't see much kayak support south of Cairo."

I agreed. "Looks like the warnings we're getting are spot on."

Gene's phone rang. After a short conversation, he filled me in. "That was a reporter from the Dubuque newspaper," he said. "She wondered if she could do an interview this afternoon. I told her we'd meet her in the museum cafe in about half an hour."

We ordered sandwiches for lunch and soon, the reporter arrived. She asked about places we served and what our days were like on the river. "You know," she admitted, "I normally don't do stories anymore about people who paddle the river. Someone's doing it all the time for the challenge and sometimes trying to earn money for one charity or another, but the story's always the same. I must admit, it's made me a little cynical." She paused for a moment and then continued, "But your trip is different. You're not asking for anything. You're working your way down the river, and your motivation is to help people along the way. That's different … that's a story."

"Thank you," said Gene. "A lot of people are interested in what we're doing. But we're not the real story. We just breeze in, help for a day or so, and then we're on our way. I suppose the way we help most is by writing about what these organizations do and putting links to their websites on our blog. The real heroes are the people we meet who volunteer to help others day after day."

"Where did you get the idea to do a trip like this?" the reporter asked.

"Actually," I began, "it was all God's idea." As I explained about getting a call in church to put service with our trip, I realized God was changing me, like Pastor Andy said he might. The old me would have worried about being too forward by saying something like that—especially to a reporter. Pushy people irritated me and I didn't want to be one. But God was growing my trust and giving me a new boldness. I was no longer wary of sharing my faith experiences with others—not to try to change them or to impress them, but to share the wonderful things God was doing. I saw some of the same changes in Gene. I was glad we were a part of this, together.

As the interview died down, the reporter gathered her notebook and electronics. Gene shook her hand. "We're happy to be a part of your story," he said, "but we'd like you to make it mostly about The Open Closet and the work that they're doing."

She assured us that she had done stories about The Open Closet and would make sure that it was a focus of this one as well. "Thanks so much for what you're doing," she said. "You've renewed my faith in people."

I took her hand in mine. "We've found people caring for others everywhere we've stopped. Believe me—there's a lot of good being done."

Saturday morning, we congregated with the other Open Closet volunteers at St. John's to get last-minute instructions. I greeted Amanda, Barb, and Jay, from the previous day, and introduced myself to volunteers I didn't know. The mouth-watering smell of fresh multigrain bread donated by an area bakery made me wish I'd eaten breakfast. Maybe I'd have some later if there were leftovers.

My friend Karen arrived, dropping several bulging bags to give me a hug. "I'm so excited to help you today," she said. "I feel like I have a little part in your trip."

"I'm glad you're here, too. What's all this?" I asked, helping her with the bags.

"I went through my closets," she said. "I have so many things that I don't wear, someone should be able to use them."

Shortly before the doors opened, Amanda addressed the volunteers. "Thank you all for helping." She smiled. "Have fun today. Let's serve with joyful hearts." She opened the doors and clients filled the lobby. Pastor Jay welcomed them and said a prayer. Then we all proceeded downstairs to the shop.

Our duties primarily included attentive assistance to the customers: helping them locate sizes, colors, and accessories and folding and bagging their selections. After dropping off her donations in the back room, Karen joined us on the sales floor, obviously in her element as a congenial personal shopper and style consultant. When Gene wasn't with customers, he busied himself keeping the displays tidy despite the clearance sale atmosphere.

I noticed a woman looking through a rack of blouses while other treasures cascaded over her arms. "May I help you?" I asked, holding a bag open for her to lessen her load.

"Thank you so much. You know, I used to bring my clothing here to donate," she confided. "I never guessed that I would lose everything and have to come here myself."

"It's my pleasure," I told her. "I'm sure that once you're back on your feet, you'll be helping again."

The sadness left her eyes for a moment and she broke out into a wide smile. "You bet I will!"

The next two hours seemed to fly by as a constant stream of customers came through, looking for clothing to fit their families' needs. The atmosphere was electric. After the customers left, we straightened up and Amanda gathered us together one last time. "Good job, everyone. We served one hundred twenty-eight customers today. Several of them mentioned to me how nice it felt to know someone cares." That didn't surprise me. The folks at St. John's offered help with compassion, dignity, and joy. It was a pleasure to serve alongside them.

Chapter 8
Poison Ivy

Aug. 4–11: Dubuque to Muscatine, IA

ON SUNDAY MORNING, Karen accompanied us to St. John's Church to worship. We always liked to attend services with new friends when we weren't on the water, and this time, two of our new friends were the pastor and his wife!

After lunch with Karen at Catfish Charlie's, we carried our bags down to the dock. Gene lay down across the boards, stretching his arms out full length to pack our clothes into the bow of the kayak. Sitting back up, he paused to roll down his sock. "Boy, this itches," he said, rubbing a cluster of tiny red bumps just above his ankle. "I think I got some spider bites."

Karen bent down to look. "I hate to tell you this," she said, "but I don't think they're spider bites. That looks like poison ivy to me."

"It can't be," said Gene. "I've walked through fields of poison ivy and never had one reaction." He scratched his ankle again. "But I'll keep an eye on it."

"We did walk through a lot of brush back on that island," I reminded him. I hoped it wasn't poison ivy. My older brother got that when we were kids. I could still remember his misery and picture both his skinny legs covered in dried pink calamine lotion.

I climbed into the cockpit, waved good-bye to Karen, and began my "coffee stroke," a gentle, take-it-easy, warm-up stroke I used early in the day. It wasn't a real paddler's stroke; the nickname came to me up in the headwaters, as I warmed up my arms while dreaming of a steaming cup of Starbucks skinny mocha.

Our trip to Muscatine had everything in the way of weather, from thunderstorms waited out in the tent, to fog and cool drizzle, to hot and sunny days. We had some wind, a few waves, and some beautiful, calm moments when the Mississippi reflected all the dazzling colors of its surroundings.

At our first overnight stay, Massey Campground, I hopped over and around puddles in the low-lying areas. It must have rained hard before we arrived. We set up our tent on the highest ground we could find and Gene started supper.

A truck pulled into the parking lot and came to a stop. Two single kayaks hung out of the open tailgate. A middle-aged, but athletic, spectacled man stepped out, walked around the truck, and tentatively approached. "Are you the kayakers we read about in the paper?"

"Maybe," I said. "Was the article about The Open Closet at St. John's? We did an interview with a reporter from the Dubuque paper."

"That was the one. It was a great article." He came closer. "My name's Dave and this is my wife, Constancia." A woman padded over in flip-flops. Her tanned arms and legs dangled out from under a colorful shift, wet in spots from her suit underneath. Her damp hair was pulled up on her head, errant strands hanging down to her neck.

"You can call me Connie," she said. "It's such a pleasure to meet y'all. I'd love to do what y'all are doing!"

Dave explained, "I used to get out on the water for some alone time, every once in a while. But then I made the mistake of bringing Connie with me. Now she always wants to come along, and when I'm done, I can't get her off the water."

"I just love it so much," she drawled. Her southern accent was striking—it felt out of place in Iowa, but because of that, it seemed exotic. "It's sooo beautiful." She stretched out the vowel sound, making her enthusiasm even more evident.

"You should paddle with us for a day," I suggested. "We'd love to have you join us."

"Really?" she asked. "I'd love to do that." She thought for a moment. "I work on Monday, but I get off at noon on Tuesday, and could kayak with you for the afternoon. How would that work?"

"That'd be awesome!" Connie and I exchanged cell phone numbers, and I promised to text her our location on Monday night, along with our Tuesday travel plans.

"We'd love to hear more about more about your trip," said Dave. "Can you join us for supper at the marina?"

"Ours is already in the oven," said Gene, pointing to our pot and burner. "But we'll come over after and join you for a drink." After dinner, we found our new friends seated at a deck table with half-empty glasses of beer. Gene ordered brown ale, along with a slice of cherry pie. I stuck with my summery gin and tonic. A few remnant clouds hovered at the horizon and the golden reflection of the evening sky shimmered off the water. Our conversation twisted and turned like the river, from our families to stories of how we met and our travel adventures. Even after a whole day on the water, Connie's passion for all of nature didn't wane. I couldn't wait to spend more time with her.

Monday, we got several messages from Connie. "I'm so excited to paddle with you tomorrow!" Then, "Where will you camp tonight?" And, "What should I bring?" I read them to Gene as they came in. The last one surprised both of us: "I told my boss about my plans to join you and he gave me the whole day off!" Monday evening, I called her, gave her our campsite location and made plans to meet the next day.

I awoke Tuesday morning to a quiet rustling outside the tent. When I peeked outside, Connie was already seated at the picnic table, drinking coffee, yarn and crochet hook in hand. I dressed quickly and crawled out to greet her. "You don't need to get up on my account," she said. "I brought my project in case you were sleeping when I arrived. D'ya want to see?" She showed me the hexagonal flower patch that she was finishing. "As I finish a row, I add it to the quilt at home," she explained. "That way, I can work on it any time and anywhere."

"You're gonna bring all that in your kayak?" I asked. I glanced at her cute little plastic boat. It was half the size of ours, with a small storage hatch in the back. Her seat and footrests were molded plastic, recessed into the deck. With no cockpit, it was ideal for suntanning, but I couldn't imagine where she might fit anything extra.

"Oh, there's lots of room. I also brought snacks, my camera"— she held up a huge SLR with a long zoom lens—"and coffee to share. Do you want some?"

"Boy, do I!" I grabbed a cup from our mess kit and Connie filled it from her pump pot. The chilly air, fog, and drizzle didn't diminish this woman's bubbly personality one bit. She wore a swimsuit under her flowing tie-dye cover-up. The natural gray accents in her long, brown hair hinted more at her real age than did her bouncy attitude, sparkling eyes, and Cheshire cat grin.

"How far are we going today?" she asked.

"We hope to make it to the campground at South Sabula Park," I said. "It's about eighteen miles."

"I think my record's about ten, but I've never been ready to stop yet! Dave said he could pick me up after work anywhere I want, but I think I'd like to try to make it the whole way."

We set off early. A thick layer of morning fog lingered over the water's surface, refusing to leave before the sun forced its hand. I heard an approaching motor and scanned the river in the direction of its sound. A small fishing boat appeared, putted past, and disappeared into the haze, leaving a V-shaped trail that soon disappeared. "Let's stay near the shore until the fog burns off," said Gene. "We're pretty near invisible to the other boaters right now." Gene was right. Even with two kayaks, we made very little noise and little wake. If we heard a boat coming, we could use evasive maneuvers, but there was no way they'd know where we were.

"Gooood idea!" Connie yodeled. The pitch of her voice lowered, and then rose again, as if her first word was made out of rubber, stretching out and bouncing back. I smiled at the energy she put into just two words.

Connie was alone in her kayak, so Gene and I took turns paddling most of the time. When we both paddled, we used coffee strokes to stay with Connie. Periods of quiet reflection alternated with lively conversation. "I'm originally from Kentucky," Connie told us, "but I've been *all* over. I met Dave in Wichita and we got married in Tampa. He was in the Air Force, so we lived in Germany for a while, where we had our two kids. Now that he's out of the military, we've settled down here in Dubuque, his hometown."

"Do you miss all the travel?" I asked.

"No, I love bein' near family. An' I can get all the adventure I need right here," she said. "The river's always got surprises for us, every time we get out here." She scanned the shore. I saw the shapes beginning to emerge from the haze. She looked back our way. "But y'all know that already."

Soon the fog lifted and the heat settled in. "Now *this* is the way I like it," said Connie as she lifted her cover-up over her head and tucked it away into the storage hatch. I followed her lead, taking off my long-sleeved top layer, and Gene stripped to the waist.

I watched the numbers on the mile markers as they passed. The Upper Mississippi started at mile zero in Cairo, Illinois, and ended in Itasca at 1340. Our eight-hundredth mile of the trip was rapidly approaching. "When we get to marker 540, can you help us document our eight-hundredth mile?" I asked Connie.

"I'd love to," she replied. As we neared mile marker 540, we eased over toward the bank and posed for a picture by the green striped marker. Connie took several pictures of us with her fancy camera, and I took one of her with my phone. After paddle high fives all around, I posted on Facebook.

"Know what we should do?" I asked. "Let's post pictures of mile markers for the next couple weeks, and do a countdown to a thousand miles." All the markers were either red or green to show the edge of the channel. But some were built up on the bank, others were on piles of rocks, and still others stuck out like tiny islands in the middle of the river. A photo countdown might help the miles move along faster—or, at least, feel like it.

Several times during the day, without warning, Connie exclaimed, "Look! Over there—critters!" She veered away, quickly at first, then stealthily, her camera around her neck. Setting down her paddle, she clicked away, shot after shot, until the animals flew or splashed away. Seemingly undaunted by their rejection, her shutter continued, documenting their departure. Then Connie paddled back over to us, her face beaming.

"Did you see that?" she always asked. "That was SOOO cool!" Her voice lilted with the accent of a displaced southerner.

By now, bald eagles were commonplace. Their beauty and strength still filled me with awe, and I quietly watched their every move. But Connie reacted to each individual animal like she was seeing one for the very first time, with a childlike wonder and excitement. Connie fanned a flame in me; she had a free spirit that I wanted to feel. I decided to follow her example, embracing the day as much as the destination.

As we rounded one bend, I had a chance to do just that. A sandbar extended out into the river, and I spied a flock of pelicans standing near the water's edge. "Let's see how close we can get," I suggested. Gene steered over toward the shore and I stopped paddling as we drifted closer. Focusing my camera, I snapped away. The pelicans waddled along the beach—their thick bodies matched incongruously with long, graceful necks. Pterodactyl heads on goose bodies. But when they unfolded their wings, raising them into the air in an uncoordinated dance, I noticed the delicate black edges along the back of their wing feathers. Wings tucked in again, I realized why I never noticed before. The black formed a faint line, barely perceptible, along the bottom of the pelican's heart-shaped back. As we drifted near, the flock evidently decided we were close enough. Running and flapping, they entered the water. Their legs slapped the surface as their powerful wings attempted to lift their cumbersome bodies into the air. A few seconds later, they completed their transition to graceful flight.

Connie caught up to us and pulled alongside. "I got some good pictures of the pelicans, and some of you taking pictures of them," she said.

"Thanks," I said. "That was awesome!"

It was mid-afternoon when we picked our way through a harbor filled with water lilies. Their pale yellow flowers urged us to stop in the middle of the maze, pausing for one photo after another, finally ending at South Sabula Lakes Park. Connie called Dave while we set up camp. She and I uploaded our pictures on each other's devices. Then we went for a walk down by the water. We watched snow-white egrets wading among the reeds. As we approached, they took flight.

"Thanks for inviting me to come along with you," she said. "I had such a good time." She gave me a hug. "Y'all *rock*!"

"You're welcome," I said. "But your coming along was really a gift to me." I explained, "I realized that I've been thinking about our goal for each day, but you focus more on the small moments and really enjoy them as they happen. I'm gonna to try to learn from you and do that more often."

Dave rolled up in his truck. He greeted Connie and listened to the highlights of her day. Then he turned to us. "Can we take you out for dinner before we leave?" he asked.

"We'd love that," Gene said. "Do you think we could stop for a few supplies, too? I'm having some trouble with my ankle. It may be poison ivy." He rolled down his sock. The tiny red dots were now pus-filled blisters. "I'd like to pick up some calamine lotion and Fels-Naptha soap—maybe more gauze bandage, too." We had a few in our first aid kit, but they wouldn't last long.

Later, bellies filled with pizza, and Gene's ankle dabbed and wrapped, we found ourselves alone again. I studied Gene's gauze-covered ankle. "We need to try to keep that dry," I said.

"Like *that's* gonna happen," he replied. "We get wet every time we get in and out of the boat."

I pulled a gallon zip-lock bag from our mess kit. "We'll try to do dry entries when we can, but if you do step in the water, wear this over your shoe. I'll wade in the deep part, but you stay shallow enough to keep your foot dry. Got it?"

"Yes, ma'am."

The following day, determined to avoid rushing to our destination. I suggested, "Let's sail for a bit." After our first sailing debacle in the headwaters, we learned to only bring it out in perfect conditions, and gained confidence controlling the sheets. With a moderate tailwind, we sailed along for a few miles on a wide straightaway. I gently guided the sheets to keep the sail full, and watched for boat traffic through the clear window in the center of the sail. Gene kept the boat in line with the channel buoys and used his phone app to measure our speed. The hull speed was consistently between four and six miles per hour without paddling at all.

"Now this is the life!" said Gene. Over my shoulder, I could see his outstretched arms and could feel the boat jiggle as he adjusted himself into a comfortable reclining position.

Pulling into the Rock Creek Marina and Campground, we set up the tent and then, as was our habit, went for a walk to explore. The trail led to a huge contemporary brick building. A sign read "Mississippi River Eco Tourism Center." A wraparound concrete ramp led up to double glass doors painted with the store hours. Wow . . . an unexpected pleasure that wasn't on our map! Gene smiled at me, a familiar gleam in his eyes. "You know what this means, don't you?"

"Ice cream?" I guessed. Two Choco Tacos later, we explored the center. We watched native catfish, bass, perch, and northern pike glide silently by the panes of an eight-thousand-gallon aquarium, and looked up at the collection of Iowa's record fish replicas displayed on the wall. In the Nature Room, we watched an artist add three-dimensional details to forest murals on the walls. Trunks and limbs of trees protruded out into the room from walls painted with foliage in most every shade of green. Birds and forest animals perched on leafy branches. I glanced up to see the hull of a boat attached to the ceiling. It appeared as if I were viewing the boat from below the surface of the river. "This is amazing!" I commented to the artist.

"Thank you," the young man said as he wiped his paint-streaked hands on his denim overalls. "The walls are almost finished, but I'm really stoked about our next project." Descending the ladder, he pointed to a plexiglass archway in the center of the room. "This'll be a turtle tank. You'll be able to view the turtle habitat from the top, and the kids'll even be able to crawl underneath the archway to view the turtles from below."

"What a great idea," I said. "I hope I get back someday to see the finished exhibit."

Back at the campsite, Gene unwound the gauze bandage from his ankle and gingerly touched his watery reddened flesh. The blisters were oozing and the rash spread around his ankle, with new spots moving up his leg. I sat down next to him, resting a hand gently on his shoulder. "It's time to see a doctor," I said. "We have a flex day before Muscatine. The Quad Cities are just ahead. Let's take a day to get you to a clinic."

Thursday, we approached Lock and Dam #14. I kept watch for the Highway 80 bridge and a rock pile along the western shore that marked the channel to the alternate lock for recreational traffic. At most locks, commercial and recreational traffic shared the facility, the right-of-way being given to barges, but both using the same enclosure. Here, at Le Claire Channel, recreational boats were encouraged to use a smaller, auxiliary lock on a side channel.

As we approached the bridge, I noticed it was draped with huge swags of plastic. Machinery and scaffolding hung over the edge of the railings. We stopped paddling to watch men standing precariously on wooden platforms and in buckets attached to long arms of cranes, diligently painting the sides and underbelly of the mammoth structure. As we passed underneath, one of the men pointed to our craft. His friend turned his head to look our way and we waved a friendly hello.

I resumed paddling, eyes scanning the Iowa shore for the auxiliary channel. "That's paint!" yelled Gene, pointing to the water. I followed the line of his arm to the water, and gasped. We were surrounded by green globs floating next to us, pulled along with us by the river current. There was no escape. The paint stretched out ahead of us and closed in from behind. Gene dipped his paddle into a green blob. The paint slid down the paddle's surface and dripped off the edge. Hopefully, the surface tension of the paint would allow it to slide off Donna in the same fashion. Gene pulled up the tail of the bowline, which was dragging in the water. The line was stained with green. So much for surface tension. We checked to make sure none of our lines or other absorbent gear touched the water. I hoped we'd get to the auxiliary channel soon.

Before long, I spied piles of rocks marked with buoys. "There!" I shouted. I maneuvered us over to the right of the rock piles, and kept us in the center of the new, smaller channel. The water surface cleared. The paint was swept along with the main current. We paddled down the deserted, narrow side channel. Three miles later, we snaked through the winding entryway to the auxiliary lock door and Gene reached up to pull the signal cord. No answer. No movement of any kind. What? Paddling around the entryway, we looked for signs of life.

A man approached and called, "Can I help you?"

"We pulled the signal cord for the auxiliary lock, but it doesn't look like anyone is here," explained Gene. "We read that recreational boats need to use this lock instead of the big one."

"Oh, this lock's only open on weekends," the man explained. "That's when there's enough rec boats out there to make it worth using both locks." That made sense, but I didn't remember reading about it. Even when we asked other boaters about the two locks, no one mentioned weekday restrictions. I tried to remember what day of the week it was. Thursday. Missed it by a day.

"Really?" asked Gene, his inflection making it seem like a ridiculous idea. I knew he was just frustrated. I couldn't blame him. "Now we have to paddle all the way back up the channel, AND back through the paint?" he asked. I hadn't thought about the paint. Gene slipped his bracelet off one wrist and onto the other, then called over his shoulder, "Ready to do this again?"

"I guess we have no choice," I grumbled. I changed my bracelet, then guided the boat back upstream.

After more than an hour, we finally locked through. When the gates opened, the river looked clean. "The churning water passing over the spillway must have dispersed the paint," said Gene. "Do you see any damage back there?"

"I think we got paint on the line, but I don't see any on the boat."

"There's one spot on the deck up here," Gene said. "I just hope the whole bottom isn't green." I leaned over, but couldn't see the waterline. We'd have to check later.

Before long, tall buildings, roads, and shoreline businesses told us we'd arrived at the Quad Cities, a group of geographically close communities on both sides of the river. Due to expansive growth, Quad Cities is actually now a misnomer, as it includes five cities: Moline, East Moline, and Rock Island in Illinois and Davenport and Bettendorf in Iowa. On our right, Bettendorf lured us with a paddleboat casino and an adjoining marina for our flex-day locale.

The first thing Gene did, after securing Donna to the dock, was to inspect her bottom for damage. "It looks like we came through that paint better than I expected," he said. "Far as I can see, it's just the one spot on top."

"Our souvenir of the Highway 80 Bridge," I added.

The following day, after two loads of laundry, we took a city bus to Urgent Care. Gene's case of poison ivy was bad, but was not infected. The doctor prescribed some oral antibiotics and steroids to supplement the treatment we were already doing. It was a relief to hear he should start feeling better soon. After a stop at Walgreens to pick up his meds, we decided to return on foot to get some exercise and see the city. We passed a beautiful golf course and a lovely city park. Gene pointed to the sky. "That front looks nasty!" I looked up.

There was a dark bank of gray clouds moving our way. Soon, we were running down the sidewalk in the downpour, pausing under trees that provided little protection against the pelting rain. Totally soaked, we took shelter under the entryway of a nearby office building.

I looked at our reflection in the window. Wet hair was plastered to our heads, dripping clothing clinging to our bodies, and sunglasses fogged with condensation. We were a comical sight. I took a couple's selfie and posted it online. Within a few minutes, I got a message from Jason in Bemidji. "NOW you look like river rats!"

After a couple doses of meds and a restful night's sleep on a hotel mattress, Gene already felt better. He changed his dressing and we took time for a hearty breakfast. We had a dry launch from the dock, paddled out of the marina, and turned toward Muscatine. Instead of starting out with a coffee stroke, Gene jumped right into his power stroke, reaching as far forward as possible and pulling his paddle deeply through the water. "Relax, hon . . . it's still early," I encouraged.

"I don't want to waste any time," he replied. "I'm only on steroids for ten days. I may as well make the most of it." I imagined him bulking out, with six hours of core workouts every day, while on doctor-approved drugs.

"I love you as you are," I said, "but go for it."

In no time, we tied up at the municipal marina. Our bag of electronics over Gene's shoulder, we set off to investigate. We found Muscatine to be a quiet river town, especially on a Sunday afternoon. Most of the streets were empty and the majority of businesses closed. Painted on the window of one store I read aloud, "Business Hours: Open When Here, Closed When Gone."

Gene laughed. "I'd like to work *those* hours," he said.

With only a few good leads for service organizations and no place to stay, we stopped at Boonie's Sports Bar for appetizers and free Wi-Fi. Walking out of the bar, not even a block away, I noticed a sign for the Muscatine Center for Social Action. "We heard good things about this place," I said. "Let's stop in and say hi. Maybe there's someone we can talk to tonight about helping out tomorrow."

The smiling bearded man at the front desk introduced himself as Mitch. I glanced at his stocky build, shock of white hair, and trimmed white beard and mustache. Off-season Santa, in Iowa for the summer. I smiled at the thought, then pulled myself back into the conversation.

"Your trip sounds interesting," Mitch said to Gene. "I don't know if there'll be anything for you to do, but you may be able to stay here. Last week, some bicyclists rode through and they stayed for a couple of nights. Let me make a call."

I leaned on the counter, between the glass partitions. My back and shoulders relaxed. I was more tired than I thought. A moment later, Mitch turned to us. "You're welcome to stay in the community room," he said. "Chris, one of our directors, can come by in the morning to show you around and tell you more about the center."

"That'd be great," said Gene. "Thanks." I was glad we could stay downtown. We would save the time and money of a hotel all the way across town and, just as importantly, be near the boat.

 Mitch led the way downstairs and turned into a huge space, like the Fellowship Hall in our church back home. "This building used to be the Y," he explained. "When it was in danger of being torn down for a parking lot, a group of private citizens bought it. They donated it to be used as housing for those in need. We've been here ever since."

I scanned the room. The cement block walls were painted light yellow, except for one, comprised of a huge mural. Lightning flashed across the black star-filled sky between the planet Earth, a human figure, and a hand in the heavens that reminded me of a contemporary take on the Sistine Chapel. On one side of the room, the gray tiles were inlaid with a dance floor of twelve-inch black and white squares. The entire floor shone like school hallways each fall before the new students entered for the first time. "Cool room," I said, gazing from one shiny surface to another.

"Sorry there's no furniture," Mitch apologized. "We just finished waxing the floors."

"No problem," said Gene. "We have mattresses and blankets. We can set up over in a corner. We'll be just fine."

August 12: Muscatine Center for Social Action

In the morning, we met Chris. We learned that the organization's name was indeed an appropriate moniker . . . a center for social action, with a mission to care for the needy in the community. "We have three separate shelters right here in this building, serving populations with different needs," Chris explained. "We have an emergency men's shelter in the gym, but we also provide private, safe areas for women with children, and over in another wing, we have thirty-five small, low-rent apartments."

"Is there anything we can do to help you today?" Gene asked Chris. "We have the whole day to do whatever you need."

"Most of the adults who work here are paid staff," Chris explained. "With the nature of our clients and the confidentiality issues, it works out better that way."

"We understand the need for confidentiality," I said. "Do you have any cleaning or maintenance that we could do?" I looked around the bare Community Room. "We could help put all the furniture back in this room, if you want."

"Thanks for the offer," he said. "The guys who stay at the shelter usually do the chores around here. It gets them a few bucks off the small nightly fee. I'll let them know you volunteered, but they'll probably want the hours."

"Usually we work at an organization for a day," Gene explained, "and then blog about what they do. Would you like us to write a blog telling what you offer? We could even add a link to your website if you want."

"That would be great," said Chris. "We pay for some of our operating expenses by renting out the gym during the days, and collecting rent and some fees, but we do depend heavily on donors. Publicity helps with that, and also gets the word out there to people who might need our services. I could give you a tour, if that would help you explain what we do around here."

Chris walked us through the building, showing us the shelter areas as well as the offices for the residents' case managers and a homeless prevention counselor, whose job was supporting at risk families in the community. He finished the tour back in the Community Room, pointing out two doors at the far end of the space. "We also have a pediatric dental clinic and an adult vision clinic. They're staffed by volunteers from the Iowa School of Dentistry and by area optometrists."

I remembered a popular quote from a few years back—"It takes a village to raise a child." The people of Muscatine were doing just that—coming together to benefit everyone in the community.

We left our phone numbers, in case MCSA needed our help later in the day, and headed off by Musca-bus for a couple of errands. We were seated on the bus when Gene's phone rang. "That was Mitch," Gene told me when he hung up. "He called to invite us to lunch to meet his wife. He said the bus stops at Walgreens. They'll pick us up there."

Soon, Mitch was introducing us to his wife, Collette. "Collette's on the board of directors for MCSA," he explained. "When I told her about your trip, she really wanted to meet you."

"My day job is pastor for the Methodist Church," she added. "So, I'm naturally interested in what you're doing. But first, where would you like to eat?"

With full plates from the buffet table at the Pizza Ranch, Collette said grace, and the conversation began. Our discussion meandered easily from one topic to another, but when speaking of the MCSA, she leaned forward and said with intensity, "I wish more people would understand that it's not about 'us' and 'them.' In a snap . . ."—she snapped her fingers, emphasizing her point— "any one of us could find ourselves in a situation where we need the help of others."

I shared about people at Grace House and at The Open Closet who volunteered and donated to these places before they needed help themselves. When I was young, my mother often said, "There, but for the grace of God, go I." Now, I saw firsthand the truth of her words.

Mitch drove us around the city for a tour, then dropped Collette off at home before returning us to the marina. Later, as Gene and I walked to Boonie's to finish our MSCA blog, he said, "That Mitch is an interesting guy. Did you know he really *does* have a job as a Santa?"

"No way!" I laughed. But after getting to know Mitch, I was sure he made a good one.

Aug. 13-20: Muscatine, IA, to Hannibal, MO

The high bluffs of northern Iowa and Wisconsin slowly transformed into rolling hills and forests. Towns were small and far between. Due to the low-lying land and the frequent and potentially devastating Mississippi floods, communities were often set back from the river behind levees. Along the banks, we saw a few year-round homes, but mostly smaller weekend and summer places known regionally as "camps." Some people owned both their camps and the property, but most leased the land from the Corps of Engineers or from landlords. The homes were built high on stilt foundations, placing them above the height of the levee and keeping them safe from floodwaters.

We no longer worried about floods. With the dry hot weather, the water level in the river dropped several inches each day. Our problems with rushing rapids and flooded campgrounds were replaced with low water, lazy currents, and hazardous wing dams. The wing dams were now visible as straight lines of riffles extending out toward the channel. This was both reassuring and alarming. We knew where the rocks were, but they were a lot closer to the surface. As we approached a submerged wing dam, the safest route was to paddle near the channel markers, past the end of the rocks. Close to shore, it was trickier. We squared up to the line of chop, stopped paddling, and floated slowly, measuring the water depth with our paddles. I often didn't realize I was holding my breath until I exhaled, once we were in the clear.

Our first campground was behind a group of islands off a narrow slough. I scanned the shore for boat ramps. "I think that's it," I called out, pointing to a blacktop ramp nearly hidden behind a curve on the left bank. We pulled the boat halfway out of the water and disembarked to scout the campground. This couldn't be the place; it was abandoned, overgrown, and downright creepy. Wooden posts with campsite markers, a winding gravel path, and an outhouse stood as vestiges of a campground that may have flourished before the Old Muddy rose to cover the land. Left in the wake of the flood were patches of caked, cracking mud and river debris scattered everywhere. The sites were overgrown with thigh-high prairie grasses, offering little space to erect a tent.

"Well, it's not much. Do you want to stay?" Gene asked. "We've got our choice of sites," he added cheerily.

"We've camped in worse," I said. "Caterpillars aren't dropping from the trees."

"And no vampire mosquitoes," he added. "How 'bout this one?" He headed to a grassy area by the river, a short walk from the outhouse. I began to unpack our gear while he went to check out the facilities.

Soon, I heard an engine and turned to watch an old, blue two-door sedan cruise slowly past. Gravel crunched under the wheels and two teenage boys, cigarette smoke swirling behind the glass windows, stared at me. As the car rolled past, I turned back to my work, listening to see if it stopped.

The outhouse door slammed and Gene returned, watching the car disappear around a bend near the end of the campground trail. "Who was that?"

"I don't know," I replied. "But I'm glad you're back." We set up camp, keeping an eye on the end of the road. I heard car doors slam and watched the two teens wander down to the water and back, but never saw them set up a tent or unload any supplies. What were they up to?

"Do you want to leave?" asked Gene.

"It's almost dusk. I don't think there's another place close. I'm sure it's fine." I tried to convince myself as much as Gene.

Before long, the blue sedan came crunching back, angled into our campsite, and stopped. Gene rose to his full six feet three and walked over. When the boys got out, I breathed a sigh of relief. Gene had 'em by a good eight inches. And they were shaking hands.

"Hi, I'm Josh, and this is Eric," the first boy said. "We love this campground. But it's been closed for over a month 'cuz of the flooding. We just came to check out the damage." We introduced ourselves, but I left out the part about suspecting them of being hooligans.

"Your kayak's awesome," said Eric. "Where're you headed?"

Gene explained our trip and we chatted with our new, previously suspicious friends. After best wishes and good-byes, they rolled off and we set about making dinner.

Twenty minutes later, the car returned and crunched to a stop. The boys climbed out and approached. "We think what you're doing is great and we just wanted to give you something," Josh began. He held out a large bag of potato chips. "We didn't know what you liked, but these are the best chips around. You can only get 'em here in Iowa. And they're our favorite. We hope you like 'em."

"Can you believe that?" Gene asked as he tore the bag open after they left. "They drove to the store just to get us a gift."

"I know. That was so sweet." I felt a twinge of guilt for misjudging them. Even though we needed to be cautious, no one we'd met along the river had given us any reason to fear. I didn't want to start now.

As the water level dropped, sand islands seemed to appear everywhere—a welcome change from the dark, sticky Mississippi mud to which we became accustomed. The beaches punctuated the river, beckoning boaters to stop for a few hours, to party with friends or to camp overnight. Camping was allowed on these sandy islands—even encouraged. And it was free! During the trip from Muscatine to Hannibal, we took advantage of several such campgrounds. My favorite by far was the first . . . a piece of heaven called Turtle Island.

Gene spied it as we rounded the bend of the river about a mile south of Lock and Dam #18. "How about that one?" The whole east end of the island was a sand beach. The rest was a thick forest, offering us a feeling of complete privacy from the mainland. We pulled Donna all the way onto the sand and set up the tent on still higher ground. We were the beneficiaries of a previously used fire pit, so Gene gathered dry wood from the forest's edge and set it ablaze. We spread out our solar blanket on the sand and chose a romantic dinner for our first island getaway. Shrimp jambalaya was still a rehydrated one-pot meal, but it *was* seafood.

The next night's island campground experience paled in comparison. The beach was smaller and the sand wetter. But even worse was a major tactical error—we chose an island near a railroad bridge. The Fort Madison Toll Bridge, the country's largest Swing Span Bridge, had two levels—one for vehicle traffic on top and one for trains on the bottom. Earlier, as we passed under its towering span, I looked up through the empty tracks, as one vehicle after another rattled over the metal grates. But what I didn't realize was that trains clattered over that bridge every twenty minutes, all night long.

The following day, bleary-eyed from lack of sleep, I looked forward to a real bed in Montrose, Iowa, at the home of a man I met only once. Mike was the father-in-law of my Mississippi-loving friend, Kathy. "You're welcome to stay at my house when you paddle the river," he said, when I met him at her house the summer before our trip, "if you make it that far." Then he spoke of dangerous winds near his home, where the river took a huge swing eastward, creating a large pool susceptible to high waves that ravaged boats far bigger than ours. "A couple years ago," he said, "a young man had to stay with me for three days just to dry out his gear." I couldn't wait to see Mike again, if only to show him that we were safe and dry.

The weather cooperated better than Mike warned. We arrived at the river's bend by early afternoon. With a brisk northerly wind, we decided to sail across the bend into the marina. As we passed the Nauvoo beacon across the river, I gave him a call. "Hi, Mike. We're at the Nauvoo light. We're under sail."

"What? You got a sail on that thing?" he asked.

"Yep. You should be able to see us soon as we come around the corner. Watch for a blue and white circular sail."

"Okay. I can't see you yet, but I'll watch for you. Meet you at the landing."

From the moment he picked us up, Mike made us comfortable. A retired lawyer and lifetime local resident with many interests, he was never at a loss for conversation. With Gene, he talked of golf, guns, and birds, and with me—books and family. As he prepared a homemade steak dinner, all three of us shared cooking stories. "If you can stay another day, we can do some sightseeing," he offered.

Mike drove us on a loop across the river and through the surrounding towns on both banks. In Nauvoo, we learned about the Mormon settlement and their exodus from Illinois to Utah in the mid-1800s. Across the river in Iowa, we visited Fort Madison, a reconstruction of a western frontier outpost originally built in 1808.

That evening, Mike took us downtown for the Montrose Watermelon Festival. We enjoyed huge hunks of free watermelon, met people from the local area, and played several games of bingo. Mike and I paid for the bingo cards, while Gene came out the big winner of the night, pocketing a thirty-dollar prize for the final game of Blackout.

"Yeah, you come to Montrose to visit and go home with all my friends' money," Mike chided. "How am I s'posed to live with them now?"

We could easily have stayed longer in Montrose, but the river pulled us back. Two miles south of Canton, Missouri, we celebrated the one-thousandth mile of our trip with a paddle high five, a water bottle toast, and a Facebook status update. Then we crossed over to the Illinois side of the river and kept an eye out for Sid Simpson State Park, where our next campsite awaited. We turned into the backwater channel by the park, but the further we paddled, the shallower it became. "That's gotta be the park," I said, pointing to the picnic benches and rolling hills of green, "but I don't see any campsites near the river." I doubted we could get there anyway. Between the shore and our boat was a swamp of silt and mud.

"The water's too low. If we go in any further, we'll get stuck," Gene warned. He turned around, and we paddled back the way we came.

I consulted the map. "It looks like there are several parks and marinas along the shoreline in Quincy," I said. "Let's head south and keep looking. I'm sure we'll find something, and maybe even take a few miles off our day tomorrow." We passed a public park and a restaurant with temporary slips for customers, but nothing suitable for camping. Soon Quincy was behind us. "There's one place south of town called the South Side Boat Club," I told Gene, "but that's our last chance before the lock." I hoped we'd find something soon. I measured the height of the sun over the horizon with my thumb. We still had over an hour of daylight, but if we had to go through another lock today, it would fade fast.

Ahead on the left bank, I saw what had to be the boat club—a long white building with a backyard deck overlooking the river. What I was most excited to see was the large grassy area by the parking lot. Perfect for our little tent. Two fishermen were gathering up their gear on the boat club dock. We fanned our paddle tips in the water to hold our position. "Hi," said Gene. "We're paddling the river and need to stop for the night. Any chance we could camp here?"

"The boat club's closed right now, but I've seen 'em let people camp on the property before. If you set up your tent over there in the corner, I don't think it'd be a problem." One of the fishermen pointed out a dark corner next to a tree line at the edge of the property.

After setting up the tent, I looked over toward the boat club. "There's a light on inside, Gene," I said. "And someone's walking around on the deck. I think we should go over and tell them who we are . . . just to make sure it's okay."

"And what if it's not?" Gene asked. "We can't go anywhere in the dark."

"Good point," I agreed, "but I still think we should let them know that the fishermen said we could stay. They'll know who we are, and that we did ask."

We knocked and peeked in the door. Behind the bar, a woman in a flowered tank top, bar towel in hand, asked, "Can I help ya?" She wiped her forehead with the back of her hand, pushing back the strands of blonde hair that fell from her clip.

I introduced myself, and then Gene, sharing our earlier conversation with the fishermen. "I saw your light on, and just wanted to make sure it's all right to stay here."

A man approached from the other end of the bar. Slight of build, he wore long shorts and a camouflage T-shirt. In his hand was a small glass of beer. "My name's Bob," he said, "and this is my wife, Rebecca. We're members of the boat club. It's not open right now; we're actually getting it ready for the grand reopening of our remodeled restaurant next weekend. Can I get you a drink?" Over gin and tonics, we told Bob and Rebecca about our trip, recounting some of the services and the people we met.

"I'm glad you stopped in," said Bob. "Before we met you, we were a little worried. We weren't sure what you were up to." I thought back to the hesitancy I felt when I first saw Josh and Eric hanging around our campground. Just a few days later, I was the suspicious stranger skulking around, frightening someone else.

"You're welcome to stay there," said Bob, "but you'll be safer over by here by the light. Why don't you move your tent by the building?" Bob and Rebecca looked on while Gene pulled up the stakes and carried the entire tent on his head over to the area by the deck. Then we wheeled *Kupendana* to the patio and secured her for the night.

"We're just about done here," said Bob. "You hungry?" Bob and Rebecca took us out for dinner, stopping at their home to let us shower before returning us to the boat club for the night. "What time are you leaving in the morning?" asked Bob. "I'd like to come say good-bye. I'll bring coffee and doughnuts."

The next morning, we arose early to break camp. As promised, Bob and Rebecca arrived with cups of steaming coffee and bakery for breakfast. Rebecca held out a leather necklace. Hanging at the bottom was a knot shaped like a ball. "I want you to have this," she said. "It's a monkey fist."

"I recognize it," I said. "My dad was a sailor, and he was always teaching me different knots." The monkey fist was originally designed to weight the end of lines so sailors could toss them more easily to someone on a dock and even to unlucky souls who fell overboard.

"It's made of one long piece of leather," Rebecca continued. "It's a sign of long-lasting friendship. When you wear it, you can think of us."

"I will." My fingers traced the smooth leather strands that wove around and through one another. I slipped it over my neck. "Thank you for everything."

"On the way to Hannibal, be sure to stop at the Purple Cow," said Bob. "The owner's great and you'll have a good time."

"Where is it?" I asked, still fidgeting with my new necklace.

"It's on the Missouri side," he said. "You'll see it."

I gave Rebecca a hug, then waved to them both as we cast off. The over-the-top hospitality we received from this couple made me wonder . . . what was it about the river angels that made them offer food, lodging, showers, and friendship to total strangers? What if more people did that, everywhere? What if I did?

Shortly after noon, I heard music and laughter drifting over the water. "Listen!" I said. "Do you think that's the Purple Cow?" The exuberant music seemed to draw us toward it. We veered closer to the shore. Hungry and ready for a break, we navigated through dozens of powerboats tied to the meager-sized dock, and found a just right inside corner to tie up.

I stared at the building nestled in the trees at the top of the stairs. It would be hard to find a building more purple . . . from the wooden siding, to the soffits and fascia, even the chimney. Only an orange neon Coors Light sign showed any sense of nonconformity. "Don't know why I'm so suddenly thirsty," Gene commented, nodding in the direction of the party. He lifted himself onto the dock, but kept his legs in the cockpit to hold the boat close while I climbed out.

"Hannibal's not far from here," I mentioned as I unfolded myself from the cockpit. "Maybe someone'll be able to suggest a service for us." We didn't yet have a plan for finding a service in Hannibal, but I knew I wanted to. I had looked forward to spending time there since we began to plan the trip. Hannibal had a special place in history as the town that inspired Mark Twain, one of America's best-known writers and a huge fan of the Mississippi River. While Gene fastened the mooring lines, I turned to the first man I saw on the dock. "Sir, are you from Hannibal?"

"No, but my son Jeremy is. He's up on the deck. I can introduce you."

"Thanks! I've gotta make one stop first; then we'll find you."

Heading inside, we threaded our way through the wild rumpus to the restrooms. The center of the room was filled with dancers, mostly women, wildly pumping the air and loudly singing, "Baaaad girrrrls!" While I waited for Gene, I briefly considered letting my inner bad girl shake my booty with the line of revelers, but my outer fatigued paddler won out. We shouted our drink orders to the barkeep, raised our glasses to the revelers, and made our way to the relative peace and quiet of the deck.

A tall young man rose from a table, where he was seated with his family. "Hi," he greeted. "My dad tells me you're looking for someone from Hannibal. I'm Jeremy, and this is my wife, Jennifer. How can we help you?" We chatted about our trip and some places we might want to check out when we got to Hannibal. I enjoyed seeing how gentle Jennifer was with her three children, and listened to the friendly youngsters talk excitedly about their day of boating.

Jennifer told me a little bit about a neighborhood after-school program she was starting. "If you're in town on Wednesday, I'd love you to come." Trading phone numbers, we planned to meet again.

Arriving at the Hannibal marina later that afternoon, we checked in to the Best Western and found a cozy little restaurant nearby. On Tuesday, we spent the day exploring the downtown area, rich with history. We wound our way through town, asking locals we met about non-profits that might like a little help. Finally, with plans to return the next morning to Douglass Community Services, we spent the rest of the day as tourists at the Boyhood Home of Mark Twain. We toured the reconstructed homes of characters from *The Adventures of Tom Sawyer*, saw the law office of Samuel Clemens's father, and even visited the famous whitewashed fence.

Aug. 21: Douglass Community Services, Hannibal, Missouri

On a sign posted outside of the Douglass Community Center, I was impressed to see the number of services offered by this community organization. We found out that it was, in fact, an umbrella organization that provided support for many programs in the eight-county area. One of these, the food pantry, was where we were scheduled to help.

We entered to find a row of shopping carts along the wall, each containing an assortment of cans and bottles. In the center of the room was an island of boxes stacked shoulder-high on pallets. A tall man appeared, dressed in jeans and a bright red T-shirt with a Milwaukee Sawzall logo across the front. "Hi," he greeted. "I'm Duane."

"You wore that for us, right?" asked Gene, explaining that we lived in a suburb of Milwaukee. We introduced ourselves and explained about our trip.

"Remind me to introduce you to Stacey before you leave," Duane said. "Her husband's a kayaker and I'm sure she'd love to talk to you."

"Thanks, we'd like that," I agreed. I nodded toward the island. "It looks like you just got a big shipment here. Where does your food come from?"

"We get our food from lots of sources," Duane replied. "There's a USDA Commodities Distribution at the beginning of each month that serves over a hundred eligible families. During the rest of the month, food gets donated by individuals, groups, and a few corporate donors. This shipment here's from Walmart."

I looked at the stacks of boxes: fruit, loaves of bread, bakery, frozen meats, condiments, canned goods, cases of granola bars, and even frozen cakes. This food pantry operation was huge. "How do you even begin to organize all this?" I asked.

"We sort it all and freeze and refrigerate what we need to," explained Duane. "We set up the grocery carts over there with the staples for each family." He indicated a row of carts along the wall. "Then, when they come to pick up the food, I ask them what else they'd like. Sometimes there's a birthday, and then I throw in a frozen cake. A roast or a turkey can make someone's day. Whenever I can, I try to add something special."

"What can we do to help?" Gene asked.

"These boxes of food in the middle of the room need to be weighed and recorded. Do the frozen and refrigerated ones first. They go in here." Duane pulled a large metal handle, opening the door to a mammoth walk-in freezer. Cool air wafted over me as it spilled out into the humid room. Duane indicated a similar refrigerator next to it. "Then we need to put the other stuff away on these shelves." Along the periphery of the room, cans and boxes were lined up neatly on metal shelving units.

Duane handed me a clipboard. "Just write down the weight of each box and we can add 'em all up later."

Gene and I set each box on the scale, recorded its weight, and then put the contents away where they belonged. Duane was an easygoing supervisor, chatting with us about the food pantry and our trip. As families came to pick up food, I heard him talking with them in the next room about how they were doing and if they needed anything special. Then he came back to get some doughnuts, a frozen turkey, a sheet cake, or other yummy items he could find to make their day a little better. He certainly was the right man for the job. At the end of our shift, we added up all our numbers. Altogether, we sorted and weighed 1,172 pounds of food!

Before we left, Duane introduced us to Stacey, as promised. "My husband would love to meet you," she suggested. "Will you be around tomorrow?"

"Yes. We still need to pick up our food box, go to the Laundromat, and blog about the services in Hannibal," I said. "We don't need to rush—we're ahead of our itinerary. We'll shove off on Friday." Exchanging phone numbers, we made lunch plans for the following day.

Aug. 21: After-School Adventures, Hannibal, MO

After freshening up at the hotel, we waited outside for Jennifer, who was taking us to help with the very first day of her new after-school program. We piled in the van with her three children and drove to a low-income apartment complex near her church. "I got to know many of the families in this neighborhood when Jeremy and I led a Summer Sunday School program here," she told us. "Now that school's starting, I want to continue to support these kids. A lot of them will come home to empty apartments after school because their parents work. If I can give them something to do on Wednesdays, that's one less day each week they sit home alone with the TV."

We helped unload bins of toys, books, and art supplies from her van into a pavilion on the property. Jennifer planned to send home flyers with any children who stopped by, telling their parents about the after-school opportunity and obtaining permission for their children to participate. It was exciting to be present at the beginning of a grassroots program like this, arising from one individual's recognition of a need and her determination to do what she could to help.

As we set up, children began to appear. They recognized Jennifer and her children and seemed comfortable joining us. The kids carefully chose their favorite ice pop colors and we introduced ourselves, chatting about their readiness for the upcoming school year and their favorite activities. As an icebreaker, we played a rousing game of Wet Tag. The dampened sponge, tossed gently at first to tag one another, became the great equalizer. Once waterlogged, it sprayed everywhere as it spun through the air. Soon, we were all dripping. We dried off and spent time together with bubbles, balls, books, sidewalk chalk, crafts, and Matchbox cars. All in all, about a dozen children of all ages joined in. Jennifer was kind and welcoming, handing out flyers and offering treats before departing. I had a feeling that next week, many of them would be back, eager to share about their first week of school and spend time together.

As we walked to the van afterward, the youngest of Jennifer's girls took my hand and said softly, "I'll miss you."

Despite the warmth of the afternoon, I could feel goose bumps along my arms. I squeezed her hand gently. "I'll miss you, too." One of the best things about our trip was making friends like these. One of the hardest things was leaving them so soon.

Chapter 9
Hot, Hot, HOT!

Aug. 22–28: Hannibal to St. Louis

BEFORE LEAVING HANNIBAL, we took a zero day to do some chores. First stop—the post office to pick up our food box. As became our custom, we sliced into the packing tape and popped the box open right on the spot. This made no sense whatsoever, since we had packed the boxes ourselves and knew what was inside. However, the prospect of a new array of edibles for the next two weeks, plus the curious expressions on the faces around us, contributed to a Christmas morning atmosphere. This time, on top of our supplies was an extra box. Written in a cursive flair on the cover was the name of our favorite family-owned chocolatier, Kehr's. "Thank youuuu, Eric!" exclaimed Gene. I immediately opened the box and scanned the assortment of rich chocolate truffles iced with drizzles of color designating the luscious flavors inside. "They won't last long in this heat," warned Gene as he popped one of the creamy confections into his mouth.

"We can't take them on the boat tomorrow—that's for sure," I agreed. "That gives us a day to finish off—how much—a pound?" I let out a groan of delight as a mocha-filled piece of happiness melted on my tongue. Then I held out the box to the staff and our fellow patrons. "We're gonna need some help here."

The rest of the day was spent eating chocolates, working on our new blog posts about the food pantry and the after-school program, doing laundry, and hanging out with Stacey and her husband, Joe. An avid kayaker, Joe eagerly agreed to spend the following day on the river with us.

Joe was waiting when we arrived at the municipal harbor early Friday morning. In his long cotton pants, long-sleeved shirt, and floppy hat, he was dressed for a sunny and warm day of paddling. For a moment, I felt guilty that I didn't protect my skin more from the sun. I used sunscreen, but I absolutely loved the warmth of the sun on my skin and sleeveless tops were the norm for me on days with temps in the nineties like this one.

We planned a twenty-six-mile day; Joe was interested in doing the whole thing. Despite the early hour, it was already warm, so we set off at a leisurely pace. Joe's day job as a biology professor at the University of Illinois at Quincy ensured that our conversations were peppered with little-known facts about the animals and plants we ran into along the river. Joe eagerly shared what he called "free lectures" along the way, including such topics as snails, cormorants, eagles, seaweed, beetles, cicadas, caddice flies, and monarchs. With over thirty years of elementary school science under my belt, I found that I could keep up with him on many subjects, but also learned some new trivia.

During one of our rest stops, Joe picked up a snail shell and handed it to me. "Do you know how snails can be used to observe the water quality in an area?"

I guessed, "If the snails are alive, it's good, and if they're not, it's bad?"

"Well, that's one way." He smiled. "But it's more complicated than that. By looking at the *kind* of snails that live in a river or lake, we can learn about the condition of the water." I nodded. I followed his reasoning, but wasn't sure what different kinds of snails had to do with it. "Place the shell in your hand with the apex, or point, away from you. Turn it until you can see the opening." He demonstrated with a snail in the palm of his hand. "If the opening is on the left, it had lungs. Since it breathed air, it was tolerant of poor water quality, such as our common genus, Physa. If the opening is on the right, it had gills and would only be found in areas of high water quality. You can remember that left and lungs both start with L. I'll test you later."

I placed the snail he gave me in my palm. The opening was on the right. "This one had gills, right? So the water quality is good here."

"Yep. You can take one of my classes any time."

"I'd love to," I said. I hoped Joe's students knew how lucky they were.

We soon approached Lock and Dam #22. "I've done a lot of canoeing and kayaking," said Joe, "but I gotta admit, I've never been through a lock."

"It's no big deal," Gene reassured him. "We'll show you the ropes."

We paddled closer, and the entrance wall soon towered above us. Joe craned his neck. "It's *huge*!" he exclaimed.

"Just wait 'til we get inside, and they lower us down," I said. "Then you *really* feel small."

Gene explained about the signal cord; Joe headed over to pull it. But the cord was a tangled mess suspended above his reach. I was worried for him, but Joe wasn't deterred. First, he tried unsuccessfully to snag the cord with his paddle blade from a seated position. Then, he raised his body to a squat with his legs spread apart and I realized he planned to stand up and reach for it. "Be careful!" I warned.

Precariously balanced, Joe stretched up to his full height and yanked on the cord. I heard the blast of the compressed air horn and watched with relief as he safely took his seat. The towering doors opened to reveal the enormous chamber. Joe caught up with us as we paddled inside. "That was fun!" he exclaimed.

"The signal's usually a lot easier than that." I lent him some reassurance that he obviously didn't need. The lockmaster dropped us lines and Joe quickly got the knack of letting the rope slip through his loose grip as the water gently lowered. Joe watched the rising walls and I watched Joe, recalling my awe at our virgin lock-through the year before.

"You did great!" I said, when the lock doors opened and we paddled through the small chop. Joe had one more experience under his belt and we had finally schooled the professor.

Later, as we glided our kayaks to a beach rest stop, I confided to Joe that I'd been hearing from locals to watch out for snakes, but I hadn't seen any yet. "Are there many snakes around here?" I asked.

He pointed to a twig sticking out from the water's surface behind a rock. "Did you see that one?"

I looked closer. The stick had eyes. A tiny snake was quietly extending its head about three inches above the surface, its eyes on us.

Joe continued, "Don't worry. That's just a little water snake. They're not poisonous, but they can be very aggressive. So I wouldn't go near it, if I were you."

"Thanks," I said. "I won't." Keeping my eye on the little master of disguise, I stepped carefully out of the boat. Now, I wondered how many other snakes were around that I just didn't see. I needed to change the direction of my thoughts. "Anyone hungry for a snack?" I asked. Raiding our deck bag, I spread a smorgasbord of almonds, salmon, crackers, and granola bars on a nearby tree stump table.

Refreshed and fueled, we crossed over from Missouri to paddle along the Illinois shore. Eventually, I saw Stacey waving from the top of our campground ramp.

After helping pull both kayaks ashore, Joe walked over to put an arm around Stacey's waist. "Thanks for coming to pick me up, hon," he said. "It was an awesome day!"

"I'm glad you could join us," said Gene, shaking Joe's hand. "It was great to meet both of you."

We watched Joe and Stacey drive off, then walked over to the campground office. The air-conditioning hit me like a cool wave as I opened the door. We filled our water bottles, bought some snacks, and perused the shelf of boating charts. The river maps we had with us were only for the Upper Mississippi. We still didn't know whether we would turn off on the Tenn-Tom, but whatever we decided to do, we'd need some new maps. I paged through the books to get an idea what was available.

"That's a beautiful boat out there," someone said. "Is it yours?"

"Sure is," I heard Gene answer. "My wife and I are paddling the river." I returned the map book and walked over.

"Name's Robert," said the owner of the voice. "I'm paddling, too—at least I *was*." He removed his camp hat, revealing a weathered face topped with curly white hair. I guessed he had a few years on us. "I'm sidelined for a few days here while I do some repairs."

I knew how that felt. "What happened?" I asked.

"Had an accident in the lock, up at Keokuk, Iowa," he said. I remembered that huge lock, just past Montrose Mike's. "Well, first ya gotta know, my boat's a little bit different. I designed it myself outa two canoes with a platform between 'em. I got the bow of one o' the canoes caught in a rung of one o' those ladders along the lock wall. As the water went down, the bow of my boat stayed in the ladder and the boat, with me on it, ended up hangin' down from the wall." He held his hand in the air at an angle, to reinforce the point. "That is . . . until the bow broke."

"Yikes!" I was horrified. I remembered how sick I felt when Donna's hull splintered. "Were you okay?"

"Yep, the boat splashed right back in the water. An' I don't know how, but I managed to hang on to both the boat and my dog. All I ended up losing was my marine radio, but I've had to do a lot o' repairs. Someone up the river helped me fix the bow, but somethin's still not right, so folks here are helping me try an' straighten out the frame."

We followed Robert over to see his boat. It looked like a cross between a catamaran and Huck Finn's raft. Metal pipes fastened two canoes side by side, and a wooden platform created a deck on top of the two hulls. "'Most days, I sit back there and face backwards to row," he explained, pointing at the stern. Two long oars rested in oarlocks on the outside gunwales of the canoes. "I gotta look over my shoulder a lot, but I sure get a good view of where I've been."

"I wish we had enough room on our kayak for a solar panel like that!" Gene pointed to a huge black and silver panel at the front of the center platform. "Ours is the size of a notebook."

"I'm glad I have it," said Robert. "It makes enough electricity for my everyday needs, and powers my trolling motor." A motor? That would have come in handy more than a few times, I thought. "I only use that if I need to get out of the channel fast," he added, "or if I need help maneuvering through the current. It's gettin' pretty strong."

I wondered what it would be like to ride this contraption down the Mississippi. With two canoes, he certainly had more room for storage than we did. His floating home was piled high with a mattress, several tarps, fishing equipment, water, food, clothing, and even a bed for his golden retriever.

"Are you planning to do the whole river?" asked Gene.

"I hope so, but I'm in no hurry," he admitted. "I'm retired, and can take all the time I want. I do about ten miles a day, and just pull my boat up on land to sleep." We wished him speedy repairs and a safe trip. I was pretty sure we wouldn't see him again, since our pace—even stopping to do service—was twice his. But I could relate to his spirit of adventure, and hoped I still had it when I got to be his age.

Sand islands continued to be plentiful and became our accommodations for most of the week. They were also primitive—no showers, bathrooms, or fresh water. The first two problems were solved with our biodegradable soap and our spade. But the latter required us to stop whenever possible to refill our water containers . . . marinas, restaurants, and anywhere else with a spigot. With daily highs pushing three digits, we were going through water like crazy, reminding each other to drink often while on the water in the sun. We arose early to get some time on the river before the day heated up and took breaks during the middle of the day when the heat was at its peak. Whenever possible, we stopped to cool off in air conditioning, shade, or even the Mississippi itself. Often, our breaks ended up being nearly as long as our paddles, but I didn't mind setting up our tent in the evening. It was much cooler.

One midday stop was the hillside town of Grafton, IL. Built right into the side of a hill, its quaint colorful buildings were arranged in horizontal rows along the face of the hillside. The town businesses, stretched along the Mississippi waterfront, took advantage of the beautiful views with docks, decks, and patios overlooking the river.

We pulled into the marina and made reservations at the restaurant before heading out to experience the town. One of the air-conditioned tourist spots to visit was a winery. After an hour of tasting free samples, we strolled back down the main street toward dinner. I noticed something all too common among little Mississippi River towns. On the side of O'Day's Fish Stop restaurant, high above the awning over the front door, hung a placard documenting the historic flood of 1993. The high water mark of thirty-eight point two written on the placard indicated the water's rise, in feet, above the normal level of the river at that location. High water marks like this were a reminder to us of the volatile nature of the river, but also served as a tribute to the resilience of the residents of these towns—a kind of badge of honor.

Some businesses proudly displayed photographs showing how high and wide the river spread, but usually, just a number was posted at the height of the crest. I extended my view from the high water mark across the river to the same level on the other shore. I imagined the sheer volume of water, the land and buildings that were submerged by the mighty river's floodwaters, and the lives that needed to be rebuilt each time it happened. I wasn't sure I would have the strength to stay.

Several days of sweating and camping on sand left us hot, tired, and smelly when we finally arrived at the Alton Marina. As we rounded the bend into the protected harbor, I could see that it was built entirely on floats. The docks, the office, and even an in-ground pool complete with umbrella tables and shower house rose and fell with the level of the Mississippi.

We tied up to the courtesy dock and freshened up in the bathroom before checking in at the office. "You can leave the boat right where it is," said the friendly woman at the desk. "No one'll bother it. And there's a grassy area near the parking lot where you can set up your tent. We don't charge river travelers. We're glad to help."

"Can we pay you something to use your showers and the pool?" I asked. She agreed on a minimal fee for the amenities, and we showered and hit the pool before we even unpacked the boat.

At the pool, I noticed several people congregating near the fence, talking and pointing in the direction of a huge powerboat tied up behind our little *Kupendana*. Then I overheard the words "beautiful wooden kayak." In the midst of this luxurious marina, surrounded by expensive motor yachts, were these people talking about our little twenty-foot, self-powered, scratched-up kayak? They were. We walked over to the railing. "That's our boat," Gene said.

"Did you build it?"

"We sure did."

"Was it hard?" asked one of the men. "I've always wanted to build a wooden boat like that." His words brought back memories of Dad saying the same thing at the kitchen table. Before we began the project together. Long before this trip.

"You should," I encouraged. I told him about the Pygmy Boats website. "There are lots of models to choose from, great directions, and good customer support, too."

Gene looked at the floating homes all around us, the extravagant yachts that we called Big Boys. "But if you *really* want one," he said, "we might be able to work out a trade."

We introduced ourselves, shared boating stories, and enjoyed cool water, company, and conversation until the sun started to fade. Showered, cooled, and rested, we set up our tent, then returned in the dark for a soak in the hot tub before retiring for the night.

It was a good thing we were well rested, because the last day of our paddle to St. Louis was not going to be easy. St. Louis was a huge metropolitan area, with a population well over three hundred thousand. It was well known for industry and as a hub for barge traffic along the Mississippi River system. North of St. Louis, there was a treacherous area of rapids known as the Chain of Rocks. To bypass this hazardous area, we planned to use an eight-mile alternate route, called the Chain of Rocks Canal. I hoped we wouldn't miss the entrance to the canal. It would be heavy with barge traffic, but that was better by far than dangerous drops over rock ridges. I was *so* done with rapids.

Our goal was to arrive at the famed St. Louis arch, where our hosts, Diane and Jerry, would meet us. Friends of a woman we met in Deerwood two months earlier, Diane and Jerry offered to host us at their home in Freeburg while we did service in the St. Louis area.

In the morning, the heat built rapidly, but a light breeze helped to cool us and we were even able to sail for a few miles. The shores were now lined with electric and gas companies. As we passed an

Illinois electric plant, a cascade of wastewater spilled into the river from an elevated pipe. Heat emanated from the water all around us. I dipped my hand into the river; normally cool and refreshing, it was warm as a Jacuzzi. A blue heron stood on the bank. I doubted it would have any luck finding food here.

We stopped to stretch on the western bank just above the Missouri River confluence. Pulling Donna onto a mud bank by several barge docks, we climbed up to the edge of Confluence Point State Park. Standing on the point of land between both huge rivers, I watched the two shades of water joining, then curving together. Upstream, the difference between the rivers was striking. On my left, park-like grass and lush foliage lined the shore, but on the right, the banks of the Mississippi were lined with mud flats, rocks, and large chunks of cement riprap. Tall metal barge docks, the reddish brown color of Mississippi mud, dappled the shores. I felt sorry for the Missouri, its pristine waters swallowed up by this industrial giant.

From our perch at the confluence, Gene spotted the entrance to the Chain of Rocks Canal. "Watch the barges," he said. "Instead of continuing down the river, they disappear into that space right over there." He pointed across to the Illinois shore. "That must be the canal. We'll have to be careful not to get swept into the Missouri current, though, or we'll have trouble getting across the river in time to make the turn."

We shot across the river to the Illinois side, then turned south along the eastern shore. Soon, I saw a large sign on the bank: CANAL—ALL BOATS ENTER HERE. Two tugs were ahead of us, already pushing their loads through the waterway. The canal was a no-wake area, so with little effort, we kept pace with the powerful push tugs. Paddling in the canal felt like being in a ditch—an eight-mile-long, straight-as-an-arrow ditch. Rocks edged both sides; above them, grass banks sloped upward. We sweated under the merciless sun. Dipping my hat in the mocha-colored water, I let it drip over my head and down my back, mingling with the rivulets of perspiration trickling down between my shoulder blades.

After a while, our companions pulled off to the side and idled their engines. "Do you think there's a wait to lock through?" Gene asked. I had no idea.

We slowed down; I wondered if protocol required us to wait in line. "I don't know, but we can't stay here," I said. Without even the slightest breeze from our forward movement, my skin sizzled like a strip of bacon in a fry pan. "Let's get to the end of the canal, and find out what's up." Carefully paddling around the sidelined barges, I decided my worry about protocol was unwarranted; I saw no evidence that anyone on the barges cared one whit about us.

The canal widened a mile before the lock. To the east, huge cranes emptied barge cargo into dump trucks and onto conveyors. Barge docks lined the west bank. Gene phoned the lockmaster, then caught me up to speed. "We were right," he said. "There's a line for the lock. But he'll put us through between them. There's one barge going down right now, and another one coming up next. He can take us down after that." Gene pointed his paddle at the pilings off to the left of the lock. "Let's wait over there. We've gotta be ready to go when the next barge comes up."

We floated for over an hour, drifting in and out of a tiny patch of shade behind a tall, cylindrical piling. Then the smooth surface turned choppy. I could picture the valves underneath the lock opening to let the water beneath us flow into the enclosure. The lock system was ingenious, really—operating entirely with gravity and water pressure. Water was added from above to raise the level, and drained into the pool below to lower it. The valves were located far below the surface, so the water inside the lock itself remained calm. But here, near the filling valves, the surging water tugged at us. We pulled over toward the bank, out of the way, and paddled backward to prevent ourselves from being sucked into the path of the barge I knew would soon emerge. Slowly, the doors swung open and the triple-wide vessel pushed its nose out into the chop. I counted as the barges appeared, like multicolored scarves from a magician's sleeve. Three . . . six . . . nine . . .

. . . twelve . . . fifteen! Finally came the tug, pushing the flotilla out of the twelve-hundred-foot-long enclosure. At last, the swirling water calmed enough for us to paddle around the corner into the lock.

The doors closed behind our tiny boat and we were all alone in the space that held such a mammoth load just a few minutes before. "Is that a Pygmy boat?" the lockmaster called down from the railing above.

"Yes. How'd you know?" I asked, impressed that he recognized our boat.

"I grew up in the Pacific Northwest," he said, "near Port Townsend, where the company's located." We chatted for a few minutes about boatbuilding during our descent. Then the metal gates opened, the air-horn sounded the all clear, and out we paddled into the metropolis of St. Louis.

The cityscape was an impressive sight. The geometric designs of bridges spanning the river framed an urban skyline above the riprap of the river's banks. Gracefully rising above all else was a sleek silver arch, the unmistakable symbol of the Gateway City. As we got closer, traffic gave me no more time to ogle the sights. Barges zigzagged across the river, seemingly on their own schedules and paths, in a water ballet we didn't understand. We skirted between and around barges and tugs, trying to make it across the river in time to pull ashore by the Arch. The last time I was this nervous, we were dodging stumps in the rapids of Minnesota. And they weren't even moving.

Finally, we arrived at Central City Park. From the river, it looked nothing like the travel brochure pictures I remembered. The water level was so low that the grassy park was no longer at the river's edge and the path leading to the shiny stainless steel Arch was now a fifty-yard cobblestone climb up the bank. We strapped on Donna's wheels and wrestled her up to the sidewalk, where we piled her contents in a heap.

Soon, I heard a shout. "Barb!" Apparently, two bedraggled, sweaty kayakers waiting by a long wooden boat were easy to identify. Jerry helped us with our things. Then Diane opened a cooler stocked with water, soda, and beer as cold as the ice mounded around the cans and bottles. "What would you like?" she asked. I picked a bottle of water, gulping half of it down in one satisfying chug. Gene followed suit. After a long, hot week, it was exactly what we needed.

Aug. 29: Timber Frame Craftsmen

With a warmth and friendliness that seemed effortless, Diane and Jerry welcomed us into their home—a beautiful timber frame structure at the end of a long winding road through the wooded hills of their property.

"This is our dream home," explained Jerry. "We built it ourselves, from the design right down to every detail of the construction."

I looked around at the towering beams and the huge hand-hewn trusses, the hardwood floors and the ironwork on the massive wooden doors. The warm interior reflected the beauty of natural stone and wood. "You built this all yourself?"

"It took a while," Jerry admitted, smiling sheepishly. With a tall hat and a little dye for his graying beard, Jerry could have made a decent Abe Lincoln double. He folded his tall, lanky frame into the soft sofa in the vaulted living room. We settled into nearby chairs and Diane poured iced tea to help combat the heat of the day. Jerry continued. "We chose the individual timbers from trees on our property. Diane was a big help."

Diane perfectly complemented her husband's modest, quiet demeanor. Her thin build and tall stature matched his, but she radiated energy and her eyes danced as she spoke. "Tell them about my birthday present!" she urged, as she pulled her legs up onto the couch next to him.

"Yeah, I got her a forklift for her birthday one year," he admitted. "But it's not my fault. She asked for one."

"And I loved it!" Diane slipped her hand around his arm. "I learned how to drive it and saved us lots of money with the stonework."

I remembered my ziggy-zaggy joy ride on the pallet dolly in Minnesota and my reluctance to even try driving the front-end loader in Ferryville. "I'm impressed," I said. "I'm not afraid to try most things, but building a house is a pretty big challenge."

"You built your kayak, right?" asked Jerry.

"Yep. But even that took years to finish. And it's only twenty feet long. We'd probably be ninety before we'd finish a house."

Diane laughed. "I don't know if Jerry'll ever be done," she teased. "It's been ten years, and he still has more to do."

"Yeah," Jerry confirmed. "I'm still working on some of the trim details. Be careful when you climb the steps to your bedroom. The railings aren't finished yet. But there's a rope to remind you. You don't sleepwalk, do you?" I didn't, but gracefulness wasn't my strong suit. I hoped the bedroom wasn't too close to the stairs.

Later in the afternoon, we climbed in the truck for a tour of the town. Diane pointed out various businesses and homes, relating stories of their history in the tiny town. "Let's stop for a minute by the *Tribune*. Maybe they'll want to do a story on Gene and Barb. It's okay, honey, if you don't want to come in," she said to Jerry. "I know publicity isn't your thing."

I smiled at Gene. Publicity wasn't really our thing, either, but maybe it would help garner attention for the programs at Peter and Paul Community Services, where we were scheduled to help the next day.

The *Freeburg Tribune* office consisted of a counter, a desk, and some file cabinets. Diane called out, "Harold . . . Helen . . . are you here?" A silver-haired man appeared and studied us over the rims of spectacles perched on the end of his nose. "Well, hello there, Diane. Who'd ya bring us today?"

Diane introduced us, explaining about our trip and why it would be of concern to the citizens of this little community. I half-listened, smiled politely, and let Gene answer Harold's questions as I glanced around the room. The most conspicuous part of the space was a brightly decorated bulletin board on the wall behind us. The plain wooden border framed an assortment of business cards, bumper stickers, and newspaper clippings, many with photos of smiling residents holding produce. I looked closer and whispered to Gene, "Take a look at this tomato!" A beaming woman held up a tomato that filled both her hands. I pointed to the picture; the wooden border of the news office corkboard effectively framed her proud form.

"That was taken right here!" exclaimed Gene.

"Yes, that's my wife, Helen's work," said Harold. "She's our photographer." He pulled out several complementary copies of past newspapers from the end of the counter and smoothed out the front pages for us to see. The same bulletin board featured other country folk, holding up super-sized pumpkins, squash, and zucchini. "Sometimes she goes out on location, but lots of times, folks just bring things right in here to get them in the paper."

"Like I brought you!" said Diane, apparently eager for our smiling faces to be inside the wood-grained frame. I resisted the temptation to make a vegetable analogy.

"We could probably run a story sometime this week." Harold hesitated. "I think we have enough information for a write-up."

Gene handed him one of our business cards. "Here's our website," he told Harold. "Feel free to take anything you want off of there if you need more background information about the trip."

Harold turned to the office door and called Helen. She grabbed her camera and lined the three of us up in front of the corkboard. "Smile!" she said, as the shutter clicked.

Back at home, after a couple of loads of laundry and a home-cooked meal, the talk around the table turned to our trip down the river. "Where you headed from here?" asked Jerry.

"After St. Louis, we we're planning on going to Cape Girardeau, but after that, we're not sure," Gene responded. "We've been advised by everyone with an opinion that we should turn off at Cairo and take the Ohio River to the Tenn-Tom."

I added, "Judging by what we've seen of the industry around here, they're probably right."

"It only gets worse from here on down," replied Jerry. "I'd say you've gotten some pretty good advice."

Later, before bed, Gene brought up the subject again. "We probably do need to make a decision about our route soon. I've been praying about it, but we seem to keep hearing the same thing. And we're running out of river."

"I know," I agreed. Maybe the advice we were getting was God's answer. But what I really wanted to hear was that staying on the Mississippi would be just fine—that there wasn't any real reason to change rivers and paddle over 200 miles upstream. "There's one more person I can think of. What if I ask Leo to look into it for us?" I suggested. Leo was my father's friend. Like Dad, he was a member of the Green Bay Power Squadron, an organization that promoted safe boating through education. They had both taught boating safety and navigation courses and each had taken his turn as Squadron Commander.

All of a sudden, I missed Dad. I wished I could call him . . . hear his voice . . . ask his opinion. I knew he would understand the lure of the Mississippi. But I could also hear him say, "Whatever you do, Toots, be safe." I wrote an email to Leo, letting him know that we were in St. Louis and inquiring about the safest route to the Gulf. I had no doubt that he would check out the options thoroughly. He'd do his best to help Hal's daughter, to take care of me for his old and dear friend. But as I hit send, I was pretty certain what to expect.

Aug. 30: Peter and Paul Community Services

Friday, we took the Metro Link train from Freeburg to downtown St. Louis. Stepping outside, I was immediately chilled by the gray layer of clouds and the dreariness of the concrete city. We found our way to the side doors of Sts. Peter and Paul Church, located in the famous Soulard District, one of the oldest neighborhoods in one of the oldest cities on the Mississippi. Jane, the volunteer coordinator, greeted us and led us down to the basement, lined with wooden bunk beds and blue metal lockers. She introduced us to Tom, the shelter director and in-house historian.

"Tom's been an advocate for the homeless here in St. Louis for the last twenty-eight years," she said. "He has a good grasp of the history of Peter and Paul Community Services and how we've evolved to meet the needs of the homeless in our city."

Tom extended his hand. If he had been barefoot, he would have fit right in on a Florida beach. He wore a dark green tropical print shirt over a black tank top, and a woven fedora with a black hatband. His tanned features contrasted with his full white beard. Suspended from the bottom of his beard was one thin braid hanging down to his generous belly. We exchanged handshakes and got a quick summary of how Peter and Paul Community Services works to address the issues of homelessness.

"PPCS currently includes five homeless support programs," he explained, "all centered in downtown St. Louis. This building right here is an emergency shelter, which provides beds, food, and showers for up to sixty men and helps connect them to community resources. There is also a meals program that serves as many as two hundred meals to homeless and low-income men, women, and children each day. We have a transitional housing program for longer-term housing and case management for the homeless who struggle with substance abuse, mental illness, or HIV and AIDS."

"That's amazing," said Gene. "I can see why your program popped up when we did research for St. Louis."

"Ya gotta understand," continued Tom, "all homeless folks aren't the same. And there's not one solution to the problem." He fingered his long braid. "Being homeless is just one symptom of many other problems and lots of them are chronic ones, like substance abuse and mental illness. You can't solve the problem just by giving someone a temporary place to stay for a while. If you don't solve the root problem, then they become chronically homeless."

Tom certainly did have a grasp of the larger picture. He continued, "All these programs have evolved as we've become more aware of the underlying needs of these people. We've developed something here we call a continuum-of-care network. It helps us place people into a program that meets their unique needs. We collect data for each of the programs; together, this helps us identify the chronically homeless. It's been a model for other major cities, too. We've even got a new program in the works . . . we're converting an old schoolhouse into twenty-five apartments to offer low-cost housing for these men and women, once they're identified as chronically homeless."

Tom couldn't stay, but we thanked him for coming to meet us and for what he was doing to help the community. He was right about the complexity of addressing the root causes of problems rather than treating isolated symptoms. I remembered the many facets of the Muscatine Center for Social Action and the community connections at Grace House in Grand Rapids. By working together, these organizations offered hope for individuals and for the community as a whole.

Jane introduced us to Cheryl and Bob, a St. Louis couple who volunteered regularly to prepare and serve meals. We helped them unload trays of grilled burgers and hot dogs, homemade potato salad, fresh green beans, huge watermelons, and soda. "Thanks for coming to help," Cheryl said. "We thought the men might enjoy a summer picnic tonight."

We got down to business. While I helped warm the food and cut the watermelon into wedges, Gene handed out toiletries, checked towels in and out, and got to know some of the men at the shelter.

After grace, we served firsts, seconds, and thirds until every diner was full. All that remained were some watermelon slices, which we polished off as we cleaned the kitchen. Saying goodnight to Jane, Cheryl, and Bob, we quietly snuck up the open metal stairway to the side door. One by one, the men at the shelter stood and began to clap. Tears clouded my eyes as I held onto the cold metal stair rail and smiled back. We did nothing to deserve applause. We just showed up. Out of love. The applause, I was sure, was gratitude for just that. It felt nice, like a warm embrace. But I was grateful as well, for the chance to help serve.

Aug. 31–Sept. 2: St. Louis to Cape Girardeau

The morning of our departure heated up quickly. The forecast showed a high of 103. After toting our dry bags to the truck, we thanked our hosts. "I bought you a little something," said Diane, handing us each a small package. "I know you don't have a lot of extra room, but thought this might help you with the heat." We opened the packages to find a pair of Frogg Toggs Chilly Pads. "You just get them wet," she explained, "and they keep you cool as the water evaporates." I hoped she didn't spend a lot; we had nothing to give in return. But no gift could have been timelier.

Diane drove us to the Chester boat ramp south of town. We packed *Kupendana*, hugged Diane good-bye, and lowered the kayak down the long, steep concrete ramp. Before we made it to the water, I was already sweaty. I dipped my Chilly Pad in the river, squeezed out the excess water, and draped it around my neck and shoulders. The dampness afforded immediate relief, but a few seconds later, it felt even cooler. "You gotta try this!" I exclaimed.

Gene dampened his and tried it on as well. As it started its magic, he called, "Thank yooou, Diane!" I glanced up, but guessed she already left. I couldn't see anything above the hill of concrete. Gene moved his Chilly Pad to his knees, where it not only cooled his legs, but also padded them from the fiberglass underside of the deck.

Back on the water, we headed for the line of channel buoys. "Look at that current!" I called over my shoulder, pointing to the green can buoy ahead. Water rushed past the mooring line and swirled around the can, straining it against its tether. With the Missouri and Mississippi flowing together, the current was stronger than ever. It felt like an old friend.

We paddled just outside of the green channel markers and watched the wing dams as they passed. The rock walls now rose above the water level and jutted out diagonally into the water from the shore, like rib bones of a twisting river spine. I guessed they were probably underwater a few months ago, when the river swelled with melting snow and heavy rain. In Minnesota and Wisconsin, surface disturbances alerted us to the underwater ridges of rock. Now we skirted along the ends of the ribs, counting them to help locate our position on our river maps and to pass the time. There was no hurry—exertion in the heat wasn't a good idea. We paddled lazily, stopping to rest, drink, and drift.

"I was thinking," said Gene. "I bet there's a Visitors Bureau in Cape Girardeau. If we call them now, maybe they could suggest a service for us once we arrive."

"That's a great idea," I said, wondering why one of us didn't think of that before we traipsed all over Hannibal to ask if anyone wanted our help. Cape Girardeau was still three days away. Maybe someone who knew the area was just what we needed—to help find a service and a place to camp.

"I found a number," Gene said from behind me. "I'm gonna call. What kind of service should I ask about?"

"We've done a lot of food pantries and homeless shelters," I said. I felt a little guilty ruling that out. It seemed hunger and homelessness existed in every community we visited. "Maybe something in the public sector—a school or a library?" I knew my way around both and they often used volunteers. "Or something really different, like a humane society?"

I listened to half of the conversation as Gene explained who were. "That'd be great. Thanks!" he said. I heard him secure his phone in its clip and twisted around in my seat to listen. "We got the right person," he said. "Cheryl's on the board at the library and doesn't know of a way we could help there, but she said her friend runs the Humane Society and is always looking for people. She'll get back to us on that. She said we can camp at the Red Star Access, a boat ramp just north of town."

"Nice!" I said. "This might just turn out to be a strategy for the rest of the trip. I knew there was a reason I brought you along."

"And I thought it was just my good looks," he answered.

Our first night was on a sand beach at Devil's Backbone Campground, named after a rock ridge abutting the property. Pulling Donna up the huge beach of soft sand to a campsite looked pretty near impossible. Gene asked the camp host if we could pay for a site, but camp near the river instead. "You don't need to pay for a campsite if you stay on the beach," she said. "But feel free to walk up and use the camp showers, and help yourself to the water. This heat wave is really somethin'."

Gene's phone rang. It was Cheryl from the Visitors Bureau. "Everything's a go for Tuesday morning," he said, after finishing the call. "Kelly, from the Humane Society, will pick us up at the Red Star at nine." He added, "Why do I get the feeling we'll be scoopin' poop?"

Inside the tent for the night, I listened to the sounds of intermittent laughter from boys around a bonfire just down the beach. Gene was still. I wondered if he was asleep. It wasn't long before the chimes of my cell phone notified me of an incoming email. The screen lit up the small space in the tent, and Gene leaned over, shoulder to shoulder. "Who is it, babe?" he asked.

"Leo wrote back," I told him. Opening the email, I began to read . . .

> "Barb—I looked up all the information I could find about the two routes you asked me about. If you really want my opinion, I wouldn't go either way. Both routes are dangerous for a small wooden boat like yours. But, if you're set on doing this, I'd advise you to turn off the Mississippi and finish the trip on the Tenn-Tom. The industrial nature of the lower Mississippi will make it hard for you to find support. But the most dangerous thing is the current. It gets very fast and strong as you get farther south. The way your boat is designed, you need to be going faster than the current in order for the rudder to steer properly. With the increased commercial traffic, this could be reckless and dangerous. I know your dad would want you to be safe. Good luck.
>
> Sincerely, Leo"

No longer tired, I sat up and crossed my legs. "Well, that's that, I guess." It was the answer we both expected, and the bluntness of Leo's response underscored the wisdom of following the advice we got from everyone else.

Gene leaned up on one elbow. "We should probably blog about the change of plan once we turn off at Cairo." Our readers had no idea that we struggled with this decision.

"I'm sure our friends will be glad we're being safe," I said, finally convinced that we made the best choice. We were abandoning the Mississippi, not our goal of paddling to the Gulf of Mexico. We'd just get there by way of Mobile Bay.

"It'll be upstream, but at least the current on the Ohio won't be as fast as the Mississippi," Gene said. That was oddly, but only mildly, comforting. He continued, "Besides ... remember all the times we've paddled into strong winds?" I nodded. "We've been reminding each other that God's making us stronger for something. Maybe this is it." I hoped we were strong enough.

The next morning, we arose early. It was still thirty miles to Cape Girardeau, and the temp was expected to be high. We planned to just go as far as we could, leaving a short paddle for day three. As we passed the twenty-mile mark for the day, however, it was still early. The current was strong, and so were we. It looked like we might make it all the way to Cape Girardeau.

About eight miles from town, we heard shouting and laughter. Beached powerboats of all sizes lined the shore of Devil's Island. Suntanned, swimsuited bodies lounged on boats, strolled the beach, and floated in the shallows. This wasn't entirely a new sight. We often passed smaller groups of boaters taking beach breaks. We waved and stayed the course in an effort to keep on schedule and stay sober. But this time, the revelers called to us, waving us in to join them.

"Whatcha think?" asked Gene. "Do we pull over or keep going?"

I knew we had to make the call soon, before the current swept us past the island. "Let's stop!" It felt impulsive, but our extra time gave us a choice. We could camp here tonight, or stay for a short break and still make Cape Girardeau before dark. A win-win. I turned the rudder and we hustled across the current toward the island beach. I steered upstream of the only open parking space between the hulls and turned into it just as the current pushed us even with the narrow available shoreline. Paddles in our laps, we slid right up onto the sand.

I didn't have time to be impressed with our own landing. We were immediately circled by shirtless men holding cans of beer and women in swimsuits and cover-ups. We introduced ourselves and joined the Labor Day weekend party in progress. "Have a Jell-O shot," one of the men said, handing us each a plastic cup filled with colorful gelatin. "But be careful—there's moonshine in there."

The cool, fruity Jell-O was refreshing; the spreading warmth of the moonshine followed. "I gotta learn how to make those," I told Gene. After swimming, visiting, and a couple more servings of Jell-O, it seemed prudent to set up camp and stay the night.

The next morning, a simple two-hour jaunt brought us to Red Star Park in Cape Girardeau. Our tent was set up by noon, but with several blogs to write, we gathered our electronics and walked the mile to town. Wi-Fi wasn't easy to find. Even the glitzy Isle Casino was a bust! Most shops in town closed for Labor Day, but we bought lunch and filled our water bottles at a small convenience store. A block west, we chanced upon the Cream of the Crust ice cream shop. All their treats were homemade, from natural ingredients. The strawberry cones were smooth and creamy, with huge chunks of real strawberries. And they came with free Wi-Fi. We lingered until the shop closed, then borrowed their signal from the park across the street until dusk called us back to camp.

Sept. 3: Humane Society of Southeastern Missouri

Kelly pulled into our campsite right on time, dressed in a gray T-shirt and jeans. Her long dark blonde hair was the color of mine, without the gray highlights. I guessed her to be in her mid-twenties, which seemed young to be the executive director of anything. On the way to the SEMO (Southeastern Missouri) Humane Society, we told Kelly about our walk into town. "We were surprised there were so few shops downtown," I told her. "It's a beautiful location, so close to the river."

"It is pretty," she said, "but things have changed. People don't have a reason to come downtown anymore. A few antiques and specialty stores stayed for the tourists, but most of the businesses moved out close to the highway where they're more accessible." This made sense, but I grieved the loss of nostalgia. I wondered if Cape (as residents called their town) would ever invest in a redevelopment initiative to revitalize the downtown area, or just let it deteriorate, taking history along with it.

Soon, we turned into the parking lot of a rather small, nondescript brick building. Kelly seemed to be reading my thoughts. "The building is small," she said. "Someday, I hope we can move to a bigger space, but this is all we can afford right now." Inside the lobby, it was tight, but homey, decorated with colorful bulletin boards and a small display case filled with T-shirts and pet supplies. "What we really need you to do, if it's okay," she said, "is to spend time with the animals. There are only two staff here today," she said. "And our time is usually taken up by people dropping off strays, coming to see the animals, or doing all the paperwork for adoptions. We'd like to give each animal time and attention, but without volunteers, it just wouldn't be possible. I hope you'll see how valuable your time is."

I noticed a bulletin board in the lobby that had the names of over fifty adoptions during the month of August. "You've placed a lot of animals," I commented. "It must feel good."

"Every match we make feels good," admitted Kelly, "but the number on that board isn't anywhere close to the number of animals that are available. Drop-offs are especially high during the summer. At this shelter alone, we took in over a thousand animals during June, July, and August. As you can see by the numbers, we can't possibly place all of them. Unfortunately, humane euthanasia is a sad part of my job. I wish I could impress on people how important it is to rescue animals from shelters and to have their pets spayed and neutered."

Gene and I spent the first half hour in the cat and kitten room. What Kelly called socialization time for the kittens was every bit as therapeutic for me. Without fail, tiny paws scampered all over each other in attempts to escape from their cages into our arms. A gray and white tabby pawed its way up to bury its head in the hollow under my chin, its oversized purr resonating through my chest. "I'll take this one," I said. I still missed Fudge, our twelve-year-old tortoise-shell, who succumbed to kidney disease a few months before our trip, and hoped, someday, to have another cat in the family. But it would have to wait. Our only home, at the moment, was a kayak.

Next, Kelly handed us a list of twenty dogs that needed walks. She gave us each a leash with a clip-on collar, and Gene opened the door to the kennels. One contagious bark, echoed immediately by the other residents, filled the room with a cacophony of yips, yelps, and loud, throaty howls.

Gene turned back to me and said, "Did I ever tell you I can't stand dogs?"

"Once or twice," I replied with a smile. I knew he had a traumatic experience during his childhood. Along his newspaper route, a charging Doberman with bared teeth and a fierce snarl once knocked the screen door off its hinges before its owner grabbed its collar, saving Gene, at the last moment, from attack. It happened long ago and was mostly forgotten, but barking or snarling dogs still set him on edge.

I tried to block the kennel noise out of my mind as I searched for a terrier mix named Myles, the first name on our list. He waited for me at the door to his pen, dressed in a sporty kerchief tied smartly around his neck. First came a few minutes of unbridled joy in the dog run. Then, after breaking in the pooper-scooper, Myles and I went for a walk around the perimeter of the property. Gene was busy with Vivian, a beautiful, but hyper Australian shepherd. I watched him lead her along the tree line at the edge of the property as Vivian turned and jumped up on his chest as if to say, "Play with me!"

During the few hours that we spent there, several cats and a couple of dogs were dropped off, an owner claimed his two lost dogs, and one was adopted. This was an especially touching special needs adoption. An elderly bulldog named Daisy, suffering from both vision problems and tumors, was leaving for her new home. I petted the old gal on the head as her new owner prepared to leave.

Daisy turned her cataract-covered eyes up toward me. She was wrapped in a soft blanket and cradled in her new friend's arms. "You're a lucky girl," I said.

"I think I'm the lucky one," replied her new owner—a senior herself—giving Daisy a gentle hug.

As we finished up the list of dogs that needed exercise, Kelly asked, "Gene, do you have time for one more job?"

"Of course," he agreed. "Anything you need."

Kelly left for a moment and returned with a pit bull—brown with a white patch on its muzzle that extended up between its eyes. "This is Mister," introduced Kelly. "He's been adopted. He gets neutered tomorrow, before his family comes to take him home. We can't bathe him right after surgery, so he needs a bath today." Gene shifted his weight and gave me a sideways glance, but Kelly continued, "The bath'll probably go better if Mister's tired, so play with him out in the run first, then give him his bath right here in this sink." She pointed to a utility sink with a sprayer hose.

We took Mister out to the play area, where he romped about a bit, but soon grew more interested in finding a patch of shade than chasing toys. "I think he's tired enough, from the heat, if not the exercise," Gene said, leading him back inside.

"Have you ever given a dog a bath?" I asked.

"Are you kidding? Never," he said. "My parents would laugh if they saw me now!" Gene leaned down, wrapped his arms around both Mister's front and rear legs, and gently lifted him into the sink.

"Hold that thought," I said, "while I take a picture of the moment, because I'm pretty sure it won't happen again." I got a quick pic to record the event and post on our blog. It would be good to give Gene's folks a chuckle. But more than that, I was proud of him. It wasn't easy for him to overcome the trauma of his past, but here he was, gently holding Mister's collar with one hand, and working the soap into lather with the other. Mister stood stoically while Gene rinsed him with the sprayer, turning his head to keep the soap and water out of his own eyes. Then he towel dried Mister's clean, brown and white dappled coat.

"Nice job," I said, as he gently lifted him down from the tub.

"I kinda feel sorry for him," Gene replied. "He has no idea what's going to happen to him tomorrow. Good luck, ol' boy." He gave Mister a pat on the head. I found myself thankful again to be sharing this experience with Gene. His desire to help outweighed his discomfort. His truly was a servant's heart.

Chapter 10
It's Not All Downstream

Sept. 4-9: Cape Girardeau, MO, to Paducah, KY

Wednesday morning, we launched from the landing at Cape Girardeau's Red Star Park for a defining leg of our journey. In fifty-three more miles, at the confluence of the Ohio River, we planned to leave the Mississippi. The Ol' Muddy had been both our companion and our home. Its sights, smells, and sounds felt as familiar by now as the rooms in our house back home. I intended to savor the few days we had left.

As our turn-off drew nearer, the moments felt saturated with nostalgia. Mile markers passed silently by, once celebrated, but now reminders of the short time remaining with our river companion. The current was swift; water lapped against the bow and swished along the sides of the hull. The sun warmed my arms and shoulders as my paddle blades dipped and pulled through the water, leaving curls on the surface that gently swirled into ripples and disappeared behind us. The sky was painted with shades of blue, blending into one another and then morphing into pinks, purples, and indigos as we set up camp on our final private sand island.

"Red sky at night, sailor's delight." I heard Dad's words come out of my mouth as we lay on the sand, watching the last sliver of pink slip below the western bank. According to sailor's lore, tomorrow would be a beautiful day.

Gene finished the rhyme. "Red sky in the morning, sailor's warning."

"Good thing it's not morning yet," I said, then admitted, "I'm going to miss this."

"Me, too," said Gene. "But you've never been to Kentucky Lake, have you?" I shook my head, and he continued, "I've been there a couple of times, when I went to Tennessee. The lake and the surrounding hills are gorgeous. You'll love it!"

I was bolstered by his optimism, and by the fact that one of us was venturing into familiar territory. In the tent, we checked our river map. We made thirty miles in one day. With good weather tomorrow, we could make the turn onto the Ohio River and camp at the state park in Cairo, Illinois, at the river's confluence.

The following afternoon, as the mile markers turned to single digits, we maneuvered to the eastern side of the Mississippi and paddled along the bank. I kept my eyes on the shoreline, watching for the cut in the land that indicated the mouth of the Ohio River. Gene veered out around the occasional docked barges that jutted into the river, then ducked back in again.

"That must be the campground!" I shouted over my shoulder, pointing to a treed bluff ahead on the left.

"Okay . . . the Ohio's just past that bluff," said Gene. "I'm going to get in as tight as I can to the shore, where there's less current, and take the corner. Tell me as soon as you can see what's up ahead. Are you ready for this?"

"Piece of cake," I said, more confidently than I felt. My paddle churned through the water as we picked up speed to make the turn.

If others were watching, they might have been impressed as *Kupendana* gracefully swung around to face our new future. I was too busy paddling. But my jaw dropped at the scene that greeted us. I heard Gene utter, "Oh, crap!" from behind me. A row of barges loomed in front of us, obscuring my view of anything beyond their steel hulls. A quick glance at their water lines confirmed what I fervently hoped—they weren't moving.

"They're moored," I reassured him. "But let's be careful, in case any of them start up." I checked the marks on the sides of the hulls to confirm that they weren't filled. They probably weren't going anywhere soon.

"Our campground should be about a quarter mile on the left," Gene said. "We'll have to pick our way around all these Big Boys to get to the landing." Slowly, we did just that. We inched our way along the sides of the mammoth vessels until we were certain they weren't under power, and then quickly scooted through the rows, scanning the bank for the boat ramp our map told us was there.

Soon, I spied a white concrete path at the top of the bluff. It wound down the side of the hill, only to end in a swamp of thick, pitted mud, extending at least twenty yards out from the shore. I pointed to the ramp. "Oh, noooo!" Too late, I realized I was whining. I'd have to change my bracelet later. "I don't think *that's* been used recently."

"There's no way we'll make it through that sludge," Gene said, echoing my thoughts. "Not in a million years. It doesn't even look like there's anyone at the campground."

I couldn't see any tents or campers, either. It was after Labor Day, but would state campgrounds be closed already? I pulled out the map. "There's another landing about three miles up, close to Cairo. Maybe we could stop there, pick up some water, and ask about somewhere to stop for the night."

The 1,340 miles of the Upper Mississippi had taught me well the value of flexibility. It was useless to dwell on plans that didn't work out. That just made it more difficult to adapt and to keep a positive outlook. There was a reason people said, "Go with the flow." With this new direction we chose, that would be as important as ever.

Before long, the barge lot was behind us. Now unprotected, we felt the full force of the Ohio River current. The water rushed by *Kupendana's* hull, but landmarks along the bank crawled by. "Let's stay out of the channel. There'll be less current near the shore," Gene said. He steered us over near the bank.

Finally, I saw the Cairo boat ramp; this one looked in much better shape. It led up the bank to a concrete wall. A large gate at the top stood open. I guessed it could be closed in case of flooding to protect the city behind it. We pulled Donna up and set her on our air-filled seat cushions. There was no place to tie up the boat—nothing around but concrete and gravel.

"That looks like an apartment building down the road. Cairo can't be far," Gene said. "Are you okay staying here with the boat if I walk down the road to see what's up? I'll try to find some water and be back as soon as I can." I agreed, and settled down to pass the time playing with my phone.

The wait was eerily quiet. I had no Wi-Fi, so after pacing around a bit, I hiked to the top of the ramp. Gene was nowhere to be seen. I hoped town wasn't as far away as it appeared. Back at the bottom of the ramp with the boat, I heard a car engine. I looked up to see the top of a blue sedan slow down at the crest of the hill, then stop. I was used to people stopping to stare at us. I waited for the sound of a door opening, ready to wave and greet the curious occupants. But I saw no one. I heard the hushed sound of crunching gravel as the car slowly crept away. Maybe they just stopped to look at the river and didn't even notice me, I told myself. A few minutes later, the car returned. Was it the same one? I put my phone to my ear, feigning a conversation. Once again, the car left. What was taking Gene so long?

After what seemed like forever, a black truck approached. The passenger door opened and Gene slid out. He pulled our water jug out of the truck bed, then shook the driver's hand and started down the ramp. "Cairo is a ghost town," he said, filling me in on his quest. "Ever since the last flood, the water in the city—and even in the state park—is contaminated. Almost everyone has moved away. Most of the buildings are even boarded up. I finally found a dollar store that was open and they still had a couple of cases of water bottles. I bought a case, and emptied as many of them as I could into our jug. I left the rest with the guy who offered to drive me back."

"That's so sad," I commented. I told him my creepy car story and we decided to cross over to Kentucky and camp along the bank. We didn't need a campground . . . just a little patch of green. But as we paddled along the Kentucky shore, we found no patch of green.

Eroded cliffs with tangles of exposed roots alternated with cracked, dried mud flats. With no other options, we set up our tent on a mud flat that smelled like musty fish. I already missed the Mississippi.

The next day, I began measuring our meager progress with landmarks along the shore. I chose a lone tree, training my eyes on it as we slowly caught up to it, then inched by. But when I rested my arms, even with Gene's paddle still digging in, we lost ground and I found myself even with the same tree once again.

Gene grumbled, "I think we could *walk* faster than this!" It was tempting to try. But I realized that if we were going to make this work, we'd have to shift a few paradigms. We were used to traveling twenty-five miles or more in a day, resting whenever we wanted, and letting the current continue to push us along. Now, we struggled to make two miles an hour and lost ground every time even one of us stopped paddling. After three months of training, we were strong enough physically, but this new challenge would certainly test our mental and emotional stamina.

We stopped in Mound City, Illinois, for lunch, and discovered Afton's Place restaurant tucked behind the massive concrete floodwall. Two of the three square tables in the cafe were taken by men hunkered over baskets of fries, talking in between mouthfuls of burgers that took both hands to hold them together. Their smudged workpants and jackets and their creased tanned faces suggested a summer of outdoor labor, perhaps on the nearby rails. "Now that's MY kind of burger," said Gene, nodding toward the feast at the next table.

"Bubba Burger," said one of the men. "Best burger around." I didn't often eat burgers, but who could resist the best one around? My single was tender, juicy, and filling. Gene ordered the Double Bubba and finished the whole thing, along with both of our orders of fries. But it was the friendly welcome and over-the-top customer service that made an impression on me. There was no Wi-Fi, but the owners invited us to update our blog on their own personal laptop, hard-wired to the Internet. We told them about our new route and they found us an Illinois state highway map, showing some river details they thought we might find helpful. As Gene wrote an announcement about our change of route, I checked out the map and asked Afton, the owner, if he had any insights about the river ahead.

"There are two dams with locks between here and Paducah," he said. "They're old wicket dams and not in very good shape."

"Wicket dams?" I asked.

"They raise and lower underwater wooden fences called wickets to control the water," he explained. "But they're hard to adjust, and constantly need repair. The Army Corps is building a new dam at Olmsted, which'll eventually replace them, but it's not done yet." With a chuckle, he continued, "It's kind of a joke around here . . . they've been working on it since 'ninety-three. It's millions over budget, and now they say it won't be done until 2020. We're bettin' even later. It shouldn't be much trouble for you, though. It'll be easy to see—just stay on the Kentucky side to get around the construction."

"Thanks," I answered. "We will. Do you know of any parks or campgrounds we could use along this stretch?"

"Nothing around here," Afton replied. "But just before Lock and Dam 52, you'll probably want to stop at Metropolis." He pointed it out on the map. "It's the home of Superman, you know. And there's a really nice state park right on the river where you could camp." Afton handed us our freshly filled water jugs and wished us luck.

Full, rested, and refreshed, we attacked the river current once more, inching our way upstream. Since we couldn't stop paddling without losing ground, we pulled over to shore more frequently for breaks. Sandbars abounded in the Mississippi, but here, we found gravel bars. The small multicolored stones sparkled in the clear water and crunched underfoot as we stretched our legs on the pebbly peninsulas reaching out from the shore. I wondered how the bottom of our hull was faring as it was repeatedly beached on the coarse grit.

During one of our breaks, Gene phoned ahead to the Paducah Convention Bureau. At the rate we were going, we didn't expect to arrive at the Tennessee River confluence for another three days, but we wanted to find out if we could arrange any services before we arrived. "She was very helpful." He filled me in. "There's a place in town called Paducah Cooperative Ministries. She'll check with them and let us know, but she said they always can use volunteers for something."

"Sounds awesome! Did she mention any campgrounds?" I asked.

"No, but there are several hotels not too far away. She also said there's an outdoor sports store called Hooper's right up the street from the landing. She suggested calling them; they've been known to store kayaks and canoes for boaters while they're in town."

Gene called Hooper's and got confirmation and directions. What a relief! Finding a place to keep a twenty-foot boat wasn't always easy. It would be nice not to have to worry about pulling her around with us. Now all we had to do was wait for a call from Paducah Ministries, and in the meantime, paddle our butts off.

Soon, I noticed unmistakable signs of the Olmsted project. On the Illinois bank, men in hard hats kept watch as others operated construction vehicles along a dirt road leading to the river. Immense concrete wall sections towered over the skyline. Cranes floated on work barges, held in place by what looked like gigantic tent stakes driven into the river's bedrock.

I was glad Afton told us what to expect. The construction congestion reached about a third of the way across the river. Gene steered right and we cranked up our speed to begin crossing to the Kentucky side, where we'd be out of the way of the crews and safe from any barges that might veer out around them.

"Is that a sand beach? Over there, right across from all the construction?" Gene asked, his voice energized.

Across the river from the Olmsted site, pilings and a concrete slab waited for the new spillway to make its way over to the Kentucky side. A beautiful ribbon of imported sand stretched downstream from the pilings, a fashionable remake of the mud-caked Kentucky shoreline. I knew it wasn't the Metropolis campground; we were still miles away from that. But it would make a nice tent site for tonight. "Are you thinking what I'm thinking?" I asked.

"We might have to put up with some construction noise, but that looks like a great site," he said. I had to admit, I was ready to stop. My elbows already felt the extra stress of the new current. We made our way over to the bank and pulled *Kupendana* onto the sand. Gene tied her to the concrete slab, and we began to set up camp. The top of the nearby generator worked perfectly for a table; I lined up our bags on the top.

Before long, I heard the hum of a skiff motoring toward us, a change from the construction noise to which I was now accustomed. I turned toward the sound. The men in the boat wore uniforms and orange life vests. As the motor slowed, one of the men reached out to take hold of the concrete and steady the craft, as another shouted out to us, "You can't camp here! This is an Army Corps construction site. Your tent is in our way."

"Even just for one night?" I asked as Gene and I approached. I wondered if we looked pitiful enough to get special treatment.

"Oh, I'm sorry," said Gene. "All the construction's on the other bank. And at the rate it's going, I didn't think you'd make it to this side by morning." I couldn't believe he said that out loud! From their stoic faces, the Army Corpsmen obviously didn't think it was as funny as Gene did. I shot him a warning glance, but he took no apparent notice.

"Sorry," continued the man in charge, no sympathy evident in his voice. "You'll have to move."

I looked down the beach. The strip of sand got gradually narrower, but maybe we could find some middle ground. "How far would we have to move?" I asked. "Could we set up our tent down around the bend, where we wouldn't be near your equipment? Pleeeease?"

The leader looked down the riverbank and I held my breath. "I suppose that would be okay, but just for tonight," he replied.

"Thank you! We'll move our stuff right away," I called. As the skiff backed away, Gene and I carried the tent and our gear down the beach to a site farther away from the spillway construction.

"You didn't like my comment?" Gene asked. "I thought it was witty."

"It was witty, all right," I agreed. "But sarcasm isn't always the best negotiation strategy, especially with the military." I added, with a smile, "I just saved us a couple more hours of paddling. I hope you're grateful."

"So grateful, I'll make you dinner." He grinned. "What are you hungry for?"

"Hmmm." I said the first fancy dish I thought of. "How 'bout Trout Amandine?"

I arranged our bedding and clothes bags in the tent, and then spread out our lightweight, reflective space blanket on the sand. Twenty minutes later, Gene presented our two plastic mess kit bowls with a flourish. "Closest thing I could find was red beans and rice with shrimp." He dropped some nuts into the bowl. "With almonds on the side."

During dinner, I brought up the subject of new goals. "It's frustrating to cover less ground," I said. Gene's face told me he agreed. "But we're just going to be disappointed every day if we keep comparing our progress to the Mississippi. Let's set an Ohio River goal for the next few days." Paddling that entire day with a break for lunch, we covered about eleven miles. We agreed on ten miles a day as a realistic temporary goal.

I watched the floodlights come on across the river as the sky dimmed. They lit up our tent throughout the night as effectively as any lantern, and the pounding of machinery made for fitful sleep. I couldn't imagine how this many people could work on a project day and night for over twenty years without getting finished. I chuckled as I remembered Gene's sarcastic remark. It seemed wittier in retrospect.

In the morning, we hurriedly packed. I was eager to put some distance between us and the dam project. Paddling past the spillway area, I noticed a fisherman dangling his legs and casting his line off the edge of the concrete slab from which we were expelled the night before. "Look." I pointed him out to Gene. "I hope they don't make him leave." I waved to the fisherman, silently wishing him luck.

Approaching Lock and Dam 53, I didn't really know what to expect. We knew the dam was constructed with underwater wickets, but didn't know exactly what a wicket was, how it would affect the water conditions, or what it would mean for us in our small craft. The lock was on the Illinois side of the river, so we approached it as we had the locks on the Mississippi. As we got closer, I could see the structure on the left, and what appeared to be a huge set of rapids in the center of the river, waves rolling and splashing like the middle of a washing machine cycle. It would have given me pause if we were going downstream. But paddling up through that would be insane. "Let's stop for a break and talk to the lockmaster," I suggested. I steered into the backwater area behind the lock. "Maybe he can give us some advice."

As we walked along the wall with the lockmaster, our predicament became clear. "The water level isn't extremely high right now," he said, "so the wickets are partially down." I looked at the rippling chop in the passageway. The water churned as it passed over the submerged wooden fences. The lockmaster continued, "If the wickets were up, we'd use the lock to bring boats up to the higher pool. But since they're down, the locks are closed. Barges and powerboats can navigate through the chop pretty easily. Boats without motors, like yours, have a little more trouble." This lockmaster was a champion of understatement.

I gazed longingly at the calm water inside the unused lock. "I don't know how we'll be able to make it through the rapids paddling against the current. Can't you just let us through the lock?

We've done the whole upper Mississippi and have lots of experience."

"Sorry," he said. "I wish I could."

"Do you have any suggestions about how we can get through?"

"I'd probably cross over to the other side and portage. See those weirs over there?" He pointed to some concrete walls extending into the river from the opposite shore. "If you pull your boat up to one of them, you can lift it over the wall and put in on the other side."

Resigned, we crossed to the other side of the river for another portage—this time, a lift-the-boat-over-the-wall type we'd never done before. The current pushed us downstream during the crossing, but we reached the Kentucky shore safely and crept back to the dam. As we approached, its structure took shape—a waist-high concrete wall, buttressed at intervals and capped at the end with a higher seawall connected to the submerged wickets. What I didn't see from across the river were the mini beaches, formed by swirling eddy currents, which beckoned from between the buttresses. I pulled Donna onto the sand, next to a fishing boat tucked in behind one of the walls. Standing on top of the outermost weir, someone was casting a line out into the rapids we just paddled. "Hey!" I pointed. "It's the fisherman from Olmsted Dam!"

Gene easily hoisted himself onto the chest-high wall. Chest high for Gene was pretty near neck-high for me, and my ascent was less graceful. Smacking my ribs on the concrete and lifting one leg to assist with a walrus roll onto the two-foot-wide seawall, I extended my arm for a hand-up from Gene. I didn't let go as I peered over the edge into the swirling water below. Gene made introductions and some small talk about fishing before explaining our predicament.

"Name's Larry," the man said. "I'd be happy to help you lift your boat over the wall. The fish aren't biting anyway. Just give me a minute to pull in my lines." While we waited for him, Gene and I removed all our gear from the boat and balanced a rainbow of dry bags on top of the wall as cushions. Larry helped us heave the kayak first onto the makeshift padding, and then down the other side of the weir. Larry climbed into his fishing boat and opened his cooler. "Need any water?" he asked. "I'm done for the day. You're welcome to take whatever I have left. You'll save me from carrying it all home." We thanked him for his help and the fresh water, made quick work of repacking the boat, and set off. I kept us close to shore for the next few miles. We weren't taking any chances on getting swept back through there anytime soon.

Our overnight stay at Fort Massac State Park in Metropolis proved to be a memorable highlight of our journey on the Ohio. Approaching the boat ramp, the first thing I noticed was the pontoon boat *Brush Creek Belle* tied to the end of the dock. If the Beverly Hillbillies had used a boat to move to California instead of a jalopy, it would have looked like this. The frame of the pontoon boat was essentially transformed into a houseboat with the use of two-by-fours, plywood, PVC tubing, and bright blue plastic tarps. Nailed to the siding at the stern was a huge, hand-painted plywood sign that read, "From Brush Creek in Andrew, Iowa, to Brush Creek in Florence, Alabama."

As we climbed out of our boat and strapped on the wheels, a gray-haired gentleman stepped out of the pontoon boat. He was of average height, but compact, as if he might have been a football linebacker a few decades ago. He wore a blue-and-white-striped polo, and his baggy khaki shorts were gathered together by a brown leather belt. "That's a beautiful boat," he called over to us. He introduced himself as Stan. "Sorry we're taking up the whole dock. We've been having some engine trouble and we're waiting for a friend to come trailer us to Paducah. Where ya from?"

We introduced ourselves and gave him the abridged version of our trip. "Are you going to be here 'til tomorrow?" I asked. "If you'll be around and would keep an eye on it for us, we could pull our boat out and lock it right here. Then we wouldn't have to lug it all the way over to the campsite."

Stan agreed, and we locked the kayak below the gangplank of the dock, then walked up to see his contraption. "It looks like you've put quite a bit of engineering into this," offered Gene.

"Sure did." Stan beamed. "My brother, Milton, and I built her from an old pontoon boat we bought last year. We added walls, bunks, a galley with a propane stove, and a head with a porta-potty." I peeked behind the blue tarp to see all his improvements. "We even have a portable washing machine for our clothes, and we hang 'em out on a line to dry." Stan reminded me a little of Robert and his double-canoe raft. They shared the same spirit of independence and creativity.

Gene pointed to the stern. "Is that a shower?"

"Yep," Stan replied. "The water goes through a purification system that we installed. It comes out over ninety-percent percent clean. We don't drink it, but we can do everything else with it." I felt a twinge of jealousy. How nice would that be—to be able to walk around on your boat and to take a shower whenever you wanted?

"Sounds like you've thought of everything," Gene admired.

"She's comfortable, but not very fast," said Stan. "She only has a fifty-horse motor, and it's been giving us some problems." I wasn't surprised. A fifty-horsepower motor would have to work pretty hard to push this pontoon-turned-houseboat. I heard footsteps on the dock and turned to see Stan's brother walking toward us. Tall and thin, he wore tropical print trunks and a white printed T-shirt. A Nikon camera swayed gently from his neck. The thing I didn't expect to see was the green Little Tykes wagon that trailed behind him, filled with plastic grocery bags.

"You even brought a wagon?" I asked, wondering where on earth they kept a wagon on their boat. I wished, for a moment, that our boat were large enough to store a few more things.

"Well, it's pretty lightweight, and some of the stores are quite a walk, as you know. We're not so young anymore."

"Neither are we," I admitted.

The next day, we wished Stan and Milton luck with their repairs and waved as we headed east to Paducah. The barge traffic was steady everywhere on the Ohio, but as we approached Lock and Dam 52, we began to see parked barges along the banks of the river. We heard from a local the previous day that Lock 52 was operational. Optimistic, Gene called the lockmaster before we arrived. The side of the conversation I heard didn't sound good.

"The lock is operating," Gene reported after he hung up, "but there's a line of thirty-three barges waiting to lock through. The wait time might be as much as three days, just for the commercial traffic. He's not allowed to lock through any recreational boats that aren't under power."

"Oh, man . . ." My spirits plunged. This river was nothing but trouble. I yearned to be on the Mississippi again—to turn around and float past the construction, past the stinky, caked mud, past the contaminated water, back to the river I knew and loved. I reached for my bracelet; any words that escaped my lips weren't likely to be positive.

Gene twisted around in his seat and smiled over his shoulder. "But he did say he can spare an extra man today and could portage us around the dam in their pickup truck. He'll have someone meet us at the takeout point behind the lock." Whew. Close call. I snapped the elastic, but left my bracelet in place—for now.

The pickup truck was waiting when we arrived. The boulder-strewn shore left us nowhere to slide *Kupendana* out of the water, so standing calf-deep, we unloaded our gear, then carried it to the pickup. We set Donna diagonally into the truck bed, padding her once again with our bags, and the Army Corpsman transported us to a safe launch upstream. I was grateful to avoid a three-day line for the lock or another portage over concrete. Thanking our driver profusely, we set off on our last leg of the trip to Paducah.

A few hours later, along the curving shoreline formed by the Tennessee River confluence, we spied the welcoming entryway to the city of Paducah. The wide, cobblestone boat ramp reminded me of St. Louis. It led up to a long seawall painted with colorful murals depicting the history of the city. A bright red and white sign over the gate in the wall welcomed us to the city. We strapped on the wheels and, with Donna in tow, hiked up the ramp and through the gate. Instantly, we found ourselves in the center of the downtown district.

Donna followed us down the sidewalk like a dog on a leash. Accustomed to the double takes we frequently received from locals, I still felt obliged to smile and raise a hand in a friendly wave. At the intersection, we set Donna's bow down gently as we waited for the light to change from red to green. "Hooper's is just ahead on the right," said Gene, pointing across the street.

"I don't know if they want us just walking in the front door with a boat," I said. "Why don't you go ahead and talk to them? I'll wait here." The light turned green. Gene jogged through the crosswalk and veered into the entranceway.

I awkwardly stood by the corner as the light turned to red, then green, then back to red again. It was bad enough that Donna and I took up the entire sidewalk, but I was pretty sure that to the casual observer, I looked lost. I shot a nervous glance over my shoulder, wondering how long it would be before someone pointed out that the river was behind me. Under a tree not far from the corner, I spied a shady bench. I walked over to check it out and the coolness washed over me like the river current. I sat down to rest, amused by the reactions of the motorists as they sighted the orphaned kayak on the corner of Broadway and Second.

After a while, Gene returned, looking puzzled by my absence. "Over here!" I called. "In the shade."

"Boy, does that look funny," he said as he ambled over and sat down beside me. "It looks like Donna's just sitting on the corner, waiting for the light to change."

"You're telling me," I laughed. "I've been watching *them*." I nodded to an approaching car as the driver's head twisted in our direction, eyes scanning the area.

"They said we can bring the boat in through the back door," said Gene. "We better get going before we cause an accident here."

We navigated Donna though the alleyway behind the store, emptied her contents, and lifted her sideways through the back door of the outfitters. Sorting through our gear to take only what we would need in town, we stretched the cockpit covers over the rest.

"Do you have a ride to your hotel?" asked the manager.

"We thought we'd get a cab after we look around downtown a bit," I explained. An exploratory walk around an interesting city was just what we needed after a few days with our legs cooped up in a narrow hull.

"I get off at five," she said. "If you want to come back then, I'd be happy to give you a ride on my way home."

"Thanks!" said Gene. "That'd be awesome." We shook hands, then turned and headed out the door. "Look!" Gene pointed across the street. A painted sign in the store window advertised "Best Cherry Pie in Town." It was time for some paddler's fuel.

Sept. 10–11: Paducah Cooperative Ministries

After a restful night at the Drury Inn, we took a cab to Paducah Cooperative Ministries. A petite and energetic woman greeted us. "Welcome, my name's Kathy. I'm the administrative assistant of PCM," she offered. We introduced ourselves, and Kathy gave us a short tour. "PCM is a cooperative effort by over fifty area churches to respond to the needs in our community," she began. "All of our cooperating churches commit to providing financial and volunteer help, and being guided by God in our service." Fifty churches all working together was pretty impressive. I wondered if there were even fifty churches in our city back home.

"Excuse me for just a minute," Kathy said as she turned to hold the door for a man in jeans and a blue T-shirt, pushing a cart of bags and boxes. "Good morning, Kenneth," she said. He returned her greeting, continuing to push the cart into the kitchen. Kathy turned back to us. "Kenneth is one of our volunteers from RSVP, the Retired Seniors Volunteer Program," she explained. "He comes in every Tuesday to work at the welcome desk. On the way in, he stops to pick up donations we're expecting that day. Today, Red

Lobster had a load of food for us." I remembered the thousand pounds of food we weighed in Hannibal and wondered what was in Kenneth's boxes from Red Lobster.

Kathy gave us a brief summary of the food, housing, and financial services that PCM provides, between interruptions to greet and direct volunteers, staff, and clients. I felt almost as if we were in the way. "How can we help today?" I asked.

"Well, we really need some painting, but before you do that, could you check with Pastor Aaron in the kitchen to see if he'd like help with the food shipment? Stop in and see me after. I'll try to gather up all the painting supplies by then."

Pastor Aaron must have started seminary early, for his youth was the first thing I noticed about him as we entered the kitchen. "Hi, I'm Aaron, from St. Matthew's," he greeted us. Small in stature, but athletically built, he was dressed in jeans and a T-shirt, rather than a traditional cleric's collar. He would have looked at home ambling through the tree-lined walkways of a college campus between classes. "We have help to put away most of the food from Red Lobster, but all these baked potatoes are frozen." He pointed to several boxes. "So we want to get them divided up into bags and into the freezer as soon as we can." As we divided the frozen baked potatoes into family-sized bags and twisted them shut, Aaron told us more about the program that provided food to over 300 households per month. Around the kitchen, bags with different amounts of food were packed and color-coded according to family size. Shelves against the walls held stocks of cans, boxes, and bags of foods, sorted and labeled for easy packing.

"Can we try packing some bags?" I asked. Aaron explained how to use the color-coded lists to pack items from the shelves into the bags. The organization made the job easy and quick. Gene and I used the system to fill a bag for each family size.

On the way to meet Kathy, we wandered into the front room, where we met Candace, a case manager for PCM's program for the homeless. "Our program is very comprehensive, because homelessness is a complex issue, with many causes." I had a flashback to the same message we heard in St. Louis. "PCM leases seven housing units, which provide shelter for up to thirty-five individuals and families. We provide case management, counseling, food, transportation assistance, and mental health services, as well as education in money management, parenting, and life skills."

I held up a framed sign on the desk, which read, "Sorry!! PCM is out of funds—'til Monday." Candace noticed my questioning glance. "We have an Emergency Relief Assistance Program for people when they just need a little extra money to get them through. Sometimes it helps with utilities, prescription medication, emergency transportation, rental assistance, or infant needs. Any county resident can get money once a year, if they need it, but the need is so great that our weekly budget, which becomes available on Mondays, is often used up in a couple of hours." It was only Tuesday.

Kathy appeared with a cart of supplies and cans of bright blue paint. Our project was to repaint the double doors and door trim at the front and the back of the building. Before we finished lining the windows and doorjamb with blue painter's tape, Kenneth approached. "I'm headed over to pick up some subs for our staff lunch," he said. "You want to ride along? You can keep me company and decide for yourselves what kind you want." His quiet, easy manner instantly made me comfortable.

During the ride, Kenneth shared more about his decision to volunteer with RSVP. "I really believe in all the things that PCM does," he explained. "And I feel like I need to help. Since I drive twenty miles to get here, I pick up store and restaurant donations on the way into town, and just stay all day on Tuesdays to help. I only greet people and answer the phones, but it gives the staff time to do all the other things they need to do." He smoothed his salt and pepper mustache, which matched the color of his hair, then added, "I've been here for over a year now, and these people are like family to me." I was glad he found a place where his gifts were well suited to making people feel welcome, and where he felt comfortable. I wondered where I'd volunteer my retirement time once I got home. All the experiences from this trip should make the decision easy, but right now, I felt paralyzed with so many options.

The conversation turned to our future plans. "Where are you going from here?" Kenneth asked.

"Thursday, we'll paddle to the Kentucky Dam," answered Gene. "There's a marina just past the dam where we can stay Thursday night. Hopefully, they'll have navigation maps for sale. Since we weren't planning on coming this way, we have no charts of Kentucky Lake yet."

"Well . . ." Kenneth hesitated "The marina probably does have the maps you need, but Kentucky Dam is closed right now for maintenance."

Oh, no.

"If you want to paddle, you'll have to go back to the Ohio and take a detour to the Barkley Dam, over on the Cumberland River. You could rejoin the Tennessee through the canal between the lakes."

I tried not to let my disappointment show while I processed his news.

"But I've been thinking," he continued. "I have nothing to do Thursday. I can borrow my friend's trailer and drive you over to the marina just past the dam. You could camp there, get your maps, and stay on schedule."

Relief washed over me, and I felt myself relax. "If it works out, we'd love to take you up on that offer," said Gene. We traded phone numbers so we could keep in touch the next day. I hoped Kenneth's friend felt generous.

After lunch, we returned to our task of the day. The painting wasn't difficult, but was time consuming . . . especially since PCM's doors were busy all day long. I think we spent as much time holding the doors open for staff, volunteers, and clients as we did applying the fresh coat of blue. Finally, we propped the doors open to dry in the afternoon sun, and began to clean our brushes and organize the painting supplies. Kathy stopped by. "The doors look beautiful," she told us. "Thank you so much!"

"It's our pleasure," I replied. "We'll work on the other set tomorrow morning."

"I don't know what you have planned after that," she said. "But Pastor Aaron is building some raised garden beds at our Fresh Start House. He could use some help with the frames and I think you might like to see one of our new initiatives." She explained further, "In a study of community needs, we found that many of the women released from jails and prisons didn't have the support systems they needed, and were soon involved in a cycle of homelessness and recidivism. To address this need, we're trying something new. We call it our Fresh Start program. None of the women have moved in yet, but I'd love you to see it."

An innovative program that came about through a systematic study of community needs? I knew we couldn't pass up the chance to learn more. "I'd love to see that. And we'd get to help build something lasting."

"Sounds like a plan," agreed Gene.

The next morning, we finished the second set of doors, then carefully pulled the painter's tape from around the windows, hinges, and doorframes. It was only a refresh, but to me, the new coat of paint looked pretty spiffy. It felt nice to see the results of our time and to know we helped brighten the environment for the staff and volunteers that worked there.

Pastor Aaron drove us across town and parked behind a single-story concrete building. Its drab exterior and chain-link fence could have qualified as a project for the Home Improvement Network, but entering the building was like stepping into a bag of Skittles. Each room was painted a different vibrant color and decorated with coordinated furnishings and boutique-worthy accents. One room sported sunflower-yellow walls with a large painting of vases overflowing with zinnias in flaming yellows, oranges, and reds. On the white bedspread was an arrangement of pillows embroidered with encouraging messages, and a crocheted afghan in colors that accented the artwork. Another room was a rich blue, with white and yellow accents. An inviting, overstuffed chair was upholstered with a delicate floral print to match the colors in the room. My favorite room, by far, was painted in lilac, with white furniture accented with black and silver.

Down the hall, a woman approached. Her yellow cowl-necked blouse and African print head scarf were as bright as the colorful walls around her. The hue complemented her mocha skin and hair. Her warm smile and gentle eyes welcomed us even before her words. "Hello," she said. "My name's Karen. I'm the director of the Fresh Start House."

As Karen gave us a short tour, I understood the disparity between inside and out. The building was a redesigned and redecorated former Army Reserve facility. "We wanted each of the bedrooms to have its own distinct personality," Karen explained. "So they were designed and furnished by different cooperating churches of PCM. We want to create a safe and nurturing environment. Rooms that feel like home are an important part of that safety."

We proceeded to the central area, where announcements of class offerings hung from a bulletin board. "Each one of the women who will be living here has already begun a program in jail called Breaking Barriers, a small-group series of classes about cognitive change," Karen explained. "Graduates of that program are eligible to come here. We want to encourage the women with programs that will support their transition back into the community by teaching them the skills they need." I glanced at the listings, ranging from cooking classes and child development to job skills and personal finance. "Volunteers sign up to teach topics they know about," Karen explained, "whenever they have the time."

We walked outside to see the site that Pastor Aaron prepared along the fence line for the raised garden beds. While Aaron went to get bags of soil, we used wooden boards and hinged corner brackets to build and line two raised beds, one six feet by four feet, and the other twice as long. When Aaron returned, together, we filled the beds with a soil and fertilizer mix, then raked them smooth.

"Thanks for your help," Aaron said as he replaced the shovel and rake in his trunk. "Now the garden's ready for planting as soon as the new residents move in." It was satisfying to help build the garden, but even more so to help build a little bit of normalcy for women deserving a fresh start.

Sept. 12–18: Kentucky Lake Dam to New Johnsonville, TN

With a borrowed flatbed trailer, Kenneth picked us up at our Paducah hotel and then we scooped up Donna from Hooper's. "Hungry?" asked Kenneth as we got underway. "There's a Cracker Barrel right on the way. They do a nice breakfast. It's one of my wife's favorites."

"I'd like to meet your wife sometime," I mentioned. "Gene and I are planning a road trip on the Great River Road when we're done with this trip. It'd be nice to get back together."

"Well . . ." Kenneth hesitated. "You might not have to wait that long to meet her. We're going to spend the weekend at our trailer, just off Blood River. If you make good time, you might pass by there during the weekend. I'll show you where it is on the map, and then you can call me if you decide you have time to make a little detour."

Kenneth helped us unload the boat and our supplies just a few hundred yards above the Kentucky Dam at the state-run resort and marina. We set up our tent on a narrow parkway, locked Donna to a nearby tree, and watched Kenneth drive over the hill to start his weekend. At the marina store, we found a map of North Kentucky Lake, then pored over it together in the tent.

The Kentucky Dam was built in 1944 to control flooding on the Ohio and Mississippi rivers. By blocking the northern flow of the Tennessee River, the water south of the dam transformed into the huge, 180-mile-long Kentucky Lake, flooding entire towns in the process. Pickwick Dam was built at the southern end to stabilize the level of the water in the lake. This formed a sportsman's paradise between the two dams, with over eighty resorts and boat docks, five state parks, and countless fishing camps. This was one of the reasons we moved over from the Mississippi to our new route. I was eager to paddle in such a hospitable locale.

As beautiful as the lake was, it had a lot of "mood swings." It took only a small change in the intensity or direction of the wind to change boating conditions. This was a lesson we learned very quickly. Friday morning started out sunny and clear. In the protected harbor, the water was calm, the surface smooth. We donned our half skirts, expecting a beautiful start to the next leg of the trip. Before we rounded the sea wall, the water became choppy, and I knew we were in for some rough conditions. It was a good decision to change to our full spray skirts, because the moment we cleared the break wall at the harbor entrance, we were paddling into crashing three-foot waves. The wind was straight out of the east and by the time the surf made it to the western shore, it was brutal. Our intended path was due south, but conditions forced us to tack, or zigzag, east and west, first bucking into the waves and then surfing with them behind us.

Two hours and only three miles later, we pulled up to a private dock for a much-needed rest. We stayed in the boat and braced to keep it from crashing into the floating pier. "Hi, there. Can I help you?" The property owner ventured to the end of the dock, zipping his coat against the raging wind.

"We just need a breather," yelled Gene. "These waves are taking a toll. Is it okay if we rest here for a few minutes?"

"Sure, no problem," he answered. "Stay as long as you like. But in this part of the lake, these waves are nothing. When the wind comes out of the north or south, we get six-foot crashers." Gene and I exchanged wide-eyed glances. We might be lucky that the waves were only three feet. "Where d'ya come from?"

"The headwaters of the Mississippi, originally. But this morning, just from Kentucky Dam," Gene answered. "We've been paddling for a couple of hours so far, but haven't made much progress at all. We need to tack so the waves don't roll us."

"We're thinking of crossing the lake and paddling south on the lee side." I raised my voice against the wind. "The shore would protect us more from the wind, and the waves would be smaller." I added, "My only concern is the middle. Will we get into higher waves because of the water depth?"

"I don't think that'll be an issue," the man replied. "By the time the waves get over to this shore, they've grown pretty wild. I think crossing's your best bet . . . unless you want to stop for the day. You're welcome to set up a tent here."

"Thanks," said Gene, "but it's still early." He turned to me. "You up for a crossing?"

The break was just what I needed. I remembered how much easier it was to paddle on the lee side of the river, sheltered by the trees along the shore. "Let's go for it." We left the dock heading due east and paddled into wave after wave, until we reached the far shore a mile and a half away. Then it was a right turn to follow the lee shore. Our decision was a good one. In the shelter of the shore, the water was choppy, but we were able to keep our heading.

As the light dimmed, we set up camp on a sandy peninsula in one of the many bays along the eastern shore, an area known as the Land Between the Lakes. As the wind died down, the setting sun painted the water with streaks of orange and red. In one of the south's most well-known recreational areas, we shared an evening of quiet solitude.

The following day, we checked the forecast and decided to stay near the same shore again. The easterly winds were still strong, and we mastered the techniques we needed right where we were. Everything was going to be fine. Then Gene got a text message from Kenneth, reminding us that he'd love us to meet his wife, Lottie, and that they'd be at their trailer on Blood River if we had time to stop by. It was Saturday and Blood River was near enough to make the stop. But it would be about a seven-mile detour and the confluence was on the western side of the lake. We'd have to cross Kentucky Lake again.

"What do you think?" Gene asked me.

I considered the pros and cons. "I'm not really keen on crossing the lake again," I started. "But Kenneth went out of his way to help us. We could go out of our way for him. And I'd like to meet Lottie."

"We do like to say that this trip is about the people, not the paddle . . ." Gene added another pro to the list. "And we'll have to cross again, but it'll be with the wind, not against it."

The decision was made. On the way back across the lake, we half-paddled and half-surfed. It was a new, pleasant feeling as the swells lifted us gently, starting at the stern and rolling along the beam to the bow. Then down we'd drop, only to be picked up and pushed along by the next big roller. Sometimes, though, I held my breath as the kayak plunged down into the water, submerging the bow. Eventually, we found the entrance to Blood River and the surface calmed as we wound our way through the backwaters.

We settled in at River's Edge Marina, where Mick, the owner, gave us a free overnight slip for Donna and a free campsite just a short walk away. "You picked a good time to visit," he said. "We've got a neighborhood block party tonight right up the road. Stop by after you're done visiting your friends. Might as well . . . the music'll be pretty loud and you won't get any sleep anyway." He laughed. "I hope to see you there!"

Kenneth appeared once more in his pickup and whisked us off for a tour of the area, followed by a picnic dinner and a campfire at his trailer. Lottie was indeed his perfect companion—low-key, without pretense, and content with the simple joys of family, health, and home.

Back at the River's Edge, we didn't need a map to find the block party. We made an obligatory appearance, mingling and drinking with Mick's neighbors, and then retired to the tent. Mick was right; we could hear the music just fine from there—long into the night.

Like on the wide sections of the Mississippi, we learned to check the forecast each day for the wind direction and strength, planning our paddle to take advantage of the sheltering shore. The current was much weaker than the Ohio, but still pushed against us. As long as we stayed well away from the channel, near the lee shore, we made the best distance—usually between fifteen and twenty miles a day. A few days' paddle from the town of New Johnsonville, we called the Visitors Bureau to inquire about a service that might appreciate our help, and chose the New Johnsonville Senior Center, a recently opened location for seniors to gather for companionship and fun.

One thing we didn't expect down here in the south was that some of the marinas would already be closed for the season. The current weather seemed typical of our northern summers, so we didn't think twice about being on the water. After finding several marinas and campgrounds closed after Labor Day, we learned to call further in advance.

This was how we learned about the Danville Bait Shop and Grill, with its accompanying campground. After getting no answer at several places closed for the season, I heard the southern drawl of a woman at the other end of the line. "Yes, honey, we're still open. But the boat raymp is easy to miss." She explained, "It's tucked up raht behind the old blowed-up railroad bridge."

"Wait a minute . . . a blown-up bridge?" I asked, wondering if I heard correctly.

"That's raht," she said. "When the river was flooded, the water was so high that the barges couldn't git under the bridge. So they blowed it up. There's a couple of sections left, but they don't go nowhere." I tried to imagine the landmark she described . . . a bridge to nowhere. That shouldn't be so hard to find. She continued, "As soon as y'all see the bridge, tuck in to the shore or ya might miss us altogether."

Her strange directions were right on target. Sure enough, along the east bank, jutting out into the river from a spit of land, I spotted two spans of a railroad bridge. The sections extended out over the water, then abruptly ended. A barricade prevented traffic from launching off the old relic into the river below. Fascinated with the sight before us, we almost missed the boat landing tucked up into a corner at the shore. We tied up to the pier and walked up to see about a campground.

Near the bait shop was an outdoor shelter, with several locals seated at picnic tables, drinking, playing cards, and chatting. They shouted a greeting and waved us over. When we joined them, I recognized we were now, officially, in the south. An oversized confederate flag hung from the rafters, and our Midwestern accents were, for the first time, in the minority. We were the strange-sounding ones. But that famous southern hospitality was at work, as we were welcomed as a part of the gang. It got late and people began to depart. A blonde woman named Bettye clasped my hand between hers. "It was so nice to meet y'all," she said. "Do y'all have any time in the mornin' before ya leave? Bobby and I'd love to take y'all fer breakfast."

We rose early the next morning, broke camp, and packed the boat before Bobby and Bettye drove up in their pickup truck. We hopped in the back seat and, before long, arrived at the Southernaire, a local restaurant and motel. Inside the lobby, various pieces of handmade wooden furniture and crafts were displayed . . . framed wildlife artwork, rustic chairs, and generously shellacked tree stump tables. As we fueled up for the day with omelets and fresh coffee, Bettye gave us some advice about paddling south outside of the channel near the east shore. "Be sure y'all stay out of the channel an' on the inside of the meeahl," she said. I had no idea what she meant, but I hesitated to respond to her kindness with a criticism of her accent. I hoped Gene had been able to understand her better than I. The meal? What the heck was a meal? We would just stay clear of the channel and we'd be fine. Maybe it would all become clear in time.

Back at the landing, we waved good-bye and launched. I asked Gene, "What's a meal?"

"I have *no* idea," he replied.

"Well, whatever it is," I said with a chuckle, "we're going to paddle inside it."

Rounding the partial railroad bridge, suddenly, everything made sense. Rising up out of the water, not far away, were the top two stories of a huge, graffiti-covered concrete building. "It's a mill!" I shouted. "An old mill!" We paddled on the east side of the mill, between the old structure and the shore. I was glad we weren't in the boat traffic of the channel; it was hard to pull my eyes away. I gazed at the sturdy construction with its pillared entry, square towers, and open windows through which I could see nothing but water and blue sky. Seagulls circled the structure, flew through the windows, and lighted on the sills.

Gene steered us as close as we dared. It would have been fun to paddle through the open areas, exploring the old structure, but how safe could a building be after standing mostly submerged for seventy years? We decided to stay clear. This must have been where old Danville stood, before the dams were built. I was sorry for the people of these southern towns, forced to move to higher ground or away altogether, leaving their entire towns to be swallowed up by progress. I imagined them demolishing their homes and businesses, then watching as the water crept higher, submerging the remnants of their lives. Our river maps marked the locations of such infrastructure features as roads, fence lines, and utility poles, which became underwater hazards for the boaters who now floated over the previously bustling towns. This reservoir and recreation area was an impressive civil engineering feat, but came at a huge personal cost to the residents of these towns.

Still wind conditions and the resulting calm water made for a gorgeous twenty-three-mile paddle, our longest since leaving the Mississippi. Wind and wave-avoidance strategies forgotten for now, I was free to fully appreciate the beauty of our new route. Along the shore, trees crept close to the water's edge, their roots breaking the cream and mocha layers of limestone into chunks of tiramisu. Staying outside the channel markers, we wove between islands of varied sizes and shapes. Once, the lake became so shallow between the islands that we stepped out into the ankle-deep water and pulled Donna behind us.

We stopped for lunch on a long stretch of pebbly island beach. The water was so still that Donna needed no grounding; she waited for us contentedly about a yard out from shore. We stretched our legs, took turns walking behind the bushes, and shared hand sanitizer, dried fruit, nuts, and granola bars. In the distance, a small-boat motor came to life, then softened and disappeared. A few minutes later, a rhythmic lapping upon our shore announced its passage with a tiny wake.

Gene put his arm around my shoulder. "Gorgeous, isn't it?" He pointed up and down the opposite shore. "I bet we can see a hundred eighty degrees." I glanced to the south and then turned right, scanning the lake and shoreline beyond. The forested hills rose and fell in waves. Hues of green dusted with hints of orange signaled nature's awareness of autumn's approach. I didn't think I'd ever tire of a view like this.

We paddled into New Johnsonville a day earlier than we expected, another first since leaving the Mississippi. I felt optimistic again; maybe the hardest part was behind us. As we tied up at the dock and climbed the steps to our little hotel, I looked forward, once again, to sinking into a real bed. We needed to find Wi-Fi and a Laundromat, but that could wait until tomorrow.

Sept. 19: New Johnsonville Senior Center

The first thing I noticed as we approached the New Johnsonville Senior Center was the beautiful sign at the entrance drive: All Seniors Welcome! The red brick exterior of the building was well kept and reminded me of an office building with benches on the front porch lending a friendly touch. Behind the meticulously organized front desk, a man leaned back in his chair, his olive plaid shirt filling out a pair of blue jean overalls, meaty fingers stuck into the pages of a magazine partially opened in his lap. He stood up, removed his camouflaged ball cap, and held out a huge hand. "Welcome," he said. "I'm Robert."

Casual, low-key Robert turned out to be the executive director of the senior center. He gave us a tour of the nearly 3,000-square-foot building, donated to the city only a year before by a relocated health care company. The renovation work on the inside of the building was completed. Painted in shades of light green, with cream and burgundy accents, the rooms were warmly inviting. The entrance area included an office and lobby with comfortable sofas.

On a coffee table, I noticed a bound book of photos of the Grand Opening, and made a mental note to leaf through it later. We wandered through the other inside spaces, flexible enough for intimate small groups or larger social gatherings. Outside, a patio area for grilling awaited completion. I wondered if we'd get to help with that. The back lawn had a horseshoe pit and an area for corn hole, a kind of beanbag toss.

"You have lots of great spaces," I said. "Do you plan activities or is it more of a drop-in opportunity?"

"A little bit o' both," said Robert. "We're open on weekdays, durin' the day. 'Cept for Wednesdays. We're closed then. We schedule activities some days, but other days, seniors jus' stop in an' see who's here. Sometimes they read a little or talk a little."

"How many people do you usually get in a day?" Gene asked.

Robert ran his fingers through his white goatee. "Oh, some days, just a few. Other days, maybe ten er twelve. We have food an' music on Friday nights, an' you should see all of 'em then." He pointed to the parking lot. "The parking lot looks plenty big now, but on Fridays, people have to park in the strip mall next door."

I smiled, imagining a rocking senior rave. I would have liked to stay another day to see that.

"We have to leave tomorrow," said Gene, "but is there anything we can do to help you today?"

"We've got bingo scheduled in half an hour," said Robert. "You can help me set up and help lead the bingo if you want." He led the way inside, and we found the bingo supplies. All was ready—we just needed some seniors.

Gene settled down on the couch with a book from the library shelves while I looked at the old photographs and articles on the walls. I was particularly interested in some framed prints of historic Johnsonville and a commemorative copy of the *Johnsonville Times*. "Come over here, hon. Look at this," I called to Gene.

I paraphrased what I already read about the naming of the old town. "Johnsonville was originally a shipping town on the river called Knott's Landing. In 1863, the railroad finally reached all the way to the Tennessee River. To celebrate, a bigwig military governor rode along on the first passenger train from Nashville. His name was Andrew Johnson." I inserted my own aside, "Turns out he had a personal agenda."

"Politicians haven't changed," said Gene.

"As the story goes, he held a ceremony when he arrived, christening the town Johnsonville, after himself." I knew a few people like that.

Gene was interested now, too. He pointed to articles about rebuilding after Civil War battles, and in the wake of Tennessee River floods. "Old Johnsonville came back from a lot," he said, "but even they couldn't survive the birth of Kentucky Lake."

The first senior we met was Merlin, a regular who told us he "stops by most every morning to visit for a bit and help out with things around the center." Later, Richard stopped by to visit and entertained us with tales of the places in the old pictures on the walls.

Lois was the only senior who showed up for Bingo. Somewhere in her seventies, I guessed, she carried her petite but fit frame in an assured manner. If I grew up in the south, she might have been my high school gym teacher. "It wouldn't make much sense to play Bingo alone," she said without cracking a smile. "Would ya like to play some rummy?" Conversation and cards were flying, and before we knew it, it was almost time to go. Gene made a trip to the strip mall for soda and carryout pizza, and we all shared a prayer and a lunchtime meal.

"You've accomplished a lot here in a short time," Gene said to Robert as he walked us to the door. "We'll have a story about the senior center up on our blog tomorrow before we leave." He gave Robert one of our business cards. "The blog address is on here. Hopefully, we'll help spread the word about what a great place you've got and the good you're doing. Is there anything you need as far as donations? We like to post a list. You never know who might read it and want to help."

"We could use a few plastic tables for the patio, once it's done," he said, "but the people here in New Johnsonville are very generous. If we let it be known that there's a need, that need gets filled. When we hold a fund-raiser, like our chicken barbeque or our yard sale, well, everyone comes out—not just the seniors."

At fifty-six, I already technically qualified as a senior. I was still pretty well plugged in socially, with family, friends, church, and work—plenty to keep busy. But as many seniors aged and lost friends and family to relocation, illness, or even death, the threat of loneliness became all too real. It was good to see this community make the quality of life for its seniors a priority.

That evening, I worked on our blog post about the senior center while Gene made a call to his daughter, Cassie, in Nashville. He sounded excited as he made arrangements to see her now that we were in Tennessee. "It's all set," he announced, placing his cell phone on the nightstand. "She'll drive out to spend the day with us Sunday. We just have to tell her where to meet, once we know where we'll be."

Gene spread our map on the bed, calculating the mileage between the next few towns. "We can wait and see how far we get, but if we stay at Cuba Landing tomorrow and camp at Mousetail Landing on Saturday, that'd give us a short three-mile paddle Sunday to Perryville Marina. We'd get there early and have the whole day to spend with her." It sounded like a good plan to me.

Sept. 20–25: New Johnsonville to Savannah, TN

During the next leg of our trip, Kentucky Lake narrowed, funneling back down again into the Tennessee River. The current was no longer spread out over the width of an entire lake, but channeled between the banks of a narrow twisting river. We were now traveling toward Pickwick Dam, the southern end of the Kentucky Lake Reservoir. Pickwick Dam controlled the water that flowed north through its turbines into Kentucky Lake, then onward toward the Ohio, and then the Mississippi. Each day of our trip, as we approached the dam, the current became stronger. Like on the Ohio, we made every effort to paddle upstream with the least amount of effort. Every day became a game of hide-and-seek with both the current and the wind. We stayed as close to the leeward shore as possible, veering out only as far as necessary to swerve around fallen trees and debris or to turn into the wake of huge pleasure boats as they powered by. The current was swifter on the outer banks of the twists and turns, so we frequently crossed the river during straightaways to take advantage of the slower current at the inside turns.

As we paddled, I noticed a variety of riverfront homes—some with long sloping manicured yards leading to the water, others with steep staircases leading up to a house perched high on the hill, and one situated at the top of a limestone cliff overlooking the river valley below. All, I imagined, had spectacular views. "How 'bout we look for a retirement home here?" Gene asked.

"I'd think seriously about that," I answered. "But I wouldn't want to deal with the erosion." On the Mississippi, the Army Corps of Engineers created a whole system of structures to control the current. But here, rocky cliffs, sandstone ledges, and enormous mud banks all bore witness to the power of the river. In an effort to control it, many of the property owners lined their shores with riprap, which seemed to work well. The rocks and broken concrete slabs prevented the soil from being swept downstream by the rushing water. But where the land was unprotected, clumps of tree roots often stood bare, like cut-away diagrams in a science textbook. I wondered how one of the trees even continued to stand, and how far out in the river we should paddle so we wouldn't get hit if it toppled over as we passed.

The Tennessee River was an oft-used water highway for pleasure boats. The preponderance of support along this route was one of the main reasons we turned off the Mississippi. At Cuba Landing, we found both a marina with a slip to tie up the boat and a nearby campground. A day later, Mousetail Landing Park offered us scenic bluff camping sites overlooking a small bay. We watched snow-white egrets wade slowly and deliberately in the shallows on delicate twig-like legs, then rise into graceful flight.

The next morning, we hurried to break camp, eager for a family day. In no time, we were gliding up to the breakwater at the Perryville Marina. I recognized the figure seated on a bench at the edge of the grassy knoll—Cassie! She gazed out at the water to the south, so we were right next to her before she saw us. "Cassie!" shouted Gene. She turned toward his voice and waved.

As we tied up at the dock, Cassie made her way down the gangplank. Gene hopped out of his seat to give her a long-awaited hug. She had her mother's ginger hair, but her dad's height. At six feet, she nearly matched his tall frame.

We threw our overnight necessities in the trunk of Cassie's Ford Escort. I slid into the back seat, leaving the front for Gene to sit next to his daughter. We stopped to reserve a room for the night at the nicer of the two modest motels we found, and then headed out on the town. On the one main street, the Save-Rite grocery store was out of business, as was the first bar/restaurant we tried.

"There's gotta be a Packer bar around here somewhere," said Cassie. "We've got several in Nashville." I appreciated the sentiment. Since I grew up in Green Bay, the Packers were as much a part of life for me as holidays with family, living by a nine-month school schedule, and vacationing near the water. If I was ever transplanted to another state, I was sure I'd find a Packer Nation there, too.

We stopped at the only bar that was open, but had to settle for watching the Titans on the big screen, while keeping up with the Packers score on our phones. Conversation drifted between Cassie's job, her southern life, and stories of our trip.

Later, Cassie dropped us off at the motel. "Love you, Dad," she said, "but some of us have to start the workweek tomorrow. Be safe."

As she drove away, I waved with one hand and put my other arm around Gene's waist. "It was good to see your baby, wasn't it?"

"Yeah, I'm proud of her. She's doing well."

"She sure is," I agreed. Gene unlocked the door to our room, holding it open for me to enter first. I was glad we were able to meet up with Cassie. She was successful, happy, and independent. In her own time, I hoped she would meet someone as special as her dad was to me.

Besides the comfort and safety of marinas, one of the fun things was meeting other river travelers. Everyone had a story. Most of them, though, weren't in kayaks or canoes. They were at the helms of sleek, well-equipped, floating vacation homes. As we left Perryville Marina, Gene pointed to a cabin cruiser leaving just ahead of us. "Look! That one's a long way from home." The white Bayliner Explorer looked to be about forty feet long. Flying from a flagpole off the stern was the red and white maple leaf flag of Canada.

"I'll say," I agreed.

"I bet they're doing the Great Loop," Gene said, "from the Great Lakes, down the American river system, and back up the Intercoastal Waterway. I've always wanted to try that."

"Let's get done with this trip before you get any ideas for another one, okay?" I was always the realist, but one of us had to be.

Later that day, we noticed the same boat moored in a side channel. The flag was a dead giveaway. As we came closer, I noticed the boat's name painted on the stern. "Ahoy, *Time & Tide!*" Gene's nautical greeting boomed across the water.

A tanned, brunette woman waved from an opening in the gray canvas cover, snapped around the stern deck. "Gary, come up here for a minute," she called. Soon, an equally bronzed shirtless man appeared, wiping his grease-smudged hands on a shop rag. He placed his forearms on the gunwale and leaned out toward us.

"Sorry," he said. "I was working on our water pump. It's been overheating lately."

"Sorry to hear that," said Gene. "We just wanted to say hello. We saw you back by Perryville and noticed your Canadian flag.

You doin' the loop?" We paddled closer, and skulled to stay near their boat.

"Yes, we're from Ontario. We're headin' down to Florida, and then to the Bahamas. I'm Gary, and this is my wife, Christelle."

Christelle leaned out next to Gary. "This is our second loop," she said. "As soon as we crossed our wake from the first loop, I said to Gary, 'That was so much fun, let's do it again!' So we took a month to get ready, and started over."

"I guess that's as good a recommendation for looping as any," I said. We introduced ourselves and told them about our trip. "We're aiming for Mobile eventually, but tonight just for Clifton Marina." We traded blog addresses and promised to check out each other's sites.

We had to book it to get to Clifton Marina before dark. The sky began to dim as we turned into the cove and slid silently past two- and three-story floating palaces along the transient docks, where travelers tied up their Big Boys for the night. Seasonal slips lined the cove; blue aluminum roofing offered protection from the elements for dozens of expensive toys. We tied up in front of the marina office. Built on a floating platform, the crisp white building with a matching blue roof was surrounded by a wraparound deck. Tables and chairs, potted plants, and swag rope railings added charm to what looked like the social center of the marina.

As we tied up to the temporary dock, a screen door slammed and a bearded man with a receding hairline approached. The evening sun cast a golden light through the white wispy curls of hair that cascaded down to the back of his neck. "Hi, I'm Terry," he said, extending a hand. His muscular, tattooed forearms extended from the sleeves of his oversized white T-shirt. "Looks like you're trav'lin'."

We told him about our trip. "Do you know if there's a place around here where we can set up a tent?" I asked.

"There's a campground up over the hill," he said, "but it's late, and there's rain comin' through." He pointed to a forty-foot Sea Ray at the transient dock. "That's our boat over there. You're welcome to sleep aboard tonight. You could leave your boat mostly packed up and just bring what you need for the night."

Another man emerged from the office, a mixed drink in hand. Dark, tanned, and solidly built, he looked younger than his companion. "Hey, Ray—over here!" called Terry. Ray joined us, then removed a pair of wraparound sunglasses from his eyes and hung them on his collar.

I wondered how Ray would feel about Terry's offer, but he agreed without hesitation. "Sure," he said. "We've got a couple of zero gravity chairs in the cockpit. We nap on them all the time. They're pretty comfortable. Want to come see the boat?"

Sleek and built for speed, the Sundancer had a surprising amount of room inside. We climbed the steps to the helm, and I imagined driving this down the river. "I can reach over thirty-five miles an hour pretty easily," said Ray. "But Terry won't let me drive her that fast and I don't get very good gas mileage at top speed anyway." I was glad that Terry was Ray's conscience. I didn't want to deal with the wake that would come from any boat at that speed.

"How much gas can you carry?" asked Gene.

"The tank is three twenty," he said. "So if I if I keep it around twenty or twenty-five, I can get about three hundred miles to a tank."

I did some mental math. Just shy of a mile per gallon. A thousand-dollar fill-up, easy—every couple days.

"We take longer," said Gene, "but we get a lot better mileage." I smiled. Gene might have a wandering eye for boats, but his loyalty to Donna was touching.

We spent the evening in the marina. Sonja, the owner and chef, made us dinner. Then we drank from Ray's stash of top shelf whiskey and hung out with other river travelers. Later, we retired to our forty-foot "boat-el." For a stomach sleeper like me, the chairs weren't quite as comfortable as Ray advertised. I spent the night flipping from one side to the other, curling up to try to stay warm in the late September chill.

"Coffee?" asked Terry the next morning as he stepped out of the cabin and handed us each a steaming mug. I could feel the warm air from the space heater inside the cabin, and wished we'd had one in the cockpit overnight. "We're both up, so come on in as soon as you're awake. It's warmer in here."

I took a sip of coffee and felt a sudden ache in my jaw. Maybe it was just temperature sensitivity. I put a finger into my mouth and pressed on the top of each tooth on the right side. A jab of pain seared into my jaw under one of the molars. "I think I have a problem," I told Gene, explaining as we climbed down the steps into the warm cabin.

"We'll be in Savannah in a couple days," Gene said. "If it doesn't go away, we'll just have to find a dentist." Terry found me some Tylenol, which took the edge off. We settled down into the cushioned comfort and chatted with Ray and Terry about our families, our jobs, and our past and present adventures.

Ray, an entrepreneur and adventurer, had decided on a whim to do the Great Loop and bought his boat just for this trip. "My kids thought I was crazy," he explained. "They wouldn't come; neither would my wife. Terry's helping me get the boat through the locks and then he's flying home." He grinned at Terry. "Unless I can convince him to stay with me a while longer." I worried for Ray, once he was left to finish the Loop alone. I wondered if his kids had a point, but then reminded myself that we set off from Lake Itasca with only a few weekends of kayak practice under our belts. Maybe we were more like Ray than I thought.

After Sonja prepared us an omelet breakfast, I finally checked the time. Eleven o'clock. We were in for another late day. More rain was on the way. Ray and Terry decided to stay for another day, but we bet on the rain to pass by to the east and set out.

The rain held off and we made it to the Riverview, a café and convenience store at Saltillo Landing. The new owner, Brian, offered us a corner of his property for our tent, outlets to charge our phones, and anything we wanted from the deli, which was about to close for the night. "We can't save this food anyway," said Brian. "Just tell me whatever you want and it's free." Instead of our usual one-pot meal, we had a picnic table feast of barbequed ribs, potato wedges, and corn bread. I popped some Advil and chewed on the left side. It was delicious.

Before leaving Saltillo Landing the next morning, we called the Visitors Bureau in Savannah, TN. We left a message, but intended to stop there even if we didn't hear back. Our food box was waiting for us at the post office, and I was pretty sure I'd need to see a dentist. With our sights set on that goal, it was knuckle down to finish the last eighteen miles to town.

Midway through the day, the phone rang. "This is Vicki, from the Savannah Visitors Bureau," a voice said. "I got your message. I have an idea of a place that might want your help—the Horse Creek Wildlife Sanctuary."

"That'd be great," I said. We'd worked with pets at the Humane Society in Cape Girardeau, but it would be fun to help out with wildlife and maybe even horses. "I'll need one more thing, too—a recommendation for a dentist. I've got a doozy of a toothache."

"I know a few. I'll check on that for you."

"Thanks. We're about three hours away from town. Is there a marina where we can leave the boat?" I didn't see one on the map, but Vicki might know.

"Not really," she said, "but I work for the museum as well, and my boss, the curator, lives on the river, just north of town. He sometimes lets people store their boats on his property. He's out of town this week, but let me call him and ask. I'll get back to you."

She called back with good news. "He said it's fine. Just pull your boat up the ramp, and you can leave it by the boathouse." I watched carefully for the landmark home and dock she described. Soon, we found the pier and pulled Donna up the long steep ramp. At the top, it flattened out and we passed through the archway of a small carriage house-turned-boathouse. A circle drive led past an outdoor pool surrounded by a wrought-iron fence and up to the riverside façade of a real southern estate. Four two-story columns stood like sentinels. I turned to see what I imagined the curator woke up to every day—a magnificent valley view, the Tennessee River sparkling below. I didn't know how old the house was, but I was pretty sure the owners never had to worry about flooding.

Soon, a black SUV crept up the drive. A petite woman lowered herself down from the seat and walked over to greet us. I noticed her African print blouse and short haircut, colored dark with streaks of blonde and nicely styled. I wondered if I should have kept mine short. I grew it long for this trip, suspecting that I wouldn't have much chance for monthly salon visits, let alone daily styling. I self-consciously checked my ponytail. This was now my go-to style, with only a rainbow of scrunchies to vary my look.

"Hi, y'all must be Barb and Gene. Welcome to Savannah." Vicki piled our bags into the back, and we climbed into the truck. Along the winding drive, we passed another estate, also with well-manicured grounds. I wasn't sure which I like better.

I was pulled out of house-hunting mode by Vicki's voice. "I hope the motel near the museum is okay. It's not very fancy, but it won't cost y'all an arm an' a leg. I wrote down a couple names and addresses of dentists. Maybe y'all want ta call an' make an appointment for Friday."

"We're planning to use Friday for errands, anyway," I told her. "We'll pick up our food box from the post office, do laundry, write out blogs . . . stuff like that."

"Go to the dentist . . ." added Gene.

"That's good. I hope y'all can get that fixed up. Can't have fun when you're hurtin'." We pulled up at the hotel lot. "See that buildin' right across the street?" she asked. "The one with the big ol' petrified logs on the porch?" I smiled and nodded. One was obviously grained, like a log, but the other looked like a hunk of charred wood from a giant's campfire ring. I couldn't wait to examine it closer. "That's the museum. I arranged for someone from Horse Creek to come by at nine tomorrow, so y'all can just walk right over in the morning."

"What can you tell us about Horse Creek?" I asked.

"It's a wildlife sanctuary and a no-kill shelter," she said, "all started by one family, through a charitable trust. It was five hundred acres, and now it's over two thousand. We're really proud of it here in Savannah. Most communities don't have anything near this nice."

"It sounds like a great place to learn more about," I said. "But they don't have horses?"

Vicki laughed. "I can see how y'all might think that, but the name comes from the creek that runs through the property, jus' south of town."

"So what's at the no-kill shelter?" I asked.

"Mostly dogs," she said. I had a strange feeling of déjà vu. I hoped they didn't have a pit bull that needed a bath.

Sept. 26: Horse Creek Wildlife Sanctuary and Animal Refuge

We barely finished greeting Vicki at the front desk of the museum and telling her about my Friday morning dentist appointment before Denise pulled up outside. On the way to Horse Creek, she confirmed Vicki's story of the Pickards, who rescued an emaciated stray beagle and were inspired to open an animal refuge. "Over the past twelve years, more than a thousand dogs have been nursed back to health and placed with loving families," Denise told us.

The majority of the land was protected and preserved as a wildlife sanctuary. Denise drove us around the winding paths, where open fields and forests provided a habitat for deer, turkeys, coyotes, foxes, snakes, owls, eagles, and water birds. "The Pickard family set up an endowment fund to make sure that there would always be money to help take care of the property," said Denise. "They take an active role in making improvements to keep the place up and serve the community. They've built a cabin for veterinary students to use while they do their studies here, and a camp house for Scout groups to use as a meeting space."

She drove us past picnic and rustic camping areas, hiking trails, a hilltop pavilion, and a bunkhouse. We walked through a day use meeting lodge complete with stone fireplace and full kitchen, and an 1800s cabin used to teach pioneer skills. "Any non-profit organization can use our facilities for nothing but a fully refundable security deposit. As long as they take care of it, it's completely free." Vicki was right, I thought. This is a gem in the community.

We drove by a large canopy being set up near a dirt road and a covered bridge. "They're setting up for a five-K run," Denise explained. "Do you want to join them?"

I remembered the miles of hilly winding paths we passed on our ride through the property. It would certainly be a scenic and challenging course for someone who liked to run. Personally, I would rather fall out of a kayak in the rapids than run farther than my mailbox. "No, thanks," I said.

Denise dropped us off at the Dog Villa, a long white building with a series of separate outdoor dog runs attached to the side. She introduced us to Kristina, the administrative manager. "I'll be back in a couple of hours," Denise said. "Have fun!"

Kristina gave us a building tour, explaining more about the care of the dogs at the villa. In the office, I noticed framed pictures of dogs on the walls and on the bookcase. "The Pickards know the names and personalities of all our residents," Kristina told us. "We send them a personal notification each time one of the dogs is adopted." Talk about hands-on owners.

"This place looks immaculate," said Gene. "How many hired staff do you have?"

"There are seven of us," she said. "We take care of the grounds, maintain the equipment, and care for the Villa residents." I liked that she used the term *residents*, and had to remind myself that she was talking about dogs. "But we do depend on volunteer help to walk and socialize them. Dogs do so much better when they get exercise and interact with people every day." I remembered the crowded kennels at the Humane Society, where volunteer shortages and lack of staff made getting a walk every day nearly impossible.

"Well, we just happen to have dog walking experience," I said, sharing our service in Cape Girardeau. "How can we help today?"

"It'd be great if you could do some walking," Kristina said. She introduced us to Kim and Tim, the kennel attendants, who gave us each a leash. Then she took us outside to explain where all the trails led.

My first companion was Jolene, a fit blue tick coonhound, with a mottled black and white coat, light brown paws, and black and brown markings on her face and back. Gene took Farley, a short, muscular hound dog mix with a shiny brown and white coat. Both dogs were sweet and well behaved. We walked them across the manicured lawn and along the winding paths through the property. When we finished, one of the kennel assistants introduced us to new companions. There were plenty of paths for long and varied walks. Sometimes we turned right along the edge of the woods, and other times, left around a fountain pond.

Once, Gene's charge was a huge flat-coated retriever named Sarah. When Gene stopped, she sat, waiting patiently for him to start again. "If I ever wanted a dog," said Gene, "it would be this one." He bent down to pet Sarah's thick fur.

"I never thought I'd see the day you pick out a dog," I teased. "Your soft side's showing."

"I said *if*," he clarified. "But I gotta admit, these dogs are all so well behaved, you can tell they've been treated well here."

We alternated walks with staff chats and refreshments from the well-stocked kitchen. Before I expected her, Denise was back. "Are you ready?" she asked. It was a lovely day and I wasn't sure I wanted to go, but our work was done. "I've got a couple more things to show you," she said, once we were on our way.

We passed a building that looked just like Dog Villa, only smaller. Instead of many small dog runs, it had only a few larger ones with grass enclosures. "That's the old Dog Villa," she said. "We call it Dog Villa T-o-o," she added, spelling out the word *Too*. "We use this smaller building for rescue dogs when they first arrive.

They need time to heal, physically and emotionally, and often aren't ready to be with lots of other dogs."

She turned down a road to a huge garage. I suspected it was for storage of maintenance equipment. Denise led the way inside and stopped by a van decorated with paintings of canines—all sizes and breeds. The dogs each had a different pose and expression, making the portraits even more irresistible. Along the top edge of the van was the Horse Creek motto, *Helping the World Through Animals.* "This is our dog adoption van." Denise beamed, obviously proud of such an unusual vehicle. "Every one of the dogs pictured here," she said, "was a resident of Dog Villa adopted into a loving family." I looked anew at the faces of each fondly remembered dog. These weren't just pets; they were forever family. Denise opened the sliding door to let us look inside. Shiny silver cages lined the walls of the van. "The van has heat and air-conditioning, and the dogs each have individual kennels," she explained. "On the first Saturday of every month, we bring them over to Memphis and have an Adoption Day at the Petco store. It started out slow, but now, people wait for us to come, and often, we'll adopt out most of the dogs we bring."

"Everyone sure knows it's you comin' down the street," said Gene.

"That's the idea," Denise agreed. No wonder this program was working so well. They had a reputation for rescuing and taking great care of the dogs, the added respect of being a no-kill shelter, and visibility in the community.

On the way home, I gazed out the window, glad Vicki recommended that we visit here, when I sat forward with a start. "You *do* have horses here!" I pointed to a stable with two horses— one white and one brown—grazing in the fenced paddock.

"Yes, did I skip that? Those are our resident horses," explained Denise. "Mike, the white one, is a Percheron Draft Horse. We call the other one LD, for Little Dude. He's a quarter horse. They probably weren't out when we came by before." She turned a corner and the horses disappeared from sight. "They're pretty spoiled living here, though," Denise continued. "In the summer, they have a lower pasture all to themselves, with a pole barn to get out of the sun and a loafing shed down by the river." A loafing shed? By a river? Someday, I wanted one of those. Whether they were spoiled or not, I was glad there were horses at Horse Creek.

Sept. 27: Open Wide

Friday morning, I awoke to painful throbbing in my jaw. "I'm glad we could get an appointment for this morning," I said, pressing gingerly on my cheek. "I think it's getting worse." I hoped it wouldn't be anything more serious than a cavity; a quick filling would solve that. Please, don't let it be a root canal, I prayed.

My appointment was with Dr. Gallien, a well-respected dentist in the area. Vicki recommended him highly—my first criteria—and he met the second as well: an office within walking distance. Mature trees shaded the sidewalk as we strolled through Savannah's historic district. I wasn't surprised by the charming old homes we encountered, but didn't expect the expansive lawns that surrounded the varied architectural styles. Long, tidy drives led past rows of manicured privacy shrubs, while edged walkways cut through large expanses of closely cropped carpets of green. "This must be the place," Gene said, pointing to a wooden sign hanging from a post with wrought-iron scrollwork. A modest white single-story with hunter green shutters was set back from the road. I wondered if this office also served as the dentist's home.

Before long, the receptionist showed me into an exam room. A spectacled gentleman, with a full head of white that matched his lab coat, stretched out his hand. "I'm John Gallien, I hear you're paddlin' the river." As well as I could with fingers in my mouth, I answered questions about our trip, our boat, and the organizations we helped.

"Youw owice is bootiwull," I said. He removed his fingers. "Do you live here?"

"Oh, no," he chuckled. "My office takes up most of this building. My house is a little north of town, actually. I live next door to the place where you're storing your kayak." The mansion next door to the curator's home was *his*.

"I saw it as we drove by!" I said. "It's beautiful. Do you plan to retire there?"

"Probably, eventually . . ." He paused. "I suppose most people would say I should retire after fifty-three years of practice." His eyes sparkled above his mask. "But I love what I do, and aim to work ten more years, God willing." Sixty-three years. Quite a testimony to loving one's work.

He snapped off his gloves. "You've developed an infection in your gums which is causing the pain. I'll give you a script for antibiotics, which should clear up the infection, and some painkillers to help you out 'til the antibiotics do their job. Sound okay?"

I swung my legs to the floor. "A lot better than I expected. Thank you. We won't be home for another month or so, but just send the bill to our Wisconsin address, and we'll pay it as soon as we get home."

"No need for that. Whatever your insurance pays will be enough. I like the good you're doing. I'm glad we could help."

I caught Gene up on the details of the visit as we walked back through town. The first stop was a pharmacy, where I began my drug regimen immediately. On the way to get some lunch, we passed a thrift shop.

"Let's go in and look," I pleaded. My wardrobe desperately needed a refresh. Half of my pants, loose last month, were now in full droop. Nearly October, daytime temperatures were cooler, and nights were downright chilly. My sleeveless tops were useless. My one warm outfit, previously reserved for sleeping, was pulling double duty. "We're going to the post office today anyway. We may as well send a few things home."

We each bought a couple pairs of long pants and long-sleeved shirts to take the place of our baggy out-of-season outfits. On the way to the checkout, I saw a rack of fleece jackets with warm fuzzy collars. "I *so* want this," I said, wrapping one around me for emphasis. "But it'll take up my whole dry bag."

"And if you get it wet," Gene pointed out, "it'll take forever to dry." He flipped through the hangers. "Look at this," he said, holding up a fleece vest with a similar collar. "Try this on. It would roll up nice and small." It fit perfectly. I turned the collar up around my neck and slipped my hands into the warm fleece pockets. It felt like Christmas.

After a brief stop at the post office, we replenished our bear vaults and reused the box to send home the excess clothing.

I checked my phone for the time. "The museum'll be closing soon," I said. "Let's go thank Vicki and say good-bye."

"Good idea."

Vicki looked up from her desk as we entered. "How'd yer appointment go at the dentist?" she asked.

I told her about the infection and my meds. "I feel better already." I smiled. "I think it's probably more due to the painkillers than the antibiotics at this point." I hoped that within a couple days, I wouldn't need prescription pain medicine. But they did really help and if they made me woozy, I didn't have to worry about operating motor vehicles any time soon.

"We're not closing for a half hour," she said. "Y'all are welcome to have a look through the museum." From the gift shop, it didn't look like there was much to see, but once we got started, the museum path wove us chronologically through rooms with stories and artifacts of the Tennessee River area, from prehistoric fossils and Native American arrowheads to Civil War battles and the steamboat economy. I was glad we stopped by to thank Vicki. She not only helped us with logistics, but like so many other river angels, she extended gracious hospitality that made our short stay so much more meaningful.

Chapter 11
Government Shutdown

Sept. 28–Oct. 2: Savannah, TN, to Fulton, MS

SINCE WE'D LEFT THE MISSISSIPPI, paddling against the current became our new normal. Sometimes strong, sometimes light, but always there, the current pushed against our every stroke. I was now content with our slower pace and lower daily mileage. But I still counted down the days until we'd pass through the Tenn-Tom Canal, signaling the beginning of our final downstream journey to the Gulf of Mexico. It would be nice to have our drift back.

We left Savannah early on Saturday, and by noon, we were only eight miles from Pickwick Dam. Hungry, we pulled over for lunch. "The water must be pretty low," said Gene. "Look how shallow it is way out here." Yards away from shore, two tree stumps stuck several feet out of the water. Gene steered us inside the stumps and we slid up onto the sand.

I stretched my legs with a walk along the beach. The striated sand was dry and clean at the top, but dark muddy sand near the water line. Debris lay along the color boundaries, like lines of seaweed I remembered along the Atlantic shore, souvenirs left by high tide.

I grabbed a Clif bar from the deck bag and straddled a dry log.

"Found a good chair, huh?" said Gene, emerging from behind a bush and grabbing the hand sanitizer from the deck bag.

"Mm-hmm." I made quick work of the snack, noticing that my jaw no longer ached when I chewed. Then I closed my eyes and let the sun warm my face.

After what seemed like just a few minutes, I stood up, stretched, and turned to look at the river. Where were the tree stumps? Had Donna drifted downstream? No, but she was floating. Checking around, all else was the same . . . except the tips of the tree stumps were barely visible. "Gene, look!" I called, waking him from his power nap and pointing at the place where the tree stumps used to be.

A look of concern spread across his face. "That water's rising fast," he said. "They must have opened up the spillways at the dam." Our beach was now under several feet of water. "We're gonna be battling the fastest current yet from here on in," warned Gene. He untied the bowline and pointed Donna upstream. "You ready for this?"

"I don't think we have a choice." I grabbed both of my armbands out of the deck bag and cinched them around my forearms.

Hugging the shore, we dug in. "Keep it steady," Gene reminded me. "Don't blow out your elbows; we've gotta keep this up for a while."

I settled into a rhythm, digging my paddle in and pulling with everything I had. "One hundred bottles of beer on the wall, one hundred bottles of beer . . ." I began to sing along to the rhythm of my paddle.

Gene laughed. "Highway 33," he said, referring to my use of the same song bicycling a few years before on an interminable windy stretch of road. This time, I soon gave up the singing, though; I needed to conserve energy.

After a long four miles, I noticed a building high up on a cliff with a deck overlooking the river. Gene steered over to the shore. "Let's take a break," he suggested. We pulled Donna all the way out of the water, in case it kept rising, and wrapped her bowline around a boulder on the shore. Then I followed Gene, scrambling over the riprap and up the stairs to the bar, aptly named The Rock Pile.

The bartender introduced us to a fisherman who schooled us on the particulars of the huge hydroelectric dam. "They have six generators," he explained. "Depending on the demand for electricity, they turn some of them on or off. The more generators they turn on, the more water they let through the spillways. The current and water level changes can be a problem for us boaters."

"We noticed," said Gene.

"I've got a website on my phone with the generator schedule," the fisherman continued. He checked his phone. "They just turned on more generators," he said. "They're letting out seventy-one thousand cubic feet more water per second now than earlier. That'd be why the water level rose so fast. D'y'all want the website?"

Gene put the website in his phone. Then we decided to modify our goal for the day. With our new friends cheering from the deck of the bar, we made a mad paddle dash across the river to the inside curve to make easier headway. We camped below the dam and checked the generator website before locking through in the morning.

As the huge Pickwick Lock doors closed behind us the next day, I heaved a sigh of relief, high-fived paddles with Gene, and posted a dam selfie on Facebook. The fifty-five-foot lift was the end of our upstream challenge, but also a significant point in our journey. Pickwick Lake was the entrance to the Tenn-Tom Waterway, and our route to the Gulf.

We celebrated a bit too early. A cold front ushered in diving temps and spitting rain. To make things worse, the wind blew from the south across twelve miles of open lake, creating six-foot waves and some impressive whitecaps. We donned our yellow rain skirts and Gene kept Donna facing directly into the teeth of the wind so the huge waves wouldn't hit us broadside. Instead, the swells raised me high in the air, then slammed me down, a wall of cold water slapping my face. "Sorry," Gene yelled over the howl of the wind. "I'm getting wet, too. That last wave went so high over your head that it hit me, way back here."

We bobbed up and down like a cork as we inched along the lake's western shore. Dad taught me to keep my eyes fixed on the horizon in rough seas, but I lost sight of it between the waves. Looking to the left, all I saw was a yawning trough that threatened to swallow anything in its way. I raised my eyes to watch the cliffs on the right, but they tipped and swayed. I hoped I wouldn't get sick. Keeping my eyes straight ahead and taking one wave at a time was the only remaining option.

"Whatever you do," said Gene, "don't lean." I sat straight as a rod in the center of the boat. If we capsized, where would we drift? We weren't far from land, but the waves crashing against the rocky shore looked anything but inviting. I wondered if Gene was as scared as I was. This wasn't the time to ask. Please keep us safe, I silently prayed as I dug my paddle down as far as I dared without shifting my weight.

Finally, we made the right turn into the bay of the Grand Harbor Marina, tied up, and dragged ourselves, freezing cold and dripping wet, into the dock store at the end of the pier. It didn't seem to bother the harbor attendant that we were dripping all over the floor. That's probably why it's concrete, I thought.

"Looks like y'all could use a warm-up," she said, ushering us to the coffee station. I took off my raincoat, but could find nowhere to put it. The attendant introduced herself as Elisa and said, "If you have time to hang around and dry off, I can open the laundry room for you. We've got a coin-op dryer." She made change and I threw in our soaked outerwear.

Between rounds of food and coffee, we browsed in the shop, choosing a book of Waterway maps and a boater's guide to the Tenn-Tom.

Elisa circled the best camping locations on our new maps, and explained how to locate the entrance to the canal. "Once y'all get through the canal, you'll be in Bay Springs Lake," she explained. "Then y'all gotta start watchin' out for gators."

"Alligators?" I asked. I expected to find some down south, on either river system we took, as we got closer to salt water. But in Mississippi?

"There didn't used to be any this far north," she said, "but a while back, there was a problem with too many beavers cuttin' down all the trees. They decided to bring in some alligators to control the beavers. Well, then the alligators started breedin'. Now, we got a new problem."

Great. I wasn't really scared of alligators. I was pretty sure they'd leave us alone, but I wasn't prepared to even think about them yet. I went back into the laundry room to check the coats. I wrapped myself in my dry, piping hot jacket. But my shorts, hanging out from under the hem, were soaked. I glanced at the timer. The dryer still had a few minutes left. A quick check of the docks outside. No one around. Keeping a lookout, I stepped out of my shorts and threw them in for a tumble. I zipped my coat, which didn't hide my cold and rosy thighs. I was sure I couldn't bend over without flashing my underwear. But if I sat down, put Gene's coat over my lap, and acted like I was just reading a magazine . . . it just might work.

"Where were you?" Gene asked as I returned to the store.

"I'll tell you later," I said, with my best mischievous smile. I handed him his coat. "Let's try to keep these dry for a while."

We camped at the closest campground to the start of the canal, hoping to finish its entire twenty-nine miles the next day. Also called the Divide Cut, this mammoth canal was a highly controversial engineering feat of the 1970s, connecting the watersheds of the Tennessee and Tombigbee rivers. It would be literally *all downhill* from there to the Gulf of Mexico.

The morning paddle started out well, but a few miles in, I was already bored. Gene was probably intrigued by the cool feat of engineering, but it looked like the Chain of Rocks Canal to me — only longer. We still had over twenty miles to go before we arrived at our campground on the shores of Big Springs Lake. I occupied my mind by picturing the lake, actually a large reservoir created by locks and dams. On the map, it looked like a prickly porcupine with fingers of flooded land sticking out in all directions, each one pockmarked by bays along the entire shore. I imagined from the water, it would look pretty confusing. We'd have to stay close to the channel markers.

The sound of machinery pulled me back from my scenic daydream to the reality of endless riprap along our straight-as-an-arrow canal. On the left bank, an excavator rolled across the terrain on its caterpillar treads, digger boom aloft. I remembered these on the Mississippi, dredging the bottom of the canal to keep it deep enough for the barges. I wondered if this one was being used for that. All of a sudden, it came to a halt. The boom pulled in, hugging the bucket close to the cab. We drifted by just as the operator climbed down, gleaming metal lunchbox in hand. "Early lunch?" I called, wondering why he was stopping in the middle of the morning.

"The government shut down," he replied. "I'm out of work."

I felt terrible. I wanted to take back my glib comment, but all I could do was shout, "I'm so sorry!" as we drifted down the canal. The canal that he probably helped to dredge.

I remembered hearing about Congress trying to reach a budget agreement as the fiscal year neared its end. Where did I hear that? TV, maybe, during the last hotel stay? News of the world seemed so far away from our everyday existence. And the government got into predicaments like that all the time, didn't it? The legislators always worked it out at the last minute. I never thought they'd really shut it all down.

"What's the date, anyway?" I asked Gene. I tried, but couldn't remember.

He checked his phone. "The first of October." Until now, that meant four months on the river, away from home, away from family. Now, it meant greeting the first day of the new fiscal year without a budget. It meant our government wasn't open for business. It meant government employees, like this man, were out of work. What did it mean for the commerce that depended on the river? What did it mean for us?

"I wonder if we're going to be able to get through the locks," I said. "Aren't the ones on the Tenn-Tom operated by the Army Corps?"

"Yep," said Gene. "I guess we'll find out tomorrow." The first of ten locks on our new waterway was at the south end of Big Springs Lake. I hoped we wouldn't have to portage.

Halfway through the canal, we came to the only boat landing indicated on our map—the one place that offered a stretch break. I paced the dock and jogged up and down the long ramp for exercise, trying to mentally prepare for the long afternoon. Gene kept watch for cars while I emptied my bladder, willing it to remain empty as long as possible. But, sure enough, a few hours later, we needed to stop again.

"I've got to get out," said Gene. I saw nothing ahead but endless water and stone. "Try to pull up sideways next to the riprap."

I guided us toward shore and made a gentle turn. Gene stuck his paddle blade into the rocks, wedging Donna between the shore and his paddle. He wound the bowline around the paddle to keep it in place. Once he got out, I did the same. Gingerly, we stepped out on the rocks to stretch. "Be careful—some of these aren't too steady," warned Gene. "We don't need any sprained ankles."

"I'm more concerned about snakes," I said. "They could be in any of these cracks." I peeked in each crevice before I moved my feet and took forever to pick my way up to a bush. "I hope we don't have to do this too often," I said as I checked for anything live inside the boat, and then settled back into my cockpit.

We got into a zone for the next few hours, but I soon noticed Gene squirming. "I'll start looking for a place to stop," I said. Then I thought how funny that probably sounded. Every place looked the same. So I began to head toward the shore. Something brown was coiled over a large flat rock. "Look at that snake!" I called out. Its dark body had a faint rust-colored pattern. It looked to be about four feet long and its girth was thicker than my wrist.

"Very funny," said Gene.

"No—*really*—look!" I repeated. This time, allowing more panic than awe into my voice. I was pretty sure it was a water moccasin, also called a cottonmouth. I could have been sure if it showed me the white coloring inside its mouth, but I was glad it watched us with its mouth closed.

"Whoa!" said Gene. "It's huge." I realized then that I stopped paddling, and that we were gliding right past. I also realized that I was at the helm—that I was the one who should be steering away. I veered away from shore and Gene helped by paddling double time. I watched to the side, then over my shoulder, as the snake slithered down the rocks and slid into the water. I remembered hearing that cottonmouths could be aggressive and would sometimes follow boats. I watched to see if it surfaced anywhere near. I had no idea where it went.

"I changed my mind about needing a break," said Gene, once we slowed down to our normal pace.

"Me, too." I wasn't about to try that again. "But you did you get a picture for the blog, right?"

Soon afterward, Gene began shifting in his seat. I felt the boat jiggle as he jerked his hips from right to left, scooting his seat cushion to a more comfortable position. Spending so much time sitting with his long legs out in front of him was taking its toll. Even though we kept our legs bent, our position was somewhat like sitting on a rowing machine for hours at a time. I knew Gene tried not to talk about it, but after four months, his hips were complaining for him. Even with regular breaks, cockpit extrusions after long stretches of paddling brought grimaces to his face that betrayed his pain and he limped gingerly to work out the kinks. Maybe we were getting too old for this.

"There's a breakwater up ahead," I said. "Let's see if we can pull over there and take turns standing up to stretch." On the left bank, a tributary stream joined the canal. The large concrete breakwater, built to help prevent erosion, made the confluence different from the previous ones on the Mississippi and the Tennessee. It looked like a huge Plinko board from *The Price Is Right*, with water spilling over the top, channeled to the left and right sides of alternating rows of rectangular concrete tiles. The effect was mesmerizing as each stream of water was diverted into two, then three, then four, decreasing the force of the stream trickling into the canal.

We steadied ourselves along the wall and took turns changing positions. "I think I'll call the Chamber of Commerce in Fulton to see about a service as long as we're stopped," Gene said. I heard one side of the conversation as he explained about our mission. He hung up, then announced, "That was Kim. She said she knows just the place for us to volunteer. It sounds like it'll be something we've never done, too. A group in town does literacy tutoring for adults. She'll check with them and call us back."

Before we finished our snacks, the phone rang. Kim gave Gene the name and number of the director at the Itawamba Learning Center. He scribbled it on the map and read it off for me to call. "I'd love to show you what we do," Elizabeth said when I called. "When will you be here?" I noticed she didn't use the southern colloquial *y'all*.

"We're planning on getting to the marina north of Fulton early Thursday afternoon," I said. "We'll get settled and then come meet you. We'll plan to spend Friday helping out with anything you need." I spelled out our website address so she could check us out and read about some of our other adventures.

"Thanks," said Elizabeth. "I'll get some ideas together for you. I have a friend from the newspaper who writes occasional stories about us. Is it all right if I ask him to stop by?"

"We're fine with that," I agreed, "as long as it helps get the word out about what you do."

I began paddling with renewed vigor as we pressed on toward the end of the Divide Cut. I was rested, fed, and stretched—but more than that, I was recharged with purpose. This trip was a mix of hard work, beautiful scenery, awe-inspiring wildlife, and challenging situations. But it was the people we met who gave the rest of the trip meaning. I was eager to meet Elizabeth and hear more about her tutoring organization.

Near the end of the afternoon, the canal opened up to a wide tree-lined lake. Just like I expected, the shoreline was peppered with long inlets and small bays. Gene spied a boat ramp leading up to a rest area with a circle drive around a large, wooden gazebo.

We tied up the boat and scouted the area. "This place is deserted," said Gene. "Look down the road. It's barricaded." Sure enough, a log gate at the entrance blocked the roadside access.

I tried the doors to the gazebo marked with restroom icons. Locked. A note on the door said the building was closed due to the government shutdown. That didn't take long," I said. "At least there's a bubbler. We can fill our water containers." I bent down and pressed the button. No water. "Guess not," I told Gene. "They even shut off the water." I climbed up on the picnic table, propped my feet on the bench, and gazed out over the lake.

Gene peeked around the gazebo to the road. "This might be a perfect place to camp," he said. I stifled my protest. We wouldn't be following the rules, but it did make sense. "There's no access from the road," he continued, "so no one will bother us. There's no sign preventing access from the boat ramp, is there?"

I glanced down by the dock, but saw no posting. "Not that I can see."

Gene continued, "It's like the river access sites in Minnesota. We won't be able to use the bathroom or the water, but there's no reason we can't put up a tent on the grass." I had to admit, even though the spirit of the law might be against us, the technicalities were with us. And it would save us a trip across the lake to our intended campground, which was probably closed, too. We set up the tent behind the building out of the line of sight from the road and had the place all to ourselves, courtesy of Uncle Sam.

The next day's paddle provided a pleasant contrast to the canal. We followed the channel markers right down the middle of the lake, but I couldn't keep my eyes off the lovely scenery along the shores. We spotted graceful snow-white egrets and cautious herons, but even more interesting were the comical cormorants. I didn't remember cormorants from the Mississippi, but they sure were plentiful here. Brown-backed, with lighter tummies and long necks, they resembled a homely mix of a duck and a pelican.

"Look," I whispered, as three cormorants perched side by side on a jagged stump sticking out of the water. Their brown webbed feet curled around the stump as they held their long hooked bills snootily into the air. They stood like wary statues. As we got closer, I noticed they shared the stump with a cluster of turtles, stepping on each other in a reptilian game of King of the Mountain. We drew near and the topmost bird threw back its head in a raucous cry. I wondered if it was a warning. The turtles plopped into the water, each following the other so quickly, it seemed like one movement. Then the cormorants took their leave. Their webbed feet slapped the surface as they half-ran, half-flew down the watery runway, leaving trails of splashy footprints behind, then rose just enough to skirt over the lake to safety, wingtips inches above the river.

Soon, the lake was behind us and the Jamey Witten Lock appeared ahead. I veered east and pulled up to a floating dock at the Damsite Recreation Area, across the bay from the lock entrance. Our book of Tenn-Tom maps included phone numbers for all of the locks; our new strategy was to call ahead whenever we could. Gene put all the numbers in his phone, so talking to each lockmaster was just a matter of speed dial. I brushed away several spiders and lay on the warm planks. The conversation went longer than I expected. With all the questions we had about current events, it was good the lockmaster wasn't too busy to talk.

"So what's the scoop?" I asked as Gene clipped his phone in place.

"He's got a barge in right now," he said, "but he'll call us about fifteen minutes before they get to the top. We'll have to be ready to go, but that should give us enough time to paddle over there before the gate opens."

"What'd ya find out about the shutdown?"

"He said the non-essential employees got furloughed, but the locks are considered essential—because of the barges, I imagine. The lockmasters have to keep working, but without pay. They're logging their hours, uncertain if they'll get back pay or not."

"That really stinks," I said. Was it complaining if it was about someone else? Probably. I changed my bracelet just in case. "But recreational boats must still be okay, huh, since he's putting us through?"

"Well, kind of," said Gene. He explained, "Boats that are purely recreational and out for the day can't use the locks. They have to stay in their pools. But they'll lock us through because we're traveling all the way down the river. He said when we call ahead, we should identify ourselves as *transient*. He's going to radio the other lockmasters and tell them to be watching for us."

"Wow. That's even better news than I hoped for." I felt relieved that we could still use the locks. But I also felt a little special. All the lockmasters on the Tenn-Tom would soon know the name of the little transient kayak, *Kupendana*.

The sun and warm dock made me drowsy, but as soon as I dozed off, the call came. Hastily, we jumped in the boat to paddle across the bay. We watched the barge emerge, then entered the cavern for the eighty-four-foot drop to the pool below. Because of the extreme drops, guide ropes weren't used in these locks. Instead, the walls were constructed with floating bollards. Vertical tracks built into the walls housed large floating cylinders, each with metal rims at the top and bottom. As the water level changed, these cylinders floated up or down in their tracks. Boaters stopped their vessel near one of the floating bollards and threw a line over the top of the cylinder to hold their boat close to the wall. Boaters with tall yachts could place a line around the top of the bollard easily. We couldn't reach the top, so Gene simply placed a fingertip grip on the flange at the bottom edge of our bollard to keep our light little boat in line.

After the lock, we found ourselves on a river once again. The Tenn-Tom Waterway now basically followed the path of the Tombigbee River, but with shortcuts added to bypass the old river's many hairpin twists and turns. The Tombigbee flowed with the Tenn-Tom for a while, then veered away like a wandering toddler returning to his parent's side before being distracted once again. Sometimes Loopers pulled into a branch of the old river to find quiet places to anchor for the night, but most river traffic avoided the shallow water, extra time, and mileage by following the newer, straighter waterway.

Loopers became a more common sight, passing by with their Big Boy water homes on their way to Mobile and then on to Florida or the Bahamas for the winter. These transient boaters were nothing like the weekend warriors we feared on the Mississippi. Once Loopers saw us, they thoughtfully throttled down, waved, and passed us at no-wake speeds. Once, a man leaned out and handed Gene a couple of fresh apples and a bag of homemade cookies. "We just baked these," he said. "Thought you might like some." I couldn't imagine baking cookies *on board*.

Most of our time, though, was spent watching out for our new nemesis—alligators. I remembered Elisa's story about stocking alligators to control the beavers. Who thought of that idea? And why didn't anyone put the kibosh on that? A beaver hunting season, maybe. Or beaver traps. But alligators?

We didn't see any alligators—or any beavers, for that matter. But we did keep a lookout for gators, snakes, and shore habitats where they might be hiding. Before each stretch break, we surveyed the available beachfront and I silently planned my getaway. Every shore-side log resembled an alligator; every stick lying on the beach became a snake. It was ridiculous to live in fear, I told myself. I made a mental note to find out more from locals when I had a chance. Maybe they'd tell me we didn't need to worry, at least not so much.

I was relieved to arrive at the Midway Marina, located at mile marker 394, on the north side of Fulton, MS. Mobile was now less than four hundred miles away. With Donna safe and secure at the dock and our belongings stowed in a little guest room above the marina lounge, we borrowed the courtesy van to drive into town and meet the folks at the Itawamba Learning Center.

Oct. 3–4: Itawamba Learning Center, Fulton, MS

The courtesy van rattled, creaked, and trembled as Gene drove out the gravel drive and headed toward town. "I can see why they don't worry that we're gonna take off with their van," laughed Gene. "I wouldn't want to go far with this."

Downtown Fulton had only a few streets going in each direction; finding the Chamber of Commerce was the easiest part of our week. Inside, we met Kim, who set us up with the Itawamba Learning Center. "I'm just cleaning up from a luncheon," she said. It must have been a fancy shindig. Her streaked hair was piled up in a bun, with strands strategically pulled down around her face. Red dangle earrings matched her necklace and the red and purple tie-dye accents on her black blouse. "Would y'all like some of the leftovers? I can't possibly eat all this."

"If you force me . . ." said Gene, twisting his arm behind his back. I smiled at his acting. Gene never needed anyone to force him to eat. I didn't either, for that matter.

"Rehydrated meals are all he ever makes me," I teased. "Homemade food will be a real treat. Thanks."

Kim filled a grocery bag with containers of soup, crackers, dessert, and sweet tea as she told us about the Itawamba Learning Center. "I thought of them immediately when I got yer call," she said. "Those people have the biggest hearts of anyone I know. They do so much with very little, really. I jus' know y'all'll love 'em!"

"How do we get there?" I asked.

"Oh, it's just across the street, right over there." She pointed out the front window at the corner. "Right next to Carl's Cleaners." Kim walked us across the street to the small storefront. The window read "Itawamba Learning Center," with a telephone number written in large, clear numerals. Just inside, we met Elizabeth. Her graying hair was pulled back in a ponytail, and large oval glasses magnified her eyes, which crinkled into crescent moons as she smiled. Her burgundy tweed jacket hung in soft folds over a yellow blouse. She gave an impression of a kind and gentle schoolmarm, interested more in comfort than pretense, shiny gold earrings an only concession to glitz. "Tell 'em about how you started this place, Elizabeth," urged Kim. "I never get tired of hearin' that story."

Elizabeth gestured to some chairs and took a seat herself. "Well, one day, I was having lunch with my friend, Nancy, and we found ourselves discussing the lack of opportunities here for adult education," Elizabeth explained. "We came up with a plan to offer free individualized tutoring to help adults learn to read, and prepare anyone without a high school diploma to take the GED. The owners of Carl's Cleaners liked our vision and donated this building space next to their business. So we opened the doors in 2009." She looked in turn at her friend Kim, then at Gene and me. "Nancy moved away, but this place is a part of me. I want to keep it going as long as we can. We have a small staff and operate on a shoestring budget of donations, but our students are the reason we're here. We hold the tutoring sessions onsite." She pointed to the cubicles behind the reception area where we sat. "But we arrange them whenever it's convenient for our students."

I glanced around the space. Several study cubicles were fashioned from freestanding bulletin board dividers. A few posters espousing literacy rules adorned the white walls. I thought of how much fun it was each fall to decorate the learning areas in my classroom, purchasing coordinated area rugs and sewing curtains to make the space warm and welcoming. But all that required money. Sometimes lots of money. And according to Kim, that was sorely missing here.

"It seems like there might be grant money that you could get for a cause like this," suggested Gene.

"The problem with grants is that usually they aren't given to religious organizations," explained Elizabeth. "Our mission is to show the love of Jesus by opening the doors of opportunity through education. We have a jail ministry that provides tutoring and free GED test registration for inmates. We pray with our clients and talk with them about faith. If we accepted grant money from public sources, it would limit our freedom to do that. I'd rather operate on a small budget and pay for things out of my own pocket than not be able to pray with our students." Working in public schools, I was familiar with the limitations she mentioned and admired her desire to live her faith.

"How can we help you tomorrow?" Gene asked.

"Well, I looked at your website," Elizabeth said. "It's pretty impressive. I think we could benefit from more visibility and easier access. Do you think you could help us set up a website?"

Gene and I shared a quizzical glance. We had learned how to create our website only months before our trip. It was successful for our purposes, but we were far from experts. "We only know about WordPress," Gene admitted. "But we could get you started with that."

"Sounds great!" said Elizabeth.

I suggested an additional idea. "While Gene's working on that, what would you think about letting me decorate a bulletin board in the reception area?" I indicated the white bulletin board divider behind the desk. "I'd love to use a warm color palette and maybe add a welcoming message." Elizabeth gave me the go-ahead, and off we went to the Tupelo Hobby Lobby for supplies.

In the morning, Elizabeth introduced us to Pat, a tutor and jail ministry volunteer, and Judy, a retired teacher, writer and volunteer tutor. A bell above the door jingled, and in walked Judy's first student of the day. "Hi, Gwen," greeted Judy. "This is Barb and her husband, Gene." She turned to us. "Gwen's worked with me off and on for two years—whenever she can make it over here. She drives a long way to get here. How many miles is it again?"

"Eighty-one," said Gwen, "each way."

Judy explained, "Gwen's already passed all the GED sections. Now we're just working on raising her cumulative score." Judy's eyes sparkled and she laid her hand on Gwen's shoulder. "When she's done, she wants to co-write a newspaper article with me about her experiences. And then—this is really cool—she wants to start a learning center like this in her own hometown."

"That sounds like a great idea," I said. "Good luck with your tests and with your future plans." I was sure that there was a need for this kind of adult literacy instruction in many communities, and it looked like Gwen had a good model to follow. I hoped she could make it happen.

Gwen politely smiled, but looked like she wanted to be anywhere but the center of attention. "Thank you," she said quietly. Then she and Judy retired to a cubicle in the back.

Soon, a young man strode through the door, setting his briefcase on the floor next to a chair. He greeted Elizabeth, then turned to us. "Are these the kayakers you told me about?" He stretched out a hand to Gene, then to me. "I'm Adam. Welcome to Fulton."

"Adam's a big Learning Center fan," Elizabeth said. "He writes an article about us every so often. He highlights some of our students and helps keep people from forgetting we're here." She showed us a small corkboard on the wall with articles and pictures of past students who met their goals, realized their potential, and changed their lives. One article told of a sixty-five-year-old man who learned to read after his wife passed away in order to be independent. Another featured a fifty-two-year old woman who tired of working at minimum wage after thirty years and got her GED in order to advance in her career. Yet another shared the story of a maintenance man who learned to read in order to take a test that was required for a better job.

Adam asked us questions about our trip and about what we were doing while in Fulton. As we answered, he jotted notes for yet another article that we'd never see. By now, that felt normal. It even felt liberating. I didn't need to worry about how I looked in the pictures, or what people thought of me. I did hope this article would result in some donations for the Learning Center, though. These women paid out of their own pockets for school supplies, books, and even testing fees. They could use some donors.

After Adam left, I lined the tackable divider with brown, teal, and gold patterned fabric, then added a border and cut out letters that announced, "All Learners Welcome." Gene worked with Pat to start a WordPress site. After a bit, I wandered back to see how they were doing.

"Look!" said Pat. "We have a website!" Her fingers flew as she typed the last few words. Her short dark hair, glasses, and petite frame made it hard to guess her age. She seemed comfortable with computers, but far from a digital native. She leaned back in her chair, a wide smile lighting up her face. At the top of the screen was a picture I took of Elizabeth in front of the center, the name and phone number on the window behind her. Basic information about their mission was clearly printed in the center of the page. I clicked on the History tab and read a short version of the story I heard the day before.

"This is awesome!"

"And it wasn't even hard," said Pat.

Gene laughed. "It was a lot easier once I set you up with an email address."

"You didn't use email?" I failed to stifle a grin. No wonder they had visibility issues. "Welcome to the Internet!" We chatted about some topics they could list on their site: volunteer bios and pictures, directions, testing dates, success stories, recommendations, and even a Donate button. Pat and Elizabeth both seemed excited—I hoped they continued to develop the site, and that an online presence would help their ministry to grow.

A few more students came in for study appointments during the morning, but one of the most touching moments occurred during our lunch break at a sandwich shop down the street. Pat excused herself to take a phone call and returned glowing with excitement. One of her jail students, released that day, called to tell her he was on the way to enroll in classes at the community college.

"I'm *so* proud of him," she said. "It wasn't easy at first. I needed to spend weeks getting his trust before I could start working with him. I prayed for him and eventually, he even let me pray with him. He's really smart, but I don't think he realized it. Once he saw what he could do and gained some confidence, there was no stopping him." She picked up her sandwich and then put it back on her plate. "Can you imagine? The day he gets out of jail, the first thing he does is sign up for *college*."

"And he wanted to tell you that," said Elizabeth. I used a fingertip to wipe the corners of my eyes, then glanced at Gene. He smiled at me through a mist of his own. No wonder this young man succeeded. He had a friend in his corner, whose faith in him and desire for him to succeed surpassed his own. Pat didn't just teach this young man. She invested in him, developing a relationship built on God that gave him the confidence to be successful. I was pretty sure Adam would soon be writing a story about another changed life.

Oct. 5-9: Fulton to Columbus, MS

We spent Saturday hanging around the marina, doing laundry, blogging, and visiting with other boaters. Many of them were residents who lived on their boats at the marina year-round. We talked to two people who told us, separately, that they stopped there for a night and just never left. In fact, the story we heard about the marina owners, Ginger and Gerald, was similar. They were cruising, stopped at the marina, and liked it so much they sold their boat and bought the place. "What's the draw, do you think?" I asked Gene, as we took an evening walk along the docks, looking at the floating homes. Some of them looked like they hadn't moved in years; I wondered if they even could.

"It would be a quiet life, wouldn't it?" said Gene. "We'd have to downsize a bit, but it sure is beautiful along the river."

I thought about our house back home. It wasn't the stuff that I would miss if I lived on a boat, but, I had to admit, it was the space. I liked having space to move around, to read on the cushion in the bay window, to warm myself by the fireplace in the living room or to sit on the swing out in the garden. A boat was a great way to travel, but I wasn't sure I could live on one.

I shivered. There was a cold front coming in. The forecast for Sunday was rain and drizzle. With the fall temperatures now upon us, it didn't look like a good paddle day. "I don't know about staying here forever," I said, "but what d'ya say we stay one more day? The weather's supposed to be miserable tomorrow. We could look for a church in the area and wait for the weather to pass."

We arrived at the Itawamba Christian Church shortly before the service began. After introducing ourselves to the few people around, we sat down to wait. As Sunday School let out and people entered the sanctuary, one after another recognized us as new faces and stopped by to introduce themselves. It felt nice to be welcomed. I resolved to be more aware of new faces in the pews at my own church back home. In the bulletin, I read that there were evening small groups. "Do you want to see if we can join a small group?" I whispered to Gene. After church, I inquired. We were invited to join a couple of members at their home south of town for dinner and discussion.

That evening, our hostess, Melanie, introduced us to her brother, Robert. He in turn invited us to come over to his house after our study to see his father's handmade cedar-strip canoe. I was beginning to see why people decided to stay in this tiny town. After a delicious potluck dinner, we began with prayers for various friends and congregation members. Then Melanie led a discussion of the sermon topic from the morning.

We ended the evening by following Robert to his home to meet his family. His father, Alan, took us in the basement to show us his canoe. The thin strips of cedar shone in different hues of amber and honey under the layers of glistening varnish. It was a beautiful craft. "I'd love to see your kayak," he said, in the lilting English accent of his homeland.

"You'll be going right by here tomorrow," said Robert. "Why don't you stop and visit? You're welcome to set up your tent in the yard." We walked outside to take a look. Their home was situated along the shore of a bay on the east side of the river. Gene got out his phone and dropped a pin at the location. It would be easy enough to find.

"We'll have to see how it goes tomorrow," said Gene. "The marina is only about thirteen miles upriver. We'd have a shorter paddle day than we planned, but it would be nice to see you again. We'll try to stop if we can."

"If you do, don't try to navigate the stump field. Just hug the shoreline." I looked out at the inky blackness. I couldn't see a thing, but wasn't worried. We'd been through stump fields before.

After a beautiful and comparatively short day of paddling on Monday, the pin on Gene's map told us we arrived at the bay. It couldn't be. This wasn't just a stump field; it was a stump forest. The entire bay was filled with obstacles of different heights protruding from the surface, and shadows of even more submerged dangers lurking below. Last night's casual warning didn't prepare us for the extensive minefield inches below the surface. Heeding Robert's advice, we stayed near the eastern shore of the bay and picked our way through the stumps to get to the Blakes' home, coasting safely to their dock early in the afternoon.

All was quiet; I imagined that everyone was still at work or school. "Let's wait on the dock," I said, pointing to two wooden lounge chairs facing the water. We tied the boat to a cleat and took our places in the sun. From the dock, the stump field looked almost pretty. Many of the sawn-off tree trunks rose a foot or two above the surface. Suckers laden with gold and orange foliage sprung from the tops like hundreds of potted plants floating randomly in the bay. I closed my eyes and let the warmth of the sun calm my nerves.

"I see you made it." An Englishman's voice interrupted my nap. I looked up to see Alan making his way out on the dock. "I'm making tea. Would you like to join me?"

Over tea and cookies, we listened to tales of Alan's childhood in England and saw photos of the picturesque little cottage on the Isle of Wight, where he and the love of his life lived together, where he cared for her until she succumbed to illness. "I love living here," he said wistfully. "It's nice to be able to spend time with my family . . . my grandchildren. But I still miss her terribly." He turned to Gene. "How long have you two been married?"

"Seven years," Gene said. "Not nearly as long as you and your wife, but even so, I can't imagine ever losing Barb."

After a couple of hours and three life stories, we decided to set up camp in the yard and stay for the evening with the Blake family. The conversation never lagged, as Robert and his wife, Vicky, arrived home from work and their three children returned after school and sports practices.

Robert walked down with us to find a place for the tent. I scanned the shoreline. "Do you have to worry about snakes here?" I asked.

"This is Mississippi. Everyone watches out for snakes," he said. "But you'll be fine. Just stay out of the tall grasses, especially near the water. And don't leave your tent unzipped." I shuddered.

"Dad just shot one last week, right down there." William, Robert's youngest son, must have followed us down the hill. He pointed to the grasses by the dock. "It was a *big* one, too."

"You do have a gun, don't you?" asked Robert.

"No," Gene said. "A few people suggested that, but we're on a mission trip. What would we do with a gun while we work at all the different services?" I was glad we didn't have a gun. I considered it before we left, mostly to protect us from bears in the north woods. But shooting snakes? I doubted I could hit a moving snake if I tried. We pulled the tent farther away from the water.

While we set up camp, William peppered us with questions about camping, paddling, and the river. He seemed at ease talking with adults. After our conversation with Alan, I expected that his presence in William's life had something to do with that.

I walked up to the house and took a long stroll around the neighborhood with Vicky, a teacher and drama director at the nearby Itawamba High School working toward her national certification. Her love for her school and students bubbled out with every story she told. When we returned, Vicky asked, "How would you like a hot bath before dinner?" I couldn't resist. She turned on some music and pointed out the bath soaps. "You take as long as you like," she said.

Relaxed and refreshed, I joined Gene and the Blake family for a steak and shrimp dinner prepared by Alan. Later, before we returned to the tent, Robert took us out on the deck and pointed out a safe route through the stump field that we could use the next day. I followed his finger, tracing a curved path toward the river channel. "You'll be fine if you head for that tree and then bend left. We used to mark it with some yellow ribbons, but we know it pretty well now, and not marking the channel gives us more privacy." I wished there were still yellow ribbons.

We woke up bright and early the next morning; due to our short day Monday, we had extra miles to paddle. Everyone else had already left for school and work, but Alan offered us the bathroom to clean up and then sent us off with a loaf of freshly baked bread and a jar of homemade jam.

I was nervous about navigating through the stump field to get back to the river. The path we saw from the deck the evening before was invisible from a water surface perspective. From the stern, I could see most of the stumps above the surface. Gene kept a lookout for underwater hazards and we picked our way around the flowerpots and jagged wooden swords.

All of a sudden, I lurched forward and the boat suddenly stopped. "What was that?" I asked.

Gene rocked side to side, then jerked his body gently forward. The boat didn't move. "We're stuck on a stump," he said. "I can feel it, right here"—he pointed toward his cockpit at the front of the boat—"under my butt." I remembered the granite rock that ripped into our hull up in Bemidji. As we passed over it, I felt the thin layer of wood flex up underneath me. But that time, we slipped off. Now, a stump was lodged underneath us.

"Are you taking on water?" I asked, afraid for the worst, but hoping to rule it out.

Gene pushed his half-skirt forward and checked inside his cockpit. "Nope. Dry as a bone."

Whew. We were stranded, but we had time. I looked toward the shore. No one was in sight. I wondered if Alan was watching from one of the windows. I kind of hoped he wasn't. This was really embarrassing. I plunged my paddle down into the water to check its depth. It didn't hit bottom. No chance to get out and walk the boat off the stump. I rocked gently side to side, but the stump was solidly centered under Gene. "I could get out and float the bow off the stump," said Gene, "but I'd rather not. I'm not sure what's down there."

"Thanks," I half-joked. "I wasn't even thinking about *that*." I didn't see any alligators or snakes around. But that didn't mean they weren't there.

Gene pushed his paddle into the water, angling it underneath the boat. With his other hand, he reached beneath the water to grasp the opposite end of the shaft. I realized it must now be positioned behind the stump. "If I push against the stump, can you paddle backwards?" he asked. He pushed the paddle shaft firmly against the stump with both hands, while I churned backwards with my paddle blades. After a series of short tugs, we finally inched off the stump.

"Nice job," I said. "I was beginning to think we might be sitting here when the kids get home from school." More carefully now, we inched through the rest of the stump field to the open waters of the channel. I turned and waved, just in case Alan was watching.

The further south we traveled, the harder it became to find rest stops. We circled all the boat ramps identified on our charts and watched for any other opportunities that arose. Passing under a railroad bridge, I spied a boat ramp on the left bank that wasn't on our map.

"Ready for a break?" I asked. Without waiting for a reply, I veered over toward the ramp. As we neared shore, I heard a faint quiet cry. "Do you hear that?" I asked. The sound became louder and more plaintive as Gene pulled the bow out of the water, holding it steady while I climbed out.

"Mew. Meowwww!" It had to be a kitten. But where was it? I followed the sound to the railroad ties that lined one side of the ramp. Cowering behind the weathered timber crouched a tiny black ball of fur. I noticed white markings on its head as its terrified eyes met mine. Moments later, it backed even more tightly into the nook between the railroad tie and soil backfill.

"It's so small; it's gotta be only a few weeks old," said Gene. "Someone must have abandoned it."

My heart ached for the little guy. Who would leave a defenseless kitten here? I wondered if he had littermates. If so, where were they? I looked around, but saw nothing unusual. "I wonder how long he's been here," I said. "He has to be hungry." I grabbed a foil packet of salmon from the ready-to-eat snacks in our deck bag, tore it open, and dropped some flaked fish into the crevice. The kitten gobbled up each bit as it landed. Before long, the whole packet—usually a lunch for two—was gone. I poured a small puddle from my water bottle onto the railroad tie. Gradually, the kitten crept out of its hiding place. It couldn't have been out in the elements for too long; its black fur was still sleek and shiny. But as it came into the light, I could see the white on the bridge of its nose, its white bib, and four snowy paws. Long white whiskers seemed out of place on its tiny baby face. "We can't leave him," I pleaded. "Maybe when we get to the next marina, we can find a Humane Society."

I didn't really want to take him to the Humane Society. I wanted to take him home. But home was over a thousand miles away, and we were heading the opposite direction.

"I think I'll call him Tom," I said. "Tom Bigbee." It seemed fitting to name him after the river where we found him.

"Good idea," said Gene. "Do you know it's a boy?"

"No," I admitted. "I don't really want to stress him right now to find out. But we've got a fifty-fifty chance."

The next thing I knew, Gene was holding the aluminum pot from our cook kit. "Let's line this with some grasses, and we'll keep him 'til we find him a home."

For the next fifteen miles, Tom entertained me from the cooking pot between my knees. I giggled as he alternated between napping and purring so loudly I wondered if Gene could hear. With my attention divided between steering and kitten watching, it was a good thing the river wasn't crowded. "A little starboard, hon," Gene reminded me more than once, correcting my errant heading before I ran us aground.

After a while, Tom became more courageous, tickling my legs as he hopped out of his pot to explore his temporary home. With all the gear stored under our deck, I knew he couldn't wander far. Soon, I heard soft snoring. I peeked into the cockpit to see him curled up in the grass-lined pot once again. After his nap, Tom ventured into my lap and poked his tiny Yoda head out from under my half skirt, alert green eyes watching the water flow by. I rested my paddle across the boat and cupped a makeshift safety railing around him with my gloved hand.

"I think I'm falling in love," I called to Gene.

"I know," he replied. "I've been trying to figure out a way we can keep him, but we still have a month left before we get to the Gulf, and I just don't think it would be fair to Tom." I knew Gene was right. As nice as it was to have Tom aboard for the day, kayaking and tent camping would be a hard life for a kitten. Knowing that he was safe would have to be enough.

That afternoon, we tied up at the floating dock of the Aberdeen Marina. Gene went to register at the office while I brought Tom to a picnic table nearby.

A young woman in jeans and a blue T-shirt approached. "Who've you got there?" Her blonde chin-length hair fell forward as she leaned over to look. Tom peeked up at her, his white mitten paws resting on the edge of the pot. "Awww," she swooned. "Can I hold it?"

The woman introduced herself as Danielle, a member of the marina staff. She cupped Tom in her hands and cuddled him in the crook of her neck as she listened to my story of Tom's rescue.

"Is there a Humane Society nearby?" I asked. "We'd love to keep him, but still have too far to travel."

"There is—but you don't need to worry about that," she said. "I'd love to take him home with me. We already have two cats, but they'll get along fine with a new kitten. And I'm sure my family will love Tom as much as I do. There's just one thing ..." She gently rolled Tom onto his back. "I think Tom's a *she*."

I imagined Danielle's children excitedly discussing potential names for their new kitten. What would they decide? I tried, unsuccessfully, to think of suitable female forms of Tom Bigbee. But it didn't really matter now. I hugged Tom close one last time, and scratched him—rather, her—under the chin and behind the ears. "You take care of yourself," I said. Then I handed the kitten I loved and wanted to the woman who wanted her, too, and would love her for us. And I said good-bye.

Back in the tent, we studied our maps for the rest of the trip. In two days, we planned to arrive in Columbus, MS. We didn't have a place to volunteer there yet, but could call the next day. Another week of paddling would bring us to Demopolis, AL. Gene was worried about the stretch after that. "I'm concerned," he said, "that we might not be able to find enough support below Demopolis to finish the trip." The maps showed only one marina in over two hundred miles between Demopolis and our destination in Mobile. The boat ramps we were using would disappear after the last lock, and we'd be left with a long stretch of swampy sea-level paddling to Mobile Bay. "We're already having trouble finding clear places to stop and stretch, and I just don't know where we'll be able to camp."

"What are our options?" I asked.

"Well, I think we should check when we get to Columbus," he said. "Maybe there's a place we could rent a car, either there or in Demopolis. We could always finish the trip by car, and still volunteer in Mobile before we go home." His eyes searched mine, for something I wasn't sure of. Understanding? Agreement? Or rather, encouragement to continue? "I hate to think about giving up," he added, "but I don't want to pass by our last opportunity, and then not be able to find safe places to stop."

I hoped he didn't want encouragement to continue, because I didn't have an argument strong enough. "I know how you feel," I said. "Paddling seems less relaxing and more anxious. I'm checking every landing area for alligators and every clump of grass for snakes. Let's see what we find out in Columbus. I'll be all right with whatever we decide." It would be nice to be able to say we paddled all the way to the Gulf, but this journey wasn't about our accomplishments. It was more about what God was teaching us. Growing our trust. Keeping us humble. Growing our compassion. Two hundred miles more or less wasn't going to change that.

Snuggled under my fleece for the night, I already missed Tom. "It would have been fun to keep Tom in the tent for a night, wouldn't it?" I asked Gene.

"It would have," he agreed. "But you know what would happen. We'd be up most of the night, and wake up in the morning with cat pee on the blankets." I could always count on Gene to provide a dose of practicality. This time, it was just what I needed.

"You're right," I said. "It was a good day, and everything worked out for the best." I pulled the soft fleece blanket up to my cheek, where Tom snuggled a few hours before. Tom would be just fine. And so would we.

In the morning, we treated ourselves to fresh hot coffee, another perk of marina life. Then we wound our way through the sloughs back to the main channel. October mornings were cool now; I shivered and zipped my new fleece vest. My fingers dipped into the water with each stroke; it felt warmer than the early morning air. A layer of mist spread over the surface like an exhausted cloud, barely able to raise itself above the water that flowed below it. I was unaware of any other boats until I heard the hum of an engine, then strained my eyes in the direction of the sound. "The Big Boys won't see us in this pea soup," said Gene. "I'm going to stay on the edge of the channel out of their way until it burns off."

The air warmed, the fog thinned, and my line of sight grew. I could now make out the form of a boat emerging from the mist, hazy at first, then looming full-sized. Usually, as soon as captains noticed us, they throttled down, their high wakes dispersing behind them, and puttered by us at no-wake speed. We'd set down our paddles, wave, and resume after they passed. But this time, the throttle-down didn't come. "They don't see us," I shouted. We waved our paddles, seesawing the blades in the air to make our presence known. Our profile was easy to see from the side, but viewed from the front or back, we were only thirty inches wide. It was our job to make sure we were seen.—and heard. Our shouts joined the visual display, and soon the boat changed course, giving us wide berth.

Later in the day, we rounded yet another bend in the river. This time, I could see a good half mile downstream. "What's that?" I asked, pointing ahead. The surface was dotted with random white buoys. As we got closer, the little dots took shape. "I think they're milk jugs!" I wondered if they were connected together, maybe fishing net buoys, but they stretched too far down the river to be connected to one net.

"I think they're anchored separately," said Gene. As we passed one near the east shore, I decided he was right. It tugged gently against some kind of tether, leaning with the current. "They're fishing lines!" he said.

"Where are the fishermen?" I wondered aloud. In Wisconsin, fishing regulations allowed us each three lines in the water, but they had to be attended. I counted the jugs I could see. There were at least fifteen scattered up and down the river.

"I think they're on the pontoon boat," Gene said. Near the far bank, a boat waited, motionless and silent. Three people milled around on board.

"Must be," I agreed. "They're about halfway between all the lines."

We heard a shout from the pontoon boat, and the motor roared to life. One of the boaters pointed and I followed the direction with my gaze. Sure enough, one of the milk jugs jerked below the surface, then up again, like a giant fishing bobber. The pontoon boat headed over, slowing down as it approached the jug. One of the fishermen knelt down, pulled up the line, and hauled in a nice-sized fish.

"Let's head over and say hi," I suggested. I never saw anyone fishing this way; I wanted to learn more. Gene turned and headed for the pontoon boat. On the way, I watched the fisherman re-bait the hook and toss the line back in the water.

"That's an awesome way to catch fish," I said, as we pulled up close to their boat.

"We're jus' juggin'," said the man. "Near everybody does it this way. Where y'all from?"

"Wisconsin," answered Gene. "A few months upriver. Are you fishing for catfish?"

"Yep—jus' pulled in a nice one. Wanna see?" He reached into the cooler and pulled out a good eighteen-incher.

"Nice," I said. I looked at its smooth, slimy body, and the flat, sucker mouth, whiskers hanging out from its face. *Yuck,* I thought. If I caught that in Wisconsin, I'd throw it back. But here in the south, it seemed to be the one thing everybody loved catching—and eating. I tried fried catfish once, but compared to the cold-water perch, salmon, and walleye I was used to, the texture seemed soft and mushy.

"Fish on!" shouted someone on the boat.

"Gotta go—nice to meet you," the man said, as he pushed the throttle forward and veered toward the new jerking jug downstream.

After that one, the men continued on their rounds to take yet another fish off a different line. "Seems too easy," I said. I wondered what it would be like to jug for walleyes. *Now there's a fish that puts up a good fight. And they're mighty good eating, too.*

We made more mileage than we intended during the day, mainly because we didn't find any spots suitable for camping. Late in the afternoon, I heard Gene exclaim, "Hey—is that a ramp?" He swerved over to the western shore, and sure enough, sheltered behind an outcropping of land was a boat ramp with an adjoining dock. I hopped out, peeled off my paddle gloves, and surveyed the area. At the top of the ramp was a picnic table, and next to that, a fire pit. This was perfect! We had an hour before sundown to set up camp. We strapped Donna's wheels around her from the dock and began pulling her up the ramp for the night.

The buzz of a scooter and the crunching of gravel alerted us that we weren't alone. An elderly gentleman, dressed in a navy blue jacket and khaki cap, dismounted and propped the bike on its kickstand. A badge on his jacket said Retired Army. "What do you think *you're* doing?" he asked.

"Just taking a break, sir," said Gene. He explained that we were traveling the river doing volunteer work and needed a place to camp for the night.

"Well, you can't stay here," he said. "The government is shut down, so the park's closed. No one can camp here."

"We've been allowed to just stay at some other government ramps," I offered. "We wouldn't use any of the facilities or the water or anything. We won't even need a fire. Just a place to put a tent up for a night. Please?"

"Sorry, but you'll have to leave. If my boss found out I let anyone stay here, I could get fired."

"*We* won't tell," said Gene. "It's almost dark and we don't have lights on our boat. It's illegal for us to be on the water after dark without lights. Where do you expect us to stay?"

"I don't care where you stay, you just can't stay here." He got back on his scooter, turned to us, and said, "You better not be here when I get back." Then off he went.

My mouth hung open, but I didn't try to conceal my shock. The parks had been closed from the roads for over a week, but we could still access them from the river. Until now. Now, we were being thrown off government property—at dusk. I tried to see the man's point of view and was even quite sure it was valid, but it still seemed mean. "I don't want to see him again, either," I said. "Let's just go. We're wasting daylight."

The Columbus Marina was still nearly five miles away. They didn't expect us until the following day, but I was pretty sure they wouldn't throw us off their property if we came in early. So we pressed ahead at urgent speed, all the while complaining to each other about the campground security confrontation. "You could tell he's used to giving commands," Gene said, "the way he bossed us around."

I wondered if he really would have gotten fired. "We wouldn't have gotten him in any trouble," I said. "We woulda left first thing in the morning."

"I can't believe that he threw us out into the night," said Gene.

"If we die, it'll be all his fault," I agreed. I stopped paddling for long enough to slip my bracelet off one wrist and onto the other. It felt good to vent.

Gene must have been thinking the same thing. "I'd change my bracelet, but I'd just have to change it right back. If I complain twice, can I just leave it where it is?"

I chuckled. "Makes sense." It felt good to have something to laugh about.

At dusk, we paddled into the harbor, located just above the John Stennis Lock and Dam. "Wow," said the dockmaster. "I'm surprised you're coming in so late. My name's Tom, but everyone around here calls me T." Gene told T about our campground misadventure as we tied up to the transient dock. "Man, this government shutdown's tough luck for you," said T. "You can set up your tent on the patio under the store, if that works for you. The Loopers use the patio for get-togethers, so it might not be real quiet, but it's safe and dry, in case it rains."

As we were unloading our supplies, a man strode quickly across the grounds and waved. I recognized his smile, his short goatee, and small gold hoop earring. "Hi," he said. "Remember me?" Before I could come up with his name, he continued, "I'm Gary, from *Time & Tide*. You passed us when we were anchored with engine trouble. It's still acting up, so we've been staying here while we figure it out."

"We'll be here for a couple days," said Gene. "T's letting us camp on the patio. Maybe we can get together and catch up tomorrow."

Gary shook Gene's hand. "Sounds good. In fact, tomorrow night, we're having a grill-out on your patio. Why don't you join us? We'll get together about five for docktails. Everyone brings their own beverages, meat for grillin', and something to share."

"We'll be there," I said. We'd need to do some shopping. Salmon packets and crackers weren't going to cut it at a Looper party, even if it was in our own backyard.

We used our Zero Day on Wednesday to our best advantage—exploring, setting up service for the following day, and socializing. Our search for a service organization led us to Patricia, the executive director of the local United Way chapter. We stopped to visit her during a courtesy van trip to town and returned with an appointment to help serve a meal with Loaves and Fishes the following day. We also brought back steak to grill, cheese, sausage, and fruit to share, and Mike's Hard Lemonade for docktails.

Dinnertime found the patio filled with boaters milling about. We introduced ourselves, but everyone else seemed to know one another. Stories of the Looper life flowed as easily as the cocktails by the docks. The boaters were from all over. Each began the Great Loop in locations near their hometowns, from Ontario, Canada, to Pensacola, Florida. One couple, nearing the end of the journey, shared the anticipation of completing the country-sized river loop, finally arriving back where they began. They sang a rousing song, composed in advance for their Crossing of the Wake party. I wondered what it would be like to do the Loop. Gene and I had already paddled a third of it. Maybe we could finish it someday, but probably not in the kayak.

Oct. 10: Loaves and Fishes, Columbus, MS

Mid-morning, Patricia arrived to take us to Loaves and Fishes. On the ride over, she told us a little more about the needs of the area. "Over twenty-five percent of our county residents live on incomes below the poverty line," she explained. "So we depend highly on both volunteers and donations." I made mental notes for blogging later.

We turned into the lot of a white steel-sided building. Simple signs identified the services inside. In addition to the United Way office and the Loaves and Fishes meal program, the building was home to the Community Volunteer Center. Patricia introduced us to Leslie, the young and energetic Volunteer Center program coordinator. I was surprised to see there was a position like this in such a small town. Paducah, KY, and Muscatine, IA, had centrally located service hubs, but they gathered financial support from wider geographical areas. "Because of the great need in our community," explained Leslie, "we qualify for a federal grant that pays my salary and helps fund this program. Any groups that need volunteers can list their needs with our office. Then, when individuals or groups want to volunteer, I match them with something they'd like to do. School groups, Scouts, and churches are big suppliers of our volunteers."

"In our hometown, the United Way has a website that does something like that," I said. I remembered going on the website, where I could make choices to volunteer at one-time events.

"Our United Way helps with that, too," said Patricia. "Since we're located in the same building, it's easy for us to coordinate services. Today, we have you two working with members of the Covenant Methodist Church to serve lunch. There'll also be a couple of gentlemen from the Mormon Church, who are doing their two-year service commitment." She walked us over to the outside entrance of the Loaves and Fishes dining room. "Just come on over to the office when you're finished."

Inside, a sea of blue tablecloths warmed the room. Posters and banners about the love of Christ and his commission to care for each other hung randomly around the room. We made our way to the kitchen, where about a dozen people busied themselves filling mustard bottles, checking pots and pans on the stove, putting out stacks of plates, and pouring sweet tea into ice-filled glasses.

"Welcome, I'm Frances," introduced one of the ladies. About my age, she had short blonde hair that framed her thin face, and her lipstick perfectly matched the bright red of her nametag. "I'm glad you can join us today," she continued. "People will start coming in at eleven thirty. At some places, food is served from a line. But here, we want the people who come to feel special, so they sit down at the tables and we wait on them. We start out with specific jobs and as it thins out, we just each do what needs to be done to get everyone what they need. How's that sound?"

I was impressed with the commitment to serve. "Sounds great," I said. "Where would you like us?" Gene was assigned to the kitchen and I got to help serve the glasses of sweet tea.

"You'll be hoppin'," Frances said, sending me over to meet my partner, already prefilling glasses. "Everyone loves the sweet tea."

Before the doors opened, we gathered for a blessing and a group prayer. Then a wave of diners entered and everything moved like clockwork. The kitchen staff prepared plates with ham steaks, mashed potatoes with gravy, green beans, bread, and dessert cake. As the diners were seated, volunteers welcomed them and set plates before them. For the next hour, nearly a dozen of us buzzed around the room with food trays and pitchers of drink, busing tables and placing silverware for new guests in our extra time. It felt more like a restaurant than a free meal program, except that we didn't have to remember menu orders. Individuals, couples, and young families chatted as they ate. Parents snuck in quick bites between assisting their young children and reminding the older ones about their manners.

At first, I carried pitchers of sweet tea and ice water, but Frances was right—the sweet tea was a hit. I soon learned which tables needed double pitchers of tea. An elderly gentleman sighed as he lowered himself into a chair that barely fit his generous form. He removed his hat and wiped his brow with an old-fashioned handkerchief, which he then returned to his pocket. "You look warm," I said. "How about some ice water or sweet tea?"

"Yes, ma'am," he said. "Sweet tea, please."

Before I got around the table, his glass was empty. "How 'bout a refill?" I asked.

"Thank you," he replied. He pointed to the empty seat next to him. "You might as well jus' stay right here, or you'll be runnin' all night. I do love my sweet tea."

As I passed by the kitchen to refill my pitchers, I inhaled the warm scents of Thanksgiving in October. Gene looked up from the sink, his hands deep in soapy water. I knew he didn't mind doing dishes, but I was glad I got to mingle with the people we served.

When all the food was gone and the dishes scrubbed, seventeen volunteers served 171 meals. It was a few less than the five thousand in the Bible story of loaves and fishes, but the generosity of the community to those in need was a tangible blessing. I couldn't wait to get busy on our blog, to share the good things that were going on here.

Back at the marina, we spent the afternoon doing laundry, blogging, and hanging out around boats with people who loved them as much as we. Down by the transient dock, boaters came and went. There was always someone to meet.

A fisherman pulled up to the dock, saw our boat, and asked about our trip. "Did y'all see any alligators yet?" he asked. I shook my head. This was getting old. "I see 'em nearly every day when I'm out fishin'," he continued. "But they're usually pretty small ones. Kinda cute, really." He pulled out his phone and flipped through some pictures. "Look—here's one I took yesterday, right over there, across the bay." He pointed to a swampy area near the opposite shore. I glanced at his photo. Sure enough—swimming right next to the side of his fishing boat was a small gator. I guess it qualified as cute, as long as it wasn't next to me.

During the afternoon, Gene found me on the porch by the laundry. "I didn't find any car rental places here," he said, "or in Demopolis, for that matter. I asked Gary, but he didn't know of any, either. If we decide to stop the trip, we may need to hire someone to drive us to Mobile, and rent a car there."

This decision weighed heavily on Gene. "We have to figure it out," I said, "but we still have time. At least another full week, maybe more, before we get to Demopolis. Try to relax. It'll work out."

"Oh, by the way," he said, heading for the tent with his dry clothes. "Gary and Christelle invited us to drop by and see *Time & Tide*. Wanna walk over there after you're done here?" I rushed to finish rolling the last of my dry clothes into fist-sized bundles and stuffed them in my bag. I only saw *Time & Tide* twice, from the water. I was eager to see the inside.

At Gene's hearty greeting, Christelle appeared at the zippered doorway to the canvas-covered rear deck. "Welcome," she said, as she rolled back the canvas. "Come on in." *Time & Tide* was more spacious than it appeared from the outside. We followed Christelle down a few steps into a dining area, which comfortably seated four. Across from the table was a galley kitchen with a refrigerator, sink, and stove. Curtains gave the windows a homey look.

"Have a seat," said Gary, rising from the bench, which surrounded the table on three sides. "Can I get you anything? A beer?" Gary handed Gene a bottle, but I declined, so he popped one open for himself and set it on the table.

Christelle turned to me. "I've got something you may like better." She reached into the fridge and pulled out a couple of hard lemonades.

"That's more my style, thanks," I said.

As Christelle sat down, a longhaired cat with a multicolored brown coat stood up from the bench, stretched, and nuzzled her arm. Christelle scratched the cat behind its head and under its neck. I could hear its purr from where I sat. "This is Josie," she said.

"We had a tortoise-shell tabby, too," I told her. "But she was a short-hair. Her name was Fudge. We lost her to kidney disease, about a month before our trip." I still missed Fudge. Eric picked her out of a farm litter when he was only seven. Actually, she picked him out, coming right to him and stretching her paws up his leg. The definition of a lap cat, she made herself comfortable the moment any of us sat down. She especially liked sitting on top of my books, newspapers, and computer keyboard. I often read and worked with my arms wrapped around her soft warm fur.

"We have two cats now," continued Christelle. "Jacob should be around here somewhere—he's probably sleeping. We had a third, but we lost her during a storm. We miss her terribly."

Gene and I shared the story of Tom Bigbee, our rescue cat. I passed my phone to Christelle. Tom's little Yoda head stared up at her from inside our aluminum cook pot. "Oh, she's SO cute! I wish you brought her here," said Christelle. "We'd have taken her in a minute."

She passed me the phone. "Do you want to see the rest of the boat?"

We followed our hosts through their home, turning sideways to squeeze by each other as we walked. The forward cabin included two bedrooms and a head, or bathroom, with a toilet, tiny sink, and small shower. A litter box was tucked in the corner. Most of the space other than the main bedroom was used for storage. I imagined that for a year of living, I'd need that much space and more. My favorite part of the boat, though, was up at the top. A stainless steel ladder aft of the cabin led us to the bridge. I found myself high above the water, looking out over the deck, hatches, and rigging. Comfortable swivel chairs faced a dashboard of navigation controls, and side benches afforded plenty of space to lounge. "Here's where I'd spend all my time," I said, "if I lived on board."

"We do," said Christelle. "But that's what Gary and I wanted to talk to you about."

Gary looked at Gene before he chimed in. "We know you're worried about paddling the last part of the river," he said. "In a few days, we should have our new part and be able to fix our engine. If the timing works out for us to meet up in Demopolis, we'd love to have you join us for the ride from there to Mobile."

I didn't expect this. I wondered if my face looked as surprised as Gene's.

"That's very generous," said Gene. "Are you sure you'd have room?"

"There's plenty of room on the deck for your kayak," Gary explained. "We could secure it right over there, along the side of the bow deck." He pointed to a space along the rails.

Christelle joined in. "The second bedroom is filled with supplies right now, but I should really clean that out anyway. It's gotten to be a mess. You could keep your own stuff in there. We could split the cost of food, too."

"All we're offering is for you to think about it," said Gary. "And to know that if it works out, we'd love to help you. You're leaving tomorrow, right? We'll keep in touch and let you know where we are. You do the same, and we'll go from there, okay?"

"Thank you," I said. I gave each of them a hug. "That's an amazing offer. It'd be fun to travel with you. We'll think about it and keep in touch." I wondered what the future held. But all of a sudden, it didn't seem so scary.

Chapter 12
Gators, Snakes, and Wild Pigs

Oct. 12–19: Columbus, MS, to Demopolis, AL

THE NEXT LEG OF OUR TRIP began with a twenty-seven-foot drop in the Stennis Lock, just south of the Columbus Marina. Each lock brought us closer to sea level now—nearer to our destination. After the drop, the lock doors opened to reveal what could turn out to be our last paddle week. Looking at the stretch of river ahead, which reminded me more of the Upper Mississippi now than of a canal, I allowed myself a moment of nostalgia. Was I ready to be finished? Despite the trials of this journey, I never felt closer to God than I did here on the river. With the tranquil moments and the sense of purpose we shared, I never felt closer to my husband, either. I remembered our last few days on the Mississippi, before we turned off. Every color seemed more saturated—every sound more distinct. I wanted this week to be like that. I wanted to grasp every moment and store it up inside. I listened to the water sounds as my paddle blades dipped and stroked—then I sliced the paddle forward through the air and watched the droplets scatter, forming ripples that swam away as we moved past.

Occasionally, Loopers passed us by, usually in pairs or small groups. They slowed down and waved, and for a few minutes, I felt like we were part of their procession. Inevitably, they vanished around a bend up ahead, the sound of their engines fading away shortly after, leaving us alone again. We passed a few fishermen, but only because they were stopped, casting near the shore, or watching their jugs. Juggers were pretty creative—we saw floats made not only of milk cartons, but anything that held air. Some of the most popular floats were made from foot-long sections of Styrofoam pool noodles in a rainbow of colors.

Wildlife was plentiful along the lower Tenn-Tom. Pelicans circled above us in a display of aeronautic precision. Matching black-tipped wings identically angled, their Blue Angel formations made it difficult to keep an eye on the river. Brown cormorants balanced precariously on stumps angling out from the surface and perched together in taller, silver-gray gnarled trees at the river's edge. Knobby-kneed herons and egrets stood in the shallows like misplaced lawn ornaments, eye movements and nearly imperceptible head turns the only signs of life.

I checked the map. "If I'm correct, we should be getting into Alabama soon." I looked at the dotted state border, and the curves of the land. "Just around this next left turn." I turned on i-maps, and placed my phone on the spray skirt where I could watch it. "This should be fun," I said. Holding the map up over my shoulder, I explained, "For the next half mile or so, the river winds back and forth between Mississippi and Alabama. We'll be in each state until the river turns again."

"If you say so," Gene said. "I'll keep paddling, and you play."

That sounded good to me. Gene made the left turn, and my blue dot crossed over into Alabama. After a paddle high five to celebrate the last state of our trip, I checked the phone again. One curve to starboard later, we were back in Mississippi. Another curve to port—Alabama. Next river bend to starboard—Mississippi. I kept Gene informed with a running commentary. Finally, the river straightened out, and we crossed over the border into Alabama for good. "That was great! I'm a little sad that part's over." I sighed.

"I'm not," said Gene. "Maybe now I can get a little help paddling?"

Mid-afternoon, I saw the buoyed channel that led to Pirate's Cove Marina, near Carrolton, AL. We followed the floating markers and pulled up to the transient dock. This was the last marina before Demopolis, but there were still recreation areas and boat ramps. I was optimistic about getting to Demopolis alive. After that, Bobby's

Fish Camp was the only marina for two hundred miles. I pushed that thought out of my mind.

Inside the small store, standing next to the counter, was a colorful, full-sized statue of a pirate, with an eye patch and a Jolly Roger on its three-cornered hat. "Hence the name, Pirate's Cove?" I asked.

"Nope, the name comes from me," said the man behind the counter. He looked to be maybe in his fifties and was dressed in jeans and a denim shirt. He stretched out his hand. "I'm Ed, the owner, and I'm the real pirate around here." We introduced ourselves and inquired about spending the night. "Yer welcome to," Ed said. "Jus' set up yer tent anywhere you'd like. The deck outside's where everyone meets up an' jus' down the path over there," he pointed outside, "are the bathrooms an' showers."

Gene surveyed the boats in the harbor, tied up along both sides of one long dock that extended into the small bay. "Couldn't you see us running a place like this in retirement?" he asked. "I've got the retail experience and we both know boats and like meeting people. This would be just about right for our first marina."

"It's fer sale," Ed said from behind us. I didn't realize he was listening. "I've got my eye on a bigger marina, further down by Mobile. I'm thinkin' about buyin' it, but don't have anyone to manage this place. If ya don't want to buy it, I'd hire ya to manage it fer me."

"We'll think about it," I laughed. I *could* see us running a marina, once we were both retired and the time was right. But I was pretty sure this wasn't it.

Some of the same people we met at the Columbus Marina docktail party were staying at Pirate's Cove, too. After dinner, we shared stories on the office deck. I liked the idea of traveling together, watching out for each other, and meeting up once in a while with other travelers on the same journey. Gene and I had met hundreds of people, and shared a day or two with many of them. I felt like some of them could be good friends, but wondered which, if any, of our paths would cross again.

Over a cup of coffee the next morning, Ed offered some advice. "After you lock through at Bevill, be sure to keep to the east shore. Just below the lock and dam, you'll see the old snag boat *Montgomery*."

"I read about that in our guide book," I said. "It's been restored, right? And it's on land now?"

"That's the one," he replied. "She was built back in the twenties—a steam-powered sternwheeler. Best-known snag boat in the south." I noticed that, like most nautical types, Ed referred to boats as "she," even if they had masculine names.

"Don't snag boats have cranes on the front?" asked Gene. "And pull the debris out of the channel to keep it clear?"

"Yep," said Ed. "An' this one was built for the job. They say in her heyday, the *Montgomery* could pull more'n a hundred fifty snags in just one day. Ya won't want ta miss seein' that."

Gene called the lockmaster before we left to let him know we were a half mile upstream. As he clipped the phone onto his deck bag, he said, "That was strange."

"What was?"

"The lockmaster said he was worried about us. Apparently, he got a radio call from Stennis after we locked through there, and expected we'd lock through yesterday. It's nice to know that they're keeping an eye out for us."

"You told him we're okay, right?" I asked.

Gene nodded. "I also thanked him for watching out for us, and let him know we were taking our time."

"Hear that, Donna? You're famous," I said. The lockmasters didn't know us, but they knew our boat.

I waved to the lockmaster from a distance as we paddled through the open waiting doors. Soon, we were twenty-seven feet closer to sea level. On the left bank, we couldn't miss the antebellum-style building that served as the Tom Bevill Visitors Center. Nearby, at the edge of the shore, sat the *Montgomery*. "Whoa, she's *huge*," I said. "Let's go over and take a look." Gene steered closer to shore.

The boat had three levels; the roof of each level was painted red. Together with a black and red hull and smokestack, the bold, horizontal stripes contrasted with the light yellow cabin color, and made the vessel look even longer than its one hundred seventy-eight feet. At the bow, a sturdy derrick held aloft a gigantic boom arm that stretched up into the sky like a reinforced fireman's ladder. I imagined its clamshell jaws ripping the gnarled roots of a tree, tangled with debris, from the mud at the bottom of the channel, clearing the way for barges laden with enormous payloads. We paddled along the length of the snag boat. I felt dwarfed by its size and quiet strength. At the stern, a black steel paddlewheel frame was fitted with wooden blades, waiting to be set in motion by the steam that now would never come.

Gene's voice broke into my thoughts. "Do you want to stop?"

"No, it's okay," I said. "Unless you do." I didn't need to see the tourist displays. It was impressive enough from the water. "But I think Ed was right. I'm glad we didn't miss it."

The morning chill evaporated, and I stripped down to my short-sleeved shirt. The Monday river was calm and quiet, resting from its weekend busyness. The sun and dappled sky played with the colors of the river—the translucent, greenish-brown hue in the sunshine darkened to a glossy black when the sun ducked out of sight.

"What's that?" asked Gene. "In the middle of the river, up ahead."

I shaded my eyes, even though my glasses already had transition lenses. "It's just some jugging lines," I said. White plastic containers were sprinkled on the surface—like milk jugs, only smaller. As I got closer, I could see they were Valvoline containers.

And one of them was moving. "Fish on!" I called, and pointed in the direction of the runaway jug. It skimmed across the water, turned, and dove under, surfacing close by and darting away again. I looked around to see if there were any fishermen attending the lines, but saw no one. "What should we do?" I asked.

"Let's find out what it is," said Gene. He was behind me, but I knew from the excitement in his voice that he was energized and ready for a chase. He turned the bow toward the oversized bobber, and off we went in pursuit. A few minutes later, Gene snatched the quart container and pulled in the line. "It's a catfish, all right," he said, "but it's just a little guy. What should we do with it?"

I grabbed my phone and twisted around in my seat to take a picture. I could see the white underbelly of the catfish, its pectoral fins splayed out to the side, and its mouth on the bottom of its crescent-shaped snout. "We can't keep it—it's not our fish," I said. "Besides, I don't even like catfish."

"I don't see anyone around, and it's so small, I doubt the fisherman would keep it anyway," he said. I clicked off a couple shots as he turned the fish belly-to-the-boat, holding it in place with his gloved hand. "Don't tell anyone, but I think I'm just going to let it go." He carefully pushed the barbed end of the hook forward to remove it, and gently released the catch. As it swam away, I wondered if we made the right decision. Where were the fishermen? Were juggers allowed to leave lines out overnight?

As the sun lowered and the afternoon light faded, we arrived at the Cochrane Recreation Area, the last Army Corps campground on the Tenn-Tom. I remembered the debacle at the campground north of Columbus. "Do you think we can camp here?" I asked Gene. "The last campground host wasn't too friendly."

"I don't know," he said. "But it'll be dark soon, and we've gotta stop somewhere. Let's check it out." We tied up at the dock. Gene hopped out, peeked over the back edge of the ramp, and walked up to the parking lot.

"How's it look?"

"Deserted," he said. "I don't think it'll be a problem."

"What if someone comes?" I couldn't help it. I was a rule follower as far back as I could remember.

Gene was better at differentiating between important rules and silly ones. He could walk in an "out" door without a second thought. In fact, he'd usually wink as he did. "I don't think we need to worry," he assured me. "Especially if they don't see us."

Taking me by the hand, he walked me to the top of the ramp. "If we tie the boat down there, behind the ramp and under the bluff, no one will see it, even if someone comes to check the ramp." I looked down from where we stood. Sure enough, the spot was out of sight from every angle. "Now we just need to find the best place for a tent. Back behind these trees would be out of sight from the road." We walked down the road in both directions, doing reconnaissance. Back by the pines, where thick shrubs obscured the road view, was the perfect site.

"Okay," I said, "we don't have much choice. But we go to bed right after supper, and leave at dawn." With the government still shut down, it bothered me to think that if discovered, we might be evicted. But we weren't hurting anyone. So I decided I'd ask for forgiveness rather than permission this time.

Speaking in hushed tones, we tucked Donna next to the cliff wall under the bluff. We took out and set up only what we needed to eat and sleep. I kept a lookout as Gene cooked and we ate dinner in the tent. A flashlight was out of the question, so we headed to bed early, planning a pre-dawn escape.

"Do you hear that?" whispered Gene. The distant sound of an engine grew louder. A truck was driving toward us along the campground road! Gene unzipped his door flap and stuck his head outside.

"What are you doing?" I whisper-shouted.

He pulled his head back in. "It's the campground host, I think. He's probably just doing his nightly rounds. But he's got a flood lamp. I'm going outside to watch."

I rolled over on my stomach—maybe pressure on my pounding heart would quiet it. Nope. I rolled back and watched the silhouette of Gene's body behind the tent, as the soft glow of the flood lamp swept by slowly, then passed by again. I listened to see if the wheels stopped, but they continued on down the road. "Is he gone?" I asked, in a voice barely above a whisper.

"For now," said Gene, a little too loudly. I let out my breath and felt my muscles relax. "But there's a roundabout at the end of this road; he'll be back." I wasn't cut out for this kind of suspense. I didn't even like scary movies.

Soon the engine sound grew louder again, from the opposite direction. I watched Gene's silhouette crouching, leaning, stretching. I pictured him peeking around the sides of the tent, his eyes reflecting in the sweep of the lamp—like a deer in headlights. I half expected to hear the tent zipper open, see the glare of a flashlight and the muzzle of a gun and hear, "Come out, with your hands up!" But none of that happened. The engine faded and then died as the truck continued on its way.

A waft of cool evening air blew across the goose bumps on my arms as Gene crawled back in. "I don't think he saw us. Wasn't that *cool*?"

Gene was obviously cut out to be the secret agent in this family. "It was . . . suspenseful, that's for sure. But I *really* don't want to do that again." I unzipped my tent flap. "I'll be right back. I gotta pee."

Early the next day, we took down the tent before the sun rose high enough to dry the dew on the nylon. We scarfed down a couple of granola bars for energy, packed the boat quietly, and were soon doing our warm-up coffee stroke through the early morning fog. "Kinda looks like Jurassic Park," said Gene. "I expect any minute to see a dinosaur head munching on trees, or a pterodactyl flying over us." The bank did resemble a movie set. Eroding cliffs stretched from the steaming water's edge up about ten feet to the dense trees and shrubs above. Spaced along the bank at random intervals, evergreens grew out from the cliff at an angle, their roots refusing to release their grip on the sparse soil that barely supported them. Tangles of bare roots hung down from the soil above, and trees that had already succumbed to the forces of wind and water jutted out from the river's surface below.

I consulted our maps to navigate the waterway. Shortcut channels bypassed miles of meandering river loops, creating a direct route for commercial traffic. From the water, these shortcuts, called cut-offs, often appeared as directional choices—like forks in the road. Our river maps were helpful, but following the channel buoys proved to be our saving grace.

The next several days, access ramps served us well as overnight stops. In a bay off the west side of the river, we found the S.W. Taylor Boat Ramp. The grassy area in the center of the circle drive provided a perfect tent site, and the wooden seawall by the bay presented a sunny spot to sit for meals. Late in the afternoon, a fishing boat with three occupants pulled up to the pier. The men gave the impression that fishing together was a common occurrence, silently going about their separate duties, but all pitching in to efficiently clean up from their day on the water. Gene and I worked that way now; we both knew what needed to be done at launches and takeouts, and while setting up and breaking down camp. Two of the men looked in their late forties—the third, a couple of decades older. The younger men took the lead, backing the boat trailer into the water and steering the boat up onto the rollers. The blue glitter probably sparkled more earlier in the day. Now it looked tired.

"Catch anything?" Gene asked, wandering over to the dripping boat. I thought maybe they were out jugging, because I saw no poles. But then, there were no floats in the bottom of the boat, either.

"Oh, we just went out today to set out our lines," said one of the younger men. "We'll go out tomorrow mornin' to check them."

"You can leave hooks unattended overnight?" I asked.

"Yes, ma'am," he said. "We just set out the string of lines one day and check it the next." He extended his hand to shake ours.

"I'm Chad, and that's Dave—and Harold." The other men waved while continuing to putz with the boat. "Where'r y'all from?" I suspected he meant, "Where would someone grow up without knowing about fishing?" I hoped the fish we let go wasn't his.

We introduced ourselves and Gene explained about our trip. "That sounds great," said Chad. He reached into the boat and pulled out a cooler. "Could y'all use some food? We've got lots of leftovers." He handed Gene some deer sausage, sandwich fixin's and chips.

"Thanks," said Gene. He gave me his all-you-can-eat smile. "Now we don't have to cook supper."

"We'll be back in the mornin'," said Chad. "We always stop and get hot breakfast sandwiches on the way. If you'll still be here at six thirty, we'll bring you some."

"We never get going earlier than that," I said. "Thanks." I loved the idea of a hot breakfast that wasn't oatmeal. I set my phone alarm for six.

The next morning, right on time, Chad and Dave returned, but without Harold. I bet he wasn't a morning person, either. "Hope you like sausage and egg muffins," said Chad, handing us a paper bag and two cups of steaming coffee. "We told them down at the M&M Market about your trip and they said to tell you breakfast's on them."

"That's really nice. Thank them for us next time you're there, okay?" As we sipped fresh coffee, I watched the fishing boat glide out of the bay and turn south. "They're going the same way we are," I told Gene. "Maybe we'll see them again."

Sure enough, about an hour later, I spied the familiar blue and white boat. We waved and paddled over to meet them. "Catch anything?"

"A few, so far," said Chad. He idled the trolling motor and we drifted next to them. "Show 'em the big one, Dave." Dave opened the cooler and hauled out the biggest catfish I ever saw. Over two feet long and twice as wide as the one we released, it had a head that looked the size of Dave's. Its meaty girth would provide a plentiful meal for several people.

"That's a monster! Congrats," called Gene, as we parted ways. Gene's allusion to *Jurassic Park* seemed even more real. Catfish like that could well have existed back then, as well as alligators and even snakes. I hoped Gary and Christelle's boat repairs were going well.

In the afternoon, we arrived at the Howell Heflin Lock and Dam, the last of the ten locks on the Tenn-Tom. We dropped thirty-six feet, exited the lock, and paddled a half mile up the Old Tombigbee River to the Gainesville Ramp.

While we were putting up the tent, a dark green ranger truck pulled up the drive and slowed. I pretended to be busy; he might keep going. But Gene, not one to shy away from authority figures, strode confidently over to the truck and introduced himself. The tone of the conversation sounded friendly. Maybe we were safe. Gene waved me over. "This is my wife, Barb." I reached halfway through the open truck window to shake hands. Gene continued. "The ranger said we don't have to move."

"It won't be a problem," reassured the ranger, whose name I must have missed. "The boat ramp isn't for camping, but we get travelers every now and again, like you, who need a place to stay overnight. As long as it's just one night and you clean up after yourself, it's fine." I liked this guy. He turned toward the wheel, as if he were going to drive away, but evidently changed his mind. "You do have a gun, right?" he asked.

"No—we're on a mission trip," said Gene. "Why?"

"I just want you to be safe. This area's primarily colored." I winced at the word *colored,* but he continued, as if it was nothing. "Just be careful's all I'm sayin'."

My affection dissolved into shock and I felt anger starting to rise. I wondered if the real danger wasn't from the prejudice that still existed—and not just in the south—between groups of people that were all too quickly and easily labeled just for being different.

"We'll be just fine," Gene said.

I changed the subject. "We've been hearing about alligators in these parts, but haven't seen any. Do we need to be worried?"

"I'd watch out for them, that's for sure," he said. He got out of the truck, stretched, and walked toward the long steep boat ramp. "I just released a thirteen-footer right down there this spring." He pointed to the bottom of the ramp where we'd waded an hour before. He went on to explain, "We got a call that it was wand'rin' through a residential area. It was a scrappy thing, too. Took a dozen of us to catch it. But then they sent only three of us to let it go. I was glad when that day was over!"

I felt like asking which way it went, but by now, it could be anywhere. It could also be bigger. "Do you think it stayed around here?"

"I got no idea, ma'am. Jus' be careful's all I'm sayin'. Watch for alligator slides, 'cuz they tend to use the same places to get into and out of the water, and the plants get pushed down kinda like a slide." I knew what he meant; I was already scanning the shore before every break stop, and planning quick getaways if anything should slide, slither, or jump at me.

"Do you know where we can get fresh water?" Gene asked. I was thankful for yet another change of subject.

"You have two choices, but they're different directions. You can walk over to the lock and dam on that road," he pointed east, "or follow the highway to Gainesville. It's only a mile or two."

Gene thanked the ranger and I watched the green truck until it turned right and disappeared from sight. "Which way do you want to walk?" I asked Gene.

"The lock and dam might have water, but probably nothing else," he said. "I was thinking town. That way, we can probably find a restaurant and get more of a feel for the area."

I agreed. Town sounded like more of an adventure. Gene and I loved meeting all kinds of people from different backgrounds. A warning from a prejudiced perspective just made me more determined to prove the ranger wrong. Maybe I *was* a little bit of a rebel after all.

We carried our empty water jugs along the shoulder of the highway toward Gainesville. At the bridge, I leaned over the rail and scanned the water below for the alligator released in spring. How big would it be now? I didn't even know how fast alligators grew. I'd have to look that up. I saw nothing but harmless current—no scaly backs gliding ominously, no stick pile nests, or even well-worn slides. I felt silly for worrying.

Soon we turned onto what looked like a main street. We passed a few nineteenth-century buildings with placards indicating historical significance. "Gainesville must've been an important town in its day," said Gene, "but it looks like a ghost town now."

He was right. The buildings looked deserted and I didn't see another soul on any of the streets. "Does that look like a restaurant down there on the right?" I asked. We walked down State Street to have a closer look. It was indeed a restaurant—with the word "Closed" displayed in the window. Across the street was the only sign of life; two elderly gentlemen sat in rocking chairs on the wooden porch of a store. Somewhere in their seventies, both were dressed in worn suit coats, dress shirts opened at the collar. A small table stood between them, but they weren't playing cards or talking. I wondered if they had been and stopped on account of us.

"Good afternoon," Gene said, as we climbed the steps of the porch. I smiled and the men nodded. Their eyes followed us into the store. I felt like a curiosity. It may have been the fact that we were the minority. It wasn't the first time, and wouldn't be the last. But I hoped that someday, I wouldn't even give it a thought. Of course, the inquisitive looks could always have more to do with our being strangers, or even river rats. I smoothed my faded blue paddle shirt.

Inside the grocery store, wire racks of snack foods stood next to meagerly stocked shelves. A plump woman wearing a white apron watched us from behind a glass case displaying some deli basics. I noticed a large ham and a block of yellow cheese that looked like cheddar, but not much else. "Hi," I greeted. "We're kayaking the river and walked into town from the access ramp. Can we get a couple of sandwiches for supper?"

"Sure," she said. "What would you like?"

"That ham looks great," said Gene. "How about ham and cheese?" In our usual pattern, I ordered one and Gene matched me and raised me one. While she made the sandwiches, we walked around the store, gleefully choosing sides. I searched in vain for fresh vegetables or fruit and Gene distracted me with junk food cravings. "Look at this," he said. "Little Debbie's . . . and ice cream!" We piled our loot on the counter—my yogurt, and his beef sticks, cookies, and an Oatmeal Pie. "I can come back for the ice cream," he said as he counted out bills for our purchase. We carried everything to a small table by the window. "What?" he asked me, in response to my where-do-you-put-it-all look. "I lost twenty-five pounds in the last four months. I can afford to splurge."

The woman carried the sandwiches over, sliding two paper plates onto our table. "You eat like that," she said, "you gon' gain it *all* back."

After Gene paid for our ice cream treats for the way home, I held up our water containers. "Is there somewhere we can fill these?" The woman directed us to a public spigot, and then we walked back to camp, our water containers as full as our stomachs.

I checked my phone. "Nothing from Gary or Christelle," I said. "D'you hear anything?"

"Not yet," Gene answered. "We're a little over fifty miles from Demopolis. It'll still take a couple days to get there, but if we are going to travel with them, I don't want to arrange a service before we know their timeline."

"Are you sure you want to take them up on the offer? If they fix the boat, I mean?"

Gene thought for a moment. "I think so. I really don't see how we'll be able to make it all the way. I can't sit in the boat for more than a couple hours before my hip freezes up and there just won't be that many places to take breaks or camp from now on."

Until now, Gene seemed to be the one struggling with the idea of stopping. I told myself—and him—that I'd be fine either way. Now, my practical side agreed with him. I wondered why I wasn't relieved. We'd come so far—and we might not finish. It felt like failure.

But was it? The purpose for this trip wasn't to finish under our own power. It was to let God lead us, to help out where we could, and to highlight the things that people were doing to serve others.

"Remember back before we even decided to do this?" I asked. "You said we'd have to guard against letting pride get in the way."

"I remember," Gene said. "That's why I always say it's about the people, not the paddle."

"Well, something just occurred to me," I said. "It would be cool to be able to say we paddled all the way. But, by accepting help, we can finish the service part of the trip and not really *have* anything to brag about."

"It's not like we have that much to brag about anyway," Gene said. "We flipped the boat twice in the first week, remember? And punched a hole in her after that."

"Good point. And we skipped Lake Winnie before we even got out of Minnesota," I added. "And then we changed our route halfway down. It seems all we have to brag about is that, somehow, God stuck with us through it all."

I wondered how Gary and Christelle were doing with their engine. Whatever happened, we'd need one more box of food. So I texted Andy and asked him to send a food box to the post office in Demopolis. In all likelihood, it would arrive there shortly before we did.

Our camps for the last two nights were, once again, at boat ramps. One was public and one belonged to a private river resident. At the first, we met a bow hunter, dressed in camo, preparing his boat for launch. "People call me Sugarman," he said. I was dying to know why, but he didn't offer.

"What're you hunting?" Gene asked.

"Deer," he said. "I have a tree stand out on that island." He pointed across the channel.

"Are there many deer in these parts?" I asked. I didn't remember seeing any along the Tenn-Tom.

"They're scarcer than they used ta be, that's for sure," he said. "The wild pigs are takin' over." *What? Wild pigs?* "They can be pretty territorial," he added, "and pretty aggressive, so if you see 'em, keep your distance."

"Thanks for the warning," Gene said. I hoped we didn't see any.

"Where ya headin'?"

"Demopolis, right now," Gene answered.

"Keep an eye out fer rattlesnakes around here," Sugarman warned. "I just shot three of 'em this mornin'—two of 'em swimmin' right in the river. Threw 'em up on the rocks over there."

"I didn't even know rattlesnakes could swim," I said.

"Oh, they sure do," he said. "They're good swimmers. But they're easy to see. They hold their heads way up, an' sometimes their rattles, too." I pictured the scene he painted with his words. I was torn between wanting to see it, for curiosity's sake, and wanting to forget I learned it was even possible.

Early Friday morning, we were treated to an amazing sight— the White Cliffs of Epes. Formed by the Selma Chalk Formation during the Cretaceous Period, these white cliffs, made even brighter by the morning sun on a cloudless day, were visible for miles. As we paddled closer, the striations on the face of the cliffs, formed by years of erosion, pulled my eyes away from the river. I shot some pictures, but knew that photos would never be as mesmerizing as the real thing.

Later in the morning, we came upon a less beautiful, but no less riveting, sight. "Over there, in the grasses by the bank," said Gene. "I think those are pigs."

I scanned the bank. Sure enough, several wild pigs rooted through the straw-colored grass—some brown, some black, and some even cream-colored. I saw the bristly hair on their backs, their folded ears, and the taper of their pointy snouts. I wanted one to raise its head to look at us, but whatever tantalizing smell propelled them forward also glued their nostrils to the ground. "I guess we won't stop there for a break," I said, remembering Sugarman's warning.

In the afternoon, we stopped at a sand beach for a stretch and a bathroom break. I rifled through our deck bag to find snack bars, while Gene walked down the beach. "Barb, come look at this," he called. He pointed to some tracks in the sand. "Those look like hooves," he said. "And those divots look like something's been rooting for food."

I looked around for familiar bristly backs, but saw nothing. If the tracks were here, though, the animals that made them would be back. "Time to go," I said.

"I'm a step ahead of you," Gene said, as he shook the water off his shoe and stepped into his cockpit.

Saturday afternoon, we paddled past the confluence of the Black Warrior River—the end of the Tenn-Tom Waterway. Barges lined the banks. I kept one eye out for boat traffic, and another for the bay that would signal our marina and the probable end of our paddle. About a mile after the confluence, we turned left into the Kingfisher Marina, our home for the next few days. We registered at the headquarters, set up our tent, and spent the rest of the daylight hours checking out the town.

Walking along the highway, we read the worship times posted on the churches we passed, hoping to find one to attend the next morning. Several were possibilities, depending how early we wanted to get up. In town, we stood at an intersection, wondering which way to walk next. We must have looked lost, because a man walking to his parked car asked, "Can I help you?"

"We're staying at the marina," I said, "and we're looking around for a church where we could worship tomorrow."

"I'd love it if you'd join us." He offered his hand. "I'm Scott, from the Presbyterian Church right over there." On the corner stood a light blue two-story colonial-style church building. "Our service isn't 'til eleven, but if you'd like to come early, we have Bible Study at nine thirty and coffee at ten thirty. You're welcome to join us for whatever you'd like."

"Thanks," I said. "That'd be great." It doesn't get much better, when you're looking for a church, to get a personal invitation from someone who notices you standing around in the street.

He continued, "Tomorrow, we're having a lunch after the service. Please plan on staying for that. I was just inside setting up. There's going to be plenty of good food."

On the walk back, Gene got a phone call from Gary. Repairs were finished and they were on their way. Barring any problems, they would pick us up at the marina on Wednesday. Gene took my hand. On our walk back to the marina, we watched the clouds along the horizon turn blue-violet. "Things are coming together," he said.

Oct. 19–22: Demopolis

We managed to arrive at the church in time to have a cup of coffee before the service. Scott introduced us to enough people to get started and by the end of the morning, a casual observer wouldn't have known that we were new. Many people asked about our trip and others offered ideas for services in town. One organization that came up often was the Bargain Box, a thrift store located in a large warehouse building downtown. We decided to stop in at the Chamber of Commerce the following morning to ask if the Bargain Box could use our help.

The potluck lunch offered an endless array of homemade dishes that stretched along one entire side of the room. One after another, the creamy textures and savory aromas begged, "Try me!" Even small servings of each rapidly filled my plate. Gene's was piled even higher, like an ice cream sundae made from scoops of deli dishes and topped with dinner rolls.

We sat across from Phil and Joyce, members involved with the mission work of their church. As Gene talked with Phil, Joyce told me about her passion for sewing and for empowering women. "I've been to Mexico several times," she said. "I love the culture, and I've developed a heart for the women who work so hard with few marketable skills. Teaching them to sew is one way I can help them to be economically secure." Joyce's efforts recently led to holding classes for sewing instructors, which she hoped would reap even more benefits.

Changing the subject, Joyce asked, "How are you getting into town from the marina?"

"It's only a couple miles; so far, we've walked," I said. "The marina has a courtesy van, too. We can sign up for that if we need to go anywhere far away."

"Tomorrow, Phil and I are leaving town for a couple days," she said. "We won't need both our cars. We were thinking ... if you had a way to get around, you could enjoy the area so much more. There are lots of nice restaurants and you could shop for supplies if you need to. Would you like to borrow our van while we're gone? We could drop it off tonight at the marina, and meet somewhere for dinner Tuesday to get it back."

"That's very generous. Are you sure?" asked Gene. Both Phil and Joyce assured us that they were more than happy to share and we made arrangements for the drop-off. I thought of my temporarily uninsured Volvo at home in the garage. I wasn't sure it would even have occurred to me to lend my car to strangers from out of town while I was gone. I was still learning about generosity from people we met along the river.

Monday morning, wearing freshly laundered clothes and driving our new borrowed van, we parked outside the Demopolis Chamber of Commerce. *Hop in the car. Go where you want in no time at all. This feels weird,* I thought. It probably wouldn't be hard to get used to first-world conveniences again. I hoped I wouldn't take them for granted.

Inside, the Chamber offices looked abandoned. I wondered how often people stopped in, and what it would be like to work in a quiet place like this. Teaching in elementary schools was often the opposite. There were days when I would have walked into a closet for some peace and quiet.

A petite brunette appeared from an adjoining office. "Hi, I'm Amanda," she said. Amanda listened to our story and seconded the idea of working with the Bargain Box, just down the street. "I'll give them a call and arrange for you to help them out tomorrow," she said. "Can you be there by nine?"

Now, we had a free afternoon. "As long as we have wheels, let's use 'em," suggested Gene. Our first stop was the post office. Gene waited in the car and I ran in to pick up our box at the counter.

"I'm here to pick up a general delivery box for Barb and Gene Geiger," I told the man at the counter. He looked on a shelf, then, with a puzzled expression, disappeared into the back.

A few minutes later, he reappeared. "Sorry, ma'am," he apologized, "but I don't have a box with that name. I looked everywhere. Maybe you could check back tomorrow?"

Walking back to the car, I recounted the days since I texted Andy. This was the fourth day. It should be here. "They don't have it," I told Gene. I sent Andy a text to make sure he sent the box. Before long, I got a reply. "He never got the text," I told Gene. I should have double-checked that it went through.

"Well, the food box system has served us well. If there's a time for the communication to break down, this is it," Gene said. "We can just add food shopping to our list of errands today."

We meandered through town, found a sandwich shop for lunch, and then wandered the aisles of the Super Walmart. We still had no means of refrigeration, but were no longer limited to our bear vaults for size. We purchased food for several meals, snacks, and drinks—not for two, but for four. "Maybe not having our dehydrated meals will turn out to be a good thing," I said, "at least for Gary and Christelle." Starting Wednesday, we'd be honorary Loopers. Now, I was excited for our new adventure.

Oct 22: The Bargain Box

We arrived at the Bargain Box shortly before they opened at 9 o'clock Tuesday morning. I wondered how old the building was; its red brick façade looked worn, even with a new coat of teal paint on its metal awning. A handful of people milled around, waiting for the doors to open. Piles of donations, probably dropped off overnight, waited at the side of a closed steel garage door.

Soon, the door opened and we filed inside. The high ceilings and whitewashed brick walls lent the interior a spacious industrial look, reminiscent of its history as a cotton warehouse. Only the dozens of cream-colored supporting columns obstructed my wall-to-wall view of racks, shelves, and tables filled with collections of donated items. I forced myself to focus on the woman who approached. "You must be Barb and Gene. Welcome to the Bargain Box!" she said with a warm smile. "I'm Kitty. How much did Amanda tell you about us?"

"Not much," I said. "But you come highly recommended by many people we met since we arrived." We explained more about our trip, our service blog, and why we were in town.

"The Bargain Box started back in 1983," she said, "by women from three different churches. Today, many area churches and groups help out, and not just women—men and young people volunteer, too."

"This is a great space," said Gene.

"This is our fourth location," Kitty replied. "We're constantly getting donations and needing bigger spaces. I think this one'll do for a while. Just watch how many people come through here in one morning. The need is great."

I glanced around the aisles. There were already shoppers milling around in most of the areas, but it didn't seem crowded. "How can we help you today?" I asked.

"Well, with so many people picking through everything," she said, "keeping the displays organized is always a job. The shoes really need to be checked for sizes and pairings." We followed her to the corner of the shop, where shoe racks lined the two adjacent walls. "If you find any without a match, just throw them in this box," she said, indicating a large, clear plastic tub. "If you have more time when you're done with that, just come find me."

"I'll start over there," Gene said, indicating the men's shoe rack. "Have fun—I know shoes are your favorite."

I gave an exaggerated groan. The assumption that women loved to shop for shoes couldn't be further from the truth, as far as I was concerned. Nothing adorable was ever available in my size. And slipping my high arch into most shoes was torture. I tried to be optimistic, but shoe shopping inevitably ended in my resignation to move to a tropical island, where I could remain barefoot for the rest of my life. I began checking sizes and reuniting lost mates. At least I didn't need to try anything on.

Soon, the shoe department was immaculate. We wandered the aisles, simultaneously looking for Kitty and nosing around for deals. Guests were everywhere, rifling through racks of clothing, hangers clicking with metronomic precision. I noticed that many items had price tags, and others, a posted price for categories—such as ties, mugs, and coffee carafes. We watched as a woman piled a cartful of clothes on the counter. The cashier folded and bagged the items, quoting a price of just over twenty dollars for two large bags of outfits. The customer checked her wallet and said, "I only have fifteen."

"Close enough," said the volunteer cashier. "Have yourself a wonderful day."

"Looks like the prices are fluid," said Gene. I would have happily pulled a five from my wallet to help the woman, but I was glad to see that this all-volunteer organization was flexible enough to meet the needs of the people it served.

Kitty found us. "How's it going? Have time to help with something else?"

"Sure, we have all morning," I said. "Then we're meeting Amanda for lunch."

"Oh, I'm sure you'll love that." She led us over toward the children's area. I bent down to pick up a shirt that lay on the floor and replaced it on a hanger. "I'm embarrassed that this area's such a mess," she began. "But when parents are shopping in this section, they usually have children with them and they don't have a lot of time to search. Sometimes they don't even have time to return things to the right places. The clothes get so mixed up, it's hard for people to find sizes they need. Can you help organize a little over here?"

"We'd love to," I said. Baby clothes would be fun, especially compared to shoes. Gene started with the larger sizes, but I went straight to the infant racks. I loved looking through the tiny outfits, checking the tags and organizing them on the boys' and girls' racks.

Parents, with babies in car seat carriers or toddlers in tow, flipped through the racks. "Are you looking for something special?" I asked. "Can I help you find a size?" Familiar with the inventory, I was beginning to feel like an expert already.

I pulled out the fancy dresses and hung them separately on spinning display racks where they would stand out. "Look at this," I called to Gene as I held up a red satin dress with lace and a bow. "Isn't it darling?"

Gene shrugged. "If you say so."

"I think you'll change your tune when there's a grandbaby in your lap," I laughed. "Why don't you work on the toys while I finish up the bottles and bedding?"

Finally, pleased with the result, I found Gene browsing in the library. Bookshelves created a corridor along the entire back wall. "Hiding out?" I teased.

"I *was* organizing," he said, "but some of these are pretty interesting. I think I'll buy one. Since we won't be paddling, maybe I'll actually have some time to read." He picked a suspense novel set during WWII. I perused a few books, but couldn't decide on any that would be more interesting than conversation with our hosts and watching the last week of the river pass by.

"Come over here," Gene said. "I know what you could use." He led me over to a rack with jackets on sale for only a dollar. I *could* use a jacket. I had a raincoat and a vest. But now that all my clothes didn't have to fit in the bow of a kayak, a warm jacket would be a luxury. A one-dollar luxury. I chose a blue zippered jacket with teal and purple accents and a soft lining that felt like a blanket against my skin. "You spoil me," I said to Gene, as he gallantly pulled out a single to purchase my heart's desire.

Over a lunch of sandwiches and iced tea with Amanda, we found out something unexpected about the Bargain Box. "One of the things that they don't tell people," she explained, "is that one hundred percent of their proceeds go directly back into the community." Thinking mostly about their service of providing clothing and necessities at bargain basement prices, I never even wondered about the proceeds. "Each year, the Bargain Box provides fifteen scholarships to area high school seniors, totaling forty thousand dollars," she said. "In addition to that, they anonymously support several local charities."

I was impressed, not only with the service they provided, but that they also gave to others quietly, behind the scenes. I thought of Matthew, Chapter 6, where Jesus taught that good deeds were best done in secret, not looking for public recognition. The Bargain Box was certainly an example of this kind of humble generosity.

Chapter 13
Salt Water

Oct. 23-30: Demopolis to Mobile, AL

Wednesday, we enjoyed a leisurely day at the marina. *Time & Tide* wouldn't arrive until late afternoon. As our last load of clothes tumbled, I took a long hot shower in the spacious women's bathroom. I dressed and sank my toes into the thick luxurious shower rug. I would miss this place. I heard that the owners had researched other marinas, incorporating the needs and preferences of boat owners into its design. It sure was a comfortable home base for us while we waited for Gary and Christelle. I brushed my teeth at the granite counter, pulled my hair back into my go-to ponytail, and checked my reflection in the framed oval mirror. The woman who looked back at me was strong and confident. She had paddled 1,800 miles, through conditions she wouldn't have dreamed she could handle, and made friends with people all across the country. I smiled back at her. The journey was about to end, but I was content.

Gene busied himself with a jigsaw puzzle, glancing every so often at the news on the TV screen overhead. I fit a couple of pieces in place, and then, hearing the dryer buzz, went to roll the toasty clothes into little bundles that would fit together in our dry bags as tightly as the puzzle pieces on the table. It still didn't seem real that we would no longer have to pack all our bags into the bow of the kayak, but instead, would have a bedroom of our own.

Gene helped to stuff the clothes into our bags. "After we get all our things together by the dock," he said, "how about a short paddle? It would be fun to take Donna out without all the bags."

"Sounds good to me." I hardly remembered what it was like to paddle Donna without almost two hundred pounds of gear filling her belly. With seat cushions, paddles, and life vests our only cargo, we gleefully zipped around the harbor like playful puppies off leash. I yearned to turn out into the river, but we needed to be ready when our ride arrived. We returned to the pier, pulled ourselves out of the cockpits one last time, and lifted Donna up onto the concrete tiles of the dock. She looked weary. Nearly five months of sun, rain, and waves had dulled her finish, giving her the weathered appearance of an older craft. I knew she had scars underneath, too, from battles with sand, gravel, and one particularly sharp granite rock. But she brought us through it all—nearly two thousand miles—and she deserved a rest.

"Ahoy, Barb and Gene!" I looked up to see Gary waving from the fly bridge of *Time & Tide*. Christelle stood on deck, a mooring line looped in her hand. Gary expertly guided the Bayliner Explorer beside the dock. Christelle tossed the line to Gene and he wrapped it around the cleat, twisting the line and giving it a firm pull. Our ride was here.

Christelle jumped down from the boat and I gave her a hug. "It's so good to see you," I said. "I'm glad everything went well with your repairs."

"Well, you know the definition of Looping, don't you?" Without waiting for me to answer, she added, "Working on your boat in exotic locations!"

I laughed. "That'd be pretty accurate for you guys, I think. You're working on it every time we meet you, that's for sure."

We lifted *Kupendana* over the safety railing onto the port side bow. She extended half the length of *Time & Tide*—all the way from the bowsprit at the front of the boat to the left side of the cabin. While Christelle and I loaded our gear, Gary and Gene wrapped Styrofoam noodles around Donna's hull and strapped it down to the bow deck. "She's not going anywhere," said Gene. We left the camping supplies we wouldn't need inside the kayak and stowed our other things in the guest bedroom, cleaned out and prepared for our stay. I perched on the edge of the mattress, where there was enough headroom to sit upright. Most of the bed was tucked under the floor of the dining area above. It might be a little claustrophobic, but felt warm and cozy.

"We even aired out the sheets for you," said Christelle. She flipped on her iPad to show us a photo of the sheets draped across the boat, hanging from the rigging.

"So where'd you put all the supplies that you had stored in here?" I asked.

"Hidden in every little nook and cranny," answered Christelle, with a giggle. "I hope I can find them when I need them." I was really going to enjoy spending the next few days with her.

Time & Tide ushered in a new pace of life. She hummed along at a little over seven miles per hour, the sweet spot at which her twin one hundred thirty horses performed most efficiently. "Each fill-up costs six hundred dollars," Gary explained. "There's no need to rush. We may as well save money where we can and enjoy the scenery along the way."

Relaxation was now our constant companion. After lifting anchor in the morning, the drone of the engines lulled both cats to sleep until we reached our anchorage for the night. Gary set Otto, the autopilot, on its course and only had to keep watch and make minor adjustments from time to time to keep the twins in sync. Free to move about the boat at will, shore-side stretches, sore tailbones, and pressed bladders became a thing of the past.

We primarily stayed up on the bridge during the day, taking trips down the cabin-side ladder to get chips, fruit, sandwiches, and zebra cakes from the galley and to visit the head. Up on the fly bridge, Gary and Christelle sat in swivel chairs at the helm and Gene and I lounged on one cushioned bench seat or another. Seventeen feet above the water level instead of six inches, we enjoyed a totally new perspective of our river environs. When I scanned the river from this height, the size of my world changed. An entire panorama of gold-tinged foliage was interspersed with occasional patches of glowing burgundy. Tall cypress trees leaned over the banks, laden with Spanish moss, like cobweb tinsel. Thirsty reeds waded into the water, crowding out the shoreline.

While our penthouse location opened up a whole new world, it also separated us from the river itself. I was used to feeling a part of the river, carried along on its surface like the curled up leaves that skittered along beside us on their backs. Now, I felt like a spectator—an athlete sitting on the bench. The knowledge that I willingly took myself out of the game made me no less anxious to get out again and play.

As I looked forward, out of the corner of my eye, I caught sight of Donna, lying tethered to the bow, hostage to our fears. I wondered, each time I saw a stretch of sand, if we made the right decision. Should we still be paddling? So far, it didn't look so bad. There were still some sand beaches and occasionally, a green patch of grass. Did we give up too soon? I longed to release Donna, take out my paddle, and be one with the river again.

Seeing Gary and Christelle work together on *Time & Tide* was as much fun as watching the scenery. Somewhere in the middle of their second trip around the Great North American Loop, having traveled over 8,000 miles together, they had cooperation down to a science. Just like in *Kupendana*, everything on board had its place and routines were completed without deviation. During the day, we joined the rotation of running errands below to fetch snacks and prepare lunch. We kept an eye on the dinghy, bouncing happily along in our wake. Christelle named it after Gary's favorite NASCAR driver, Jimmy Johnson, because, as she said, "He's always behind."

It was easy to tell that our hosts loved being on this adventure together. As Gene and I developed, over the summer, a collection of common experiences, shared memories, good friends, and inside jokes, so it was with Gary and Christelle. Spying a blue heron, they often called out in unison, "Cranky pants!" in reference to the raucous call that the herons make as they take flight. At the trigger of a memory, both of them would smile fondly, then share the memory with us through a story of their Looper life. Several times,

Gary stretched, leaned back, and sighed, "I love my life . . . and I love my wife!"

With the help of an online navigational program called Active Captain, Christelle planned an anchorage for each night—a calm place down a side channel or tributary stream, safe from the river's current and the wake of other boats. When anchoring at night or lifting anchor in the morning, she took the helm and Gary donned his life vest to walk out on deck. He stood near the bowsprit, where the award flag they received for completing their first loop still flew. With mostly hand signals and an occasional "That's good, love!" he directed her to creep forward, then stop, as he released the anchor, and then reverse to set it in place.

After the day's travel was finished and the engines were silenced, the two cats woke, stretched, and waited at their dishes for dinner. Once their dishes were empty, Christelle unsnapped the canvas cover around the boat, and out they hopped onto the deck. I watched them through the cabin windows and again from the deck, as they checked out our new anchorage. Jacob moved regally to the bow, wrapped his fluffy brown tail around himself, and sniffed the rigging. Josie found a high perch on *Kupendana*'s stern, alertly inspecting the shore. The cats were both sure-footed, but I understood why netting hung down from the life lines around the entire deck and why our friends checked each night to make sure both cats were back inside before closing the canvas.

Gary stuck his red-capped head outside. "We're going to take Jimmy out for a spin to check out the anchorage. Wanna come along?"

I looked out at the bay. The calm, quiet water was still brightly lit by the afternoon sun. Lush lime reed beds, accented with drifts of bright yellow flowers, enticed me closer. "Absolutely!" After Gary climbed in and took a seat by the motor, Christelle folded down a wooden seat in the bow. Gene steadied me with an outstretched hand as I took a seat next to him in the middle. The rubber gave a little, but I felt comfortable and secure. "Jimmy's stronger than he looks."

My camera shutter clicked as we puttered around the backwaters surrounding our bay. We passed a small, square fishing shack that seemed abandoned, except for what looked like a fresh coat of paint—bright robin's egg blue. One corner of the shack tipped down to touch the water, as if it the whole building might slide off any minute. Plastic stretched over the two window openings that I could see, and the tarpaper on the roof was curled up on one corner. "I think I'd be afraid to fish from that," I said.

"Look over there," Christelle said, as we came around a bend, "on the sand." I turned my head in the direction she pointed. The back half—actually everything but the head—of an alligator rested on the sandy spit of land at the end of a small reed bed island. Its visible hind foot was turned upside down, as if it was sleeping. I wondered how fast it could move from that position. I strained to see if its eyes were open, but couldn't see its head behind a tuft of willow branches. I zoomed in with my camera to get a better look. Gary brought us a little closer. "No," shrieked Christelle. "I don't want to get *closer*!"

The gator lazily uprighted its leg and pushed off, slipping into the water behind the spit of land. Gary quickly turned the other way. "That was fun," he said.

"Let's just get out of here!" Christelle voiced her sentiments and mine.

We motored by one of the drifts of bright yellow flowers. They reminded me of my coreopsis back home. Gary turned Jimmy toward the flower patch. "There's a bobber," he said. "I'll get closer, love, and you grab it, okay?"

Christelle turned to explain. "It doesn't matter where we are, if Gary sees a fishing bobber, he'll go to any lengths to get it." My brother and his two sons would be able to relate; they did the same thing. Besides fishing equipment, they had huge collections of lost sports paraphernalia, including golf balls and Frisbee golf discs.

The bobber was caught in some water lilies in front of a coreopsis bed. "Maybe we should leave this one, hon," said

Christelle, pointing beyond the water lilies. I looked through my camera lens. All I could see behind the grasses and lilies was a crisscross pattern of scales. Neither head nor tail was visible, but I knew immediately what it was.

"She's right," I agreed. "There's a gator back there—in the weeds."

"We're almost there," said Gary. "Just reach out and get it, quick! Then I'll back up." I couldn't believe it. All for a grimy fifty-cent bobber.

Christelle backed away, but Gene leaned over the side of the boat, snatched the bobber, and said, "Go!" as he pulled in the prize. In reverse, Jimmy backed away slowly. I finally released my breath as we turned and headed for *Time & Tide*. My desire to paddle again—to be one with the river—subsided. I no longer felt sorry for Donna, or wistful about not finishing the trip under our own power. Gene still had both his arms, and I still had Gene. That was the way I wanted it to stay.

Upon our return, it was our turn to cook. Gene and I made a traditional spaghetti dinner. But first, we treated our hosts to rehydrated shrimp gumbo, partly as an appetizer and partly to give our Looper friends a taste of kayak living. "This is actually pretty good," said Gary. "Wouldn't want to have to live on it, but it's not bad."

After dinner, Christelle brought out a deck of cards. "Hearts or euchre?" she asked.

"She never loses at hearts," warned Gary. Turned out he was right.

As we traveled farther down the river, the shoreline became less hospitable and alligator sightings became more common. With all his experience, Gary was an expert at spotting them, but it was a new skill for me. Whenever I saw something long and brown on the shore, I'd ask, "Is that a gator?" Then I'd train my telephoto lens on it to get a better view.

"It's a log," Gary would reply, often with a smile and a wink.

Later, Gary would point and say, "There's one."

I teased him once by asking, "A stick?" But he was always right. As we got closer, the stick would develop stubby legs and a scaly back, a thick tail, and a wide toothy grin. I watched with fascination as we passed, wondering if we would have seen that one from the kayak.

Eventually, the river widened and the shore became even swampier. "We never would have made it through this," said Gene. I looked out the window at the shoreline. Trunks of tall, lean cypress trees grew right out of the water. Behind them, reed beds offered no solid ground, as far as I could see. Had we been paddling, there would have been absolutely no place on either side of the channel for us to pull Donna over to stretch or camp.

Boat traffic increased and the river opened into the salt water of Mobile Bay. Crisply painted, tire-lined tugboats waited patiently along the docks. Pallets of colorful storage containers sat at the loading dock, waiting for passage on one of several enormous ocean liners.

"There's the convention center," said Gene, pointing to a contemporary concrete and glass building. The Mobile Convention Center, located at Mile Zero of the Tombigbee River, was our previous paddle goal. A small voice inside wanted to yell, "Stop," so we could put the boat in and paddle up to the convention center, celebrating the end of our five-month journey. But I knew it would be an empty victory, like the time I walked my bicycle up Wisconsin's famed Cardiac Hill near Maiden Rock, only to hop back on and ride the last fifty feet to the top. It felt good, but meant nothing.

We followed the channel markers toward the middle of the bay. Flocks of water birds followed shrimp boats to feast on their catch and dolphins swam playfully in the wakes alongside the boats. Before we knew it, we turned west to follow the channel into Dog River, where Turner Marina awaited the arrival of *Time & Tide*. As we pulled up to the dock and unloaded Donna, our cross-country journey down more than 2,000 miles of river came to an end.

"We're going to stay here for a while," said Gary, "to clean and repaint the hull. Then it's on to Florida and the Bahamas for a few months." It sounded like a nice way to spend the winter. Gary turned to Gene. "What's next for you?"

"Nothing that exciting," Gene answered. "We want to work with a service here; then we need to find a way home. Our kids could come get us if we wait 'til Thanksgiving break, but it's still October, so we'll probably check into rental vehicles."

We traded thanks, handshakes, and hugs. "You might want to check with the office upstairs about keeping your kayak here. They'd love to help, and it'd make it a lot easier for you to know it's safe while you're in town."

We spent the next few hours in the marina office, on the phone and online. We soon had reservations to help the next day at the Ronald McDonald House of Mobile, but finding a way home was not so simple. "Renting a vehicle big enough to carry Donna will cost us over two thousand dollars," Gene reported, "and that's only one way. Shipping the kayak and driving or flying home would be even more than that. I'm running out of options."

"Your transmission's going out on your Tribute anyway, right?" I asked. Gene's Mazda was on its last legs, and before the trip, he had started looking at used cars to replace it. "What if we take a look at used cars down here? If you find something you like, buying it here instead of at home will be like getting it a couple of grand cheaper." It sounded funny to think of saving money by spending it, but if he found a car he liked, it made sense to me.

Oct. 31: Ronald McDonald House of Mobile

On Thursday morning, the accordion doors of the city bus opened to a park-like neighborhood with a historic residential feel. I turned and checked with the driver. "This is the stop for the Ronald McDonald House, right?"

"Yes, ma'am," he said. "Just past those gardens, you'll see the sign."

Gene and I meandered along a path through the arboretum of manicured bushes, fragrant floral arrangements and brass sculptures. Near a gazebo, an angel held her hands in prayer, her face lifted to the heavens. In a clearing, time seemed suspended as a line of children, their arms raised and legs frozen in mid-stride, played a forever game of Follow the Leader across a log bridge. Perhaps my favorite, though, was a sculpture of a young ponytailed girl in overalls, holding a trowel in one hand, her other arm curled around a garden pot. Surrounded by a visual symphony of bright red, white, orange, and pink shrub roses and impatiens, clumps of purple veronica and flame-red spikes of celosia, her loving gaze was on the lone live plant in her brass pot. It reminded me of the love God has for us. In the midst of a crowded, complex world, God's loving gaze, like the girl's on her plant, is fixed on each of us.

We walked up the front steps and Gene rang the doorbell of the restored brown brick mansion. The large wooden door opened. "Welcome," said a petite brunette, wearing a black sequined headband with a single black feather. "I'm Amanda." The rest of Amanda's flapper wear included a short dress with layers of swishing red fringe below a red sequined belt. My expression must have looked more surprised than I realized. "Sorry for the outfit," Amanda said, "but we're all dressing up today for Halloween. Don't worry—everyone's not this outrageous."

It hadn't even occurred to me that this was Halloween. "No problem," I said. "I wish we knew. We would have dressed up."

Gene laughed. "Like kayakers. That's all we got."

We followed Amanda's swaying fringe as she introduced us to the other staff in the office and gave us a tour. "The first Ronald McDonald house started in Philadelphia," she explained, "to provide a comfortable place to stay and healthy meals for families whose children were being treated in area hospitals."

"I know we have one in Milwaukee, but I've never been there," I admitted.

"People sometimes don't, until they have a reason to," said Amanda. "Once people see firsthand how comforting it can be, they're on board for life." I glanced around the family room. Comfortable beige leather seating was arranged in several areas: around a wall-mounted TV screen, around a coffee table in the center of the room, and off in a corner near a window. Definitely more homey than a hospital waiting room, I thought. I refocused my attention as she continued, "We didn't open here until 2000. We originally had twelve rooms, but in 2011, we added on. Now we can be a home away from home for thirty-eight families."

Amanda led us down the hallway with original hardwood floors and moldings. Quilts and artwork adorned every wall. Framed pictures done by children were hung next to photo boards with pictures of past residents and colorful inspirational messages. I stopped to look at one framed crayon drawing of a square house with a triangle roof. Stick figures held hands outside the home, and written at the top, in kindergarten spelling, was the message, "I LOVe THis Hous a LOT."

We passed a large kitchen with bright blue cheery walls, individually wrapped breakfast breads still on the counter. "Volunteer groups sign up to provide lunches and dinners each day," Amanda explained. "Families can eat together as a group, but sometimes their hospital schedule doesn't allow for that. They can use the kitchens in their suites or come down and use this one any time they want to make their own meals."

A man passed by, following a woman with a blue oversized shirt and a floppy red hat. "Nice outfit, Mary," called Amanda. They stopped and turned to us.

"I'm Curtis, on vacation," said the woman, pointing to her Halloween costume nametag.

"I don't think I believe that Curtis takes vacations," said Amanda. She turned to us. "Curtis is our custodian; it seems like he's always here."

"Well, he should take one," Mary said, taking the baseball cap off Curtis's head and replacing it with her floppy headwear. Curtis grinned from underneath the bright red hat. The combination of his full, gray mustache and his new outfit made me smile.

Amanda turned to us. "If you still have some time to help us, I'm going to hand you over to Curtis. No, not you, Mary," she said to the woman. Curtis and Mary switched back hats. "He'll give you what you need to get the rooms ready for tomorrow's new guests. Then, after you're done, come join us for lunch. You may even get a chance to talk to some of our families."

Curtis took us past the laundry to a wing of rooms that needed to be cleaned. "What made you want to work here?" I asked.

"Well, that's a good story," he said. "The first time I came here, I was a guest. My wife and I stayed here while my granddaughter was getting treated at the hospital. It was such a blessing to us that I wanted to be that for someone else. And I know what the guests are going through, 'cuz I've been right where they are now."

"That *is* a good story," I said. "Amanda told us that to be a guest, your home has to be twenty miles away. How far do you commute?"

"Oh, I actually live in Mississippi," he said. "It's about an hour's drive each way. But this is where I'm supposed to be. It's my calling. My wife works here, too, on weekends, as a relief manager." I was impressed with the empathy of his experience and the strength of his conviction.

"Here's everything you need," he told us, rolling over a canister vacuum, sheets, and a tote of cleaning products. "Replace the sheets and towels, do the whole bathroom, the kitchen, and then the floors. Don't forget to wipe down the blinds and the refrigerator. Those are the ones most people forget."

Gene and I divvied up the chores and went to work. I wondered how hotel maids cleaned rooms so quickly. The refrigerator took me the most time; I think it must have been forgotten once or twice. Gene wheeled the garbage-sized Coca-Cola canister vacuum around behind him, using the wand to clean behind the dressers. When he switched it off, the silence was deafening. "I think I'm done here," he said. "You?"

I turned to do a visual sweep of the room, then peeked into the kitchen and bathroom. Everything looked guest-ready. "Looks good," I said. After cleaning our two assigned suites, I felt grimy. "Let's wash up and head for lunch."

A lasagna lunch, provided by a local civic group, waited on the counter, complete with cheesy garlic bread, lemonade, sweet tea, and cookies. We loaded our plates. *Now that we're done paddling, I have to stop eating like this,* I thought. But everything looked so good. On the way to Wisconsin, we planned to visit two of our favorite Mississippi River cities, missed due to our change of route—New Orleans, renown for signature powder-sugared beignets, gravy-laden gumbo, and spicy jambalaya, and Memphis, the Barbeque Capital of the World. This was not the time to worry about my waist.

A few groups of people sat at dining tables, eating and talking softly. One elderly man sat alone. I caught Gene's eye and tilted my head in his direction.

"May we join you?" I asked, slipping my tray onto the table across from him. He seemed glad for some company. Nonetheless, as we talked, his story came out in quiet, wistful words. "My granddaughter's over at the Children's Hospital," the gray-haired gentleman said. "The doctors say she's got leukemia." His voice faltered. "My son and daughter-in-law are there right now."

"How old is your granddaughter?" I asked.

"She's five," he said. A momentary smile brought life to his face, then vanished. "Too young for this." I didn't even know this man, his children, or his granddaughter, but my heart ached for them all.

The smile came back, more determined to stay. "But she's a fighter. I never saw anyone stronger."

"I'm sure it helps that you can be with her," I said. "Are her parents staying here, too?"

"They are. I don't know how we'd be able to do it without this place. We live hours away, but here, we're only a couple minutes from the hospital. We can be there for every procedure and I can visit to give her parents time to rest. It's such a blessing."

Before leaving, we sat outside, flanking a cross-legged life-sized Ronald McDonald, red-and-white-striped sleeves draped over the back of the bench. Across the playground, in a tangle of arms and legs, giggling children scrambled across the equipment, their young mother smiling while keeping watch—a moment of normalcy in the midst of a family health crisis I knew nothing about.

"I can't help thinking about those little yellow Ronald McDonald House donation boxes," Gene said. "You know the ones in the restaurants?"

"Mm-hmm. What about them?"

"I've passed by those millions of times, without much of a thought. Now that I know how much good they do, I don't think I'll ever go by one again without dropping something in the box."

"Me, too," I agreed.

Oct. 31–Nov. 1: On the Road Again

Gravel crunched under my feet as we walked hand in hand down the frontage road, where car dealerships lined up like Main Street bars in small-town America. I stopped to dig some errant stones from my sandals, wishing I wore my close-toed tennies, even on this warm sunny afternoon. To buy or not to buy—we would decide today, and next week's travel depended on our decision. I was glad Gene was the one whose car needed replacing; rapid high-priced decisions weren't my forte. But I was determined to be his cheerleader, encouraging him to pull the trigger if he found anything he liked.

"Can I help you?" asked a suited salesman, hurrying transparently to claiming dibs on any commission.

"I hope so," said Gene. "I'm interested in buying a used car to replace my Mazda Tribute. I'm thinking SUV, and it has to have a roof rack that can hold a twenty-foot kayak."

"Do you have a trade-in?"

I couldn't help but chuckle.

"No," said Gene, pointing to his shoes. "We came by Nike. And if we find something we like for a good price, we'll drive it home." I bet not many people kayaked in and walked over to buy a car. I knew Gene enjoyed the novelty of our situation, and I had to admit I did, too.

One dealership after another, we narrowed down the search. Too many miles, not big enough, no room to bargain. On the third try, Gene pointed to a red SUV parked away from the rest, over by the building. "Is that one for sale?"

"I suppose it could be," said the manager. "One of my salesmen is using it right now as a personal vehicle, but it's scheduled to be sent to another dealership next week." A 2004 Buick Rainier with just over a hundred twenty thousand miles, the price was right and the body looked clean.

"That's one nice thing about buying a car down south," said Gene, "We don't have to worry about rust from salt on the winter roads. Bet we couldn't find a nine-year-old car in Wisconsin this clean." It had all of the things Gene wanted, for less than he expected to spend. And the No-Need-to-Rent-a-Car discount helped even more. The car was in excellent condition, with only a couple of quirks—a crack in the dashboard, and an intermittently functioning gas gauge. What would have been deal breakers for me were only minor challenges for Gene. On the way back to the hotel, he said, "I think I'll name her Lucy."

I took the bait. "Why?"

"'Cuz she's a redhead, beautiful to look at, but something always goes wrong." He launched into a Ricky Ricardo imitation, "Lucy—you got some 'splainin' to do!"

The next day, it was off to the marina to load Donna and wish Gary and Christelle safe travels. I wondered what it would be like to spend the winter in the Bahamas, but even the lure of beach living didn't match my desire to spend Thanksgiving with our family after being away for so long.

"Are you the kayakers we've heard about?" I turned to see a thin woman approach, dressed in gray slacks and a light blue wicking top. Gray steaks in her shoulder-length hair framed her tanned and freckled face. She had to be a boater.

"Probably," I said, leaving Gene to finish tying Donna onto the rack of his new car. "What'd you hear?"

"You were on a mission trip?" she half-asked, half-stated.

I nodded. "We paddled from the Mississippi headwaters," I said, "and stopped at charities along the way." I introduced myself and called Gene over.

"I'm Anne," she told us. "My husband, Jeff, and I are getting ready to start a mission trip, too. We'd love to talk with you. Would you have time to stop over by our boat and share some stories before you leave?"

"Sure," I said. "We'd love to." I wondered where they were headed and what their plans were.

"Her name is *Joyful*. She's the Pilot Saloon on the hard, over there." She pointed to a group of boats, their keels resting on land, support jacks pressed up around the hulls to keep them upright while out of the water. Gary and Christelle had pulled *Time & Tide* out and put her on the hard, too, so they could clean, paint, and wax the hull. I wondered how that was going.

Joyful was easy to find. From the ground, she towered above us. Gene's head barely rose above the gray section of hull that, with the keel, would normally be under water.

"I bet that looks really sleek in the water," said Gene. Its white, streamlined hull, black accents, slanted stern, and angular cabin windows did indeed create an impressive sight. Forty feet in length, *Joyful* was eight feet longer than any of the sailboats I'd sailed with Dad. I wished that he could see it with me. I shaded my eyes to look up the full height of the mast, complete with all the rigging.

"Ahoy!" I heard a familiar nautical greeting, and noticed Anne leaning out of the cabin. "Come around on the port side. There's a ladder. But hold on with both hands; it's a little rickety." I kicked off my flip-flops—a rickety ladder was no place for floppy footwear. Lacing my fingers through the sandal straps, I climbed barefoot up to the deck.

As we all sat around the small table in the salon, Anne and Jeff told us about their upcoming trip. Dressed in jeans and a collared shirt, his bare head circled with close-cut white hair, Jeff had a gentle manner that seemed a good match for his wife. They sat side by side comfortably in the close quarters, their conversation like a familiar well-rehearsed dance. "We're going to sail around the world with Blue Planet Odyssey," Jeff explained. "It's an organized three-year sailing rally to bring awareness to climate change and ocean conditions."

Anne continued, "We'll be taking measurements and water samples for scientific studies, but since we're both Christian musicians, we decided to take our music ministry to the places we stop. We try to follow 1 Peter 4:10." She quoted, *"Just as each one has received a gift, use it to serve one another as good stewards of the varied grace of God"* (NET). I couldn't help but think back to all the volunteers we met who were doing just that—giving their time and special talents to serve others.

"What instruments do you play?" I asked.

"I play classical guitar and Jeff plays keyboard," Anne told us. "We hope to be able to use our gifts to make music wherever God leads us."

"And God will lead you, all right," said Gene. "When we said yes to God's call, we did the same thing. We turned over the rudder." Jeff nodded. I knew he understood, as a captain, how important the rudder was to the boat's direction.

"It's been pretty amazing to trust God to put people in our path," I added, "and then to meet all the people who helped and encouraged us. Some of them even told us *they* felt a call in their hearts to go out of their way to meet us or help us."

"We had our share of screw-ups," said Gene, "but there's no doubt in my mind that God was with us . . . every paddle stroke."

"You're going to write a book about your trip, aren't you?" Anne's question caught me off-guard. A few other people had asked us about that, but I never really considered it seriously.

"I don't know—probably not. A book about a five-month trip wouldn't be an easy thing to write."

Anne persisted. "I didn't say it was easy, but it's an inspiring story. You can let it end here or keep it alive by writing a book. God can still touch lives through your story, even after your trip is done." I never thought of it that way before. Maybe I could.

We wished Jeff and Anne safe travels, then stopped by *Time & Tide* to do the same for Gary and Christelle. "Thanks for everything," I said, giving Christelle a last hug. "Keep in touch. Wisconsin's on the way to Canada, you know."

We drove along the Gulf shore, past miles and miles of white sand beaches in Alabama and Mississippi. I was struck by the expanse of the Gulf of Mexico, and the number of homes and lots for sale along the coastline. I chose a white stucco estate, with a veranda overlooking the water. "I'll take that one."

"We'll have a lot of windows to board up when the hurricanes come," Gene warned.

He did have a point. "Okay. Let's just rent it for a couple months during the winter."

We stopped for the night at Buccaneer State Park. The campground was nearly deserted; we had our choice of sites. The ones near the water were devoid of trees, exposed to the chilly evening breeze. But for several months, the lure of salt water had pulled us, like a carrot on a stick, toward our goal. Now that we were here, I wasn't about to head for the trees. After dinner, I zipped my Bargain Box jacket and watched the moon's shimmering reflection float on the surface of the undulating waves.

"Beautiful, isn't it?" Gene's baritone voice echoed my thoughts and his hand enveloped mine with warmth.

"Mm-hmm," I agreed. "I can't wait for our paddle tomorrow." I snuggled into his side, as much to share his body heat as to share the moment.

"Me, too," he said. "I've been thinking about it since Lake Itasca." I rested my head on his shoulder, but a minute later, he turned with a start. "Hey, I just thought of something!"

"What's that?"

"We survived for five months together in a divorce boat!" If I hadn't been able to see his grin in the reflected light of the night, I still would have known from his voice.

"We did, didn't we? That's probably some kind of Guinness record," I teased. "But we've still got tomorrow." Of all the things I worried about, divorce was never one of them. Gene and I didn't always agree about everything, but the important things lined up pretty well, and we made a good team. We retired to the warmth of the tent and our familiar fleece. As I drifted off to the rhythmic lapping of the surf on the shore, I couldn't imagine this journey with anyone else.

Nov. 2: Salt Water

Launching from the beach into the Gulf of Mexico felt familiar, but at the same time, new. We'd launched hundreds of times over the last few months, but always with a place to go. This time, we had no destination; we were already there. The boat was empty, our journey over.

We waded Donna into the chilly water. The sandy bottom felt firm underfoot. "Can you believe it?" asked Gene. "We're here!"

"How do you feel?" I asked.

"Honestly, I'm not sure," he said. "For over a year, we planned and prepared, and then paddled. On the one hand, I'm glad it's over. But, on the other hand, I don't want it to end."

His words gave voice to my feelings. "I know what you mean," I said. "So let's stretch it out a little longer and find out how it feels to paddle in salt water." I stepped into the bow cockpit, and Gene took the stern. "Which way?" he asked. "Your choice."

I scanned the wide expanse of water. There was land behind us, but ahead, only open sea. On the river, since the very beginning of our trip, we had a heading—a direction. Meandering, maybe, but always between two banks, toward the Gulf. Finally here, the horizon opened to infinite directions, infinite choices.

"Well, we could always paddle over to Florida," I said, pointing southeast. "And then up the Intercoastal Waterway, through the Great Lakes, and cross our wake in the Mississippi."

"Okay. East it is." Gene turned left and we followed the shoreline to the east, toward the longest fishing pier I ever saw. I assumed it was so long because of the shallow water and maybe the tides. At intervals along the pier were pagoda shelters. As we got closer, I could see a couple standing under one of the roofs, lines in the water. Gene turned away from their lines. I stopped paddling and waved.

"There's an offshore north wind," said Gene. "Do you want to sail for a bit?"

"Sure," I said. "But not too far out. We still have to get back before dark."

"If we get too far, we can just keep going," Gene said. "We'll eventually hit Mexico."

"Yeah, your hip would love that," I teased. "I don't know of any rest stops between here and there."

I felt the gentle tug of the breeze filling the sail and tightened my hold on the sheets. I was grateful for this time that we had to surround ourselves with nature. The wind, water, and earth were inextricably woven together with all that lived. For the past five months, I felt more a part of God's creation than ever.

I heard splashes behind me and sensed Gene was eager to paddle once more. A glance over my shoulder confirmed we'd been sailing longer than it seemed. The beach was a faint line, Lucy only a red speck. "Ready to head back?" he asked.

"We probably should. Give me a minute to fold up the sail." I pulled the sail down to empty the air, folded it with much more ease than in June, and tucked it under the crossed bungee cords.

"Where to?" Gene asked, as he turned the boat around to face land.

From the water perspective, the shore felt welcoming. The slight curve to the land pulled us in, like sheltering arms. *This is it*, I thought. *We're going home.* "We've already gone over by the pier. Let's head toward the casino on the west side," I suggested, "and then we can paddle east along the shore to the car."

The Silver Slipper Casino took shape as we paddled closer, its glittery namesake sign sparkling off the water. Under other circumstances, I would have probably liked to drop a few coins in the penny slots. But not tonight. The side of the building facing the water was lined with windows. "I bet they have a beautiful view," I said.

"Ours is better," Gene replied, turning the kayak to head east again, up the beach.

"It certainly is," I said, over my shoulder. Our view was *from the water*. The sea wasn't outside a window. We could feel it, smell it, see it.

I heard the thunk of the rudder onto the stern, and knew that Gene had pulled it up for the last time. My paddle blades hit bottom, and Donna's hull slid up onto the sand beach, coming to a slow stop. "*That* was fun," Gene said. "Thank you." The boat jiggled, and I felt the stern float up as he stepped out into the chilly seawater.

"It *was*, wasn't it? We waited a long time to paddle in the Gulf." Before standing up, I ran my finger over the brass plaque on the wooden brace by my hip. In my mind's eye, I saw Dad's eyes twinkle as he said, "What a beautiful day to be on the water." I hoped that somehow, he knew we made it.

I hugged Donna's bow as we carried her to the car, and then helped hoist her onto the J-cradles we bought at the sporting goods store. Tipped up onto her side, her shape still looked graceful. But she'd need some work to get back the shine she had when we slid her into the cold Itasca stream. Besides the splotch of green paint from the Highway 80 Bridge, her deck was spotted in places with a cloudy white mineral haze. I rubbed the varnish with a wet finger, and she shined right up, but faded again as her surface dried. A good sanding and a few coats of varnish would return the luster to her finish. The cockpit covers were a dark gray now, instead of black, faded from the sun—like our life jackets, raincoats, and most of my paddle shirts.

I walked around the SUV to secure the straps and toss them back to Gene. The bottom of the boat looked even worse than the deck. Scratches were everywhere, like the scribbles of a toddler on an artist's easel. The edges of the giant fiberglass patch tried, with marginal success, to blend into the fiberglass hull. I tugged the straps, then patted her hull. She was a survivor. *Well done, Donna.*

Gene held open Lucy's front door for me; I climbed in and settled comfortably in my seat. He walked around the car, tugging on Donna's lines for good measure. I looked past him to glance at the Gulf, glowing now with reflected radiance from the late afternoon sun.

"I think we need to celebrate," Gene said as he slid into his seat. "I know a great place in New Orleans for café au lait and beignets."

"Sounds good to me," I said. "And then it's time to head home." I snapped my seat belt into place. My thoughts turned from the past to the future. It was time to take the lessons of the river back home to our own community. Our family and friends beckoned. And now, I had a book to write.

The End

Acknowledgments

FIRST, I MUST THANK the One who created the rivers we paddled, the wildlife we witnessed, and the beautiful places we camped. The One whose Spirit gently nudged us to give our journey purpose by stopping along the way to serve others, placed people in our path for us to meet, and changed our hearts through the experience. Thank you, God.

All along our journey, we encountered river angels who offered food, shelter, assistance, and encouragement. At every charity organization, we met volunteers who eagerly welcomed us, teaching us lessons of love and generosity. I am incredibly grateful to all of them, not only for their help and friendship, but also for the wonderful stories they gave me to write.

On the river, my husband, Gene, was an amazing friend and paddle partner. His unquenchable love of adventure and steadfast sense of purpose made each day more meaningful and fun. I relied heavily on him for help throughout the writing of the book to ensure the authenticity of the details, descriptions, and conversations to the best of our memories.

We are grateful to our family members, our friends, and our St. Mark's Church family, who supported us, watched over things at home, visited us in cities along our route, and prayed for our safety.

I am indebted to my writing coach, Kathie Giorgio, and to my many colleagues at AllWriters' Workplace & Workshop for their critiques of my work, draft after draft. Their feedback helped me bring every revision closer to the version it is today and their encouragement kept my hope alive during the process. I would also like to thank Liz Smirl and Chris Beck, beta readers of my final draft.

Finally, I am grateful to the staff at eLectio Publishing for believing in me and in the merit of this story. I admire their mission and the quality of the books they publish. I am honored to count mine among them.

CPSIA information can be obtained
at www.ICGtesting.com
Printed in the USA
FFHW020957280219
50731109-56144FF